THE
RANDOM HOUSE
HANDBOOK
fourth edition

Frederick Crews

UNIVERSITY OF CALIFORNIA, BERKELEY

RANDOM HOUSE • NEW YORK

THE RANDOM HOUSE HANDBOOK

fourth edition

Fourth Edition
987654321
Copyright © 1974, 1977, 1980, 1984 by Random House, Inc.

Library of Congress Cataloging in Publication Data
Crews, Frederick C.
   The Random House handbook.

   Includes bibliographical references and index.
   1. English language – Rhetoric.   2. English language –
Grammar – 1950-   .   I. Title.
PE1408.C715   1983   808'.042   83-21091
ISBN 0–394–32395–5

Manufactured in the United States of America

Cover design: Jurek Wajdowicz © 1980

FOR BETTY
again and always

PREFACE

From its first publication in 1974, *The Random House Handbook* has tried to perform two functions that are rarely found together. Like many other composition handbooks, it has offered substantial information about the grammar, usage, and punctuation of standard written English. Yet it has also attempted to guide the student writer through the composing process and to explain in detail how ideas can be sharpened and made rhetorically effective. By now many readers seem to agree that one book can serve as both a "handbook" and a "rhetoric." The three previous editions of this text have acquired a large body of friends—including friendly critics who have helped to make each edition more practical in the classroom than its predecessor.

As my book enters its second decade of existence, it continues to evolve in response to its users' needs. Instructors who have taught from the third edition will find that this text incorporates all the essential features of its predecessor, but they will also notice some major improvements:

- The college essay as a genre is more fully explained (Chapter 1), with due emphasis on the writer's options of voice and stance as well as tone.

* A new chapter (2) is devoted to description and narration as essay modes.
* Each of the modes that dominate college writing, explanation (exposition) and argument, now receives a full chapter of its own (3 and 4).
* A new chapter, "Getting Started," shows how to use such techniques of invention as freewriting, brainstorming, and the posing of reporters' questions (Chapter 5).
* A whole chapter (6) covers the drafting and revising of essays, and all aspects of revision—conceptual, organizational, and editorial—receive balanced treatment.
* A popular feature of the second edition, "One Essay from Start to Finish," has been revived, tracing a new student essay through the entire work of composing (Chapter 6).
* In the chapters on paragraph and sentence structure (7 and 8), terms and concepts have been made more accessible to the freshman writer.
* The chapter on library use (14) now covers such innovations as microfiche and on-line catalogs and computerized source materials, and it gives more attention to helpful research strategies.
* Chapter 15, on documentation, follows the MLA Advisory Committee on Documentation Style in offering a reference-list form of citation (that of the American Psychological Association) along with the traditional notes-and-bibliography form.
* Chapter 16 now contains *two* research papers that grew out of investigations discussed in the library chapter. The sample papers illustrate different modes (explanation and argument) and citation styles (MLA and APA).
* Two new chapters (18 and 19) explain how to write business letters and prepare résumés.
* Throughout the book readers will find many new and lively examples of essay prose, drawn from both professional and student writing.
* The number of exercise sets has been increased by more than 75 percent.

Since most composition students are asked to produce essays in the early weeks of a course, the *Handbook* begins by considering what college essays are like, how their modes differ, how they can be composed, and what stylistic resources they call upon. Chapters 1 through 9 can be assigned in order, with detours as necessary to the "handbook" chapters that follow. Many students and instructors, however, will want to begin with Chapters 10 through 12, which review the fundamentals of grammar, usage, and punctuation.

For this edition I have brought Ann Van Sant's helpful *Instructor's*

Manual up to date. The *Manual* offers advice about the day-to-day conduct of classes and includes model schedules for the teaching of key chapters. Professor Van Sant has also prepared the fourth, significantly reconceived, edition of *The Random House Workbook,* a supplementary text offering thorough exercises in those fundamentals of writing that prove most troublesome to students. Both the *Workbook* and Robert Atwan's *Random House Diagnostic Test of Composition,* a proven tool both for identifying student problems and for testing progress through a term or year, are keyed specifically to the *Handbook.* On request, Random House will provide instructors with all of these materials, including ditto masters for reproduction of the *Diagnostic Test* in its two versions, which can be used to measure students' progress in specific areas.

The Random House Handbook has long been indebted to such influential theorists as Francis Christensen, Mina Shaughnessy, E. D. Hirsch, Jr., Ken Macrorie, and Peter Elbow. To those names I must now add those of Linda Flower and Elaine Maimon, who have left their mark on this edition by means, respectively, of a fruitful conceptual framework and a wealth of generously proffered advice. I also want to thank Lois Pryor for essential research assistance. Within Random House, Steve Pensinger, Elisa Turner, and Jennifer Sutherland have been faithful and patient guides. For new advice and examples I am beholden to Mitchell Breitwieser, Alan Mac-Gregor, Sandra Schor, Robert Shelton, Murray Sperber, and Beverly Voloshin, among others.

The following knowledgeable teachers of composition helped me by preparing critiques of the third edition or commenting on my draft chapters: Gary L. Aho, University of Massachusetts, Amherst; John D. Bencich, Brevard Community College, Cocoa Campus; Portia Brown, University of Delaware; Santi V. Buscemi, Middlesex County College; James V. Catano, Tulane University; Bill Connelly, Middle Tennessee State University; John Cooke, University of New Orleans; Mary Jane Dickerson, University of Vermont; Russell M. Griffin, University of Bridgeport; Richard Hannaford, University of Idaho; Constance W. Hassett, Fordham University; Maj. William C. Jeffries, United States Military Academy; William Monday, Mount Royal College, Alberta; Judith Moore, State University of New York at Oswego; Al Nicolai, Middlesex County College; Mary Cathryne Park, Brevard Community College, Cocoa Campus; Linda Peterson, Yale University; Kenneth C. Risdon, University of Minnesota; Art Simpson, University of Wyoming; Craig Snow, University of Arizona; Stephen J. Spector, University of Bridgeport; John Spradley, Metropolitan State College; Ruth Warden, University of Arizona; and Nancy T. Zuercher, University of South Dakota. They all have my deepest gratitude.

Frederick Crews

CONTENTS

PART II COMPOSING 81

5 GETTING STARTED 82

6 DRAFTING AND REVISING 112

PART III UNITS OF EXPRESSION   149

7 PARAGRAPHS   150

8 SENTENCES   176

9   WORDS   208

PART IV CONVENTIONS   239

10   A REVIEW OF GRAMMAR   240

13   SPELLING AND OTHER CONVENTIONS

PART V   RESEARCH 373

14   USING THE LIBRARY 374

PART VI PRACTICAL WRITING 459

PART I
ESSAYS AND THEIR MODES

1

THE COLLEGE ESSAY

LOOKING AHEAD

If you are like most students entering a composition course, you arrive with a mixture of hope and worry. The hope is that the course will help you to put your thoughts into written words with greater precision and effect. The worry is that nothing of the sort will happen and that you will have to go through a painful, humiliating ordeal. Essays, you know, will be required of you on short notice. Will you be able to write them at all? Looking ahead, perhaps you experience a feeling that assails every writer from time to time—the suspicion that words may fail you. (And if words fail you, the instructor may fail you, too.)

It may seem odd at first that putting your thoughts into words should be so challenging. Since childhood, after all, you have been speaking intelligible English. When you talk about things that matter to you, the right words often come to your lips without forethought. Again, in writing letters to friends you scribble away with confidence that you will be understood. But in writing essays you find yourself at a disadvantage. You know that your prose is expected to carry your reader along with a developing idea, but you don't have a clear notion of who that reader is. Instead of exchanging views with someone who can see your face, interpret your gestures, and tell you when a certain point needs explanation or support, you have to assume a nonexistent relationship and keep on writing. It is almost like composing love letters "to whom it may concern" and mailing them off to "Occupant" or "Boxholder."

Faced with this real but manageable challenge, some students make matters worse by conceiving of "good writing" as a brass ring to be seized or, more probably, missed on their first and only try. Condemning themselves in advance as people who lack a writer's mysterious gifts, they imagine that their function in the months ahead will be merely to produce errors of expression so that their instructor can continue to believe that the language is going downhill. For them, the game is over before its rules have been explained.

To stave off such defeatism you need only realize that effective prose is not like a brass ring at all; it is more like the destination of a journey, approachable by steps that anyone can follow. People who turn out dazzling work without blotting a line are so rarely found that you can put them out of your mind. Everyone who writes for a living knows what you too should remember: by and large, *writing is rewriting*. Even the most accomplished authors start with drafts that would be woefully inadequate except *as* drafts—that is, as means of getting going in an exploratory process that will usually include a good many setbacks and shifts of direction. To feel dissatisfied with a sample of your prose, then, is not a sign of anything about your talent. The "good writer" is the one who can turn such dissatisfaction to a positive end by pressing ahead with the labor of revision, knowing that niceties of style will come more easily once an adequate structure of ideas has been developed.

Thus it is also a mistake to think of yourself as either having or not having "something to say," as if your head were a package that could be opened and inspected for inclusion of the necessary contents. We do not *have* things to say; we acquire them in the process of working on definite problems that catch our attention. If you grasp that crucial fact, you can stop worrying about writing in general and prepare yourself for writing *within a context*—that is, inside a situation that calls for certain ways of treating a typical range of questions.

contextual clues from the discipline . . .   Everything you encounter in a college course provides elements of context, helping to make your writing projects less like all-or-nothing tests of your inventiveness and more like exercises in the use of tested procedures. Before long, in any course that calls for written work, you will have picked up important clues about characteristic subject matter and issues, conventions of form and tone, and means of gathering and presenting evidence. And as you do so, you will find yourself not only writing but also thinking somewhat like a historian, an economist, or whatever. That practice in operating within the idiom, or accepted code, of various disciplines is a good part of what a successful college experience is about.

. . . and from the instructor   In a composition course, most of your contextual clues will be gleaned not from readings or lectures but from your instructor's way of explaining assignments, discussing common problems, and commenting on your submitted work. It is essential, therefore, that you get over any lingering image of the composition teacher as a mere fussbudget, hungry to pounce on comma faults and dangling modifiers. If you arrive with that stereotype in mind, you may start out by writing papers that are technically careful but windy and devoid of feeling. In other words, you may think that the game is to be won through negative means, by producing the lowest possible number of mistakes. You should realize instead that your instructor's standards, like your own when you pick up a magazine, are chiefly positive. It is perfectly true that English teachers prefer correctly formed sentences to faulty ones; so do you. But you also expect an article to engage you in a lively and well-conceived topic, to show a consistent point of view, and to convey information clearly and efficiently, without needless pomp. Your instructor will hope for nothing less— and nothing fancier—from your own papers.

As it happens, the teaching of collegiate writing has recently been undergoing a transformation that will almost certainly affect the way your own course is conducted—just as it has affected the emphasis of this book in its four successive editions. Instead of waiting to receive final copies and then passing judgment on them, instructors are now more likely to attend to the whole composing process, from the search for a topic and thesis through the revising of drafts. They know that student writers need strategies for developing usable ideas; that revision ought to be a continual effort, not just a last-minute tidying-up of spelling and punctuation; and that standards of acceptable prose depend largely on the writer's audience and purpose.

WRITING FOR AN AUDIENCE AND A PURPOSE

This last point may require some getting used to. Many college-bound students have been taught to aim at a prissy, rule-bound, rigidly formal notion of "good English." The outcome is prose that sounds as if it were meant to pass a parade inspection rather than to win a reader's sympathy or agreement. In college and beyond you will find that no single formula can suit the variety of writing contexts you will meet. The rules you may have memorized in high school— *avoid the passive voice, never use* I *and* me, *do not begin a sentence with a conjunction or end it with a preposition*—must now be reconsidered in the light of shifting audiences and purposes.

To illustrate, let us apply some common, supposedly universal, tests of "good writing" to two very different paragraphs:

A.   Asked to compare the benefits of academic jobs with jobs in government or business, over 90% of humanities graduate students cited greater flexibility in the use of time. Two-thirds or more mentioned freedom to do as one wished, opportunities to experiment with differing life-styles, and ability to flout social conventions. On the down side, one-quarter to two-fifths expressed suspicion that a teaching job would carry less social prestige and less job security. They were divided almost evenly on whether teaching would involve less leisure or more. The chief drawback to the academic career identified by the majority was relatively lower earning power.[1]

B.   Eating the catered meals they serve on airplanes is always a memorable experience. In the first place, you have to admit it is exciting to open that little carton of salad oil and find a stream of Thousand Islands dressing rocketing onto your blouse. Then, too, where else would you be able to dig into a *perfectly* rectangular chicken? And let's not forget the soggy, lukewarm mushrooms which are accused by the menu of having "smothered" the geometrical bird. They look and taste exactly like the ear jacks that are forever falling off your rented headset. Come to think of it, what *do* they do with those jacks when the flight is over?

Is one of these passages better written than the other? If we go by "the rules" without regard for audience and purpose, we could object to both passages:

Passage A

Rule 1.   *A paragraph should show clear subordination of all other sentences to one main, controlling sentence.* But all the sentences in passage A seem to have roughly equal emphasis.

Rule 2.   *A writer's language should be vivid and concrete.* But this whole paragraph is consistently abstract and colorless.

Rule 3.   *The writer's point of view should always be apparent.* But here we can detect no point of view at all. The paragraph merely summarizes some findings without passing judgment on them.

Passage B

Rule 4.   *A writer should make defensible assertions and support them with evidence.* But the assertions in passage B are exaggerated and unsupported.

Rule 5.   *A writer should take a moderate, reasonable tone, without signs of agitation, sarcasm, or insincerity.* But here the writer uses farfetched language (*rocketing, accused*) and italics (*perfectly, do*), implying an excitement which she probably doesn't feel.

Rule 6. *Written prose calls for a consistent, middle level of diction.* But here we see a swerving between relatively "high" language (*memorable, rectangular, geometrical*) and more casual expressions (*let's not forget, Come to think of it*).

The point is not that passages A and B are bad prose; in fact, they both look good if we reverse the two sets of standards. The point is that standards are relative to occasions. The authors of passage A, writing for an audience of professors and university administrators, are trying to report some survey results with maximum clarity and objectivity; they are being dry and neutral for good reason. Writer B, by contrast, is trying to amuse her instructor and classmates in a composition course; she "breaks rules" in order to achieve a calculated effect of whimsy.

rhetoric   In your own writing, you will always want to adjust your **rhetoric** to the specific audience and purpose you have in mind. That advice may leave you uneasy if you think of rhetoric in its casual meaning of insincere, windy language, as in *Oh, that's just a lot of rhetoric.* But in its primary meaning rhetoric is simply *the strategic placement of ideas and choice of language*—the means of making an intended effect on a reader of listener. Rhetoric need never call for deceptive prose; it calls, rather, for making a strong case by satisfying your audience's legitimate expectations.

Understandably, many students would rather be handed a formula than be told to write in different ways for different audiences and purposes. How are they going to tell in advance what is expected of them? But within any one context—the laboratory, the business or government office, the sociology course, and so on—audiences and purposes for writing tend to be well defined and predictable. Even in a composition course, where practice with various forms of writing is the goal, you at least know who your audience for every assignment will be. It is your instructor—not, however, as a unique individual, but as someone who will try to represent generally accepted standards of careful, sympathetic reading. Later in this chapter we will begin to see that there is nothing mysterious, tricky, or impossibly hard about making a good impression on such a reader.

classmates as audience   Nevertheless, like many another freshman student, you may feel ill at ease addressing this still unknown and potentially troublesome person. Very well: don't even try. You can get the desired results if, while you compose, you think of your classmates, not the instructor, as your audience. This is not to say that you should write in dormitory slang. The point is that if you think of trying to convince people of your own age and background, you will get a reliable sense of what needs proving, what can be taken for granted, and what tone to adopt.

In all likelihood your classmates *will* get to read some of your work in duplicated form. When they do, you will discover that writing for classmates is by no means a holiday from standards of usage and style; once those students have memorized some rules, they will apply them with a fanaticism that may make your instructor look easygoing by comparison. But your classmates share your world in important ways, and you can use them as touchstones of reality and good sense. If the student sitting next to you would choke on some contrived generalization, leave it out. If you suspect that the class as a whole would say *Make that clearer* or *Get to the point*, do so. I can guarantee that your instructor will be delighted by any paper that would impress most of your classmates.

EXERCISE

1. Think of a topic that you would have to handle very differently for different audiences. For example, if your topic were nuclear disarmament you would not say exactly the same thing to a peace rally on the one hand and to Defense Department strategists on the other. Gun control, tax reform, affirmative action, open admission to college, government loans to students — whatever topic you choose, you should be able to think of two audiences that would expect to hear quite different presentations. Briefly indicate which topic and which two audiences you have in mind. Then write two paragraphs, one addressed to each audience, in which you take the same position, but do so with the attitudes and expertise of your different audiences in mind.

CONFRONTING THE ESSAY

By the end of your composition course you will almost certainly be better able to write papers for any other course, regardless of its subject matter. For now, however, you will not be asked to write such "disciplinary" papers. Instead, your instructor will call for *essays* conveying a characteristic blend of opinion and evidence, of intimacy and objectivity.

the essay defined   An **essay** can be defined as *a fairly brief piece of nonfiction that tries to make a point in an interesting way:*

  1. It is fairly brief. Some classic essays occupy only a few paragraphs, but essays generally fall between three and twenty typed pages. Under that minimum, the development of thought that typifies an essay would be difficult to manage. Above that maximum, people might be tempted to read the essay in installments, like a book. A good essay makes an unbroken experience.

2. *It is nonfiction.* Essayists try to tell the truth; if they describe a scene or tell a story, we presume that the details have not been made up for effect.

3. *It tries to make a point* . . . An essay characteristically tells or explains something, or expresses an attitude toward something, or supports or criticizes something—an opinion, a person, an institution, a movement. A poem or a novel may also do these things, but it does them incidentally. An essay is directly *about* something called its **topic** (see p. 83), and its usual aim is to win sympathy or agreement to the point or **thesis** (see p. 84) it is maintaining.

4. . . . *in an interesting way.* When you write an answer to a question on an exam, you do not pause to wonder if the reader actually *wants* to pursue your answer to the end; you know you will succeed if you concisely and coherently satisfy the terms of the question. But a full-fledged essay tends to be read in another way. Its reader could agree with every sentence and still be displeased. What that reader wants is not just true statements, but a feeling that those statements support an idea worth bothering about.

As an essayist, then, you should aim to harmonize reason and rhetoric, trying to be at once lively, fair, and convincing. You must

tell the truth ⟶ but first make people interested in hearing it;
write with conviction ⟶ but consider whether the ideas will stand up under criticism;
supply evidence ⟶ but not become a bore about it;
be purposeful ⟶ but not follow such a predictable pattern that the reader's attention slackens.

the essay justified   But why, you may ask, should you have to write essays at all? No doubt they provide good training for students who want to become professional essayists, but what about future nurses or computer programmers or social workers? I think there are four reasons for the persistence of the essay in freshman English:

1. In a population of freshmen who have varying career plans (including, in some cases, no plan at all), it is impossible to have all students write the kinds of specialized papers or reports they will be producing in their majors.

2. Writing that draws chiefly on opinion and personal experience can spare you the inconvenience of having to do outside reading for every writing assignment.

3. All college writing tasks place a premium on certain common

points that are highlighted by the essay: coherence, clarity, logical order of presentation, and correctness of usage and punctuation.

4. More generally, practice in defending opinions is also practice in forming them—in thinking clearly, weighing objections, and preferring solid evidence to prejudice. In this sense, learning to write a persuasive essay is an experience that can carry over into the rest of your college work and indeed the rest of your life as a citizen in a democracy.

ESSAY MODES

Whole essays and parts of essays have traditionally been divided into four basic types or **modes**, each calling for its own kind of rhetoric. Beyond the paragraph level, those modes—*description, narration, explanation* (or *exposition*), and *argument*—are rarely found in pure form. A representative essay will cross boundaries, setting a descriptive scene for an explanation, showing how a narrated incident lends support to an argument, and so forth. You needn't worry, then, about suddenly slipping out of one mode and into another; that is what good essayists do deliberately whenever it suits their purpose. Yet it remains useful to isolate the modes and practice them one by one. If you can learn to describe, narrate, explain, and argue with some assurance, you will have the essential resources needed for any kind of writing.

modes, tasks, and aims Here in schematic form is a view of the four modes in relation to the tasks and aims for which they are typically used:

Mode	Task	Aim
1. **Description**	Picture	Make vivid
2. **Narration**	Recount	Tell what happened
3. **Explanation**	Define Divide Illustrate Analyze a process Compare and contrast Analogize Show causes and effects	Make understandable
4. **Argument**	Defend a position	Win agreement

Note that the first two modes, description and narration, are presentational; they ask the writer to call scenes or episodes to the reader's mind. The third mode, explanation, encompasses most writing assignments outside of freshman English. For college courses deal mostly in method, classification, and information, all of which are explanatory. The pursuit of knowledge is by and large the pursuit of explanations of one sort or another. And argument, the final mode, appeals to facts, descriptions, narrations, and/or explanations in order to support a position on an issue.

To see the logical relations among the four modes, we can locate them on a scale with immediate experience at one end and abstraction from experience at the other:

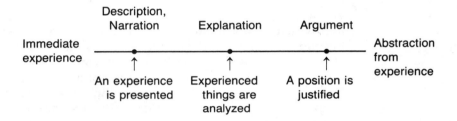

This diagram is not meant to imply that argument is the most important or difficult mode. It does suggest that you can use "distance from experience" as a way of grasping the four modes:

Does a given passage aim chiefly to represent something that can be remembered in its physical actuality? Then it must be either *description* or *narration*.

Does the passage aim chiefly to help us understand the nature or function of something or to see its relation to other things? Then this is a passage of *explanation*.

Does the passage try to convince us that a certain view or policy is preferable to another? Then we are dealing with *argument*—the rhetorical mode that stands at the greatest distance from immediate experience.

Suppose, for example, you were thinking about discussing the subject of *bubonic plague:*

In a *description* you might give your reader a detailed, physically vivid account of the symptoms: fever, boils, discoloration, chills, etc.

In a *narration* you might tell how the plague swept through Europe in 1348–1349—or, in a personal vein, how you had to change your camping plans when health authorities found that rodents were dying from the disease.

In an *explanation* you might show how the plague bacillus is transmitted by rats and their fleas.

And in an *argument* you might support as essential, or oppose as no longer necessary, public health regulations designed to prevent outbreaks of the plague.

In the three chapters following this one, we will indicate in detail how the four modes customarily serve an essayist's purposes.

VOICE, TONE, STANCE

Once you have decided what you want to say in an "English essay," you must decide *how* you want to say it. Even with a fixed audience you have some options to choose from. Do you prefer to write in an intimate, cordial manner or with a touch of formality? Will you show anger, amusement, enthusiasm, detachment . . . ? Would you like to be taken at your word, or would you rather pretend (with the reader's understanding) to be supporting one idea while really supporting its opposite? All of these possibilities are open to you if the assignment seems to allow them.

To sort out the main options, three somewhat overlapping terms are handy: *voice, tone,* and *stance.* Because they do overlap, you needn't worry about exactly where, say, voice ends and tone begins. Simply take note of the rhetorical opportunities discussed below, and review them if you like when deciding how to approach a given writing project.

Voice

Literally, of course, your voice is just your voice; anyone who knows you can recognize it as soon as you speak. In a more extended sense, however, your speaking voice changes according to the occasion. Think, for example, of the different ways you sound in phoning home, in arguing politics with a friend, in applying for a job, and in answering a police officer's questions about an accident. In discussing written prose, we will follow this extended meaning and say that **voice** refers to the "self" projected by a given piece of writing. And for simplicity's sake we will recognize only two voices, the *impersonal* and the *personal.*

impersonal voice   The authors of passage A on page 5, wanting to show a serious, well-informed audience that they are reliable transmitters of facts, adopt a strictly impersonal voice. They do not refer even distantly to their own experiences, opinions, or feelings; nor do they ask their readers for anything beyond attention to the reported results. In this deliberately neutral prose, "the facts speak for themselves"—not because facts really do anything of the sort, but because the authors want to leave that impression. The absence of intimacy is a deliberate stylistic effect, well suited to the businesslike work of conveying information. Whenever that is your chief purpose, you will want to adopt an impersonal voice.

To do so, you should try to keep yourself out of the picture, not just by avoiding *I* and *me*, but also by weeding out any expressions of attitude or mood. You should draw conclusions modestly and soberly, letting your reader understand that those conclusions are compelled by the facts of the case, not by any special commitments on your part. And you should choose neutral-sounding or technical language rather than words that convey emotion. All these devices risk making your essay too dry to be interesting, but you can call on them when liveliness is less important to you than an air of sober reliability.

personal voice   Passage B on page 5 illustrates a highly personal voice. The writer everywhere implies that she is drawing on her private experience, and she addresses her reader as an individual: *you have to admit; your blouse; where else would you be able; your rented headset.* Since the "facts" in that passage are not facts at all but witty exaggerations of widely shared inconveniences, the writer wants us to gather that she is saying at least as much about her own wry, mildly cynical attitude toward life as she is about airline food.

The personal voice has its high-serious uses as well. A writer who is moved by an issue or directly affected by it can mobilize individual experience and feeling to good effect. The issue is no longer something abstract and remote; it has been tested on a person who is making a claim on our sympathy. Thus Martin Luther King, Jr., addressing a "letter" to eight Alabama clergymen who urged him to proceed cautiously at the height of the desegregation crisis, stepped forward in his own person to testify:

> We know through painful experience that freedom is never voluntarily given by the oppressor; it must be demanded by the oppressed. Frankly, I have yet to engage in a direct-action campaign that was "well timed" in the view of those who have not suffered unduly from the disease of segregation. For years now I have heard the word "Wait!" It rings in the ear of every Negro with piercing familiarity. This "Wait" has almost always meant "Never." We must come to see, with one of our distinguished jurists, that "justice too long delayed is justice denied."[2]

Here is the rhetoric of a writer who knows that he cannot bank on much agreement from his immediate readers; after all, they had just written *him* a highly critical letter. Instead of swallowing his feelings, King defiantly stands on his own authority: *I have yet to engage in a direct-action campaign that was "well timed". . . ; for years now I have heard the word "Wait!"* He and other black activists *know through painful experience* what the eight timid clergymen will never know about how freedom is won; and he and *every Negro* have a personal basis for asserting that *"Wait" has almost always meant "Never."*

Tone

The way a piece of writing sounds—the quality of feeling it conveys —is called its **tone**. You can think of tone as a mood expressed by language. If voice indicates the kind of authorial self (personal or impersonal) we are expected to picture, tone indicates the emotional state of that self. The writer's actual emotional state while writing is, of course, unknown to the reader. Tone is a *projected* mood—a coloration of feeling meant to guide the reader's response.

We might reach for several adjectives to characterize the tone of any given sample of prose. Thus we could call the tone of passage A (p. 5) dry, sober, neutral, formal, and matter-of-fact. The following terms would help to pinpoint the tone of passage B: light, informal, droll, wry, relaxed, conversational, intimate, facetious (mockingly joking), and sarcastic. And any number of other tones are imaginable: playful, somber, placid, agitated, modest, proud, thankful, bitter, and so on.

What matters, with respect to tone, is not that we all use the same terms in analyzing it, but that we have a general sense of the picture we are creating of ourselves as writers. Tone is not something to fuss about in the early stages of writing an essay. Once you have finished a draft, however, try to reread it as if you didn't know the writer, and ask yourself, "What is this person's mood?" Frequent underlinings, dashes, and exclamation points, for example, are signs of excitement. Is that the effect you want to create in the final version? In revising, you may decide you would rather show composure and control. On the other hand, if your draft sounds like the work of a bored and listless writer, you can look for ways of showing more engagement.

For further discussion of tone, see pages 74–76.

Stance

forthright In most papers and essays the writer's tone (apparent mood) is meant to be taken "straight." Readers sense a forthright **stance**, or rhetorical posture; they know they are expected to respond according to the text's obvious emotional signals of approval or disapproval, belief or doubt, enthusiasm or reserve. In the following paragraph, for example, the writer gives us no reason to doubt that she means what she says about the *exciting* and *disturbing* attributes of Houston, Texas:

> What Houston possesses to an exceptional degree is an extraordinary, unlimited vitality. One wishes that it had a larger conceptual reach, that social and cultural and human patterns were as well understood as dollar dynamism. But this kind of vitality is the distinguishing mark of a great city in any age. And Houston today is the American present and future. It is an exciting and disturbing place.[3]

ironic stance   Sometimes, however, a writer says one thing in order to convey a different or even opposite meaning. Thus, instead of weighing pluses and minuses, the analyst quoted above could have *ironically* praised Houston in this fashion:

> Everyone knows that a great city should be a challenging place to live. Houston, judged by this standard, may be one of the greatest cities ever to congeal on the crust of this planet. Its heat waves alone would be challenge enough for most faint-hearted citizens. But for the very sturdy, Houston offers Olympic-caliber tests: political violence, racial strife, a sports-mad populace, and a total absence of zoning, enabling the city to grow with all the sophistication and tact of a malignant tumor.

Here you can see the usual mechanism of irony: a jarring contrast between cheerfully positive claims (*a great city, challenging, one of the greatest cities, Olympic-caliber, sophistication and tact*) and deflating realities (*heat waves, violence*, etc.). The same work of ironic undercutting appears in passage B (p. 5), which refers to *a memorable experience* whose *exciting* elements include soiling one's blouse and eating a rectangular chicken.

If you found the second "Houston" paragraph disagreeable, you now know why many instructors are reluctant to encourage attempts at irony. To be effective, irony has to be handled with a light touch; it requires more control over tonal effects than straightforward writing does. You need only scan the letters column of your campus newspaper to see how easily the ironic stance can become overbearing: *We must all be grateful for the dean's efforts to turn this school into a concentration camp*. . . .

Your wisest course, then, may be to pass up chances to write whole essays governed by an ironic stance. Try instead, if you wish, to get occasional effects of irony through understatement. In an essay on fallout shelters, for example, you might reflect ironically that *Recovery from an all-out nuclear attack would not be quite the routine project that some officials want us to believe*—after which you could go back to straightforward discourse about the likely effects of such an attack.

EXERCISES

2. In identifying only two voices, the impersonal and the personal (pp. 11–12), we have left out of account the range of possibilities between those extremes. This book, for example, is written in a voice that is neither entirely personal nor entirely impersonal; the intent is to show engagement *and* to be objective about standards and problems of composition. With this intent in mind, reread the opening paragraph of this chapter (p. 2) and study its effects of voice. Then write and submit two alternative versions of that paragraph, the first taking a *more impersonal* voice and the second taking a *more personal* one.

3. Using any handy source—for example, a science textbook—locate some facts or ideas that

might bear on a controversial topic (creation, evolution, energy development, environmental protection, abortion, foreign aid, etc.). Submit two connected paragraphs dealing with some of that material. In the first, make use of an *impersonal voice*. In the second, continue to develop a position, now using a *personal* voice to indicate your involvement or conviction.

4. Look through your local and campus newspapers for two editorials, syndicated columns, or letters that strike you as illustrating quite different uses of *voice* and *tone*. Clip or duplicate the two items, and submit them along with two or three paragraphs of your own explaining (a) how the two writers have used different features of expression to create different effects of voice and tone, and (b) how those effects are suited (or inappropriate) to each writer's apparent audience and purpose.

5. As we have seen, any number of adjectives might be used to characterize the tones to be found in essays—for example, *serious, playful, urgent, detached, sarcastic, bullying, sly, angry, menacing, cordial, joyous, mournful*. Indicate *any five* of these (or other) tones that you intend to illustrate. Choosing any topic, write a sentence conveying the first tone on your list. Then, keeping as much of the original statement as you can, write four more sentences, each using one of the other tones you have named.

6. Take *any one* of the five sentences you wrote for Exercise 5, and build a whole paragraph around it. Try to support your main idea, using a voice and tone that you consider appropriate for a college essay.

7. Here are three passages illustrating very different tones:

   A. Yes, you CAN stop drinking! I tell you it's really possible! The fact that you're reading these words means that you have the MOTIVATION, the WILL POWER, to make the change now—*today!*—and to STAY ON THE WAGON *FOREVER!!* Think and believe, *I am just as good as everybody else! I don't NEED that bottle!* It's really true. You have more potential than the HYDROGEN BOMB! Just take yourself in hand *today,* and by tomorrow you'll start feeling like a NEW PERSON—the person that you really are inside!

   B. While it has seemed probable that addiction to alcohol is at least in part due to the development of physiological tolerance to the drug, there have been to date no clear demonstrations that alterations in the blood level of alcohol alone (without concomitant experiential factors of taste and ingestion) were sufficient to produce a lasting enhancement of alcohol preference subsequent to treatment. Here we report a method capable of producing a lasting enhancement of alcohol preference without concomitant oral stimulation. . . .

   This enhancement of preference has been achieved by prolonged passive infusion of alcohol into the stomach of rats. After recovery from surgical preparation, the rats were placed in a Bowman restrainer cage to adapt for 24 hours. After this initial period each rat was connected to a pump. . . .[4]

   C. A man who once developed printed circuits for computers begs on street corners for enough coins to buy another bottle of cheap port. A woman whose husband walked out when she couldn't stop drinking at home sits stupefied on a park bench, nodding senselessly at passers-by. An anxious teenager raids her parents' liquor closet at every opportunity. These people, though they have never met, suffer from the same misfortune. If they were placed together in a room, each of them might recognize the others as alcoholics. Yet what they have most in common is their inability to see *themselves* as alcoholics—and this is the very worst symptom of their disease. For until the alcoholic's self-deception can be broken down, not even the most drastic cure has a chance of success.

Study passages A, B, and C, and then submit an essay in which you discuss their differences of tone, pointing to specific uses of language in each case. Include an assessment of each writer's probable audience and purpose.

8. Submit a paragraph or two in which you take an *ironic stance* (p. 14) toward any of the issues you have dealt with straightforwardly in Exercises 3, 5, or 6.

9. Here are the opening sentences of perhaps the most momentous scientific paper published in the past half-century:

> We wish to suggest a structure for the salt of deoxyribose nucleic acid (D.N.A.). This structure has novel features which are of considerable biological interest.[5]

Study this brief passage as an example of style in scientific reporting. What are its qualities of voice, tone, and stance? How far, if at all, do you think the authors were allowing themselves to go in revealing their excitement over having won the race to publish the structural formula for DNA? Submit a paragraph answering these questions by referring to specific features of Watson and Crick's language.

THE MIDDLE WAY

Despite your many options of voice, tone, and stance, you don't need to start from confusion every time you get a new writing assignment. The rule of *writing to convince your classmates* (pp. 6–7) can give you a workable model for just about any "English essay." The norm would be a straightforward stance, an earnest, unpretentious tone, and a voice that expresses your personality but also shows respect for evidence and for other people's views. Here is a reliable "middle way" of writing, situated between informal conversation on the one hand and technical academic discourse on the other. Yet the middle way is not a compromise designed to give least offense. On the contrary, it is the manner cultivated by the most creative professional essayists—those writers who engage us not just in a well-covered topic, but also in their personal responses to it.

To see how accessible the middle way can be, look at the following paragraph from a freshman essay:

> Twelve or fifteen years ago, somebody who admitted to being a fraternity member could expect to be treated like an outcast. The frat man was "rah rah" or "Joe College"; if you wanted people to believe that you were against the Vietnam War or in favor of civil rights, the easiest way was to put down fraternities. Today, however, everything has changed. Somewhere along the line, the idea took hold that fraternity men don't automatically resign from the human race when they recite their pledge.

This is not the work of a future English major, yet it strikes an appropriate and comfortable note for a freshman essay. Consider some of its features:

1. *The writer uses standard written English* (pp. 240–241), not a dialect of speech, and he observes the conventionally correct forms of punctuation and spelling.
2. *The language is drawn largely from a middle level of diction* (pp. 218–219). A phrase like *frat man* dips slightly below that level, but in general the writer's language is neither *slangy* nor *formal*. He doesn't say, for example, *people dug* or *the conception was crystallized;* he says *the idea took hold.*
3. *A point is developed.* The writer doesn't just blurt out his main point and follow it with another one. He has shaped his paragraph around a contrast between conditions twelve or fifteen years ago and today. Note how the transitional word *however* marks a break, a turn toward the central idea. The whole paragraph shows a care for controlling the reader's expectations.
4. *The writer comes through as a person.* Notice how some of his language, like *frat man, put down fraternities,* and *somewhere along the line,* keeps the feeling of a speaking voice, and notice his active and direct way of stating things.
5. *The writer shows engagement with his topic, not agitation about it.* You can tell that he cares about the good name of fraternities, but you can also tell that he feels no need to take a bullying tone.

And here, finally, is a fuller example of the middle way—a complete essay for you to examine on your own. Its author, Abigail Zuger, was a senior when she wrote this piece, which was published in a national magazine. (In Zuger's title, *acrophobia* means "fear of heights.")

ACROPHOBIA IN THE IVORY TOWER

My father, who has not set foot in a college classroom in almost fifty years, occasionally wakes up in the middle of the night in a cold sweat, shouting loud and unintelligible phrases into the darkness. At breakfast he tells us that he was somewhere on his college campus, racing blindly up a walk, two hours late for an exam and stark naked. Someone has taken all the knobs off his bureau drawers, and he has spent two frantic hours looking for his clothes. Stomach churning, he pounds on the door of the exam building. His advisor has told him that the outcome of this exam is crucial to his professional career. The door remains locked, however; the jeers of the passersby resound in his ears, and his professor peers out of an upstairs window, face convulsed in laughter. Fifty years have done nothing to quell the horror of this dream.

In 1973 *Harvard Magazine,* a bulletin for Harvard alumni, published a short article on pre-exam nightmares and received a staggering number of congratulatory letters. Harvard men of all ages wrote in that their subconscious minds still regularly treated them to these dreams. Graying businessmen found themselves seated for an art-history exam without ever having taken the course. Feeble doctors habitually galloped across the campus searching for a Bio. 1 exam no one seemed to have heard of. Lawyers by the score showed up for freshman English and found the exam written in Chinese. To a man they seemed to be saying that to live through these dreams was a thousand times more grueling than anything they had experienced since leaving college.

The ivory tower, as college students—and psychiatrists—across the country will testify, is not nearly so pleasant an abode as it appears from the outside. It shelters its inhabitants from some of life's pedestrian difficulties, but at the same time creates new traumas and problems, which take on, in such closed quarters, an importance of which the real world cannot conceive. The legendary tower of learning is not a stable structure: it is buffeted by the high winds of exam periods, by the gales of preprofessional competition; it shakes with the constant underground rumblings of adolescent crises. What shall I be? What shall I do? Will I succeed? At times it sways so forebodingly that the unfortunate standing on top sees his future in a heap of broken bones and ivory rubble.

Every student has his own mechanism for coping with the panic which invades even the most sedate college existence. It is a kind of panic difficult to describe except by example, a panic of which there is no real equivalent in the nonacademic world. It comes after forty-eight hours of sleepless labor, with the realization that the paper must be completely reorganized; or on the day before the exam, with the realization that a human being cannot read 5,000 pages in one day; or on the Friday before the Monday, with the realization that an academically respectable job on the given topic is the work of a lifetime, and not a weekend. It is the lucky student who can internalize his worries and convert them into an occasional nightmare. Others resort to desperate means.

When the federal law giving students the right to see their own records went into effect last fall, colleges across the country began to sort painstakingly through student files for confidential letters of recommendation, which must be returned to the writer for a signature before being released to the student. At Harvard, several professors received letters of recommendation they had never written, urging that a student named [deleted] be considered for admission to various medical schools, for Phi Beta Kappa, for a highly desirable scholarship. Admitting to the forgeries, ——— was requested to leave the school.

His saddened coworkers in the lab announced they were forced to question the validity of experimental work he had done; his friends were baffled. He had been an enormously talented, straight-A student, had celebrated promising lab results over champagne with Dr. James D. Watson, could probably have gotten into any medical school in the country. The recommendations he had written for himself, it was whispered across Harvard, were couched in far less glowing terms than the recommendations other professors had written for him. ————, accounting for his "highly regrettable acts," explained that he had lost all perspective on his life and his work. "Almost constant pressure . . . , spending excessive time in the laboratory, and a demanding course load," he admitted, "caused me to see events in desperate terms."

————'s desperation is only an ironic exaggeration of the desperation that pervades college campuses in other forms. It is at the root of the notorious pre-med gangsterism, of the flourishing term-paper companies, of the waiting lists in college psychiatric facilities, of the occasional sad college suicide that never makes the front page. Some students survive their college traumas with enough equanimity to mold it all, under the benign influence of time, into part of the best years of their lives. The others wince as they remember, and dream unsettling dreams.⁶

EXERCISES

10. Review the qualities that typify a college essay (pp. 7–9), and see how many of those qualities are to be found in Abigail Zuger's essay (above). Submit a paragraph or two in which you name those qualities and illustrate them by referring specifically to Zuger's prose.

11. Study Zuger's essay (above) for its *rhetoric*—that is, for its strategic placement of ideas and choice of language. In what ways does the essay hang together? How has the writer guided our expectations? Does she shift between essay modes (pp. 9–11), and, if so, to what effect? Submit several paragraphs analyzing Zuger's rhetoric and judging how successful you think it is.

12. Find a magazine article that shows most or all of the qualities that characterize a typical college essay. Submit (a) a page or two of that article, with underlinings and marginal notes to indicate the features you want to isolate, and (b) two or three paragraphs discussing those features and their effect on the reader. Is the article perfectly characteristic of the "middle way," or is it more formal or informal than that model?

13. Pick a subject that you know something about—it could be anything from ten-speed bike derailleurs to teenage unemployment—and write two paragraphs about it. Paragraph A should be as impersonal and dry as possible. In paragraph B restate roughly the same information, but this time try to follow the "middle way" of the typical college essay. Try, in other words, both to be accurate about the subject and to engage your reader's feelings.

14. Here is a set of facts about solar heating, presented without emotional emphasis. Using some of these facts, along with some reflections of your own, write a paragraph about solar heating that would be appropriate for a college essay. Use your own words, making new sentences that engage your reader's interest and reveal an attitude toward the topic.

About one-fourth of American energy is used for the heating of buildings.

Heat from the sun, as it strikes most buildings, could easily supply the energy necessary to heat them.

The relative cost of solar heating, as compared to the costs of conventional fuels, has been rapidly dropping.

Oil and gas shortages have focused a new interest in solar heating.

Government inducements, such as subsidies and tax incentives, could make solar energy more attractive than it is today.

The future of nuclear power has become clouded by controversy in recent years.

American dependence on foreign sources of energy is widely recognized as undesirable.

NOTES

[1]Ernest R. May and Dorothy G. Blaney, *Careers for Humanists* (New York: Academic Press, 1981), p. 71.

[2]Martin Luther King, Jr., *Why We Can't Wait* (New York: Harper & Row, 1964), pp. 82–83.

[3]Ada Louise Huxtable, *Kicked a Building Lately?* (New York: Quadrangle, 1976), p. 149.

[4]J. A. Deutsch and H. S. Koopmans, "Preference Enhancement for Alcohol by Passive Exposure," *Science,* 179 (1973), 1242.

[5]J. D. Watson and F. H. C. Crick, "A Structure for Deoxyribose Nucleic Acid," *Nature,* 171 (1953), 737.

[6]Abigail Zuger, "Acrophobia in the Ivory Tower," *Harper's,* Oct. 1975, pp. 4–5.

2

DESCRIPTION AND NARRATION

Vividness

When you write descriptively, you aim to *make vivid* a place, an object, a character, or a group. That is, instead of trying simply to convey facts about the thing described, you want to give your readers a direct impression of it, as if they were standing in its presence. Your task is one of translation: you are looking for words to capture the way your senses have registered the thing, so that a reader of those words will have a mental picture of it.

Early in a composition course you may be asked to write a descriptive sketch of one provocatively simple thing, such as a pencil or an apple. If so, your opening move will be to set aside everything you already know about the object and to open your senses to its physical characteristics. As soon as you do, you will be surprised by its endless particularity: the lopsidedness of the apple, its creases and scars and speckles, the fuzziness of its stem, and so forth. And you will begin to appreciate the real lesson your instructor has in mind, namely, the value of language that serves vividness by being both concrete and specific.

descriptive language A **concrete** word or phrase denotes an actual, observable
concrete versus thing or quality such as *skin* or *crunchy*. Words of the opposite sort,
abstract like *nutrition* or *impossible assignment*, are called **abstract**; they address the mind without making any appeal to the senses. Concrete (or **sensuous**) terms are essential to description because they are the only ones that can bring the perceived thing to life in your reader's imagination. And among the possible concrete terms you might use,
specific versus the relatively *specific* ones will call up sharper images than the rela-
general tively *general* ones. Specific language gets down to particulars: not *red* but *greenish-red*, not *too soft* but *dented by my thumb print*. Note, incidentally, that although we can distinguish clearly between concrete and abstract language by the test of "appeal to the senses," a word is specific only by contrast with a more general one. Thus, *hound* is specific by contrast with *dog* but general by contrast with *bloodhound*.

creating a picture Detail alone, however, does not make for vividness, as you can tell from these opening sentences of a book about baseball:

> It weighs just over five ounces and measures between 2.86 and 2.94 inches in diameter. It is made of a composition-cork nucleus encased in two thin layers of rubber, one black and one red, surrounded by 121 yards of tightly wrapped blue-gray wool yarn, 45 yards of white wool yarn, 53 more yards of blue-gray wool yarn, 150 yards of fine cotton yarn, a coat of rubber cement, and a cowhide (formerly horsehide) exterior, which is held together with 216 slightly raised red cotton stitches.[1]

Here we have an abundance of concreteness and specificity. The baseball is not just *made of different materials inside* but *made of a composition-cork nucleus encased in two thin layers of rubber . . .* ; it is not merely *stitched* but *held together with 216 slightly raised red cotton stitches*; etc. Yet the effect created is not descriptive but remote. Why?

The answer is that the writer has made no effort as yet to *show* us the baseball. Rather, he is analyzing its components in the spirit of a statistical review. Note, for example, how little appeal to our senses is made by the difference between 2.86 and 2.94 inches or by the idea of 150 yards of wound yarn or of 216 stitches. Even though the stitches are on the surface of the ball, we could never see more than a fraction of them at a time. The implied point of view, then, is not that of someone who is looking at a baseball, but of someone who knows the manufacturer's secrets.

This writer, who knows how to be as vivid as anyone, is here deliberately adopting a dry analytic stance, holding in check his enthusiasm for baseballs and baseball so that we will be struck by the release of that enthusiasm a few sentences later:

Pick it up and it instantly suggests its purpose; it is meant to be thrown a considerable distance—thrown hard and with precision. Its feel and heft are the beginning of the sport's critical dimensions; if it were a fraction of an inch larger or smaller, a few centigrams heavier or lighter, the game of baseball would be utterly different. Hold a baseball in your hand. As it happens, this one is not brand-new. Here, just to one side of the curved surgical welt of stitches, there is a pale-green grass smudge, darkening on one edge almost to black—the mark of an old infield play, a tough grounder now lost in memory. Feel the ball, turn it over in your hand; hold it across the seam or the other way, with the seam just to the side of your middle finger. Speculation stirs. You want to get outdoors and throw this spare and sensual object to somebody or, at the very least, watch somebody else throw it. The game has begun.[2]

Once again we find highly concrete and specific diction: *just to one side of the curved surgical welt of stitches, there is a pale-green grass smudge, darkening on one edge almost to black. . . .* But now the definite language presents something we can take in, moment by moment, with our senses; the writer *is* being vivid. Even though quite a bit of his language is abstract (*purpose, precision, the sport's critical dimensions, memory, speculation,* etc.), our attention is occupied not by analytic findings but by the ball itself as we would see and feel it.

The key to vividness, then, lies less in a certain range of language than in a certain relationship with one's reader. The idea is to invite the reader into the scene and make it believable as immediate experience. Notice, for example, how convincingly a zoologist describes the way a digger wasp typically paralyzes a tarantula in order to provide nourishment for a "descendant" wasp:

When the grave is finished, the wasp returns to the tarantula to complete her ghastly enterprise. First she feels it all over once more with her antennae. Then her behavior becomes more aggressive. She bends her abdomen, protruding her sting, and searches for the soft membrane at the point where the spider's legs join its body—the only spot where she can penetrate the horny skeleton. From time to time, as the exasperated spider slowly shifts ground, the wasp turns on her back and slides along with the aid of her wings, trying to get under the tarantula for a shot at the vital spot. During all this maneuvering, which can last for several minutes, the tarantula makes no move to save itself. Finally the wasp corners it against some obstruction and grasps one of its legs in her powerful jaws. Now at last the harassed spider tries a desperate but vain defense. The two contestants roll over and over on the ground. It is a terrifying sight and the outcome is always the same. The wasp finally manages to thrust her sting into the soft spot and holds it there for a few seconds while she pumps in the poison. Almost immediately the tarantula falls paralyzed on its back. Its legs stop twitching; its heart stops beating. Yet it is not dead, as is shown by the fact that if taken from the wasp it can be restored to some sensitivity by being kept in a moist chamber for several months.

After paralyzing the tarantula, the wasp cleans herself by dragging her body along the ground and rubbing her feet, sucks the drop of blood oozing from the wound in the spider's abdomen, then grabs a leg of the flabby, helpless animal in her jaws and drags it down to the bottom of the grave. She stays there for many minutes, sometimes for several hours, and what she does all that time in the dark we do not know. Eventually she lays her egg and attaches it to the side of the spider's abdomen with a sticky secretion. Then she emerges, fills the grave with soil carried bit by bit in her jaws, and finally tramples the ground all around to hide any trace of the grave from prowlers. Then she flies away, leaving her descendant safely started in life.[3]

This description compels our interest on several levels. Most obviously, we *see* everything that can be seen; each recounted action is as vivid and unavoidable as the previous one. Second, we join in the scene psychologically, dreading the mechanistic invincibility of the wasp, chafing at the tarantula's strange helplessness, and then sharing in the tarantula's descent from being merely *exasperated* and *harassed* to being *desperate* and finally comatose, doomed. And though the battle is recounted clinically, without sentimental human touches, we do get clues for a general response to the scene. The wasp's business is a *ghastly enterprise*, and the combatants rolling across the ground make a *terrifying sight*. (Note, again, the shift into abstract language, not to interrupt the description but to guide our feelings toward it.) Much as we might like to, we are no more able to escape the writer's intended mood than the spider is free to avoid paralysis and live burial.

participation The second "baseball" passage (p. 24) illustrates one frequently used technique for heightening vividness. The writer addresses the reader directly, commanding certain imagined actions (*Pick it up; Feel the ball, turn it over . . .*) and responses (*You want to get outdoors*). Such commands would sound bullying if they went on for one paragraph after another, but when sparingly used they can make for involvement.

An effective description, whether or not it calls the reader *you*, typically contains multiple cues for reaction to the scene:

A single knoll rises out of the plain in Oklahoma, north and west of the Wichita Range. For my people, the Kiowas, it is an old landmark, and they gave it the name Rainy Mountain. The hardest weather in the world is there. Winter brings blizzards, hot tornadic winds arise in the spring, and in summer the prairie is an anvil's edge. The grass turns brittle and brown, and *it cracks beneath your feet.* There are green belts along the rivers and creeks, linear groves of hickory and pecan, willow and witch hazel. *At a distance in July or August the steaming foliage seems almost to writhe in fire.* Great green and yellow grasshoppers are everywhere in the tall grass, popping up like corn *to sting the flesh,* and tortoises crawl about on the red earth, going nowhere in the plenty of time. *Loneliness is an aspect of the land.* All things in the plain are isolate; *there is no confusion of objects in the eye, but* one *hill or* one *tree or* one *man. To look upon that landscape in the early morning, with the sun at your back, is to lose the sense of proportion. Your imagination comes to life, and this, you think, is where Creation was begun.*[4]

Everything we have changed to italics here enlists the reader's participation, beginning with a sense of physical hardship and ending with a general awe at a landscape that frustrates every wish for comfort, moderate weather, gentle scenery, sociability, and human scale. The effect, once again, is not just vividness but inescapability.

the revealing action When the thing to be described is a person or animal, you would do well to include a characteristic action—either a revealing incident or a habit. Note, for example, how a student writer characterizes her stepfather by telling a little story which puts his best-remembered quirk into a form that the reader, too, will be likely to remember:

Poor Harvey meant well by all of us, but the truth is that we made him uncomfortable—especially as we grew into gangly adolescence and began changing shapes and voices. Youthful bosoms and peach-fuzz mustaches across the dinner table were too much for his suspicious, uptight nature to bear. He could hardly criticize us for getting older, but he *could* take his nervousness out on Blacky the dog, who was forever scratching wherever he pleased in a carefree, immodest way, as dogs will do even while grace is being said at Thanksgiving. Harvey would sit at the head of the table, not knowing how to control the squirming and giggling teenagers he had acquired as relatives, but then he would spot Blacky off in the corner scratching away most indecently, and he couldn't contain himself. "Blacky, Blacky!" he would yell, *"Stop it! Stop that right now!"* Blacky would stop scratching for just a moment—long enough to stare back at Harvey as you would too if a lunatic were trying to interrupt your normal life for no reason—but when he started up again, he had a large and appreciative audience.

description through metaphor If the purpose of describing is to render things exactly as they are, it would seem to follow that descriptive prose should always be **literal**; that is, the words should represent what they describe without poetic embellishment. Such is the case, by and large, in the paragraph above—even though it is possible to find minor figurative touches in practically any prose. Accurate literal writing can be an important means of winning a reader's trust, so that you may be given the benefit of the doubt when you become more speculative or poetical.

In practice, however, some of the most intense and memorable descriptive effects result not from literal but from **figurative** language (pp. 230–233)—especially from **metaphorical** expressions, those that render one thing in terms of something else. And this is not surprising if we recall that our minds are constantly making sense of experience by comparing something new to something already known. Metaphorical writing makes such comparisons in shorthand form, as you can see by examining the emphasized words below:

> The sun is up and the pens are empty. As the deck is hosed down and the trash fish pitchforked overboard, the noise from the birds rises *hysterically—barnyard sounds*, shrieks, whistles, *klaxon horns*.
>
> Now the birds can be seen flying in a circle around the boat. Each can hold position for only a few moments beside the point where the remains of fish are washing over. Then it falls astern and has to come up to windward on the other side of the boat, cross ahead and fall backward to the critical point. The birds pumping up the windward side *look like six-day bicycle riders, earnest and slightly ridiculous,* but when they reach the critical point there is a miraculous moment of aerobatics as the birds brake, wheel and drop in the broken air.
>
> Gulls snatch, gannets plunge, but the little kittiwakes balance delicately, their tails spread *like carved ivory fans.* There is *a column* of descending, shrieking birds, *a scintillating feathered mass.* The birds revolving about the boat *have made themselves not only guests at the feast but have formed the wreath as well.*[5]

The elements in italics here, by proposing how an imaginative observer would relate the sea birds to more familiar, landlocked experience, turn the reader into that observer. If the images of the six-day bicycle racers and the wreath of birds are somewhat daring, the accuracy of literal description elsewhere in the passage encourages us to trust their appropriateness.

Similarly, another writer combines precise literal details with figurative effects in order to rivet our attention on the object described—in this case, a performer who dives from a forty-foot ladder into a play pool of twelve-inch-deep water:

LaMothe dives, however—doesn't jump—into water that scarcely reaches his calves as he stands up, his hands in a Hallelujah gesture. His sailor hat never leaves his head, his back stays dry unless the wash wets him, and yet so bizarre is the sight of a person emerging from water so shallow that one's eye sees him standing there as if with his drawers fallen around his feet. As he plummets, his form is as ugly and poignant as the flop of a frog—nothing less ungainly would enable him to survive—and, watching, one feels witness to something more interesting than a stunt—a leap for life into a fire net, perhaps.[6]

This writer combines sharply rendered particulars with a continual appeal to our imagination. First LaMothe is said to assume *a Hallelujah gesture*, as if he were in a revival meeting. Then we see him *as if with his drawers fallen around his feet*; nothing of the sort has actually occurred. Then LaMothe's fall is likened to *the flop of a frog*, and finally we regard the whole jump as if it were *a leap for life into a fire net*. The writer has gained effect not just from close observation, but also from freely relating what he perceives to other forms of experience.

Most metaphorical language is local and fleeting; the figure of speech lasts just long enough to make one aspect of the object vivid, and then the description either reverts to literalism or launches into a fresh metaphor. Sometimes, however, a writer will extend a metaphor, using it as an organizing principle. The effect can be illuminating if it stops short of being mechanical and overelaborate. One writer, for example, used the image of a bird to order her memories of the great dancer Pavlova:

As her little bird body revealed itself on the scene, either immobile in trembling mystery or tense in the incredible arc which was her lift, her instep stretched ahead in an arch never before seen, the tiny bones of her hands in ceaseless vibration, her face radiant, diamonds glittering under her dark hair, her little waist encased in silk, the great tutu balancing, quickening and flashing over her beating, flashing, quivering legs, every man and woman sat forward, every pulse quickened. She never appeared to rest static, some part of her trembled, vibrated, beat like a heart. Before our dazzled eyes, she flashed with the sudden sweetness of a hummingbird in action too quick for understanding by our gross utilitarian standards, in action sensed rather than seen. The movie cameras of her day could not record her allegro. Her feet and hands photographed as a blur.

Bright little bird bones, delicate bird sinews! She was all fire and steel wire. There was not an ounce of spare flesh on her skeleton, and the life force used and used her body until she died of the fever of moving, gasping for breath, much too young.[7]

Here the idea of Pavlova as a bird doesn't simply recur in certain phrases; it informs the entire passage, including the writer's own birdlike manner of *quickening and flashing* from one descriptive phrase to the next.

Descriptive Order

How should you go about arranging the elements of a description? Your best course is to see if those elements lend themselves to some dramatic order:

1. If you are rendering a landscape or an object, ask yourself what is most impressive about it, and try to save that feature for last. If it is a small detail, begin with larger ones; if it lies in the foreground, begin in the distance; etc.
2. Similarly, if one fact about a described person stands out as more imposing than the others, look for a way of leading up to it (Pavlova's early death).
3. If you are recounting a typical action, follow that action to its climax or conclusion (the burial of the paralyzed tarantula). If it is a single incident, give it an introductory context so that your reader will understand why it is typical (Harvey's yelling at the dog). Alternatively, you could plunge your reader into the incident and then supply the context, as in a "baited opener" (pp. 126–127).
4. If you want to convey a certain mood or idea, look for an order that will gradually develop and intensify the desired response without giving it away at the outset (the mysterious effect of Rainy Mountain).
5. If you want to "command" your reader's participation in the scene (pp. 25–26), begin with physical activities and work toward conclusions (from holding the baseball to wanting to play).
6. And if you have an important surprise to reveal, think how you can introduce it by stages, drawing your reader into a puzzle that you will eventually solve:

He is big. He has always been, over six feet, with that slump of the shoulders and tuck in the neck big men in this country often affect, as if to apologize for being above the democratic norm in size. (In high school and at college he played varsity basketball. In high school he was senior class president.) And he looks healthy enough, blue-eyed behind his beard, like a trapper or a mountain man, acquainted with silences. He also grins a lot.

Odd, then, to have noticed earlier—at the house, when he took off his shabby coat to play Ping-Pong—that the white arms were unmuscled. The coat may have been a comment. This, after all, is southern California, where every man is an artist, an advertiser of himself; where every surface is painted and every object potted; where even the statues seem to wear socks. The entire population ambles, in polyesters, toward a

Taco Bell. To wear a brown shabby cloth coat in southern California is to admit something.

So he hasn't been getting much exercise. Nor would the children have elected him president of any class. At the house they avoided him. Or, since he was too big to be avoided entirely, they treated his presence as a kind of odor to pass through hurriedly, to be safe on the other side. They behaved like cats. Of course, he ignored them. But I think they were up to more than just protecting themselves from his lack of curiosity. Children are expert readers of grins.

His grin is intermittent. The dimples twitch on and off; between them, teeth are bared; above them, the blue eyes disappear in a wince. This grin isn't connected to any humor the children know about. It may be a tic. It could also be a function of some metronome made on Mars. It registers inappropriate intervals. We aren't listening to the same music.

This is the man who introduced me to the mysteries of mathematical science, the man I could never beat at chess, the man who wrote haiku and played with computers. Now there is static in his head, as though the mind had drifted off its signal during sleep. He has an attention span of about thirty seconds.[8]

> In reading this passage we begin on a generally positive note, with only faint misgivings about a man—actually the writer's older brother —who *looks healthy enough*. His truly drastic state is revealed only by degrees—the unmuscled arms, the shabby coat, the children's catlike wariness in his presence—whereas we are told directly what he used to be like. The effect is gripping, much more so than if the writer had begun *My brother is now a schizophrenic with an attention span of about thirty seconds*.

EXERCISES

1. Write a descriptive paragraph about an object within your view as you sit at your desk. Begin the paragraph with a sentence supplying an idea to cover the details that follow.

2. Choose an activity with which you are closely familiar, and write a paragraph describing that activity in a way that gives your reader a sense of being present as that activity is performed.

3. Think of a place you are fond of; it could be as small as your bedroom or as large as your home town. Write two descriptive paragraphs about that place. In the first one try simply to "give the facts" in a neutral, precise way, without any special emphasis. Then convey the same information in a vivid, engaging paragraph. You may find that you have to add some further details in the second version.

4. Think of someone you know who can be identified by a habit or quirk. (The person could even be yourself or your instructor.) Then, like the writer of the "Harvey" passage on page 26, write a descriptive paragraph about that person, using the characteristic action as a point of focus.

5. Choose any two of the six listed principles for ordering a description (p. 29), and submit two descriptive passages, each following one of those two principles. Indicate which principle you are illustrating in each instance. If you wish, you may use some of the same descriptive material in both passages.

6. Here is a passage from Mark Twain's *Life on the Mississippi,* reflecting on the way his training as a steamboat pilot changed his understanding of the river:

> Now when I had mastered the language of this water, and had come to know every trifling feature that bordered the great river as familiarly as I knew the letters of the alphabet, I had made a valuable acquisition. But I had lost something, too. I had lost something which could never be restored to me while I lived. All the grace, the beauty, the poetry, had gone out of the majestic river! I still kept in mind a certain wonderful sunset which I witnessed when steamboating was new to me. A broad expanse of the river was turned to blood; in the middle distance the red hue brightened into gold, through which a solitary log came floating, black and conspicuous; in one place a long, slanting mark lay sparkling upon the water; in another the surface was broken by boiling, tumbling rings, that were as many-tinted as an opal; where the ruddy flush was faintest, was a smooth spot that was covered wtih graceful circles and radiating lines, ever so delicately traced; the shore on our left was densely wooded and the somber shadow that fell from this forest was broken in one place by a long, ruffled trail that shone like silver; and high above the forest wall a clean-stemmed dead tree waved a single leafy bough that glowed like a flame in the unobstructed splendor that was flowing from the sun. There were graceful curves, reflected images, woody heights, soft distances, and over the whole scene, far and near, the dissolving lights drifted steadily, enriching it every passing moment with new marvels of coloring.
>
> I stood like one bewitched. I drank it in, in a speechless rapture. The world was new to me and I had never seen anything like this at home. But as I have said, a day came when I began to cease from noting the glories and the charms which the moon and the sun and the twilight wrought upon the river's face; another day came when I ceased altogether to note them. Then, if that sunset scene had been repeated, I should have looked upon it without rapture, and should have commented upon it inwardly after this fashion: "This sun means that we are going to have wind to-morrow; that floating log means that the river is rising, small thanks to it; that slanting mark on the water refers to a bluff reef which is going to kill somebody's steamboat one of these nights, if it keeps on stretching out like that; those tumbling 'boils' show a dissolving bar and a changing channel there; the lines and circles in the slick water over yonder are a warning that that troublesome place is shoaling up dangerously; that silver streak in the shadow of the forest is the 'break' from a new snag and he has located himself in the very best place he could have found to fish for steamboats; that tall dead tree, with a single living branch, is not going to last long, and then how is a body ever going to get through this blind place at night without the friendly old landmark?"
>
> No, the romance and beauty were all gone from the river. All the value any feature of it had for me now was the amount of usefulness it could furnish toward compassing the safe piloting of a steamboat. Since those days, I have pitied doctors from my heart. What does the lovely flush in a beauty's cheek mean to a doctor but a "break" that ripples above some deadly disease? Are not all her visible charms sown thick with what are to him the signs and symbols of hidden decay? Does he ever see her beauty at all, or doesn't he simply view her professionally and comment upon her unwholesome condition all to himself? And doesn't he sometimes wonder whether he has gained most or lost most by learning his trade?[9]

Submit several paragraphs in which you discuss this passage, attending to its leading idea, its use of language, its effects of comparison and contrast, and any other features you find noteworthy. Your remarks should show familiarity with the kinds of diction (abstract and concrete, general and specific) treated on pages 23–25.

7. Simply by growing up and acquiring skills, all of us have undergone something like the loss of "poetic" perception that Mark Twain discusses (Exercise 6). Think especially of some area (a job, a sport, a field of study) that has made you think more practically or systematically about some aspect of the world. For example, a course in meteorology or oceanography may have changed your way of considering clouds or waves. Submit two descriptive paragraphs about the same material. In the first paragraph, use concrete language to convey a sense of immediate experience. In the second, allow your description to reflect the knowledge or skill you have acquired.

NARRATION

Narration, or storytelling, is one of the basic and universal human activities. Every culture, literate or nonliterate, has its favorite tales, myths, and jokes; if we face a choice of hearing some lesson directly stated or having it embodied in a story, nearly all of us would gladly opt for the story. For you as a writer, narration offers one of the most promising chances to build a sense of community, of shared experience, between yourself and your reader.

Outside a composition course you may not find many opportunities to write whole essays of narration—or of description, either. Yet essays of explanation and argument, precisely because they tend to be analytic and abstract, can be usefully illustrated through storytelling. Thus, if you are explaining how hard it is for a high-school student to make a wise choice of career, you can give your essay concreteness (p. 23) by narrating your discouraging experiences in a summer internship program. Or suppose you are arguing that the present minimum wage is too high because it makes teenagers unemployable in summer jobs; here again you can give the point authenticity by telling how you were treated by hiring agencies.

Much that bears saying about description applies equally to narration, for both modes aim at reproducing experience. Indeed, we have already seen that the recounting of characteristic actions is a common means of describing. What makes the story of the tarantula's fate (pp. 24–25) a description, for example, is simply the fact that the action occurs *typically*, not just in some bygone period but for as long as wasps and tarantulas will be on the earth.

Means of Telling

choice of tenses   A narrator's decision to use the customary past tense (*went, did*) or the less usual present (*goes, does*) should rest on whether or not a special effect is desired. Since narrated actions are always "over," the past tense is generally appropriate and expected. Thus the writer of the following paragraph, recalling how he once counterattacked neighborhood bullies who had been tormenting him, uses the past tense to create a clear sense that the story is being recalled from an earlier period of his life:

> They closed in. In blind fear I let the stick fly, feeling it crack against a boy's skull. I swung again, lamming another skull, then another. Realizing that they would retaliate if I let up for but a second, I fought to lay them low, to knock them cold, to kill them so that they could not strike back at me. I flayed with tears in my eyes, teeth clenched, stark fear making me throw every ounce of my strength behind each blow. I hit again and again, dropping the money and the grocery list. The boys scattered, yelling, nursing their heads, staring at me in utter disbelief. They had never seen such frenzy. I stood panting, egging them on, taunting them to come on and fight. When they refused, I ran after them and they tore out for their homes, screaming. The parents of the boys rushed into the streets and threatened me, and for the first time in my life I shouted at grownups, telling them that I would give them the same if they bothered me. I finally found my grocery list and the money and went to the store. On my way back I kept my stick poised for instant use, but there was not a single boy in sight. That night I won the right to the streets of Memphis.[10]

For past actions that were typical or recurrent, the auxiliaries *would* and *could* are serviceable: *I would cry every Saturday night,* etc. The following student paragraph shows the auxiliaries in action:

> When I was a child I could always tell what the next day's weather would be. If, for example, rain was on the way, I would know it many hours in advance, without having to listen to weather forecasts. Sometimes I would notice a small change in the sky, such as the arrival of the first wisps of cirrus clouds that come before a front. Or again, I would realize that the flies around our apartment were acting sluggish in a way that usually spelled rain to me. Most often, though, I would simply feel "rainy inside," as I called it; the drop in barometric pressure would take down my mood and my energy level before there were any visible signs of a storm.

A shift into the present tense creates a more immediate effect, giving readers a sense of participating directly in the scene:

> It is high noon. The sand burns the feet of the little children, who leave their palm leaf balls and their pin-wheels of frangipani blossoms to wither in the sun, as they creep into the shade of the houses. The women who must go abroad carry great banana leaves as sun-shades or

wind wet cloths about their heads. Lowering a few blinds against the slanting sun, all who are left in the village wrap their heads in sheets and go to sleep. Only a few adventurous children may slip away for a swim in the shadow of a high rock, some industrious woman continues with her weaving, or a close little group of women bend anxiously over a woman in labor. The village is dazzling and dead; any sound seems oddly loud and out of place. Words have to cut through the solid heat slowly. And then the sun gradually sinks over the sea.[11]

Sometimes, too, a narrator will choose the present tense to suggest that the events being told are still fresh in memory and that they are accompanied by strong feelings. Thus a student writes:

I turn on the public television station, expecting to hear a thoughtful program on Africa scheduled for this hour. But tonight there is a fundraising "special" instead. I am annoyed, but I try to be understanding; after all, the station needs extra contributions to survive. But before long I am completely fed up with the whole undertaking. It seems that the station manager has asked every unemployable comedian and punk band in town to put in an appearance. They are "special," yes—in just the way that marked-down loaves of yesterday's bread are "special" in the supermarket.

Notice how the writer's impatience is made more convincing by his telling the story as if it were occurring as he writes.

dialogue versus indirect discourse   One frequently used feature of narration is the reporting of speech exchanged between two or more people. If you render that speech directly, with quotation marks, you are employing **dialogue**:

"Mayday! Mayday! We're going down!" Those were the captain's last recorded words.

"Try to make it to the runway," pleaded the flight controller. "We've got the fire trucks on line for you." But there was no reply; the plane had already begun its fatal plunge.

The obvious advantage of such quotation is that you give your reader the impression of being right on the scene.

Note that a paragraph of dialogue can be as brief as one speaker's remark. It is customary to begin a new paragraph with every change of speaker.

If your purpose is merely to convey *what* was said, without reproducing speech patterns and tone, you can use **indirect discourse** instead of dialogue:

In his last recorded words the captain declared that the plane was going down. There was no reply to the flight controller's plea that he try to reach the runway; the plane had already begun its fatal plunge.

Compared with the dialogue version, this is colorless. But no writer needs to be colorful at every moment—and no reader could stand it. In many situations you will find that indirect discourse suits your purpose perfectly well.

For punctuation rules governing the presentation of dialogue, see page 334.

Order of Telling

straightforward   Because every story occurs in a time sequence, the most natural order of telling is a chronological one, from the first incident at the outset to the last one at the end. That is the easiest order to master, and in many cases it is also the most effective one. The stark and manly impression made by the "Memphis" paragraph (p. 33), for example, would have been spoiled by any juggling of the order of events. So, too, all the other examples of narration thus far reviewed show how a narrator typically allows the telling to follow the action as it actually occurred.

anticipatory   Once you feel comfortable with straightforward narrating, you can experiment with an order that requires more forethought but also offers greater possibilities for securing a reader's curiosity. Instead of proceeding from beginning to end, you can choose a climactic scene and start there, revealing just enough about it to provoke interest. After that act of *anticipation*, you can move both forward and backward in time, filling in the circumstances that led to this major event and then carrying it through to the end.

Thus one writer, in an essay dealing with his decision to flee Germany shortly after Hitler came to power, begins with a later incident:

In the days of Hitler Germany's collapse, a short item on an inside page of *The New York Times* caught my eye. It ran somewhat as follows:

Reinhold Hensch, one of the most wanted Nazi war criminals, committed suicide when captured by American troops in the cellar of a bombed-out house in Frankfurt. Hensch, who was deputy head of the Nazi SS with the rank of Lieutenant General, commanded the infamous annihilation troops and was in charge of the extermination campaign against Jews and other "enemies of the Nazi state," of killing off the mentally and physically defective in Germany, and of stamping out resistance movements in occupied countries. He was so cruel, ferocious, and bloodthirsty that he was known as "the Monster" (*Das Ungeheuer*) even to his own men.

It was the first time since I had left Germany in the winter of 1933 that I had heard or seen Hensch's name. But I had thought of him often. For I had spent my last evening in Germany in the company of "The Monster."[12]

Could anyone read this tantalizing opening without wishing to have the rest of the story filled in?

movement broken by commentary   But just as a good description usually contains more than bare details of scenery, so a good narrative may contain interruptions for reflection or highlighting:

During the first few days of my sojourn with the wolves I stayed inside the tent except for brief and necessary visits to the out-of-doors which I always undertook when the wolves were not in sight. *The point of this personal concealment was to allow the animals to get used to the tent and to accept it as only another bump on a very bumpy piece of terrain.* Later, when the mosquito population reached full flowering, I stayed in the tent practically all of the time unless there was a strong wind blowing, *for the most bloodthirsty beasts in the Arctic are not wolves, but the insatiable mosquitoes.*[13]

The lines in italics are commentary, not narration in the strict sense of advancing the story. As you can see by reading the paragraph without those lines, however, they supply important elements of motivation.

comparison and contrast   In many cases, what makes an event meaningful is its relation to similar events that it calls to mind. Notice, in the following student paragraph, how the order of narration is successfully governed by a comparison-and-contrast pattern:

The tornado that struck our farm in 1978 looked at first just like the one I had seen four years before. The nearby clouds had the same dark and jumbled look, and the thin, twisting, black funnel appeared much the

resemblances   same, like some kind of putty-like upside-down vacuum cleaner sucking things out of the sky on the horizon. But that time, the funnel *stayed* on the horizon until it veered out of sight, and I never knew what it was doing on the ground until I saw the television reports of the damage. This time the tornado came right at us, quietly at first and then with a

differences   sickening roar. We all ran for the shelter, of course, and we made it with time to spare; the funnel couldn't have been moving faster than about thirty miles an hour. Even so, leaves and straw were already flying about wildly as we pulled down the hatch. And when we peeked out ten minutes later, we saw that our truck had been overturned; two walls of the barn had collapsed; and half the roof of our house was lying in the field a quarter of a mile away.

Notice how the recounting of a calamity becomes more dramatic by contrast with a similar event that passed the writer by.

For further discussion of comparison and contrast, see pages 52–53.

The Implied Narrative Thesis

In telling any story you will necessarily be expressing an attitude or position of some sort: admiration or anger, compassion or detachment, a sense of urgency or of helplessness to change the inevitable. Sometimes a narrator will put such editorializing directly into words, but too many statements of opinion can slow a story down and break the reader's spell of curiosity. The trick, then, is to color the narrated events within the very telling of them. Thus, for example, the writer of the "Memphis" paragraph (p. 33), by bunching actions together without commentary, lets us feel how desperate and possessed he was when he took on the neighborhood bullies. By contrast, the "wolves" writer (p. 36), by supplying reasons for each of his actions, points to the analytic, experimental character of his arctic sojourn.

To see how a thesis or leading idea can saturate the details of a story, consider the opening paragraph of an essay about a famous murder and trial in southern California:

Imagine Banyan Street first, because Banyan is where it happened. The way to Banyan is to drive west from San Bernardino out Foothill Boulevard, Route 66: past the Santa Fe switching yards, the Forty Winks Motel. Past the motel that is nineteen stucco tepees: "SLEEP IN A WIGWAM – GET MORE FOR YOUR WAMPUM." Past Fontana Drag City and the Fontana Church of the Nazarene and the Pit Stop A Go-Go; past Kaiser Steel, through Cucamonga, out to the Kapu Kai Restaurant-Bar and Coffee Shop, at the corner of Route 66 and Carnelian Avenue. Up Carnelian Avenue from the Kapu Kai, which means "Forbidden Seas," the subdivision flags whip in the harsh wind. "HALF-ACRE RANCHES! SNACK BARS! TRAVERTINE ENTRIES! $95 DOWN." It is the trail of an intention gone haywire, the flotsam of the new California. But after a while the signs thin out on Carnelian Avenue, and the houses are no longer the bright pastels of the Springtime Home owners but the faded bungalows of the people who grow a few grapes and keep a few chickens out here, and then the hill gets steeper and the road climbs and even the bungalows are rare, and here

—desolate, roughly surfaced, lined with eucalyptus and lemon groves—
is Banyan Street.[14]

Here the writer guides our responses not only with an open editorial
remark—*It is the trail of an intention gone haywire, the flotsam of the new
California*—but also by her choice of landmarks in a make-believe trip
to the murder scene. Instead of feeling controlled by a possibly biased
point of view, we are caught up in a rapid sequence of images.
When we finally reach the *desolate* area of the crime, we are psychologically prepared for the writer's tale of shallow, confused values
and unchecked impulses.

Our final example of narration, a whole essay by a freshman student, shows how storytelling can powerfully convey a central concern without spelling it out at all:

"You should fix everyone's coffee or tea. You know, add the sugar, etc.,
and pour it. If the meat is hard to handle, you should cut it for the patient," instructed my predecessor. "After you've passed out the trays,
you feed Irene and Molly."

"That's Granny Post in there. She's 106. Even though she's not particularly senile, she's lost her teeth and must be fed with a giant eyedrop-
per." I discovered just how clear Granny Post's mind was when I tried
to feed her. The dear old lady wasn't hungry and spat it back at me.

After that first day at the convalescent hospital, I was on my own.
Irene was eager to please and partially fed herself, but I dreaded feeding Molly. She was blind and pitifully thin. "I'm sick. I'm sick," she'd
cry. "Don't make me eat any more. Please, I'm sick."

"But Molly, you've got to eat so you can get well. Come on, one more
bite. Here, hold my hand. It's not so bad." And I'd coach one more bite
down her before gathering the sixty trays onto their racks and wheeling
them back to the safety of the kitchen. The rest of the evening I cleaned
the coffee pot, set up the breakfast trays, scoured sinks, and mopped
the floors. I didn't mind sitting on the floor scrubbing at the oven or
making the juices and sandwiches for the evening nourishment. It was
when I confronted the elderly people on the other side of that kitchen
door that I became nervous and awkward.

In a few weeks I mastered the hospital routine, the names of most of
the patients, and their idiosyncrasies.

Opposite the kitchen was what was fondly called "the ward." Dora, a
small, white-haired woman who was continually nearly slipping out of
the bottom of the wheelchair to which she was tied, was the ringleader
of this group. She cussed up a storm at anyone who came near her and
perpetually monotoned, "What can I do? Tell me, what can I do?" May
accompanied her with "Put me to bed. I want to go to bed." One eve-

ning as I entered with dinner, the woman across from Dora was gaily slinging her waste matter about the room, especially at anyone who threatened to come near her. A nurse and some aides calmed her down.

As far as the two sisters in room twelve were concerned, they were traveling on a huge ocean liner. When I brought their trays, they always asked, "How long till we get to port?" or "I'm sorry. We can't eat today because we're seasick."

John mumbled perpetually about the batty ladies in the TV room. He liked his smokes and his sports magazine.

Mr. Harrison fed a stray cat that stayed outside his sliding-glass door. He loved his cat and I gave him leftovers to feed it. One day a car rushed down the hill and struck his cat. Mr. Harrison told me his cat ran away, but it would come back as always. He stood at his door watching for it.

There were two Ethels. Dora advanced to feeding herself so I began feeding Ethel Irene. Ethel Irene was small, roly-poly, and had gray-black hair cut short like a little boy's. She liked to joke and use large words. Sometimes when she grasped for a word, it just wouldn't come and great big tears would form in her eyes. She liked sunshiny days and the sound of birds singing. She liked me to sing to her, too. Always clamped tightly in her hand was the buzzer to call the nurse. It was Ethel Irene's lifeline. Occasionally it fell out of her hand and she became so frantic she couldn't speak, only pointing and crying.

I tried to regard the other Ethel as just one of the many patients to whom I delivered food. When I brought dinner, I fixed Ethel's tea, cut her meat, and tucked in her napkin. Then I'd clearly shout, "Enjoy your dinner." But instead of letting me leave, she'd pull me down to her and in a low, halting voice struggle out, "I like you. Can I kiss you?"

It became increasingly difficult to leave Ethel. She'd refuse to release my arm, purposely eat slowly so I was forced to return just to retrieve her tray, and cry when I succeeded in making my exit. To avoid upsetting her, I began sneaking into the room to take her tray or sending someone else. If she realized the deception, she'd let out an anguished cry and begin sobbing. I couldn't bear to pass Ethel's room and see her arms reaching out for me.

Many of the patients were lonely like Ethel and starved for attention. Some were on welfare and had few or no relatives. Most were just forgotten.

Ethel's son visited one day. Roaring drunk, he first tried to get fresh with me and then stomped into the kitchen demanding food.

Molly had visitors once, too. When I reached work and dropped by to see Molly, two or three of her relatives were standing about her. Molly was breathing laboriously, her nose and mouth were attached to an oxygen tank. She was dying now. The relatives left shortly. Molly's bed was empty when I returned the next day.

I worked in the convalescent hospital only sixteen hours a week for eight months. The old people remained there twenty-four hours a day for months or years, depending on how "lucky" they were. They were fed, diapered at night, and sponge-bathed in the morning. But what they needed most . . .

The age is gone when three generations occupy the same house. Young people want a life of their own.

My parents are nearly fifty now.

This essay has some minor flaws, but they are outweighed by its compassion and control. The memorable description of Ethel Irene with her "lifeline" buzzer and the understated recounting of Molly's death seem like reality itself. And the apparent disorganization covers a subtle and effective movement engaging the reader in the writer's own ordeal of first learning her chores, then coping with the patients' oddities, then facing the ultimate fact of death, and finally turning her thoughts to her own parents, who "are nearly fifty now" and may someday be like Molly and Mr. Harrison. Will she look after them in their senility? The abrupt ending leaves us troubled, not only by grotesque and tender images from the convalescent hospital, but also by conflicting feelings toward parents who deserve our care but who threaten to invade "a life of [our] own."

EXERCISES

8. Here are the opening paragraphs of an essay about young radicals and terrorists of the early 1970s who suspected the writer of being a government agent:

> It is a warm August night in Ann Arbor, Mich., in 1970. The house I have come to visit looks like so many other houses built for the returning heroes of World War II: a rambling split-level, with a flagstone path that leads to the front door. Beyond that door, however, the lighting is dim, mattresses are scattered about on the dusty floor. The smells are reminiscent of a bazaar: overripe fruit, marijuana, baby formula, gasoline from freshly mixed Molotov cocktails that are lined up on the bookshelves like soda pop in a grocery.
>
> Men, women and children wander about the rooms as aimlessly as house cats. They eat when hungry, sleep when tired. On this night, however, two of the men have a purpose. They have backed me so close against the wall that I can count the whiskers in their beards. To my right and to my left is a photo gallery of F.B.I. agents and policemen across whose faces have been scrawled: "Off the pigs. . . . Mash the pigs. . . . Stick the pigs."[15]

Write two or three paragraphs discussing the rhetorical effect of this narrative beginning. Consider such matters as the writer's use of tenses, anticipation, contrast, and significant detail. How has she involved us in her story?

9. Think of a significant incident that once occurred in your life, and narrate it in one or two paragraphs, using a straightforward time sequence and the past tense.

10. Choose a person to write about—either someone you know or someone you have seen in public life—and write a narrative paragraph that (a) shows the person in action, and (b) uses the present tense.

11. Tell part of the same story you told in Exercise 10, but this time mix your narrative with interpretive commentary, as in the "wolves" example on page 36.

12. For your own reference, make a list of events that would form a unified story. Ask yourself which event in the sequence seems most important. Then write a narrative of two or three paragraphs, beginning with that important event and then moving backward and forward in time.

13. Think of a real or imaginary story that would lead to some perception or generalization. Put that point into a sentence at the top of a page. Then skip some lines, and write the story in two or three paragraphs (or more, if you use dialogue) so that the story implies your point without stating it.

NOTES

[1] Roger Angell, *Five Seasons: A Baseball Companion* (New York: Simon and Schuster, 1977), p. 11.

[2] Angell, p. 12.

[3] Alexander Petrunkevitch, "The Spider and the Wasp," *Scientific American,* 187 (1952), p. 23.

[4] N. Scott Momaday, *The Way to Rainy Mountain* (Albuquerque: Univ. of New Mexico Press, 1969), p. 5.

[5] William G. Wing, "Christmas Comes First on the Banks," *New York Times,* 24 Dec. 1966, p. 18.

[6] Edward Hoagland, *Red Wolves and Black Bears* (New York: Random House, 1972), pp. 19–20.

[7] Agnes De Mille, *Dance to the Piper* (New York: Da Capo Press, 1980), p. 43.

[8] John Leonard, *Private Lives in the Imperial City* (New York: Knopf, 1979), pp. 93–94.

[9] Mark Twain, *Life on the Mississippi* (1883; rpt. New York: Signet, 1961), pp. 67–69.

[10] Richard Wright, *Black Boy: A Record of Childhood and Youth* (1945; rpt. New York: Harper & Row, 1969), p. 25.

[11] Margaret Mead, *Coming of Age in Samoa* (New York: Blue Ribbon Books, 1928), pp. 16–17.

[12] Peter F. Drucker, *Adventures of a Bystander* (New York: Harper & Row, 1978), p. 158.

[13] Farley Mowat, *Never Cry Wolf* (New York: Dell, 1963), p. 79.

[14] Joan Didion, "Some Dreamers of the Golden Dream," in *Slouching towards Bethlehem* (1968; rpt. New York: Washington Square Press, 1981), pp. 20–21.

[15] Lucinda Franks, "The Seeds of Terror," *New York Times Magazine,* 22 Nov. 1981, p. 35.

3

EXPLANATION

Description and narration, we have seen, can be considered together as the representational modes—those that aim to show the immediate reality of a given object or person or event. In turning now to explanation we move from that concrete purpose to an abstract one: not creating a physical impression or report of something, but proposing an idea about it that will make it understandable.

Needless to say, as essayists we can never hope to make an object of explanation totally understandable. Rather, we adopt one or more of the following particular strategies, each of which involves performing a specific explanatory operation on the object at hand (x):

Defining	Distinguishing x from everything else
Dividing	Showing the parts that make up x
Illustrating	Naming instances of x
Analyzing a process	Showing how x works or is properly done
Comparing and contrasting	Relating x to other things that are closely associated with it

| Analogizing | Presenting *x* in terms of something else |
| Showing causes and effects | Indicating how *x* came about or how it affects other things |

Each of these seven strategies can occupy as little space as a paragraph or as much as a whole essay. For now, however, we will put whole essays aside and simply introduce the basic means of explaining. Since most college papers are in fact essays of explanation, you will find such essays discussed at length in the section on composing (Chapters 5 and 6).

DEFINING

In **defining** a writer specifies exactly what a certain thing or idea is, so that it cannot be mistaken for anything else. Definition of things or ideas always involves two basic steps:

1. *classification,* showing what kind of thing *x* belongs to:

- A snail is a mollusk of the class *Gastropoda,* . . .

2. *differentiation,* showing how *x* differs from all other members of its class:

- . . . having a spirally coiled shell of a single valve and a ventral muscular foot on which it slowly glides about.

These two steps are fundamental because they encompass the mind's most common procedure for making sense of the world. To decide what any unfamiliar object is, we must first align it with already familiar things having the same general nature or purpose: all snails are mollusks, and among the mollusks all snails fall within a smaller grouping, the gastropods. But precisely because there are other gastropods, we must spell out features of the snail which, taken together, apply to *no other* gastropods. When that has been done, the definition is adequate.

Again, if we want to say just what a hammock is, we cannot avoid beginning by classifying it as a type of bed. Then we will want to locate the smallest possible subclass of beds to which every hammock belongs: *it is a hanging bed.* Yes, but an upper bunk in a ship or prison may also be a hanging bed. Since the subclass contains members which are not hammocks, we must specify features that show hammocks to be a unique kind of hanging bed: *A hammock is a hanging bed* (classification) *made of canvas, netted cord, or the like* (differentiation).

Exact definition is of the utmost importance in legal and scientific writing, where there must be no possibility that different readers may construe a term in different ways. That is why, for example, legal prose is so full of cumbersome-sounding repetition and elaboration; the idea is to "close loopholes" by making sure that all possible instances of the term are covered and that no false instances are included. Such ponderousness would be out of place in essay prose, but there, too, definition can be an important means of securing agreement.

It is, in fact, just because readers tend to grasp the same idea in diverse ways that definition is a powerful rhetorical tool. If, for instance, the idea in question is *murder,* think how many issues hinge on its definition. Is it murder to kill a fetus, and if so, at what point after conception does the concept apply? All arguments about abortion revolve around this point. Again, is it murder to kill someone on a sudden uncontrollable impulse, or in revenge or fear after decades of wife beating, or under the influence of a drug unknowingly taken, or behind the wheel of a car, or on the orders of a superior officer? Definition turns out to lie at the heart of many a longstanding public debate. And this means that a writer who can convincingly show why a key term deserves to be understood in a certain way has won a commanding advantage.

In a paper of explanation, for example, a student wanted to maintain, despite a contrary view held by some expert researchers, that apes and dolphins do not truly possess language. He was in no position to challenge the research cited by the "pro-language" advocates, but he *could* ask whether they were using too open-ended a definition of language. Note how the following passage moves from classification *(a language is simply a communication system . . .)* to differentiation (*. . . which meets four conditions . . .):*

> If a language is simply a communication system, then apes and dolphins certainly use language. So, for that matter, do ants, bees, and termites. We might even say that flowers are using a language—of color, shape, and smell—to summon the bees to their pollen. But when we allow a term to include so many different things, it ceases to be interesting or useful.
>
> Clearly, we want a definition of language that stays fairly close to the human capacity for speech. From our readings this term, I gather that a communication system is a language only if it meets all of the following conditions:
>
> 1. It must contain a large number of signals.
> 2. Those signals must not be mere cries triggered by inner states; rather, they must be symbolic, *referring* to such things as non-present objects, ideas, and past and future states.

3. The system must be syntactic; that is, the *order* of the sounds made will affect their meaning.

4. The system must be conversational; when two parties use it together, they will be able to take turns and respond to the meaning of each other's signals.

To insist on all four of these conditions is to acknowledge how radically different a true language is from animal communication in general. And it is also to pose a suitably difficult test for apes and dolphins to pass. In this demanding sense of the term *language,* I have yet to read a convincing case for the existence of animal language, either natural or produced through human training.

EXERCISES

1. Submit dictionary definitions for any five familiar terms (e.g., *opera, cancer, handbag,* . . .), indicating in each case which part of the definition is *classification (C)* and which part is *differentiation (D).*

2. Ask yourself which, if any, of the following activities ought to be regarded as *sports:* hiking, chess, bowling, body building. Then write a paragraph or two in which you resolve that issue by carefully defining what you mean by the term *sports.* (Must a sport be physical, competitive, etc.?)

3. Choose a term, such as *freedom* or *democracy* or *patriotism,* that you find to be interpreted *positively but very differently* by different individuals or groups. (For example, leaders of nations with entirely opposed political systems regard those nations as *democracies.*) Using your dictionary, your memory, and any other handy sources, gather as many different senses of your chosen term as you can locate. Then submit several paragraphs in which you define the term as *you* think it should be construed, showing why you prefer that definition to other possibilities.

DIVIDING

In **division** the work of explanation proceeds by a spelling out of the parts or stages that make up some whole. Since the parts of one thing will always differ in some way from those of anything else, division can be close in function to definition; naming all the parts is a means of grasping what is unique about the object or idea. Thus the writer who specified all the ingredients of a baseball (p. 23) was using division to indicate what the ball *must* contain to be properly considered a baseball and not, for example, a softball.

Especially when used near the beginning of an essay, division can perform the simple but useful function of indicating the range of a subject:

> The predators—insects that kill and consume other insects—are of many kinds. Some are quick and with the speed of swallows snatch their prey from the air. Others plod methodically along a stem, plucking off and devouring sedentary insects like the aphids. The yellowjackets capture soft-bodied insects and feed the juices to their young. Mud-dauber wasps build columned nests of mud under the eaves of houses and stock them with insects on which their young will feed. The horse-guard wasp hovers above herds of grazing cattle, destroying the blood-sucking flies that torment them. The loudly buzzing syrphid fly, often mistaken for a bee, lays its eggs on leaves of aphid-infested plants; the hatching larvae then consume immense numbers of aphids. Ladybugs or lady beetles are among the most effective destroyers of aphids, scale insects, and other plant-eating insects. Literally hundreds of aphids are consumed by a single ladybug to stoke the little fires of energy which she requires to produce even a single batch of eggs.[1]

Observe how the writer has first defined predator insects and then divided them into various kinds. Yet instead of making a dry, listlike effect, she has sustained interest by descriptively capturing each species' most typical action. More important, she has demonstrated her wide knowledge and laid a foundation for her main point, disclosed in a later paragraph: that indiscriminate spraying of pesticides kills a great many insects that would otherwise help to control agricultural pests.

By dividing a subject into its parts, you can also bring order out of apparent confusion. Look, for example, at how a student writer leads into a discussion of buying a ten-speed bicycle:

> What should you look for when shopping for a ten-speed bike? It is easy to get confused by glossy advertisements saying that you can't do without the latest molybdenum frame and cantilever brakes. But you can bring some sense into the matter if you keep in mind that all ten-speed bikes are designed primarily either for *touring* or for *racing*. Which activity do you prefer? The answer will tell you whether to go for a stiff frame or a more comfortable one; whether you want tight steering or a capacity for no-hands cruising on the highway; whether you should be more interested in quickness of shifting or in having a low enough bottom gear for hauling luggage up a mountain road.

Here the act of division—separating all ten-speed bikes into touring and racing cycles—leads to a series of further distinctions, each of which can be developed in a subsequent paragraph.

As we will see in Chapters 5 and 6, division is as much a means of gathering and organizing ideas as it is a rhetorical strategy. Once you have broken any subject into parts, new relations come into view, and you have in hand a variety of possibilities to work with. The paragraph above, for example, could find a place in a whole essay about racing bikes, or about touring bikes, or about innovation in design, or about the inevitable tradeoff between speed and comfort.

Again, a student who wanted to write about hang gliding but who felt at a loss for a precise topic was able to find one as soon as he had *listed all the skills* that make for competence in that sport. The skills, he saw, bore no resemblance to the recklessness that many people associate with hang gliding:

> When they see somebody careening beyond a steep cliff on a hang glider, most people probably think they are watching a person with a death wish. Hang gliding *is* dangerous; I don't recommend it for everyone. But after three years of improving my skills in that sport, I think I can say that foolhardiness has nothing to do with it. The qualities required if you are going to get anywhere with hang gliding are, first, an ability to be decisive without being reckless; second, muscular control; third, patience; and last, a thorough understanding of your equipment. These are not exactly the makings of a suicidal personality.

The essay went on both to describe hang-gliding maneuvers and to narrate instances from the writer's experience. Those details, however, were recounted not for their own sake but in illustration of the thesis that four qualities are required by hang gliding. Thus it was the original division of a general subject, *competence in hang gliding,* that gave the essay its coherence.

EXERCISES

4. Take a public problem or issue, such as air pollution or gene transplants or the arms race, and break that problem or issue into what you consider to be its component parts—namely, the narrower issues that go to make it up. (If the issue were abortion, for example, the sub-issues might be the rights of the unborn, how to determine when human life begins, parents' right to control family size, religious prohibitions, health risks to mothers, and the effects of making abortion legal or illegal. But now that this example has been supplied, you should choose a different issue.) Underline the items on your list that strike you as deserving the most concern, and then write the introductory paragraph to an essay about the issue, emphasizing the important subissues. Hand in your underlined list along with the paragraph.

5. Write several paragraphs in which you divide college or high-school teachers into a number of main types (e.g., the lawgiver, the prima donna, the chatterbox, the pal). You need not worry about being especially fair-minded. Try to include at least one characteristic action to illustrate each of your types.

ILLUSTRATING

A third explanatory strategy is **illustration,** or the providing of examples to back up an idea. Here the point is not to distinguish one item from all others or to name its parts but to offer a sample of *instances.* The sample should be small enough to be rhetorically manageable but large enough to inspire trust that the writer's idea is grounded in cases:

> Foreigners are buying America. It's no longer just the smart money or the tax-evasion money. It's the savings of a Bavarian innkeeper who can earn only 3.5 per cent a year at his bank at home; it's the British Airways pension fund, which owns a shopping center in Houston. It's the oil money of Iranians, among them a sister of the Shah, who have bought so many of the million-dollar homes in the Trousdale Estates section of Beverly Hills that the natives call it "the Persian Gulf." And it's the Eurodollars in the coffers of polyglot multinationals in Stockholm and Stuttgart, using the profits from their exports to the U.S. to build and buy factories here. The Germans make Volkswagen Rabbits in a Pennsylvania factory that Chrysler had to abandon. The Japanese bottle Coca-Cola in New Hampshire, raise cattle in Utah and make soy sauce in rural Wisconsin.[2]

The opening sentence of this paragraph, stating its theme, is meant to be a shocker. By the end, however, having been subjected to a battery of impressive examples, we are sure that the idea (however overstated) rests on real evidence. It is easy to picture this single explanatory maneuver being expanded into a whole essay in which each example would have a paragraph to itself.

A humorous or whimsical thesis stands in just as much need of illustration as a serious one:

> "I eat bread sparingly," writes Tom Osler. "In the summer, I consume large quantities of fruit juices. . . . I do not use salt at the table or at the stove. I do not use sugar, because it seems to make my skin break out in acne." In an article titled "Running Through Pregnancy" in *Runner's World,* we learn that runners "have little trouble with irregularity. Some even experience a frequency increase in bowel movements." In the pages of the same magazine Joe Henderson reports that he thinks of a running high "as the way we're supposed to feel when not constipated." If one did not know what was being talked about—running—one might feel like an eavesdropper listening in on conversations in a nursing home for the elderly.[3]

EXERCISES

6. Look through the readings assigned for this course—or, if you prefer, through recent newspapers and magazines—for an article or column that uses substantial illustration to support a thesis. Submit a paragraph in which you state that thesis, and back it up with several of the instances cited in the article or column. Be careful to use your own language, not the writer's.

7. Think of some general statement you would feel comfortable defending (e.g., *Students on this campus are more interested in parties than in books*), and jot down as many illustrative instances as you can think of. Then write a paragraph in which you set forth your idea and illustrate it with a number of specific cases.

8. Submit a paragraph which, like the passage about runners on page 48, uses illustrative points to build toward a conclusion at the end.

ANALYZING A PROCESS

Sometimes the stages to be covered in an explanation are actions or steps which, performed correctly and in a certain fixed order, make up a routine for accomplishing some end. Thus the student who wrote in defense of hang gliding (p. 47) could have submitted a **process analysis** of his favorite recreation, specifying the measures needed for successful takeoff, flight, and landing.

A process analysis can serve its purpose only if all of the essential steps appear in their necessary order. If, for instance, you were teaching your reader how to drive a stick-shift car, you might decide that the essential parts of the process are (1) familiarizing oneself with ignition, clutch, brake pedal, accelerator, and emergency brake; (2) starting and stopping; (3) steering while remaining within one gear; (4) shifting gears; (5) making turns; and (6) backing up. If item 1 appeared farther down the list, or if item 4 were missing, or if a triviality like *reading the odometer* were thrown in, the analysis would be flawed.

Process analyses occur frequently in technical writing—for example, in reports of experimental procedures or in operating instructions for new equipment. When essayists use the same strategy, they usually have some further idea in mind. Thus one writer analyzes a motorcycle mechanic's diagnostic steps, not in order to teach motorcycle repair, but to show that the mechanic uses exactly the same principles of reasoning as a scientist:

Skill at this point consists of using experiments that test only the hypothesis in question, nothing less, nothing more. If the horn honks, and the mechanic concludes that the whole electrical system is working, he is in deep trouble. He has reached an illogical conclusion. The honking horn only tells him that the battery and horn are working. To design an experiment properly he has to think very rigidly in terms of what directly causes what. This you know from the hierarchy. The horn doesn't make the cycle go. Neither does the battery, except in a very indirect way. The point at which the electrical system *directly* causes the engine to fire is at the spark plugs, and if you don't test here, at the output of the electrical system, you will never really know whether the failure is electrical or not.

To test properly the mechanic removes the plug and lays it against the engine so that the base around the plug is electrically grounded, kicks the starter lever and watches the spark-plug gap for a blue spark. If there isn't any he can conclude one of two things: (a) there is an electrical failure or (b) his experiment is sloppy. If he is experienced he will try it a few more times, checking connections, trying every way he can think of to get that plug to fire. Then, if he can't get it to fire, he finally concludes that *a* is correct, there's an electrical failure, and the experiment is over. He has proved that his hypothesis is correct.[4]

What distinguishes such a paragraph from sheer narrative is its reference, not to something that happened once, but to a procedure that must be followed every time a certain problem arises.

Sometimes, however, you can include elements of process analysis within prose that *is* primarily narrative, saying in effect *This is how I used to do* x. Notice, for example, how one writer zeroes in on a process as he recalls his boyhood days as a yo-yo champion:

The greatest pleasure in yo-yoing was an abstract pleasure — watching the dramatization of simple physical laws, and realizing they would never fail if a trick was done correctly. The geometric purity of it! The string wasn't just a string, it was a tool in the enactment of theorems. It was a line, an idea. And the top was an entirely different sort of idea, a gyroscope, capable of storing energy and of interacting with the line. I remember the first time I did a particularly lovely trick, one in which the sleeping yo-yo is swung from right to left while the string is interrupted by an extended index finger. Momentum carries the yo-yo in a circular path around the finger, but instead of completing the arc the yo-yo falls on the taut string between the performer's hands, where it continues to spin in an upright position. My pleasure at that moment was as much from the beauty of the experiment as from pride. Snapping apart my hands, I sent the yo-yo into the air above my head, bouncing it off nothing, back into my palm.[5]

Again, here are the reflections of a karate expert who succeeded in breaking cinder blocks only after he had stopped consciously "try-ing" to:

> Thus, when I now approach a stack of three two-inch cinder blocks to attempt a breaking feat, I do not set myself to "try hard," or to summon up all my strength. Instead I relax, sinking my awareness into my belly and legs, feeling my connection with the ground. I breathe deeply, mentally directing the breath through my torso, legs, and arms. I imagine a line of force coming up from the ground through my legs, down one arm, and out through an acupuncture point at the base of my palm, through the stone slabs, and down again into the ground, penetrating to the center of the earth. I do not focus any attention on the objects to be broken. Although when I am lifting or holding them in a normal state of consciousness the blocks seem tremendously dense, heavy, and hard, in the course of my one- or two-minute preparation their reality seems to change, as indeed the reality of the whole situation changes. I am no longer a thirty-two-year-old American writer in basketball sneakers doing strange breathing exercises in his suburban back yard in front of a pile of red patio blocks: I am a spiritual traveler, making the necessary preparations for a journey to a different world.[6]

In the first of these passages, the writer reveals more about his own mind—one that takes delight in the hidden order of things—than he does about yo-yoing. In the second, the writer is not so much "explaining" a karate feat as he is endorsing a non-Western approach to the relation between body and mind. These are only marginal instances of process analysis—but so are most uses of that strategy in essay prose.

EXERCISES

9. Think of some result that is usually arrived at by stages (e.g., developing a conscience, losing one's innocence, understanding computers, becoming an alcoholic). Write a paragraph of process analysis in which you set forth those stages in their usual order.

10. Think of some process that you have mastered or are trying to master (e.g., juggling, cooking an omelet, writing computer programs), and jot down the stages of that process—either the stages of learning it or, if you prefer, the stages of executing it. Then write a paragraph or two in which you analyze the process by describing those stages as accurately as possible.

11. Think of a general point that could be supported by one of the analyses you wrote for Exercises 9 and 10 (e.g., *There are no shortcuts to learning how to program computers* or *Anyone can become a juggler, but only by mastering the relevant skills in their necessary order*). Submit a paragraph in which you make that point, including as much process analysis as you find necessary for illustration.

COMPARING AND CONTRASTING

In a sense, we could say that all thinking comes down to **comparing** (matching things that are alike) and **contrasting** (pointing out differences). We cannot have an idea about anything without setting that object of thought beside similar things and then asking ourselves how it differs from them. Not surprisingly, then, comparison and contrast can be found at all levels of writing, from the structure of sentences and paragraphs through the central purpose of an essay or book. Definition, as we saw, works by comparison and contrast, and so does many a passage of description and narration (see, e.g., pp. 31, 36–37).

A typical essay of comparison and contrast might be called "American Dance Crazes: Then and Now" or "Country Living Is Best" or "Fashion Changes for the Later Eighties." Even though the title might not express the contrast in so many words, in each case the essay would pivot on significant differences. If country living is best, it can only be best by contrast with city living; and a fashion *change* would be meaningless without a discussion of the trends being replaced.

In an extended comparison and contrast, it is common to find whole paragraphs devoted to *either* resemblances or differences. And because the differences are usually more significant, the whole paragraph of resemblances generally comes earlier so as to establish a basis for the points of contrast. Thus an essay about the differences between two famous pitchers included the following early paragraph of sheer comparison:

> Both Seaver and Palmer have been World Series heroes. Both are handsome, intelligent and articulate men who are team leaders and spokesmen. They share a scholar's curiosity about their game and probably are the two best all-around pitchers in baseball today. Certainly many of the men who bat against them think so. "Seaver's the best pitcher around," says the Cards' hard-hitting Ted Simmons. "Palmer's top in the American League in my book," says Lee Stanton, even though one of his Angel teammates is the reigning fastballer, Nolan Ryan. But last year Seaver had an 11–11 record and Palmer was 7–12. They were at the abyss.[7]

Again, a student writer who wanted to show how different Hamlet and Laertes are devoted a richly detailed early paragraph to showing that the two characters deserve to be considered together:

> We need only abstract Laertes' five brief appearances in order to see that he and Hamlet are meant to be taken as parallel figures. In Act I, scene 2, Laertes asks the King for permission to return to France; in the

same scene we learn that Hamlet has asked the King for permission to return to Wittenburg. In Laertes' second appearance he reproaches his sister for her receptivity to Hamlet; Hamlet later gives a comparable lecture to Gertrude. Hamlet's loss of a father through murder is mirrored by Laertes' loss of Polonius to Hamlet's own sword, and in Act IV, scene 1, Laertes reappears with the Hamlet-like idea of killing his father's murderer. Again, Laertes' cries of grief at Ophelia's funeral are travestied by Hamlet, who leaps after him into the grave. And in Laertes' fifth appearance, in Act V, he and Hamlet square off for a duel of offended sons—and the result of the scene is that both of them die and both are avenged. Laertes, we might say, scarcely exists apart from Hamlet. Superficially, at least, they harbor the same desires and grievances, love the same woman, behave alike, and are drawn into a single fate at the end.

Having established such strong parallels, the writer went on to show how Laertes' reckless passion stands out against Hamlet's doubts and hesitations.

Whichever element comes first—resemblances or differences—we can be fairly sure that the *second* element will receive major emphasis. This rule applies, for example, to paragraphs that include both elements. Thus, seeking to dwell on the differences between the American Bill of Rights and the *Communist Manifesto*, a student writer wisely began her paragraph with comparisons, not contrasts:

resemblances

differences

The authors of our Bill of Rights and of the *Communist Manifesto* shared an idea that previous forms of government had protected injustice and inequality. Both were determined to write a charter for a new kind of society in which ordinary people would be free from tyranny. The two documents, however, are absolutely opposed in their conceptions of human liberty. The Bill of Rights seeks to limit the powers of government by specifying the rights of individuals, whereas Marx's *Manifesto* seeks—chiefly by denying the rights of inheritance and private property—to protect the masses from powerful individuals. We will see that this difference of philosophy runs straight through the two documents, making one of them, the *Manifesto*, a list of what *must* be done and the other, the Bill of Rights, a list of what *must not* be done to interfere with the will of citizens.

The pivotal word *however* doesn't simply divide this writer's paragraph in two; it correctly predicts that in her essay the differences between the *Communist Manifesto* and the Bill of Rights will outweigh the characteristics they share.

---

12. Looking through magazines and newspapers, find two editorials or columns expressing opinions about the same public issue. Submit copies along with two or three paragraphs of your own in which you compare and contrast the two pieces, emphasizing the points of opinion or style or tone that you find most significant.

13. Write two paragraphs about two movies that seem to you alike in certain ways and different in others. Use your two paragraphs to establish the most important resemblances and differences. You can deal with themes, leading characters, techniques, or effects.

14. Think of two individuals or groups that are often considered to be extremely different (e.g., two famous public figures, men and women, babies and old people, Texans and New Yorkers). Jot down all the ways in which you could show that the seeming opposites are really alike. Then submit a paragraph in which, beginning with the obvious points of difference, you emphasize the little-noted similarities.

ANALOGIZING

A writer who analogizes is calling attention to likenesses of a special kind. Instead of pointing up resemblances between two things that are clearly alike in certain ways (comparison), the writer asks us to see one thing—the only one actually being considered—*in terms of* an obviously different thing. If a comparison says that *x* is like *y*, an analogy says that you can grasp something important about *x* if you think about *y* in a certain way. The *y* term is not itself an object of study, as in a comparison. Rather, it is a figure of speech (see pp. 230–233)—a means of clarifying or emphasizing a point about *x* that the writer already believes to be true.

To illustrate, let us consider the nuclear arms race. A writer who likened that competition to the struggle between the United States and Japan for dominance in the electronics industry would be *comparing* two things that are similar enough to be considered together. But suppose, instead, the writer said this: *In their nuclear arms race, the U.S. and the U.S.S.R. are like two men sitting in a pool of gasoline. One of them has seven matches and the other has only five.*[8] That would be an **analogy**—that is, *an extended likeness purporting to show that the rule or principle behind one thing also holds for the quite different thing being discussed.*

Why bother with analogies when more direct forms of explanation are available? The "arms race" example tells why: a good analogy makes a point vivid, memorable, and easy to comprehend. One immediately sees what is foolish about stockpiling matches while sitting in a pool of gasoline, and the mind readily transposes that lesson to the arms race. If a nuclear war will destroy both nations, neither of them should be trying to produce the bigger arsenal.

But this same example also shows the limited force of even the best analogies. An analogy can be persuasive on an emotional or imaginative plane, but it can never prove the intended point. An opponent is always free to brush the analogy aside and talk about factors that the analogizer has left out of account. An advocate of nuclear "parity," for example, could maintain that the theory of deterrence has prevented another world war for some forty years now, whereas the theory of nuclear disarmament faces many untested difficulties. For every analogy urging one side of the case, a contrary analogy could be devised: *The U.S. and the U.S.S.R. are like two men who hate each other but have to act cautiously because they live together in a room full of TNT. The advocates of nuclear disarmament would take away the explosive and leave the men alone with their guns and knives.* Which of the two analogies is "right"? Neither. Both of them are simply means of dramatizing beliefs that rest on other grounds.

Even so, there is something about a well-turned analogy that inspires trust. At the very least, we sense that the writer has thought carefully about the topic. And when the topic is complex or controversial, the analogy can overcome resistance by permitting us to think in less clouded terms. Thus, for example, an investment adviser who believed in going against market trends made a strong impression by writing *If all the children sit on the south end of the seesaw because that's the end going up, it can't go up.*[9] Once again the analogy proves nothing—market trends, after all, do not always reverse themselves as soon as everyone follows them—but the writer has found an apt image to convey *his* logic about investment strategy.

Do not conclude that analogies are good only for argumentative position taking. On the contrary, their main function is to make something clearer by putting it in simpler and more pictorial terms. Wherever you are worried that things may be getting too complicated for your reader to follow, you can consider resorting to this device. Here, for example, a writer who is seeking to explain a disastrous conjunction of weather fronts uses the more readily apprehended image of an automobile crashing into a wall:

> The real problem with forecasting the generation of a storm such as this is gauging its severity. It is not like following a fully developed storm for several days as it moves across the ocean, watching it weaken or strengthen with some sort of regularity. It is more like watching a car about to crash into a brick wall; you know there is going to be a crash, there is an 80 percent chance the gas tank will explode, but you don't know how much gas is in the tank! Just as with the car, the measure of a storm's severity is gauged by its ingredients; the existence of a front (the brick wall), the amount of cold air coming down behind the front

(speed of the car), and the degree of circulation in the upper air approaching the front (amount of gas in the tank).[10]

Note how carefully this writer has developed the elements of his analogy, drawing out its lesson without pursuing it to the point of tedium or overelaboration.

EXERCISES

15. Examine and, in a paragraph or two, evaluate the use of analogy in the following paragraph by a writer who wants the oil industry to be subject to fewer regulations:

> To return to our analogous world of the entertainment industry, we may ask why it is fair that someone earn a fortune because he is born with flexible hips and durable vocal cords. To my knowledge, most people do not chastise entertainers for making a fortune rocking in the jailhouse in blue suede shoes. We accept that market outcome and fuss very little about its equity. Why is it that we place emphasis on political justice in petroleum but not in amusement? When we have answered that question, if we can, and when we have decided to allow petroleum companies and consumers the same rights we grant rock musicians and their audiences, I strongly suspect we will find the public better served.[11]

16. Think of an activity, hobby, sport, or business that you might want to explain to someone who knew nothing about it. Jot down as many analogies as you can think of, and write a paragraph in which you use the most promising-looking of those analogies to make the topic clear to an outsider.

SHOWING CAUSES AND EFFECTS

A final strategy of explanation—one so basic that we rely on it in every aspect of our waking lives—is the isolating of causes and effects. All of our decisions rest on beliefs about the consequences (effects) of this or that action. Rhetorically, the investigation of causes and effects has a place in any number of contexts, from the reporting of experimental results and the analysis of historical events to arguments for or against a given policy.

Most writing about cause and effect proceeds from known effects —that is, from accomplished facts such as a burst dam or an economic recession or a change in climate—to supposed causes, which are usually multiple. The following student paragraph shows a common pattern of beginning with the effect, disposing of relatively minor causal factors, and then treating the factors that seem weightiest:

the effect to be explained   In recent decades the reported death rate from cancer has been rising dramatically. How alarmed should we be by this statistical change? One

cause #1	cause of the mounting curve is probably the simple fact that we are
	more conscious of cancer now than we used to be, and less ashamed to
cause #2	mention the feared disease. Another cause may be the fact that more
	and more people are dying in hospitals and undergoing autopsies: in
	earlier times the comparable deaths at home from cancer might have
the more	been attributed to "old age." But factors like these take us only so far.
serious causes:	Eventually we have to admit that cancer has been gaining on us in an
	absolute sense. If so, the real causes must be environmental: the contin-
#3, #4,	ued increase in smoking, the use of dangerous pesticides and food addi-
#5	tives, and increased pollution from automobiles and industry. Some of
	those sources must be more responsible than others, but until we know
	more than we do, we had better give urgent attention to all of them.

After this strong introduction, which showed a proper caution about making one-to-one connections between causes and effects, the writer devoted the rest of her essay to the three causes she had identified as most significant.

It is possible as well to begin with something already known or proposed and to ask what its effects are or would be. Here, for example, a student writer focuses on the effects of jogging—effects that lead to a general conclusion at the end of the paragraph:

effects: #1	Tests show that joggers have significantly lower resting heart rates than
#2	nonjoggers and that their recovery time after exertion is much briefer.
#3	Heart attacks, which some people still wrongly associate with the en-
	larged "athlete's heart," are more common in the general population
#4	than among joggers. Then, too, every jogger experiences an exhilarat-
	ing sense of well-being and vitality, not just while running but through-
	out the day. A daily half-hour of jogging is time invested at the highest
	rate of return.

post hoc explanation   You should bear in mind that two events or conditions can be associated in time without being related as cause and effect. Perhaps this seems obvious, but most of us become superstitious when partisan feelings or pet beliefs are involved. Democrats claim that Republican administrations "cause" economic recessions; Republicans call their rival "the war party" because most wars have erupted when Democrats were in power; and zealots of various kinds support their dogmas by arguing that their dreams were fulfilled or that some good result followed the performance of a ritual. This fallacy goes by its Latin name, *post hoc ergo propter hoc:* "after this, therefore because of it." It was most memorably exemplified by the Canadian humorist Stephen Leacock: "When I state that my lectures were followed almost immediately by the union of South Africa, the banana riots in Trinidad, and the Turco-Italian war, I think the reader can form some opinion of their importance."

correlation Much treatment of causes and effects wisely steers away from flat assertions that *x* is *the* cause of *y*. Instead, the writer significantly associates, or **correlates**, *x* with *y*, leaving open the possibility that factors *a, b,* and *c* may also have played a part in producing *x*. In the paragraph above, for example, the writer does not claim that jogging is *the* preventive against heart attacks, but that the incidence of heart attacks is low among joggers. The door is left open to other factors, as it should be—for joggers tend to be nonsmokers, and smoking in its turn has been correlated with heart disease.

Consider the following student passage, which correlates a popular dance style with various characteristics of the 1970s:

> The clearest example of all is provided by disco dancing, which became a national craze in 1978. In several respects disco is the perfect expression of the decade that produced it. For one thing, the seventies combined a rediscovery of "roots" with an easing of the racial tensions that were so explosive in the sixties. Black and Latin in its origins, disco has remained somewhat ethnic in flavor, yet it has been accepted by the whole society. Second, disco is a high-technology form; its amplified sounds and its dazzling lights suggest the network of electronics that many people have recently felt to be their real environment. Third, disco expresses "the me decade" both in its demand for physical fitness and in its emphasis on display. And finally, disco is more disciplined than the do-your-own-thing dances of the sixties. Disco swept the country at a time when nearly everyone who had once joined "the counterculture" was ready to give the sense of order a second chance.

Observe that in this passage, cause-and-effect reasoning merely *associates* a complex of factors with a certain result. The writer wisely refrains from risking everything on only one of four possible sources of the 1970s' disco craze—the emphasis on *race, technology, self,* and *discipline.* By including all four factors, he shows both an acquaintance with the decade and a regard for the limitations of his insight into it.

EXERCISES

17. Think about something you have done that now strikes you as wrong; it can be either a specific act or the adoption of a habit or prejudice. What were the probable causes, or determining factors, leading to your act or habit? Write a paragraph in which you proceed from *what* you did to *why* you think you did it.

18. To explore relations between intended causes and effects, find an advertisement that implies a strong but farfetched connection between an advertised product and an appealing image, personality, or style of living. Submit the advertisement or a photocopy of it along with two or

three paragraphs analyzing what you take to be the intended effect of the ad. (Of course, the ultimate intended effect is that people buy the product. You should concentrate on the immediate intended effect—namely, to link the product with a desirable feeling.)

19. Find a news story about an event that probably had at least three separate causes, and write two or three paragraphs summarizing the event and revealing what you take to have been its main causes.

NOTES

[1]Rachel Carson, *Silent Spring* (Boston: Houghton Mifflin, 1962), pp. 249–50.

[2]"The Buying of America," *Newsweek*, 27 Nov. 1978, p. 78.

[3]Joseph Epstein, *Familiar Territory: Observations on American Life* (New York: Oxford Univ. Press, 1979), pp. 159–60.

[4]Robert M. Pirsig, *Zen and the Art of Motorcycle Maintenance: An Inquiry into Values* (New York: Morrow, 1974), p. 110.

[5]Frank Conroy, *Stop-time* (New York: Viking, 1967), pp. 114–15.

[6]Don Ethan Miller, "A State of Grace: Understanding the Martial Arts," *Atlantic*, Sept. 1980, p. 88.

[7]Ron Fimrite, "Kings of the Hill Again," *Sports Illustrated*, 21 July 1975, p. 15.

[8]Adapted from quotation of Barbara Boxer by Herb Caen, *San Francisco Chronicle*, 27 May 1982, p. 37.

[9]John Train, "Lessons of the Masters," *Harvard Magazine*, May–June 1982, p. 19.

[10]Rob Mairs, "How the Storm Developed," *Yachting*, Nov. 1979, p. 120.

[11]Edward J. Mitchell, "Oil, Films, and Folklore," *Chevron World*, Fall 1978, p. 25.

4

ARGUMENT

ELEMENTS OF PERSUASION

The fourth traditional mode of rhetoric is **argument**, or the reasoned defense of opinion about a topic of controversy. As the diagram on page 10 suggests, argument in its central purpose is the most abstract of modes, stepping back from the data of experience to convince us that a certain view or policy is preferable to another. If a typical argument nevertheless contains concrete details, that is because arguments usually *incorporate* more immediate kinds of writing as evidence for the case being made.

Let us think, for example, of *drug abuse*. In a typical instance of description or narration, we would be told what it is like to abuse drugs. In an essay of explanation, the writer might show us the causes or effects of drug abuse or divide the subject into a number of categories. In arguing, by contrast, the writer might try to convince us that certain banned drugs should or should not be made legal. In order to support that argumentative thesis, the writer would have to include such evidence as *description* of withdrawal symptoms, *narration* of significant case histories, and *explanation* of how the changed law would affect tax revenues, the incidence of crime, and so forth.

Every argument asks either that we choose between competing goals—for example, having a championship football team or expanding the library—or that we decide on the best way of reaching an agreed-upon goal. If we want a winning team, which measure is more urgent: aggressive recruitment of players or hiring a new coach? Whether the issue is ends or means, the writer of an argument always hopes to move the reader away from a neutral or differing opinion so that the two of them will share a conviction. That is why argument is sometimes called **persuasion**. To persuade is to move to action. Although no action is necessarily demanded of readers who accept an argumentative thesis, the word *persuasion* does capture that idea of moving people from one attitude into a different one. We can think of argument, then, as the attempt to persuade readers to share the writer's attitude toward an issue.

The term *argument* may nevertheless sound odd if you are used to thinking of arguments as quarrels involving raised voices and frayed tempers. Actually, quarrelsomeness need not enter into argumentative writing at all. The ideal is to present supporting evidence pointing so convincingly to the correctness of your stand that you can afford to be civil and even generous toward those who believe otherwise.

Some arguments, it must be said, succeed because they trigger the prejudices and emotions of a highly susceptible audience. It is no great feat, for example, to argue convincingly for patriotism when your country has just been invaded. In college writing, however, arguments are supposedly addressed to a neutral reader—one who is open to cogent reasoning without having a prior stake in a certain position. The classic virtues of argument, which sometimes get brushed aside by zeal, are worth cultivating because they carry the best hope, not of arousing the faithful, but of appealing to the sympathies and common sense of people in general.

main principles of argument These are the principles of arguing to convince a wide audience:

1. The thesis, or central idea, is prominently stated, carefully limited in scope, and plausible.
2. The weightiest objections are answered, either by concession (granting the truth of a statement without agreeing to its supposed importance) or by refutation (proving a statement untrue).
3. The evidence, or body of supporting statements, is strong.
4. The tone is controlled. The essay may be impassioned, but it makes its point without coercive appeals to emotionalism.

In the rest of this chapter we will touch on these requirements one by one, suggesting how each of them can be translated into effective rhetoric.

ARGUMENTATIVE THESIS

The thesis of an effective argument is always a stand for or against a certain position or course of action. Readers must be left in no doubt that it *is* the thesis; it needs to be stated explicitly, emphatically, and early enough for the writer's unfolding logic to be clear. That is, no doubt should remain that such-and-such points are being included because they support the thesis or that certain others constitute objections to be disposed of without causing serious damage to the thesis. In a word, if the thesis lacks prominence, the argument lacks coherence.

How do you find a suitable thesis, and how can you tell it from a fatally weak one? These questions are so important that they will occupy much of the following chapter (pp. 86–103). For now, let us emphasize that a good argumentative thesis is *not* found merely by asking yourself what you believe most strongly to be true and important. Since your purpose is to win agreement, not to blow off steam, your choice of a thesis should have as much to do with your imagined reader as with yourself. You should seek a common argumentative ground with that reader—a neutral territory where you can communicate without appealing to sheer prejudice.

In practice, this means three things. First, you should try to argue about something in which your reader could readily take an interest. If, say, your general subject area is *video game arcades*, you want to think twice about arguing that such-and-such a game is more fun to play than such-and-such another one; that preference involves no public issue. If, in contrast, your thesis is that *Video arcades are a useful means of reducing juvenile crime* or that *Video arcades should be closed down* or that *Video arcades should be located well away from public schools*, you have a reasonable expectation of gaining your reader's interest. Not many adult readers are video fans, but everyone supposedly cares about the social environment of children and teenagers.

Second, your thesis should be *testable* by appeal to experience that you and your reader are both willing to count as valid. This principle is violated, for example, by the thesis x *We must make every preparation for the prophesied end of the world.* The prophecy in question may prove true, but until a prophecy is fulfilled it remains an article of faith, not evidence. If the reader must join your sect in order to agree with your thesis, you have not yet found a common ground for argument.

And third, you must steer between the *empty* and the *implausible* thesis. On the subject of poverty, for instance, a typical empty thesis would be x *We must do whatever we can to eliminate poverty.* That statement is so indefinite that it could cover any action—or inaction. ("Whatever we can do" may turn out to be nothing.) You want your thesis to be at least somewhat controversial. Otherwise, why bother? Yet at the same time you want to avoid the wild or implausible thesis: x *The government should erase poverty by giving a direct grant of $100,000 to every low-income citizen.* Here the problem is no longer emptiness but extravagance; you would face an impossible task of showing that this "erasing of poverty" would be a net benefit to the society as a whole. Choose a thesis that could be made plausible by a relatively limited fund of new evidence—for example, *We should abandon the "trickle-down" theory of helping the poor by giving tax breaks to the rich* or *Able-bodied recipients of welfare should be required to work in exchange for their subsidies.* You need not agree with either of these statements in order to see that they fall within the "arguable" range.

Avoiding the Unfair Thesis

Nothing is easier than to "win" an argument that has been stacked in your favor from the outset. Such a victory will be not only hollow but boring as well. Readers cannot take an interest in the rejection of claims that are identified from the first as outlandish. Your argumentative thesis should reflect your judgment that a real point remains to be settled.

fallacies to avoid Although common sense is all you really need to avoid the unfair thesis, it is useful to be aware of the classic **fallacies**, or shortcuts of reasoning, that readers consider illegitimate. If your thesis or indeed any part of your argument shows one of the following traits, you need to address the issue more squarely.

begging the question Beware of settling an issue in advance by posing it in "loaded" language. Such **begging the question** (prejudging the issue) is apparent in each of the following theses:

> x A. It is inadvisable to let hardened criminals out of prison prematurely so that they can renew their war on society.
>
> x B. Society has no right to lock up the victims of poverty and inequality for indefinite periods, brutalizing them in the name of "rehabilitation."

Writers A and B are addressing the same issue, but each of them has settled it in advance. The word *prematurely* already contains the idea that many convicts are released too soon, and other terms— *hardened criminals, renew their war*—reinforce the point. For writer B there is no such thing as a criminal in the first place. When *victims* have been *brutalized,* it isn't hard to decide whether the brutalization should be prolonged. The trouble is that both A and B, in their eagerness to sweep away objections, have shown at the outset that their "investigation" will be phony. If you want to engage your reader's mind, you have to state a thesis with which some sane people might reasonably disagree.

Of course your thesis should convey an attitude, but it should do so in fair language:

- A. The policy of releasing prisoners on probation has not justified the social risks it involves.
- B. If the goal of prisons is to rehabilitate, the prison system must be considered on balance to be a failure.

Note that these two versions are just as hard-hitting as the ones they replace; the difference is simply that their language doesn't beg the question.

misstating the opposing case: the straw man   Another form of unfair argument is to exaggerate or misrepresent the opposing position. Such a falsification turns that position into a **straw man** that can be all too easily toppled. Thus, if the question is whether students should be allowed to serve on faculty committees, a writer would be creating a straw man by arguing that *Faculty efforts to keep the student body in a state of perpetual childhood must be resisted.* Here the specific issue—the pros and cons of student participation— has conveniently disappeared behind the straw man of wicked faculty intentions. A fairer thesis would be *If faculty members really want to make informed judgments about conditions on campus, they ought to welcome student voices on their committees.*

attacking personalities: ad hominem argument   Still another fallacious shortcut is to attack the people who favor a certain position rather than the position itself. This is known as *ad hominem* (Latin, "to the man") argument. Sometimes such an argument tells us real or invented things about somebody's character or behavior. The implication is that if we disapprove of such shamefulness, we had better reject the idea that has become linked with it. More often the writer simply mentions that a despised faction such as "communism" or "big business" supports the other side:

x By now we should all recognize the dangers of national health insurance, a scheme for which subversives have long been agitating.

x To vote correctly on this antipollution initiative, one need only realize that the oil and highway lobbies are doing everything in their power to defeat it.

Compare:

- To judge from the British example, national health insurance might impose an intolerable burden on our economy.
- Although it will involve extra costs in the short run, this antipollution initiative will eventually prove economical by reducing expenditures for sick leave and disability.

As politicians realize, *ad hominem* attacks do often have their desired effect. Because none of us has time to think through the pros and cons of every public issue, we sometimes rely on surface clues; if certain "bad guys" are revealed to be on one side, we automatically favor the other. As citizens, though, we ought to recognize that the *ad hominem* appeal is a form of bullying. And as writers, we ought to get along without the cheap advantage it affords. If you *can* win an argument on its merits, do so; if you cannot, you should change your position.

either-or
reasoning

Finally, make sure your thesis does not forbid disagreement through **either-or reasoning**—that is, by pretending that the only alternative is something awful. Thus a writer favoring legal abortion might claim, x *We must legalize abortion or the world will become disastrously overpopulated,* and a writer on the opposite side might reply, x *We must prevent legal abortion or the family will cease to exist.* Both writers would be delivering an ultimatum. *Which do you choose, overpopulation or legal abortion? What will it be, legal abortion or the survival of the family?* The choice is supposed to be automatic. All a reader must do, however, to escape the bind is to think of one other possibility. Is there no means to control population except through abortion? Might legal abortion have some lesser consequence than the destruction of family life? Your wisest course would be to admit that people favoring an opposite stand from yours have good reasons for their view—reasons that you do not find decisive. If the issue *were* one of total right versus total wrong, you would probably be wasting your time writing about it.

For further fallacies, see pages 99–100.

EXERCISES

1. Drawing on some or all of the following general subjects, submit five theses that strike you as appropriate and workable for an essay of argument:

   A. Drunken driving
   B. Effects of immigration on American life
   C. The increased rate of football injuries on artificial turf
   D. Treatment of patients in irreversible comas
   E. Costs and benefits of the space program

2. Submit a paragraph explaining why any of your five theses (Exercise 1) is appropriate for an essay of argument. Contrast that thesis with two versions that would be considered (a) "empty" and (b) implausible.

3. Mark a whole sheet of paper as follows (p. 66), leaving ample spaces between the lines. Review the fallacies discussed on pages 63–65. Then, choosing any topics except those used in the text, make up four unfair theses of the indicated types. For each unfair thesis that you write in the left column, add an improved version in the right column.

	Unfair Thesis	Improved Thesis
Begging the Question		
Straw man		
Ad Hominem		
Either-or		

CONCESSION AND REFUTATION

Since an argument always takes a stand, it always implies the existence of an opposing stand. A writer who simply ignores that contrary position is gambling that readers will not be able to call it to mind. If they do—and they usually will—it will weigh more heavily with them than if it had been openly discussed. The wiser course is to *concede* or grant points that count against one's case and to *refute* or disprove points that can be shown to lack merit. Ideally, an argument will confront the very strongest objections and, by showing that they are either wrong or not very damaging, clear the way for the making of a positive case.

concession   Thus, for example, someone who wants to argue in favor of nuclear power plants would do well to concede that in general, nuclear wastes retain their toxicity far longer than do the wastes from conventional plants. Since that point is undeniable, the writer's task is not to sweep it under the rug but to admit it and assess its importance. Is the problem of waste disposal as horrendous as many people think? Perhaps not, for reasons *a, b, c.* . . .

It is never enough to concede the merit of an opposing point; the writer must then limit the damage by restoring the dominant, positive point of view. You can observe the two essential steps in the following paragraphs from an essay arguing that we must place controls on population so as to avoid degrading the "carrying capacity" (ability to support species) of the lands they occupy. First the writer admits that until this point he has been oversimplifying the issue:

> Before proceeding with the inquiry we need to note one way in which
> the previous analysis is deficient for the human situation. The diagrams

and the argument that accompanied them implicitly assumed that carrying capacity (ignoring fluctuations) is static. For most species most of the time, that is true. That was the assumption Malthus made when he wrote his *Essay on Population* in 1798. Unfortunately for Malthus' reputation, the carrying capacity of the earth for human beings has grown fantastically since his day. In part, it has increased because new lands have been opened up to human settlement (but this process is almost at an end). Even more important has been the growth of science and technology. Irrigation, fertilization, and new genetic strains of plants and animals have greatly increased productivity per hectare. So why worry? Can't this go on forever?

But a paragraph later he returns to the attack. Even if carrying capacity *is* expandable, he says, the *quality* of life is jeopardized by ever larger populations:

> Living is an expensive game, and the greater the density of population the more expensive it becomes. If we want reasonably pure air and pure water the carrying capacity of the earth is much less than it is if we do not care what we breathe and drink. More generally, for the human population, once it numbers in the hundreds of millions, what we call the carrying capacity is inversely related to the material standard of living we choose. He who says "The earth can support still more people" is always right; for, until we reach absolute rock bottom, we can always lower the standard of living another notch and support a larger population. The question is, which do we want: the maximum number of people at the minimum standard of living—or a smaller number at a comfortable, or even gracious, standard of living? We are our own caretakers: the choice is ours.[1]

refutation   A shrewd arguer will always ponder as many objections as possible and then concentrate on the most important or imposing ones—those that appear to threaten the entire positive case. Some of those points may have to be conceded (and minimized), but others can be *refuted*, or shown to be untrue.

In one argument, for example, a student writer was defending the thesis that *People should sign agreements donating their organs, at death, to patients in need of transplants.* Having stated her thesis, she proceeded at once to refute the main objection to it:

> I believe that reluctance to enter into such humane agreements usually stems from a fear that overeager surgeons will pluck out one's heart or eyes or kidneys while one is "still alive," presumably with a chance of recovery. That is a prospect to make anyone squeamish—but it is simply unrealistic. Organs have never been removed before a state of brain

death has been declared, and in the entire history of medicine there is *not one* documented case of a patient returning to life after that diagnosis. The stories we hear about miraculous recoveries involve only a loss and resumption of heart function, not of brain wave activity.

Again, a writer opposing gun control laws realized that many readers would resist his argument because of the famous English example: "Banning handguns must work, because England does and look at its crime rate!" To concede the force of that example would have been rhetorically devastating. But the writer had in hand a 1971 Cambridge University study enabling him to challenge the direct cause-and-effect relation between British gun control and a low crime rate:

> The Cambridge report concludes that social and cultural factors (not gun control) account for Britain's low violence rates. It points out that "the use of firearms in crime was very much less" before 1920 when Britain had "no controls of any sort." Corroborating this is the comment of a former head of Scotland Yard that in the mid-1950s there were enough illegal handguns to supply any British criminal who wanted one. But, he continued, the social milieu was such that if a criminal killed anyone, particularly a policeman, his own confederates would turn him in. When this violence-dampening social milieu began to dissipate between 1960 and 1975, the British homicide rate doubled (as did the American rate), while British robbery rates accelerated even faster than those in America. As the report notes, the vaunted handgun ban proved completely ineffective against rising violence in Britain, although the government frantically intensified enforcement and extended controls to long guns as well. Thus, the Cambridge study—the only in-depth study ever done of English gun laws—recommends "abolishing or substantially reducing controls" because their administration involves an immense, unproductive expense and diverts police resources from programs that might reduce violent crime.[2]

This paragraph does not in itself make the writer's case against gun control, yet in effectively using refutation to clear away a major obstacle to that case, it may well be the most important element in his essay.

EXERCISES

4. Go back to any one of the five theses you wrote for Exercise 1 (p. 65). Think of as many likely objections to that thesis as you can, and then submit two or three paragraphs in which you deal with the most important of those objections by using either concession or refutation or both.

5. Choose a topic of controversy about which you feel strongly. In one sentence write down

your position on that issue. Then list as many possible objections to that position as you can, and place check marks beside the points that you would want to concentrate on if you were defending your position in a written argument. Be prepared to explain why you checked certain points instead of others.

6. Write a paragraph or two in which you deal with one of the checked objections (Exercise 5) by means of concession. Make sure that your discussion not only grants the point but also "limits the damage" by reasserting the merits of your own stand.

7. Take any of the checked objections (Exercise 5) and refute it in a paragraph or two.

ARGUMENTATIVE EVIDENCE

It should be clear by now that a writer making an argumentative point cannot afford to say in effect, *Believe my thesis because I am telling you to* or *Believe it or else.* Readers expect to be shown that the thesis rests on sound reasoning about established facts. This is not to say that argumentative prose must be self-consciously "logical," laboriously spelling out premises and conclusions in every paragraph. It means instead that the writer must be ready to back significant points of opinion with statements that a reader would be likely to find relevant and believable.

The most significant point of opinion is the writer's thesis, which by its nature "remains to be seen." And the most crucial stage in the composing of an argument is consequently the weighing of available evidence to make the thesis believable. It is not enough that the writer believe the thesis; a given thesis should not be put forward at all unless adequate supporting statements can be marshaled.

Forms of Evidence

"facts and figures" When most people think of evidence, they call to mind "facts and figures"—statements and numerical data that are beyond any dispute. The truth is that useful argumentative evidence goes well beyond such items—yet there is something especially compelling about an argument that seems to have sprung directly from unquestionable findings.

The great virtue of "hard information" is that it puts the real world in the writer's corner. Suppose, for example, you suspected that minorities and women are scarcely better off today than they were twenty years ago. Personal testimony about lost opportunities and experiences of discrimination would be helpful, but a reader could always dismiss that testimony as unrepresentative. Armed, on the other hand, with a report of the U.S. Commission on Civil Rights entitled *Social Indicators of Equality for Minorities and Women*, you could put to use facts like these (here summarized in a weekly news magazine):

Median family income among blacks is 63 percent that of whites, no higher than it was in 1968.

White male teenager unemployment has risen from 10.6 percent in 1970 to 15 percent—bad news, but not as bad as the figure for blacks during the same period, which skyrocketed from 20.5 percent to 47.8 percent, and for Puerto Rican youths, more than half of whom—55.2 percent—lack jobs.

Occupational segregation—herding members of a group into a limited variety of jobs—has increased substantially among minorities and women since 1970.

Fifty percent more black high-school graduates than whites have jobs for which they are overqualified.

Minorities do not receive equal pay for equal work. Black males receive 85 percent of the wages of white males in the same job with comparable qualifications; even white women receive only 57 percent of the white male salary, just as they did in 1959.[3]

To see how an array of facts and figures can add substance to an argument, consider two passages, the second of which was written by a student:

In 1976, Americans threw out 70 *billion* beverage containers, many of which wound up on our roadsides, beaches, and parks or polluted our streams and lakes. Even the ones that are "disposed of properly" burden our landfills and cost us nearly $500 million per year in extra garbage collection costs. The problem of solid waste is one that many California cities are now confronting. Oregon's roadside container litter has been reduced by up to 80%, and tourists vacationing there are amazed by the lack of litter. The bottle bill would penalize those who actually litter and reward those who pick up empty containers. The California Legislative Analyst has estimated that such a bill would reduce our litter disposal costs by $2 million (tax dollars) a year.[4]

Yes! Every second, the sun fuses four million tons of hydrogen into helium, producing 380 billion trillion kilowatts of power. Of this power, 173 trillion kilowatts reach the earth's atmosphere; 85 trillion kilowatts reach the surface of the earth. On the average, the earth receives 1.395 kilowatts of power per square meter. If we could capture the solar energy dissipated on earth in forty days, we would have enough electricity to last a century. The energy shed on the earth in three days is greater than the total amount of energy contained in the world's fossil fuel supply.

Neither of these passages constitutes a sufficient case for each essay's thesis—in the first instance that a container deposit law should be passed, and in the second that solar energy should be favored over other types. An opponent could raise any number of objections not covered here. Yet both writers are strengthening their credibility, if only by demonstrating that they have some firm statistical evidence on their side. It would not occur to many readers, for example, to object that the second writer has said nothing about *actually recoverable* solar energy. So long as the facts and figures keep on reeling past one's mind, the arguer remains in rhetorical control of the situation.

quotation   We have already seen (pp. 34–35) how quoting someone's spoken words can be a lively means of description or narration. In explaining and especially in arguing, quotation of spoken *or* written words is a standard means of presenting evidence. Quotation is especially useful to argument because it appeals to authority. That is, the writer is not simply reproducing some positive testimony but reminding the reader that someone of consequence appears to be on the better side of the issue.

Consider, for example, this writer's quotation of an expert who shares his dismay over the involuntary subjection of mental patients to heavy drug dosages:

> In late 1973, Richard Cole, then a third-year law student at Boston University, arrived with permission to open a legal-services office on the hospital grounds. Soon appointed head of the institute's civil-rights committee, he found no lack of patient interest in his services. According to Mr. Cole, one of the patients' most frequent and disturbing complaints concerned the involuntary administration of antipsychotics. "When patients were treated against their will," says Mr. Cole, now a lawyer at Greater Boston Legal Services in the city's Roxbury section, "they felt their humanity being offended. I have met many former patients who tell me that because of their experience with involuntary treatment and the loss of self-respect and feelings of powerlessness it engendered, they never want to see a psychiatrist again. I think that's sad, because many of them really need some help."[5]

Faced with such a judgment from an informed source, a reader who believed that psychiatric patients *should* be treated against their will would probably feel obliged to come up with equally knowledgeable contrary testimony. Thus the writer has used quotation to put the ball in his adversaries' court.

Sometimes it is good to cite the words of an eminent figure even if those words were not originally addressed to the issue at hand. Notice, for example, how the writer of the following passage draws her examples together with a concluding reflection from the admired humanitarian Albert Schweitzer:

> Strontium 90, released through nuclear explosions into the air, comes to earth in rain or drifts down as fallout, lodges in soil, enters into the grass or corn or wheat grown there, and in time takes up its abode in the bones of a human being, there to remain until his death. Similarly, chemicals sprayed on croplands or forests or gardens lie long in soil, entering into living organisms, passing from one to another in a chain of poisoning and death. Or they pass mysteriously by underground streams until they emerge and, through the alchemy of air and sunlight, combine into new forms that kill vegetation, sicken cattle, and work unknown harm on those who drink from once pure wells. As Albert Schweitzer has said, "Man can hardly even recognize the devils of his own creation."[6]

Sometimes, finally, the source is anonymous—quoted, we hope, honestly and accurately as well as pertinently:

> The handicapped—the blind, crippled, deaf, mentally retarded—have mobilized into a civil rights movement for the 1970s. They have organized and lobbied for what most Americans take for granted: a drink of water at a public fountain, access to buses or subways, a way in and out of buildings, the right to attend the schools of their choice, and the freedom to live independent lives with dignity. The disabled constitute a unique minority, embracing every race and religion, both sexes and all ages. And, as handicapped groups like to point out, membership can be conferred on anyone at any time—by disease, by accident, by heart attack or stroke. "Not anyone can become black or a woman," says one movement leader. "But anyone can become handicapped. You could, tomorrow."[7]

Observe how, through the device of quotation, the writer has sent an unsettling personal message to every reader: if you think of the handicapped as a breed apart from yourself, think again!

explanatory strategies   Note, too, that argumentative evidence can consist of *reasoning* on the writer's part. Since many explanations already contain the germ of an argumentative thesis, it is hardly surprising that the various strategies of explanation can be incorporated into arguments. Without much trouble, for instance, we could take some previously discussed explanatory passages and think of argumentative theses that they might serve:

STRATEGY	EXAMPLE	ARGUMENTATIVE THESIS
Definition	What is a language (pp. 44–45)	Tests for animal language should be made tough enough so that mere "communication in general" is not counted as truly linguistic
Division	Skills required for hang gliding (p. 47)	Regulations against the "reckless" sport of hang gliding are unnecessary
Illustration	Instances of foreign purchase of American assets (p. 48)	Laws should be passed to control foreign purchase of American assets
Process Analysis	How a mechanic checks a hypothesis (pp. 49–50)	Students should be introduced to scientific logic through study of mechanics' procedures
Comparison and Contrast	*Communist Manifesto* versus U.S. Bill of Rights (p. 53)	We must preserve the uniquely individualist spirit of our Constitution
Analogy	How a collision of storm fronts is like a car crash (pp. 55–56)	Weather experts should not be fired for failing to predict the ferocity of every storm
Cause and Effect	Environmental sources of the increased rate of cancer (pp. 56–57)	We should focus the greater part of our anticancer efforts on removing environmental carcinogens

EXERCISES

8. Find an article that contains an abundance of factual evidence, and jot down the facts and figures used there. Then submit a paragraph or two in which you use some of that information as evidence in support of an argumentative position. Use your own language, not the author's.

9. Find an article that looks reasonably convincing to you; any topic will do. (You can use the article cited in Exercise 8 if you prefer.) Submit an argumentative paragraph in which you quote the author to good effect, thus strengthening your own position.

10. Review the diagram showing explanatory strategies, sample passages, and argumentative theses (p. 73). Submit two paragraphs in which you (a) practice *any one* explanatory strategy and (b) make argumentative use of your explanation.

ARGUMENTATIVE TONE

Once in a while an essay written in apparent anger is so eloquent that nobody misses the usual virtues of argumentation. Different contexts call for different tones; it would be useless, for example, to ask that revolutionary manifestoes sound sweetly reasonable at every point. Again, controlled sarcasm is sometimes more effective than a weighing of pros and cons—provided the writer can count on the reader's general sympathy. Hence the abrupt and cutting tone in much commentary found in magazines whose audience consists of a single political faction. A master of withering scorn such as Nicholas von Hoffman or William F. Buckley, Jr., writing only for partisans of the left or right, can chop up opponents with unrelenting efficiency, and the result can be great fun for the already converted.

But what about the unconverted? In college argumentation, where the instructor and one's classmates try to impersonate that mythically neutral character, "the reader," it is unwise to adopt the tone of someone who cannot possibly be wrong. The goal—one that will present itself in any number of other contexts—is to allow one's ideas to prevail by their soberly demonstrated superiority to other ideas *which are treated just as fairly.* Since no prior sympathy can be taken for granted, a posture of open-minded fairness—of letting the better case win on its own merits—actually produces better results than smug certainty would.

avoiding emotionalism   In any case, the chief threat to effective argument comes not from strong emotions but from **emotionalism**, the tone of someone who is too upset to think clearly. Compare, for example, the following passages:

x A. The slaughter of whales is butchery pure and simple! Can you imagine anything more grotesque than the hideous, tortured death of a whale, shot with a grenade-tipped harpoon that *explodes* deep inside its body? *And for what?* Why the sadistic murder? Because certain profiteers want to turn the gentlest creature on this planet into *crayons, lipstick, shoe polish, fertilizer, margarine,* and *pet food,* for God's sake! If this doesn't make you sick—well, all I can say is that you must be ripping off some of those obscene profits yourself.

The second passage shows at least as much conviction—probably more—but the emotionalism of passage A is nowhere to be seen:

- B. The killing of a whale at sea isn't pleasant to witness or even to contemplate. Hunted down through sonar and other highly specialized equipment, the whale has no more chance of escape than a steer in a slaughterhouse. The manner of his death, however, is very different. A grenade-tipped harpoon explodes deep within his body, often causing prolonged suffering before the gentle giant, whose intelligence may be second only to our own, is reduced to a carcass ready for processing into crayons, lipstick, shoe polish, fertilizer, margarine, and pet food.

    The inhumane manner of death, however, is the least part of the scandal known as the whaling industry. Much more important is the fact that the killing is quite unnecessary. Adequate substitutes exist for every single use to which whale carcasses are currently put, and although some 32,000 whales are killed every year, the sum of commodities they provide is insignificant in the world's economy. Indeed, two already wealthy nations, Russia and Japan, account for eighty percent of all the whales "harvested" annually. Though the Japanese claim that whale meat is a vital source of protein for them, less than one percent of the Japanese protein diet actually comes from that source. Yet the slaughter goes on unchecked. The alarming truth is that one of the noblest species on earth is being pressed toward extinction for no justifiable reason.

If you already agree with the author of passage A, you may find yourself aroused by his overemphatic prose. In that case nothing has been gained or lost. If you disagree, you find yourself insulted as a profiteer. And if you are neutral, wondering which side possesses the strongest argument, you may notice how little relevant information is offered here. Should whaling be stopped because of the mere fact that whales are slaughtered and turned into commodities? Don't many other animals endure a similar fate? In his outrage the writer has neglected to supply a reasoned argument that would keep him from being regarded as a sentimentalist.

The sober language of passage B is much more effective than the exclamations and italics of passage A. Take the description of a whale's death: we see, not the writer emoting over the fact, but the fact itself, which becomes more impressive without the signs of agitation. Similarly, by not calling special attention to the list of commodities from *crayons* through *pet food*, passage B achieves a powerful quality of *understatement*, whereby the mere reality appears more expressive than any editorializing about it would be. And above all, note that writer B provides detailed, dispassionate *evidence* for the belief that whale slaughter, whether or not it revolts us, is economically unnecessary. In reading passage A, our only options are to share or reject a fit of temper. But even if we lean at first toward a pro-whaling stance, we find it hard to dismiss writer B's objectively reported facts. Here and elsewhere, reasons prove to be not just fairer but also more persuasive than fits of sentiment.

Finally, consider a student paragraph that successfully maintains a moderate tone, and notice how that tone accompanies an actual movement of thought between pros and cons:

a problem is recognized	By and large, Americans pay no attention to the national speed limit of 55 miles per hour. Nor do they hold back from buying heavy, gas-guzzling automobiles just because the government wants them to con-
one solution is rejected	serve fuel. Extra taxes on the heavy cars would not discourage would-be purchasers, who like to be considered big spenders. What really pains them is the thought of not being allowed to use all that horse-
a new proposal is offered	power. Suppose the government had two different speed limits, one for cars that get over 30 miles to the gallon and a much lower one for cars
effect #1 a drawback	that do worse. If strictly enforced, such a law would cause some resent-ment and confusion at first, but before long it would begin having bene-
effect #2 positive	ficial effects. The glamor of big cars has a lot to do with their horse-power; if buyers realized that a huge, expensive model wouldn't be allowed to go as fast as a small, economical one, sales of the big cars
effect #3 positive	would quickly dry up. The savings in fuel would more than offset the losses from higher speed limits, and Americans would be spending less
effect #4 positive	useless time puttering along on superhighways.

This writer is not only committed but also confident, and thanks to his confidence he can take a calm, thoughtful tone—one that invites his reader to weigh alternatives without feeling any emotional coercion. If you disagree with him, you will have to come up with reasons more impressive than his own.

EXERCISES

11. The following passage may serve as an extreme example of argumentative emotionalism:

> Supermarket prices are a damn ripoff! The middlemen and store managers take us customers for a bunch of suckers! Hamburger "extended" with soybeans but labeled as pure meat costs more than steak did a few years ago! Hey, man, don't try to tell me it's just inflation! The filthy con artists shake you down for all you're worth! "Specials" in bins turn out to cost more per item than the cans on the shelves, for God's sake! I've *had* it with those dudes! Have you seen the way they put candy right by the checkout coun-ter, where your kid will grab it and throw a tantrum if you don't buy it?

Write a paragraph of your own in which you express some or all of this writer's grievances, but in a tone suitable for a typical college essay.

12. Looking through the sample theses and passages used in this chapter, find an argumentative position with which you might readily *disagree*. Taking a moderate tone, submit several para-graphs in which you show your reasons for rejecting or questioning that position.

A COMPLETE ARGUMENT

Bearing in mind the four classic virtues of a sound argument (p. 61), note how they are embodied in the following brief but complete student essay:

PROTECTING THE RIGHTS OF NONSMOKERS

the issue is announced

It has been many years now since the United States Surgeon General announced the finding that cigarette smoking is a direct cause of lung cancer. That finding has been reinforced many times over by later studies. Radio and television advertising of cigarettes has been banned since 1971, and all cigarette packages and advertisements carry the stern (though sometimes nearly illegible) message, "Warning: The Surgeon General Has Determined That Cigarette Smoking Is Dangerous to Your Health." All this official concern, however, has had little effect. No doubt many would-be smokers have thought twice about taking up the habit, but cigarette sales have kept right on climbing. Some fifty-three million Americans, we are told, now consume a record two billion tons of tobacco per year.

the writer prepares us for her thesis

she states that thesis

Regrettable as it is, this fact in itself doesn't necessarily call for further regulation. It could be argued that people have a right to poison themselves, or risk poisoning themselves, by any means they choose. Unfortunately, however, smokers like to indulge their habit wherever they happen to be, in public as well as at home; their cigarettes are not just a poison but a pollutant as well. In recent years we have begun to recognize that "used" smoke endangers the health of nonsmokers who have no way of escaping it in crowded restaurants, elevators, theater lobbies, offices, and factories. I believe the time has come for the law to recognize that smoking in most enclosed public places is not private, harmless conduct, but public conduct that endangers a significant number of victims.

now she fairly states the strongest objections to her thesis . . .

Opponents of antismoking laws greet such proposals with several answers, some of which look very impressive at first glance. The new laws would be unenforceable, they say; smoking is an irrational addiction, and millions of smokers would simply defy the law. The government, we are told, should direct its efforts not to hiring Smoke Police but to developing harmless cigarettes. Furthermore, we are reminded that regulation of smoking would cause economic hardship for tobacco growers, advertisers, and people connected with bars and arenas— places where smoking is so customary that a ban on smoking would affect patronage. Above all, the defenders of smoking point out that no studies have yet demonstrated a connection between lung cancer and *accidentally* inhaled smoke. Perhaps, then, we who favor new laws have failed to distinguish between a mere annoyance and a health hazard.

. . . and takes two paragraphs to answer those objections with evidence

Let us review these arguments in turn. Is it obvious, first of all, that antismoking laws couldn't be enforced? People said the same thing about "pooper scooper" ordinances directed at dog owners, but those ordinances are actually working in New York City and elsewhere. It is not a question of hiring more police, but of using the law to raise consciousness, make violators feel criticized, and bring about voluntary compliance. To say that the government should try to develop safe cigarettes is true but beside the point; we must decide what to do *until* such cigarettes are on the market.

Again, the "hardship" argument has some merit but is not decisive. If smoking did decrease, farmers could be compensated and aided in switching crops; advertisers would surely continue to get cigarette accounts; and bars and arenas could be exempted from the law on the grounds that most of their patrons *voluntarily* expose themselves to smoke. As for the lack of proven connection between second-hand smoke and lung cancer, we should remember that lung cancer is by no means the only disease associated with cigarette smoke. It *has* been proven that people who suffer from heart and respiratory diseases can be seriously affected by a smoke-filled environment. It is these people —not the rest of us who just find smoking distasteful—whose rights are at issue.

now she offers further evidence on her side

Of course, those already sick would not be the only people to benefit from a partial ban on public smoking. If you are a nonsmoker who has ever tried to enjoy a restaurant meal while waving away smoke from a neighboring table, you can appreciate my point. Being free from other people's smoke would be like not having to listen to somebody's turned-up stereo all night. (And note that the law already protects you from *that* kind of pollution.) Smokers themselves, furthermore, would profit from consuming fewer cigarettes per day; some of them might even be nudged into quitting the habit at last.

she then reinforces her thesis by reassuring us that the effects would be positive

The central point, however, is that public smoking jeopardizes the lives of citizens who already have health problems and who presently find it dangerous to be in most public places—even, in some cases, the places where they have to work. Laws to protect those citizens would be no more oppressive than the laws that once taught people to stop tossing their garbage directly into city streets. The effect of regulating smoking would be much the same: not to fill the jails with offenders, but to encourage people to change their practices for the sake of other people's health and comfort.

13. Do you agree or disagree with the point being defended in the "smoking" essay? Write a paragraph supporting or challenging the writer's argument.

14. Study the features of the "smoking" essay that are marked in the margin. Then choose an argumentative thesis of your own; if you like, you can draw it from a previous exercise in this chapter. Then submit an essay displaying as many of those classic features as you can include without strain. Leave a wide left margin, and use the blank space to mark your major rhetorical strategies, as in the sample essay.

NOTES

¹Garrett Hardin, *The Limits of Altruism: An Ecologist's View of Survival* (Bloomington: Indiana Univ. Press, 1977), pp. 57, 58–59.

²Don B. Kates, Jr., "Against Civil Disarmament," *Harper's,* Sept. 1978, pp. 29–30.

³"Unwelcome News," *Saturday Review,* 25 Nov. 1978, p. 7.

⁴Trician Comings, "Can, Bottle Deposit Law Is Proposed," [Berkeley, Calif.] *Co-Op News,* 5 Mar. 1979, p. 1.

⁵Paul S. Appelbaum, "Can Mental Patients Say No to Drugs?" *New York Times Magazine,* 21 Mar. 1982, p. 51.

⁶Rachel Carson, *Silent Spring* (Boston: Houghton Mifflin, 1962), p. 6.

⁷Sonny Kleinfield, "The Handicapped: Hidden No Longer," *Atlantic,* Dec. 1977, p. 87.

PART II
COMPOSING

5

GETTING STARTED

COMPOSING: AN OVERVIEW

So far we have been discussing the classic modes of essay prose and exploring their various uses. It is time now to turn to the actual work of composing—to begin seeing how to find workable ideas and to carry them through the process of drafting and revising.

In doing so, however, we will narrow our focus to just two modes, the ones that dominate college writing: explanation and argument (pp. 42–59, 60–79). Those are the modes best suited to making a point —or, in our terms, to *supporting a thesis.* Thus they are also the modes that require the most forethought. In description and narration much of what you want to say is "already there" in a remembered scene or sequence of events, and your chief problem may be choosing an effective order of presentation (see pp. 22–41). But in explanation and argument you must decide above all *what idea* you want to pursue.

Essential Terms

To be sure that you have a real idea and not just some material to cover, you must be alert to the differences among three things that are often confused: a *subject area*, a *topic*, and a *thesis*.

subject area A **subject area** is a large category within which you may hope to find your actual topic—the specific question you will address. Thus, if you are asked to "recount a personal experience" or "discuss an issue of civil liberties" or "write a paper about *Catch-22*," you have been given, not topics, but subject areas: *a personal experience, an issue of civil liberties, Catch-22*. A subject area is too large to be usefully made a topic in itself. If you find yourself muttering "I can't say anything about such a ridiculously broad topic," perhaps it *isn't* a topic but a subject area. Think of a subject area as a large unopened sack of topics, and consider how awkward it would be to write an essay about an as yet unopened sack.

topic The **topic** of an essay is the question or focused subject it deals with. Thus, within the subject area "Open Admission to College," some workable topics might be:

The effect of open admission on "high potential" students

My debt to the policy of open admission

Why did open admission become popular in the late 1960s?

The success (or failure) of open admission

Open admission as a means to social equality

Notice that these topics take up considerably more words than "Open Admission to College." Potential "topics" expressed in few words may be subject areas in disguise. A topic is definite, and definiteness means spelling something out.

Here are further instances of the contrast between subject areas and topics:

SUBJECT AREA	TOPIC
Agricultural production	The effect of mechanization on farm employment
Genetic research	Major developments in genetic research since 1970
College life	The transition between the senior year of high school and the freshman year of college
Moby-Dick and *Huckleberry Finn*	A comparison of the young narrators in *Moby-Dick* and *Huckleberry Finn*
Drug abuse	Behavioral effects of "angel dust"
Federal water projects	How federal water projects get approved or canceled

. . . versus thesis The **thesis** is the one leading idea you are going to propose *about* your topic. Thus, a thesis is never subject matter to be investigated; it is always *an assertion.* As such, it lends itself to expression in one clear sentence:

a. The right to privacy, broadly conceived, is the most fundamental of civil liberties in a democracy.

b. Known criminals should not be excused from punishment merely because of technical errors in the way they were arrested and tried.

c. After my night in jail I will have more respect for prisoners' rights.

d. When government officials place innocent citizens under observation and routinely tap one another's phones, everyone's civil liberties are threatened.

e. Civil liberties have not been a major concern of the Burger Supreme Court.

Of all the aids to writing effective college essays, having a sound thesis is the most important. Lacking a thesis, you will be lucky to come up with anything better than assorted remarks. Possessing one, you will be confident that you can take your reader somewhere, and your knowledge of that goal will help you across all the remaining hurdles of composing.

The Composing Process

Perhaps the need for a strong, clear thesis suggests to you that every explanatory or argumentative essay should be preceded by a stage of sheer thinking—of waiting for the light bulb to flash over your head. But merely furrowing your brow will give you nothing except wrinkle lines. Ideas are generated not from sheer inspiration but from activities that place one thought into relation with another— and one of those activities is writing itself. In the labor of writing you are forced to zero in on connections, comparisons, contrasts, illustrations, contradictions, and objections, any of which can point you toward a thesis or alter the one you began with.

Thus the finding of a thesis is not a fixed early stage of the composing process, but a concern that is urgent at first and will probably become urgent again when you run into trouble or realize that a better idea has come into view. The sooner you arrive at a thesis—by any means, including random writing—the better; but your choice has not been fully tested until you are ready to type up the final copy of your essay. At any moment you may find yourself having to take more notes, argue against a point you favored in an early draft, or throw away whole pages that have been made irrelevant by your improved thesis. Do not imagine that such annoyances set you apart from other writers; they put you in the company of the masters.

So, too, the other "stages of composing" normally leak into one another. Although you cannot complete your organizing, for example, until you have arrived at a thesis, unexpected problems of organization may point the way to a better thesis. Even a simplified flow chart of your options at such a moment would look complex:

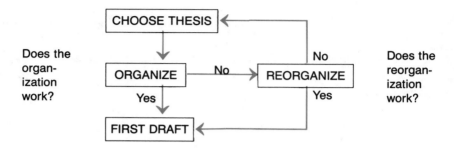

And even the revising of paragraphs for internal unity may prompt a more fundamental change of direction. Writing is almost never a linear process; it typically doubles back on one phase because a later one has opened new perspectives.

Thus, though we can (and will) break composing into a certain logical order of steps, its actual order defies summary. At nearly every point you are free either to move ahead or to reconsider any previous decision:

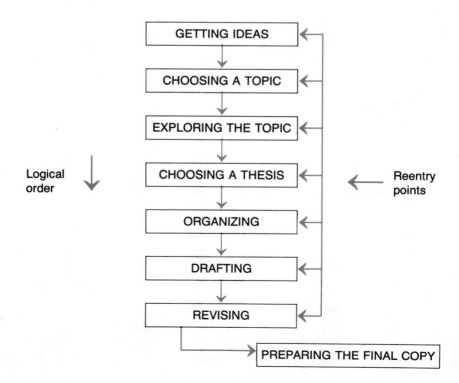

The lesson here is that, wherever your composing hits a snag, it is normal and useful to double back. Such rethinking is nothing to be alarmed about; it is the usual means by which weak ideas and structures give way to stronger ones.

EXERCISE

1. Each of the following is either a *subject area*, a *topic*, or a *thesis*:

    A. Mass urban transportation
    B. The space shuttle should not be used primarily for military research
    C. Protection of rape victims from harmful publicity
    D. Network news programs
    E. The return of the convertible car

Submit a whole sheet of paper that you have first marked as follows, leaving ample space between the horizontal lines:

	Subject Area	Topic	Thesis
A.			
B.			
C.			
D.			
E.			

For each letter matching the items listed, (a) put a check in the appropriate column, and (b) fill in examples for the two remaining columns. Thus, if you think that item A is a topic, check the "Topic" column and add a related subject area and thesis.

WAYS OF BEGINNING

Starting from Experience

When you are given a free assignment, you should think at once about your own interests and areas of special knowledge—activities, skills, attitudes, problems, and unique or typical experiences. The reason is simple: what doesn't interest you isn't likely to engage a reader. Although it is possible to *become* interested in a new project, an already existing concern can give you some relatively well-developed ideas and a fund of relevant examples.

course work One source of interest may be your work in this or some other course. Have you come across a significant problem in your assigned reading? Do your lecture notes contain questions or observations that could lead to a thesis? Wherever you have recorded doubts or strong agreement or connections with ideas of your own, you may have in hand the beginnings of an essay.

miscellaneous reading So, too, you can search for topics in the books and magazines that happen to be within easy reach. The goal, of course, is not to copy someone else's words or ideas (see pp. 404–407), but to find an issue that meets up with experiences or knowledge or opinions of your own.

diary or journal Your search for ideas will be easier if you keep a **diary**—a random record of your day-to-day life—or, still better, a **journal**—a running account of your experiences and thoughts within a certain area. A typical journal, for example, might trace your progress in understanding music theory or mastering computer skills; alternatively, it could store your reflections about life in general, your plans and ambitions, your ideas for short stories you hope to write, and so forth. You may even be asked to keep a journal about your efforts and problems in this very course. Whatever material it deals with, a journal can point you toward a topic by reminding you of already developed interests and opinions.

Freewriting

If you have ever told yourself or others *I don't know what I want to say until I've written it out,* consider yourself normal. Writing is a primary way of arriving at ideas, and teachers have increasingly been recognizing that fact instead of pretending that composition is a lock-step march from planning to writing. By forcing yourself to hook up nouns and verbs, subjects and predicates, you can draw forth insights that you didn't know you possessed. Whenever you feel that you must "stop thinking and write," go ahead and do so. The urge to commit words to paper is usually a signal that some key idea is tunneling toward the surface of your mind. The prose that results will probably be awkward and rambling, but that won't matter unless you confuse unrevised exploratory writing with a final draft.

You can even begin writing before having any idea of what your topic will be. When you feel stymied, assign yourself a ten- or fifteen-minute stint of **freewriting**. The trick is to begin scribbling at "Go" and to keep it up until "Stop" *without pausing between sentences or sentence fragments.* Once the words begin flowing, you will be surprised to see how easily each sentence suggests the one to follow. More important, you will usually find a possible topic beginning to come into view.

There is nothing magical or foolproof about freewriting or, for that matter, about any other source of ideas. Especially at first, you may find yourself writing mostly about the artificiality of freewriting itself—not the most alluring of possible essay topics. But such self-consciousness quickly wears off. Even if one freewriting session appears to take you nowhere, a second one, started a few minutes later, may pick up on thoughts that weren't quite ready for expression in a first effort.

Here, for example, are two passages of freewriting that a student produced in quick succession:

First freewriting:

> Well, what do I have to say? Not much it appears! Sitting here "free" writing, so they tell me. How free is freewriting on demand, with the stopwatch ticking? Freedom in general—it always confuses me. I never know whether it's supposed to be freedom to go out and do something you'd like to, or freedom to keep somebody else from doing something mean to you. Anyway, would sure like to be free from freewriting! What is so sacred about exactly ten minutes worth of this stuff? How about nine or eleven? Stuck for ideas—ugh! Well, just keep pushing this pencil until time's up. . . .

Second freewriting:

> OK, maybe something here after all. Idea of freedom. *Total* freedom is empty, unattractive, boring—we always have something in mind to be free *for*—i.e., something that won't leave us so free any more. E.g., religious freedom usually means spending that freedom on some belief and/or practice—some "service." Or does it? What about unbelievers? I guess they have a right to a freedom that stays negative: no, thanks. . . . But historically, the fighters for freedom have always been people with strong beliefs of their own. Luther, Jefferson, Lincoln, King. . . . Maybe an essay here? "Freedom For or Freedom From"?

Notice several typical features here:

1. Neither of the two passages has the continuity and logical development of finished essay prose, yet, under pressure to come up with something, the writer has forced himself to focus on a possible topic and to begin weighing ideas about it.

2. The writer begins with strained feelings about an imposed task, but he pushes ahead until he finds a likely-looking idea.
3. That idea emerges unexpectedly from a "hostile" context. By letting his thoughts play over an uncomfortable situation, the writer has been able to reach back for some material that may take him beyond his discomfort.

You can see that the drill-sergeant aspect of freewriting—whether the taskmaster is your instructor or yourself—is one of its key virtues. If you *must* keep writing for a specified period and then *must* do so again, the odds are that your mind will shake off its sleepiness and come to your rescue.

Brainstorming

Instead of freewriting, you may find your best source of first ideas in **brainstorming**, a similar technique for drawing out undeveloped thoughts. In freewriting, ideas are teased forth by our natural tendency to link one sentence—either by development or by contrast—with the one before it; freewriting is thus invention by means of continuity. Brainstorming works by the opposite principle—discontinuity. To brainstorm is to toss out suggestions with as little regard as possible for their connections with one another. Since no development is called for, nothing stands in the way of your seizing a fresh possibility.

You can brainstorm by yourself, scribbling across a note pad or talking into a tape recorder. Or you can work in a group, either among roommates and friends or in the classroom, where the "note pad" is a shared chalkboard. In discussion or reflection certain ideas will begin to look more fruitful than others—and you are on your way toward a topic.

When brainstorming works, it sometimes evolves naturally into freewriting as one hastily mentioned idea starts to look more interesting than the others:

> Freedom / freedom fighters / free-for-alls / freed slaves / "free gifts" / I.e., come-ons for renting (or buying) a car, going to grand opening, etc. What's really free—nothing! Who pays? The customers, of course; extra costs added back into prices. Notice that "free gifts" come only when the customers aren't buying. . . .

Taking Notes

If, after whatever efforts of invention, you still feel that you have nothing to say, the chances are that you haven't been using notes to record your fleeting ideas. Once you develop the habit of taking notes *as you think,* you will realize that your mind *was* at work when you "couldn't get an idea"; the problem was that you were skipping nervously from one thought to another without writing any of them down. Once you have a variety of ideas recorded on note cards or scraps of paper, you ought to feel better about the rest of your task. Your notes, taken together, will suggest more possibilities than you could have kept in mind at any moment. Instead of confronting an awesomely large subject area, you will now be able to refer to your own familiar notes—discarding certain hunches, pursuing others, and building confidence as you gradually understand where you are headed. And you should continue to take notes throughout the composing process, raising previously unforeseen questions, commenting on earlier notes, jotting down changes of plan, and reminding yourself of the next two or three points you ought to cover. Even if you are working from an outline, your notes can overrule any segment of it.

When your essay is supposed to deal with an assigned text, your note taking should begin during your reading of the text. Do you own the book? If so, mark it up, underlining passages that look significant and writing comments and questions in the margins. Wherever one part of the text helps you to understand another part, make a marginal cross reference such as "see p. 134." And as soon as you have finished reading or, preferably, rereading, get your miscellaneous impressions onto paper so that you can begin dealing with *them* instead of with the whole elusive text. You will need to keep returning to the text, but now you can do so with specific, pointed questions in mind.

Some writers use uniform-sized *index cards* (3" × 5", 4" × 6", or 5" × 8") for all their notes, restricting themselves to one idea per card. That system allows you to rearrange the cards and test a variety of possible structures for your essay. You can even sort your cards by headings you have written in the top corners, so that you can quickly draw together all the thoughts you have been developing about one aspect of your topic or another.

But you may also want to use full pages of scratch paper for jottings that might not fit on a card. I myself resort to cards only to organize and reorganize ideas that have been scribbled out at random on haphazard-looking pages. I am more worried about premature tidiness—getting an illusion of purpose and order before enough thinking has been done—than I am about burying my desk in paper. In this, as in every other, aspect of the composing process you should suit your own inclinations; all that matters is the outcome.

In your notes you can perform a number of helpful operations:

Quote passages from articles and books:

> Loercher (p. 14) cites Ronsard as saying: "There does not live a man in the world who so greatly hates cats as I with a deep hatred. . . . I hate their eyes, their brow, their gaze."

Summarize facts or conclusions from those and other sources:

> Montaigne (Loercher, p. 14) once asked himself whether his cat wasn't more amused with him than he with her.

Analyze texts that have to be interpreted:

> Consider Chateaubriand's praise of "the independent, almost un-grateful character of the cat, . . . the indifference with which it moves between salons and the gutters of its origin" (Loercher, p. 14). Relate to Ch's noble origins and adventurous period in America?

Draw distinctions between apparently similar things:

> Felix the Cat grows out of Krazy Kat visual tradition—but note the political and counterculture emphasis of the 1960s.

Launch trial theses that will be approved or rejected later:

> My guess is that the eras that produce sentimentality about cats are the same ones in which the "evil cat" image flourishes. Cf. periods when cats are depicted as just cats. A thesis here?

Express doubts and warnings that will have to be met:

> Watch out for exclusively Western emphasis. Loercher, e.g. (p. 14), cites Buddhist, Hindu, and Muslim traditions of esteeming cats.

Record random observations that may or may not prove relevant:

> Any chance of tossing in something about T. S. Eliot's *Practical Cats*?

Comment on earlier notes, developing a dialogue of pros and cons:

> Forget about starting with idea that cats figure prominently in the art of every civilization. According to Loercher, cats have practically no place in Bible and the lit. of ancient Rome (p. 14).[1]

EXERCISES

2. Writing once a day for a week, keep a journal of your thoughts about any one subject that interests you—a world crisis, for example, or your own work habits, or the problems you face as a student writer. Submit your entries along with a paragraph or two about the experience of journal keeping. Did you find that one day's entry responded to the previous one? Did your ideas become more definite as you went along? Did the existence of the journal affect the rest of your life in any way? Have you found the possible makings of an essay?

3. Write freely for ten minutes without planning or pausing. After a brief rest, read what you have written and then write for ten more minutes, this time taking off from any promising-looking idea in the first passage. Submit both passages along with a carefully revised paragraph that turns the second passage into typical essay prose, with consecutive development of a central idea.

4. Take some notes reflecting on any recent experience of yours that you think you could make interesting to readers. Submit the notes along with a paragraph developing one idea you have selected from those notes.

5. Using either cards or pages, take notes on anything you find significant in a piece of writing assigned by your instructor. Submit your notes along with a paragraph that develops one idea you have selected from those notes.

CHOOSING A TOPIC AND THESIS

Exploring Possible Topics

narrowing the subject area   Once you recognize that you have been given a subject area rather than a topic, you can work toward possible topics by dividing and subdividing the subject area. That maneuver will not in itself present you with a topic. "Chicago," for instance, is narrower than "Illinois," and "Lakeshore Drive" is narrower still, but all three lack a suitable focus; they remain subject areas because no question has yet been asked about them. Yet the process of breaking a large subject area into several smaller ones may bring such questions to mind.

If all you have to go on is the vast subject area "Education," for example, start by noting as many *categories* of education as you can:

Education
  private / public
  religious / secular
  vocational / academic
  lower / higher

Which of these categories do you feel most comfortable with? Write it down, and run through the categorizing operation again:

Higher education
  undergraduate / graduate
  science / humanities / engineering
  privately supported / state-supported / federally supported

Now study each item in your second list, and ask what *issues or questions* it raises in your mind. One of them should prove to be an acceptable topic. Thus, if you are looking at *federally supported education*, you might ask these questions:

Have universities become too dependent on the federal government?

How much influence does the government exercise over the direction of university-based research?

Has the program of federal loans to students been cut back too far?

Can the government put an end to traditional biases in academic hiring and promotion?

To what extent can the government insist that men's and women's athletic programs be equally funded?

Suppose, again, you are asked to write about sports, and suppose your favorite sport is skiing. So far so good—but "Skiing" is just as much a subject area as "Sports." By multiplying categories, however, you can tease your mind into posing some topic questions. Thus you might start by dividing skiing into its two main types, downhill and cross-country. Already a workable topic is in view: the relations (likenesses and differences) between those two kinds of skiing. Again, you can enumerate the functions or purposes of skiing: recreation, sport, exercise, social encounters, and so forth. Or suppose you want to write about *skiing equipment* but lack a clear focus. Through categorizing you can isolate such components as skis, bindings, boots, and poles, any one of which might be definite enough to sharpen your thinking. Or, equally, you can concentrate on one of the qualities people look for in ski equipment, such as speed, flexibility, maneuverability, or safety. Those qualities are not topics, but they can readily lead to topics—for example, the tradeoff between greater maneuverability and reduced speed in the short skis now used for teaching beginners.

trial topic Once you are sure you have arrived at a topic rather than a subject area, you may feel so relieved that you yearn to start the actual writing of your essay. But that would be a mistake. In the first place, your writing will quickly bog down if you don't yet have a thesis—a main point that answers your topic question. And second, how do you know that the first topic to come to mind is the best one for your purpose? Your trial topic should stay on probation until you are sure it can pass five tests:

1. Is this topic likely to sustain my interest throughout the writing project?
2. Is it appropriate to my intended audience?
3. Can it lead to a thesis of the expected type (usually explanatory or argumentative)?
4. Does it involve enough complexity—enough "parts"—for development at essay length?
5. Do I have enough supporting material to work with?

If you can answer all of these questions positively without further thought, consider yourself lucky. But probably, you will need to *explore* your trial topic by one or more of the following means.

focused freewriting or brainstorming   If freewriting and brainstorming can lead to preliminary ideas for an essay, they can also help you to explore a trial topic. The same rules apply (see pp. 87–89). The only difference is that now you begin with a definite focus and try to keep it—developing, not miscellaneous thoughts about anything, but every angle on the trial topic. As before, the idea is to set aside worries about correctness of organization and expression and to see what happens. Something always will. Even if you end by discovering fatal objections to the trial topic, your time will have been spent efficiently. The real misfortune would be to make that discovery after hours of struggle with a draft of your essay.

asking reporter's questions   Another simple but helpful way to expand your view of the trial topic is to run through the standard list of questions reporters are supposed to answer in covering a story: *who? what? when? where? how? why?* Unlike a reporter, you are not trying to make sense of a single event, yet the procedure can work because it makes you return to the same material from fresh perspectives.

Suppose your trial topic were the merits of a proposed bottle deposit law. Asking the six standard questions, you might come up with answers like these:

Who? The elected officials of your community or state.

What? Pass a law requiring a five-cent deposit on every returnable bottle.

When? At the next session of the city council or legislature; law to take effect at start of next calendar year.

Where? Only within the boundaries of this community or state.

How? Fix penalties for noncompliance by sellers of bottles, give the law wide publicity, warn first offenders, then begin applying penalties.

Why? Reduce waste and pollution; raise public consciousness about conservation; cut prices through use of recycled glass.

Even if there is nothing here that you didn't already know, one or two points might catch your attention in a new way as you sketch your answers. Given inflation, for example, will a five-cent deposit be large enough to ensure returns? Will there be special problems associated with putting the law into effect so soon? If the law applies only within a small geographic area, will consumers take their business elsewhere? Are the penalties for noncompliance too strict? Not strict enough? Any of these questions could carry you beyond your first thoughts, giving you a more solid basis for assessing whether you should settle on this topic.

applying explanatory strategies Finally, whether or not you intend to write an essay of explanation, you can explore your trial topic by considering it in the light of the seven explanatory strategies we reviewed on pages 42–43: *definition, division, illustration, process analysis, comparison and contrast, cause and effect,* and *analogy.* These strategies are so basic to thinking in general that you can hardly fail to stimulate new trains of thought by reviewing them in turn.

Thus, staying with the "deposit law" example, you might come up with results like these:

Definition: How does a law differ from a regulation? A misdemeanor from a felony? What kinds of containers would be included or excluded?

Division: What are the separate provisions of the bill? What types of stores would be affected?

Illustration: Which communities and states have already established deposit laws? What reports of success or failure are available? Do we have case histories of bottling companies and grocery chains that have accommodated themselves to the law, of individuals who were prosecuted, of others who have made a subsistence living by collecting other people's empty bottles for refund?

Process analysis: How will violations of the law come to public notice, arrive at a prosecutor's desk, and be subsequently handled? Does the law allow unknowing violations to be treated differently from outright defiance? If so, at what point would such a difference be recognized? And what flow of payments and reimbursements is expected among the consumer, the grocer, and the distributor?

Comparison and contrast: In what ways does this law resemble others that have been enacted elsewhere? How does it differ from them? Are the conditions (commercial, political, environmental) in this community or state like those elsewhere, or must special factors be taken into account?

Cause and effect: What events and trends have made passage of the law likely or unlikely? What differences in consumers' behavior would the law bring about? Would littering be significantly curtailed? In the long run, would prices of bottled products go up or down?

Analogy: How can the positive or negative aspects of this law be dramatized by statement in terms of some different measure?

Any number of good possibilities could grow out of such questions. Thus, *definition* of a misdemeanor might help you to decide whether the law carries adequate or excessive penalties for noncompliance. After *division* you could ask whether "mom and pop" stores would be more inconvenienced by the law than supermarket chains. Examples *illustrating* existing laws elsewhere could be powerful evidence of workability or unworkability. *Process analysis* might show how flexible or inflexible the proposed law would be in implementation. *Comparisons and contrasts* could have obvious relevance to judgments about the wisdom of the law. *Cause and effect* reasoning could extend your thoughts in two directions, back to origins and forward to consequences; the latter would be crucial for an essay of argument. And once you decided which side you were on, you could draw an *analogy* to emphasize your position:

Pro: Asking people to recycle bottles is like asking them to subsidize medical care for the aged. Some will want to, many won't, and the program will get nowhere. In one case as in the other, the goal of *general* compliance requires that a tax be imposed.

Con: A swimmer who ties her feet together may feel especially noble and self-sacrificing, but she isn't going to win a race. If we pass this deposit law, we, too, will think ourselves morally superior to neighboring communities (states)—and we, too, will find that we are handicapping ourselves right out of business.

Trying Out Theses

By now you know that the search for a topic shouldn't be artificially set apart from the search for your key asset in composing, an engaging *thesis* or leading idea. (Indeed, if you can go directly from first ideas to a good thesis, so much the better.) To repeat: a topic, whether or not it is phrased as a question, is in effect a question to which the thesis is the answer. Thus you should never settle on a topic until you are reasonably sure you can match it to a sound thesis.

trial thesis   To the concept of the trial topic, then, we must add that of the **trial thesis**, a would-be leading idea which is still untested. To check it adequately, you cannot simply mull it over in your head; you must write it out in one clear sentence that you can examine from several vantages. Typical trial theses about the bottle law, for instance, might be these:

EXPLANATORY TRIAL THESES

Increased alarm over environmental pollution and over the scarcity of raw materials has provided broad-based support for laws requiring deposits on returnable bottles.

The passage or failure of bottle deposit legislation in any given state or community can be directly correlated with the proportion of voters under age thirty.

ARGUMENTATIVE TRIAL THESES

The minor inconvenience of paying a deposit and having to return empty bottles to a store is far outweighed by the benefits that all citizens would receive from a well-drafted law requiring the deposits.

A deposit law would not only hurt small business people by adding to their expenses and reducing their sales, but would also result in more, not less, pollution because of the increased trucking it would require.

None of these four examples is good or bad in itself; everything would depend on whether the writer had appropriate material on hand to make a convincing case.

There are, however, certain further tests that you can and should apply to any trial thesis:

1. *Does the sentence I have written make* only one *assertion?* If it makes more than one, start over. Your essay must cohere around a single main idea. (Note, however, that a trial thesis can give *several reasons* for the one opinion it puts forward.)

avoid the weaseling thesis . . .

2. *Does it make a* definite *assertion?* It had better. Beware of the *weaseling* thesis, which expresses little more than the writer's wish to stay out of trouble: × *Topic A is very controversial;* or × *Although some people approve of A, others do not.*

the circular thesis . . .

Watch, too, for the *circular* thesis, which doubles back on itself, saying only what is already implied by some of its own language: × *The growing popularity of sports shows that people are more interested in athletics than ever before;* or × *Contact sports should be banned because they involve the violent impact of one body on another.* If the popularity shows the popularity or if contact is bad because it involves contact, the trial thesis is biting its own tail instead of moving onto fresh ground.

Compare: *The growing popularity of sports expresses nostalgia for a more physically challenging existence; Contact sports should be banned because they whet an unhealthy appetite for violence and harm.* Whether or not you agree with these revised versions, at least they escape circularity.

. . . and the sweeping thesis

3. *Is it properly limited?* If the purpose of explanation and argument is to make a thesis believable, you would do well to *limit* your theses so that you will not have to support impossibly broad ideas. Many student writers, however, imagine that English essays must be lofty and grand, and some others want to hide their uncertainty behind huge assertions. And so they come up with theses like × *The decay of our culture has been accelerating every year,* or × *The West is guided by Christian morals,* or × *The purpose of evolution is to create a higher form of man.*

Encyclopedias of support could not establish the plausibility of such theses. Consider: (1) What universally recognized indicators of "cultural decay" do we have, and how could anyone show that cultural decay has been "accelerating every year"? (2) Can something as vague and various as "the West" be said to be "guided" by certain "morals"? How will the writer explain away all the brutalities of the past twenty centuries? (3) How has the writer been able to discover a purpose hidden from all professional students of evolution?

When you write out a trial thesis, examine it for danger words like *all, none, no, any, always, never, only,* and *everyone.* Such all-inclusive terms usually signal the presence of **faulty generalization,** the illegitimate extension of *some* instances to cover *all* instances of something. Suppose, for example, you want to argue that *There is no reason to delay immediate adoption of a national health insurance program.* Ask yourself: No reason at all? Will I be anticipating *all* possible reasons in my essay? Maybe I can avoid unnecessary trouble by making my thesis more modest: *Adoption of a national health insurance program would answer needs urgently felt by the poor, minorities, and the chronically ill.*

One usual cause of the needlessly sweeping thesis is overconfidence in the general applicability of the writer's own experience. If the question is whether the human species has an innate aggressive instinct, you may feel inclined to look in your heart and say either yes or no. To do this, however, would be to rely on guesswork and an inadequate sample of just one case. The same lapse occurs when a foreign-born writer asserts *The idea that immigrants want to become "Americanized" is contradicted by all experience,* meaning *I, for one, don't want to be Americanized.* Someone else writes *Professors actually enjoy making students suffer,* meaning *I had an ugly experience in History 10.* Personal experience can usefully *illustrate* a thesis, but you should be wary of generalizing from it.

Never pass up an opportunity to scale a broad thesis down to manageable size. The less you assert—without reducing your thesis to triviality—the more you can defend. Thus one student writer eliminated multiple problems she discovered in the following trial thesis: *The safe and efficient way to meet America's present and future energy needs is to replace all existing plants with geothermal ones.* Her eventual thesis was this: *Intensive development of geothermal energy could prove to be an attractive alternative to relying on expensive and dangerous nuclear plants.* Note the differences:

FIRST TRIAL THESIS	REVISED TRIAL THESIS
Geothermal power is the safe and efficient way to meet all present and future needs; it should replace all existing plants.	could prove to be one attractive alternative to one source of power.

EXERCISES

6. Suppose you are asked to write a 750-word essay on a topic of your choice. The following eight possibilities occur to you, but you begin to see that four of them are *subject areas* rather than topics. Indicate in writing which four will require significant narrowing before they can yield topics. As for the four genuine topics, recast each of them in question form, anticipating a specific thesis.

    A. How to Watch a Solar Eclipse
    B. World Peace
    C. The End of the Pac Man Craze
    D. Making Do with Less Gasoline
    E. A Woman's Role
    F. American Arms Sales to Underdeveloped Countries
    G. The Olympic Games
    H. Air Pollution

7. Take one of the items from Exercise 6 that you judged to be a subject area rather than a topic. Think about ways in which that subject area could be divided and subdivided during the process of searching for a topic. Then submit subdivided lists like those on page 92, using different indention to show how the subject area at the left can be broken into smaller and smaller units. Try to include at least three levels of generality in your list. On the lowest level of generality — the one where you hope to find usable topics — include three items.

8. For each of the three items that resulted from the last step of Exercise 7, write out a possible topic for a 750-word essay.

9. For each topic developed by Exercise 8, write out a *trial thesis.* Then in a paragraph or two explain why you would find one of those trial theses more promising than the other two. Assume once again that you are looking ahead to a 750-word essay. Your discussion should deal with the *interest* of the three trial theses and with the *support* each one would require.

10. For any topic that interests you, submit a page on which you briefly answer each of the standard "reporter's questions": *who? what? when? where? how?* and *why?*

11. Submit a paragraph or two showing how any *one* of your answers in Exercise 10 could yield useful material for an essay. Be sure to mention the essay's thesis and to explain how this material supports it.

12. Submit a page on which you explore the same topic used in Exercise 10, this time employing any three *explanatory strategies* (pp. 95–96). For each of the three strategies, indicate how your newly developed material might be put to work in an essay.

13. Mark a whole sheet of paper as follows:

	Faulty Thesis	Improved Thesis
weaseling		
circular		
sweeping		

Review the tests for trial theses on page 97, where *weaseling, circular,* and *sweeping* theses are characterized. Then, choosing any topics except those used in the text, make up three defective theses of the indicated types. For each faulty thesis that you write in the left column, add a corrected version in the right column.

14. For each of the following five trial theses write a brief comment explaining why you find it suitable or unsuitable for an essay of any size.

> A. Although some people disapprove of welfare reform, others do not.
> B. Vanilla ice cream makes me break out all over.
> C. The United States can no longer afford to have its energy prices dictated by foreign powers.
> D. People who think that Communists should be allowed to teach schoolchildren are completely crazy and should be locked away in asylums.
> E. Hospitals should spend less money on "showcase" equipment and more on clinical services for the poor.

DEVELOPING A THESIS STATEMENT

Suppose now that you have definitely arrived at a thesis for your essay and that it takes this form: *Intensive development of geothermal energy could prove to be an attractive alternative to relying on expensive and dangerous nuclear plants.* At last, you think, you are ready to begin planning the essay's organization. But to organize you must first have *parts* that require sorting out, and this thesis doesn't indicate what those parts might be. Suddenly, just when it appeared that nothing could stop you, you are adrift between two big phases of the composing process.

from thesis to thesis statement

Never fear. To get going again, all you need do is recast your thesis into a full **thesis statement**—that is, a sentence that not only conveys your main idea but also indicates what the major parts of your presentation will be. The "geothermal" thesis, you notice, already hints at such parts by mentioning that nuclear plants are (a) expensive and (b) dangerous. Ask yourself: Can I add other grounds for preferring geothermal power? At least one other reason comes to mind, giving you the following thesis statement: *Geothermal energy deserves to be developed intensively, for it is cheaper, safer, and more abundant than its main rival, nuclear energy.* Now, though your organizational work still lies ahead, you have at least shown yourself what needs organizing: a broad comparison of two energy sources and three specific reasons for choosing one over the other.

thesis statement stands alone

A full thesis statement, then, is *always complex*—a fact that may trouble you if you think of the thesis statement as one sentence within the essay. Won't that sentence be awfully cumbersome? Often it will, but there is no need to include it anywhere. The thesis statement is a private guide to the rest of the composing process; its only audience is you as you go on to draft your essay.

Sometimes your core thesis will already possess the complexity that can carry you into the work of organizing. We have already met one such thesis/thesis statement: *A deposit law would not only hurt small business people by adding to their expenses and reducing their sales, but would also result in more, not less, pollution because of the increased trucking it would require.* Here we see three crucial factors begging to be made structurally prominent: added expense, reduced sales, increased pollution. The writer is ready to decide on an effective order for these main supporting points.

More often than not, though, a core thesis will be too simple in form to serve as a thesis statement. The remedy is not to toss in miscellaneous verbiage, but to spell out some of the large considerations that made you adopt the thesis in the first place. You can add *main details, reasons,* and/or *objections,* all of which will become prominent organizational units of your essay.

main details Suppose your trial thesis, now tested and approved, is a sentence as plain as this: *Chinese farming methods differ strikingly from American ones.* You may or may not have all the major differences clearly in mind, but the way to be sure is to work them into a full thesis statement. And since you will eventually have to decide which order they should follow, why not decide right now? As a rule, the final

emphatic last position position is the most emphatic, whether the unit be a sentence, a paragraph, or a whole essay. Think, then, about the relative importance of your points, and arrange them accordingly within your thesis statement:

> Chinese farming differs strikingly from American farming in its greater concern for using all available space, its handling of crop rotation, its higher proportion of natural to manufactured fertilizers, and, above all, its emphasis on mass labor as opposed to advanced machinery.

The implications of this sentence for organizing a brief essay are so obvious that you could probably move directly from such a thesis statement to writing your opening paragraph.

reasons: the <u>because</u> clause Not every trial thesis can take on complexity through more detailed recasting of the main statement, but you can always find "parts" in the reasons why you think the thesis deserves to be believed. Suppose, for example, you intend to maintain that *The first year of college often proves to be a depressing one.* That is a fair beginning, but it tells you only that *x proves to be y.* How is a whole paper going to result from such a simple declaration? Ask yourself, then, *on what grounds* or *in what ways* you find that year typically depressing. If you list those grounds or ways in one or more *because* clauses, your thesis statement becomes an organizational blueprint:

The first year of college often proves to be a depressing one, because many students have moved away from their parents' homes for the first time, because it is painful to be separated from established friends, and because homework and grading are usually more demanding than they were in high school.

Now you have laid out the nature of your explanation; you are reasoning from an effect (depression) to its causes, which you will discuss one by one in your essay.

objections: the *although* clause But you need not stop with reasons. You may also want to *grant the objection* that some students find their freshman year exciting and rewarding. That will be a shrewd point to make before getting into those reasons for depression, for it will serve to limit your thesis (pp. 97–98), making it less exposed to rebuttal. In order to remind yourself that this limiting point belongs in the essay, add it to your thesis statement by means of an *although* clause:

Although some students find their freshman year exciting and rewarding, many others find it depressing, because they have moved away. . . .

argumentative thesis statement Our introduction to argument has already called attention to *although*s and *because*s. An *although* clause expresses a *concession,* admitting the truth of some nonessential point on the other side; a *because* clause contains *evidence,* or the reasons why you still have confidence in your main assertion. In planning essays of explanation you *may* place both concessions and reasons within your thesis statements; in argument you should do so routinely. Why? Because an argument is by definition the defense of one position against another. If your thesis statement merely announces your own stand, it will give you no help in meeting the two cardinal requirements of argumentation: to consider objections and to provide evidence. The *although/because* formula, demanding as it may be, obliges you to think about both of those requirements before beginning to write.

Let us say that you intend to maintain that the government should not insist on equal expenditures for men's and women's athletic programs in colleges. You know that to argue persuasively, you will have to blunt the force of at least one strong point on the opposite side. Get that point into your thesis statement, add your positive reasons, and you have a complete thesis statement:

Although men and women in college should certainly have equal opportunities to participate in sports, the government should not insist on equal expenditures for men's and women's athletic programs, because some colleges have many more men than women, because a football program requires disproportionately high expenditures, and because that program can produce income to support the entire spectrum of men's and women's athletics.

Quite a mouthful! But again, since a thesis statement is only a roadmap, not an excerpt from your essay, you needn't try to make it concise. It will succeed in its purpose if it allows you to move confidently into the next phase of planning.

EXERCISES

15. In the left column of a sheet of paper write out the three revised trial theses you presented for Exercise 13. In the right column write *full thesis statements* possessing enough complexity to serve as organizational guides for the writing of brief essays.

16. Submit a full thesis statement whose *main details*, like those in the expanded "Chinese farming" statement on page 101, give the statement an adequate degree of complexity.

17. Jot down an *explanatory trial thesis* that, like *The first year of college often proves to be a depressing one*, lacks the complexity of a full thesis statement. Then expand that core thesis by surrounding it with an *although* clause and one or mroe *because* clauses. Hand in your complete thesis statement.

18. Reread the "smoking" essay on pages 77–78, and hand in a fully developed thesis statement for that argument. The argumentative thesis statement on pages 102–103 can serve as a model.

19. Hand in an argumentative thesis statement of your own, dealing with any topic. Your statement should be comparable in development to the example on pages 102–103.

ORGANIZING

Ordering an Explanation or Argument

A full thesis statement, we have said, can help you start organizing and can even settle the order in which main points of evidence should be presented. Even so, you will usually face further structural choices. The longer your essay, the more freedom you will have to depart from an expected pattern. Still, it is important to know what that pattern is, for you can always have recourse to it when you notice that something needs fixing.

a general model To see essay structure in its broadest contours, you need only put yourself in a reader's place. Beginning in ignorance, the reader wants to know certain things that fall into a natural order:

1. what is being discussed
2. what the writer's point is
3. why objections, if any, to that point are not decisive
4. on what positive grounds the point should be believed

As a flow chart, then, the most common and reliable essay structure would look like this:

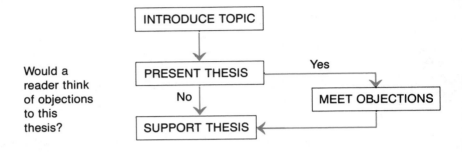

Would a reader think of objections to this thesis?

If you try to rearrange this order you will come up against difficulties. How, for example, could a reader want to know the writer's point before knowing the issue at stake? Why ask for supporting evidence before knowing what it is evidence for? Even the optional part of the sequence, the handling of objections, falls into a necessary place. When (as in any argument) it does become important to address objections, the logical place to do so is right after the thesis has been revealed—for that is where the objections are most likely to occur to the reader and hence to threaten the writer's credibility.

thesis statement as guide   Note that by following this model you can derive the structure of a *brief* essay directly from a full thesis statement (pp. 100–103):

The *topic*, the first element of the model, is known from the thesis statement because it is the question answered by the thesis.

The *thesis* is directly named in the thesis statement.

If the thesis contains an *although* clause, at least one important *objection* has been isolated.

Because clauses in the thesis statement specify the final element of structure, the main points of support for the thesis.

limitations of the model   But there are things the model cannot do, choices you must settle either through a detailed outline (pp. 105–109) or through problem solving as you work your way through a draft. Specifically, the model

does not tell you how to catch a reader's interest

does not say how many objections, if any, you should deal with or whether they should be met by concession or by refutation (pp. 66–68) does not say how much space you should devote to any single point

does not indicate whether you will need a formal concluding paragraph

Thus your sense of problems, opportunities, and paragraph-by-paragraph tactics, rather than any fixed formula, should be your final guide. Suppose you notice that the best positive evidence for your thesis consists of points that also answer main objections. In that case it would be wasteful to treat objections and supporting evidence separately. Or again, the decision to include or skip a summary paragraph at the end is a matter of weighing available alternatives. If your essay is long and complex, a conclusion is probably called for. But if you have saved a decisive point of evidence, a revealing incident, or a striking sentence, you may be well advised to end dramatically with that clincher.

Outlining

Outlines, like automobiles, are useful contrivances, but only to people who can keep them pointed toward their destination. Otherwise they end in the junkyard of vague purposes. Let us first consider why so many teachers are justly suspicious of the outline as an aid to composition.

The trouble with most outlines is that they short-circuit the necessary work of the full thesis statement. A writer goes directly from a subject area or topic to an outline, as follows:

x Europe
  I.   Germany
  II. France
  III. Spain
  IV. Holland
      (and so on)

What is wrong with such an organization? Well, what is right about it? No point is being addressed; the writer has used the outline as a lullaby for dozing off. An explanatory or argumentative essay, you recall, must *pursue an idea* from beginning to end. The "Europe" outline compounds the main procedural error we warned about at the outset, confusing a subject area or topic with a thesis (pp. 83–84). An essay that you organize according to the subdividing of a subject area will be no more engaging than a demonstration that each of your feet contains exactly five toes.

scratch outline   A truly useful outline is one that derives from a thesis statement and reveals whether or not that thesis statement needs revising. Let us say that you have been asked to write a 600-word essay of comparison and contrast dealing with television and radio. You already have a fully developed thesis statement: *Although both television and radio are private and domestic media, television is more intimate, better able to give us the illusion of being present at events, and therefore able to get by with less commentary about those events.* On the basis of this thesis statement you could draw up a simple *scratch outline,* reminding yourself of the order in which you intend to place the elements of the thesis statement:

1. Resemblance: TV and radio both private and domestic
2. First difference: TV more intimate
3. Second difference: TV gives more illusion of presence at events
4. Third difference: TV needs less commentary

A scratch outline merely puts your intended points in order without indicating which ones are most important. Even so, laying things out in sequence can bring hidden problems to light. Looking at the scratch outline above, for instance, you might see two possible weaknesses. First, you haven't yet caught the most obvious difference between the two media—namely, that TV is predominantly visual while radio is entirely verbal. And second, you have mixed your emphasis between comparing the two media in general and comparing them in one specific area—their coverage of public events.

Wrestling with these deficiencies, you may be able to come up with a more sharply focused thesis statement: *Although television and radio both cover news developments and sports events, their styles of coverage are necessarily different, because television can show us what radio can only describe.* Your revised scratch outline can now follow suit:

1. TV and radio cover many of the same happenings—e.g., news developments and sports events.
2. Thesis: But the two styles differ, because TV can show what radio can only describe.
3. News developments (film clips of speeches, interviews, battles, etc.): on TV, the events speak for themselves.
4. Sports events: TV, relatively free from reporting what is happening, includes more commentary than radio does.
5. In summary: TV coverage doesn't abolish the spoken word, but because we can see, the balance tips toward "editorial" as opposed to "reportorial" coverage.

Now your thesis is more pointed; you have clearly told yourself where it is to be revealed; you know you will follow it with discussion of the chosen categories *news developments* and *sports events;* and you look ahead to a concluding paragraph that won't just restate the thesis, but will reinforce that thesis from an informed perspective.

subordinated outline   So long as you are writing relatively brief essays, the scratch outline ought to serve you well enough. But for longer essays you may find it useful to **subordinate** certain points to others by indenting them and listing them according to a different set of numbers or letters so as to remind yourself which ideas are major and which are not.

sentence . . .   Suppose you had decided to write a thousand-word argument opposing rent control of off-campus housing and you were satisfied with the following thesis statement: *Although off-campus rent control is aimed at reasonable rents for students, it would actually produce four undesirable effects: establishment of an expensive, permanent rent-control bureaucracy; landlord neglect of rental property; a shortage of available units; and a freezing of currently excessive rents.* Knowing that your argument would have to be relatively complex, you might want to draw up a full outline such as the following one:

> I. The Problem
>> A. Students are currently subject to rent gouging.
>> B. High rents force many students to live far from campus.
> II. The Promise: Rent Control Aims at Guaranteeing Reasonable Rents Near Campus
> III. The Reality: Actual Results of Rent Control
>> A. An expensive, permanent rent-control bureaucracy would be established.
>> B. Landlords would neglect rent-controlled property.
>> C. The shortage of units would *worsen*, because
>>> 1. Owners would have no incentive to increase the number of rental units.
>>> 2. Competition for rent-frozen units would be more intense.
>> D. Currently excessive rents would be frozen, thus ruling out any possible reduction.

Notice that this outline establishes three degrees of importance among your ideas. The Roman numerals running down the left margin point to the underlying structure of the essay, a movement from *problem* to *promise* to *reality*. The indented capital letters subordinate specific ideas to those larger units; the problem, says Part I of the outline, has two aspects: rent gouging and the forcing of students to seek lower rents far from campus. By listing those aspects as A and B, you assign them parallel or roughly equivalent status in your argument. Points A through D in Part III are also parallel, but one of them, C, is supported in turn by two narrower points. By assigning those two points Arabic numerals and by a further indention from the left margin, you indicate to yourself that these considerations go to prove the larger idea just above them. Thus the three sets of numbering/lettering and the three degrees of indention clearly display the intended logic of your paper.

The example just given is a **sentence outline**, using full sentences to state every planned idea. (Note that the Roman headings I and III, which are not in sentence form, introduce *categories* rather than ideas; the substance of the argument has been put into sentences that are subordinated to those categories.) A sentence outline is the safest kind, because its complete statements ensure that you will be making assertions, not just touching on subjects, in every part of your essay. But if you are confident that you won't lose your way, you can use the simpler **topic outline**, in which sentences are replaced by concise phrases:

... versus topic

> I. The Problem
>   A. Rent Gouging
>   B. Students Forced to Live Far from Campus
>   (etc.)

The form you choose for an outline is hardly an earthshaking matter. Just be sure the outline gives you enough direction, and do not waste time elaborating an outline that is more intricate and hairsplitting than your essay itself. While writing a draft, be ready to depart from the outline wherever you discover flaws in it. When you do so, however, take time to recast the outline so that you will still have a complete conception of the essay to consult. And if, like many writers, you find that you simply cannot work from an outline in your first draft, make an outline of that draft when you have finished it. There is no better way of spotting redundancies and inconsistencies that need fixing.

If you do use subordination in your outlines, observe that a heading or subheading in an outline should never appear alone—no *I* without *II*, no *A* without *B*. The reason is that headings and subheadings represent divisions of a larger unit, either a more general point or the thesis of the whole essay. It is impossible to divide something into just one part. If you have a lonesome *A* in a draft outline, work it into the larger category:

ILLOGICAL:

> I. Problems
>   A. Excessive Noise
> II. Cost Factors
>   A. Overruns

BETTER:

> I. Problem of Excessive Noise
> II. Cost Overruns

In addition, you should always check a draft outline to make sure that all the subheadings under a given heading logically contribute to it. Do not try to tuck in irrelevant items just because you find no other place for them. That would defeat the whole purpose of outlining, which is to keep your essay coherent and logical in moving from one idea to the next.

Whether or not you find outlines useful, the more organizational thinking you do before undertaking a draft, the better chance you will have of finishing that draft without time-consuming setbacks. With that lesson in mind, we can turn now to the actual work of drafting and revising.

---

20. Suppose you wanted to write essays based on the following five theses. In which instances would you include a discussion of *objections* to the thesis? Briefly justify each of your answers.

   A. Recurrent images of rottenness and disease help to convey Shakespeare's thematic emphasis in *Hamlet*.
   B. In the interest of public safety, Congress should pass a law requiring the installation of restraining air bags in all new automobiles.
   C. Although soccer has grown enormously in popularity, it is still largely boycotted by the major television networks.
   D. The decline of the Roman Empire, so often attributed to loose living and military errors, was in reality caused chiefly by lead poisoning from toxic earthenware.
   E. Airlines should not be held financially liable for problems of hearing loss experienced by people who live close to major airports.

21. For any one of the theses appearing in Exercise 20, submit a full thesis statement (pp. 100–103) and a scratch outline for an essay.

22. From the fully developed explanatory thesis statement required for Exercise 17 on page 103, write out a *subordinated sentence outline* (pp. 106–108) for an essay. Resubmit the thesis statement with the outline.

23. From the fully developed argumentative thesis statement required for Exercise 19 on page 103, write out a *subordinated topic outline* (p. 108) for an essay. Resubmit the thesis statement with the outline.

24. Write out a full thesis statement for a 750-word essay comparing and contrasting your present life with your life of a few years ago. Along with that thesis statement, hand in a *subordinated sentence outline* of the essay itself.

25. Suppose you have been taking notes for an essay defending the private automobile against those who regard it as a social menace. Your notes include the following miscellaneous statements:

   We could find new fuels and impose limits on horsepower.

   Cars waste precious energy.

   We don't have to make all-or-nothing choices between private cars and mass transit.

   Congestion and smog are real problems.

   Cars give people initiative and individualism.

   Thousands of people are killed every year in traffic accidents.

Without cars, no one could live outside major population centers.

The government can require stricter safety standards.

Abolish the dangers and inconveniences, not the cars themselves.

Using some or all of these statements—and a few more, if you like—write a full thesis statement for your essay, and submit that thesis statement along with a subordinated outline of the type (sentence or topic) preferred by your instructor.

NOTE

[1]The sample quotations are from Diana Loercher, "The Cat: Friend, Villain, Enigma?" *Christian Science Monitor*, 16 Mar. 1976, p. 14.

6

DRAFTING AND REVISING

TOWARD READABLE PROSE

According to a certain old-fashioned conception of writing, someone who has drawn up a cogent outline has only one remaining task: to translate that outline into fleshed-out, rhetorically connected paragraphs. Composing was thought to have two distinct steps: the organizing of ideas and their subsequent expression in "good English." But we now realize that this was only a teacher's daydream. Actual composing is a messy, intermittent process whereby the writer continues to struggle toward clarity and persuasiveness—goals that, at any given moment, may be better approached by discarding one's outline map and looking around than by poring over it as one steps off the edge of a rhetorical cliff.

We have some distance to go, then, before completing our review of composing. The key term from here on must be **revision**. Though the previous chapter could be said to deal continually with revising (of one's first ideas, one's topic and thesis, one's organizational plans), it now becomes more urgent to insist that the essence of writing is rewriting. For the temptation to shut down one's critical powers, to settle for anything, is strongest at the completion of a draft—the first moment when one can seriously imagine that the whole job is finished.

Unpracticed writers usually hold both of the following opinions: *I will never be able to say what I mean* and *What I've just written will do, because it's mine.* One of these ideas replaces the other as a first draft limps toward completion. Writers are so relieved to find the page before them no longer empty that they draw a protective curtain across it: *I have suffered enough: here are my precious thoughts, exactly as they flowed from my brain.* And so they insulate themselves from advice about revision. Having discovered that they aren't completely blocked, they prefer not to ask whether people will be likely to accept what they have written.

Another way of characterizing this defensiveness is to say that writers invest *themselves* in their first draft. They see it, not as a collection of sentences and paragraphs, more or less intelligible and convincing, but as an expression of their inner worthiness. What they feel is a normal dread of rejection, but their way of coping with the feeling is to fantasize that the work has already been approved. All writers, no matter how experienced, get temporarily swept up in this false success. A veteran differs from a novice only in being more willing to descend from the clouds and begin rewriting. Eventually the veteran comes to share Mark Twain's resigned opinion: "The time to begin writing an article is when you have finished it to your satisfaction."[1]

That sentence probably sounds absurd to you. It will make more sense if you consider that "your satisfaction" refers to that initial relief over having made it all the way through a draft. You are really aiming at a more remote target, your reader's satisfaction—and readers, you may have already learned, don't care at all about your victory over writer's block. They expect to be interested and convinced by lively, technically correct prose. Your job, therefore, is to put yourself in your reader's place insofar as you can. You cannot do so fully while you are struggling to get something—anything—down on paper; revision can accelerate after the first draft has assured you that your mind hasn't rusted out since your last assignment.

Early in this book (p. 4) we referred to a fundamental change of attitude that has been transforming the teaching of composition. The heart of that change is a recognition that first-draft prose, with all its predictable limitations, is not so much incorrect as incomplete; it represents a necessary stage in the writer's progress toward finished work. Accordingly, many instructors now want to intervene at that stage, not in order to ferret out dangling modifiers and split infinitives, but to help students move from what Linda Flower has called writer-based prose to reader-based prose.[2] Let us explore the practical meaning of these terms.

Writer- and Reader-Based Prose

As the name implies, the audience of writer-based prose is the person who writes it—someone who is not yet single-mindedly concerned with convincing or impressing others. Writer-based prose is exploratory. It is a means of discovering how much one has to say—perhaps even *whether* one has much to say. Thus—and this is important to bear in mind—insofar as your planning has been thorough and shrewd, you will not be producing a pure version of writer-based prose even in your first draft. But that draft will inevitably contain some writer-based features. No cause for alarm. You need only be on the lookout for those features in revising.

Eventually we will consider some detailed ways in which writer- and reader-based prose differ. For now, here are paired traits that should give you a general sense of the two kinds:

WRITER-BASED	READER-BASED
1. Relatively undeveloped ⟶	Relatively developed
2. Attention to parts ⟶	Attention to whole
3. Associative order ⟶	Logical order
4. Assume context ⟶	Supply context
5. Assume evidential basis ⟶ for ideas	Establish evidential basis for ideas
6. Assume interest ⟶	Create interest
7. Imprecise language ⟶	Precise language

Everything in the left column relates to a writer's basic situation in trying to work out ideas and get them into sentences at the same time. Writer-based prose is (1) *relatively undeveloped* because ideas are still being isolated and named, not modified and illustrated. It attends to (2) *parts* because the whole that might unify them is not yet apparent even to the writer. It is (3) *associative* because one thought leads directly to another without leaving the writer time to see which of them is more important. It (4) *assumes a context*—a sense of the writer's larger purpose—because that context is already known to the intended audience, the writer, and hence it need not be set forth on paper. For similar reasons, writer-based prose takes for granted both (5) the *evidential basis* for the ideas presented and (6) *the reader's interest*. And if the proposer of ideas and the audience for those ideas are the very same person, the language conveying them can be (7) *imprecise*. It need only refer in an offhand way to thoughts that are securely stored away in the writer's mind.

In all these respects writer-based prose is at once efficient in getting something down and inadequate as rhetoric. The task of revision consists in taking what has been recorded for one's own sake—prose that makes full sense only when joined to unexpressed considerations—and making it independently communicative. For, once the essay reaches a reader who has nothing to go on but the words on the page, the whole production must be clear, informative, and persuasive on its own merits. To pass from writer-based to reader-based prose is to turn a halting conversation with oneself into an ordered presentation for others.

EXERCISES

1. If you have on hand the two samples of freewriting required for Exercise 3 in Chapter 5 (p. 92), submit them. If not, do that exercise and submit the two passages. Add a separate paragraph or two in which you (a) point out what you think are writer-based features displayed in those two samples of freewriting, and (b) indicate specifically how the passages could be made more reader-based.

2. Write a paragraph or two (on any topic) displaying as many writer-based features as you can manage to include. Submit that passage along with a revised one in which you have transformed the writer-based elements into what you take to be reader-based ones.

THE FIRST DRAFT

Overcoming Inertia

Even after much preparation, you may feel some resistance to launching into the actual prose of your first draft. If, as often happens, the opening paragraph looms as an especially big obstacle, why not skip beyond it and start with a slightly later one? Again, if you are worried about losing inspiration in the middle of a sentence, you can use a private shorthand, keeping your mind on the continuity of thoughts instead of on the missing words. And instead of writing, you may find it easier to talk into a tape recorder and then transcribe the better parts. Whether you write or dictate, do not be afraid to include too much, and do not be embarrassed by imperfections. What matters is that you get the draft finished—and that you understand how much more work remains to be done afterward.

Nothing is more normal than a feeling of reluctance and anxiety during the writing of a first draft. Those first few paragraphs will prove especially troublesome. Since the great enemy of the first draft is uncertainty, however, you will find your work much less awesome if you have on hand ample notes, a fully developed thesis statement, and an outline that arrives somewhere. These are your safe passes into that forbidding realm, the Not Yet Written. Knowing (from your thesis statement) that you have a clear and interesting point to make, and knowing (from your outline) that the paragraph you are sweating over now belongs in an ordered sequence, you can talk back to that little demon who keeps saying *You're stuck, you're stuck, you're stuck.* . . .

Planning versus Improvising

The work you have put into outlining will obviously be wasted if you set the outline aside while writing. Use the outline to judge, not only what each paragraph ought to be saying, but also where it ought to be leading. That is, look ahead to the next outline category and try to make each paragraph end in a way that will allow a smooth transition to the next one.

Remember, though, that an outline should always be your servant, never your master. As you approach each new paragraph, the outline offers you one direction for proceeding—in most cases the best one. But your sentence-by-sentence work of composing will sometimes show you unforeseen possibilities that deserve weighing. One sentence calls for further elaboration; another will sound misleading unless you immediately qualify it; and now and again you may find yourself on a completely new train of thought that may prove more fruitful than your original plan.

Good writing results neither from planning nor from improvising, but from the two in mutual tension. That is why many a classic essay, when studied for its supposed logical rigor, turns out to have a crooked line of development. The writer has mastered the art of putting each sentence and paragraph into dialogue with the previous one, and our pleasure in watching a lively mind at work blinds us, on a casual reading, to any inconsistencies. Perhaps we dimly recognize and admire the writer's capacity to be carried away—to follow a new idea wherever it leads.

But this is not to say that your own reader is going to be thrilled by sheer disorganization. You want to give the impression both of thinking on your feet and of reaching a known destination. Instead of discarding your plan, then, you should return to it and see how much rearranging is called for. Your reader will welcome all signs of close engagement with ideas, but only if your total presentation keeps a reader-based coherence and pointedness. To that end, continual revision is called for even at the first-draft stage.

THE REVISING PROCESS

Many students are willing to revise their work but are held back by two misconceptions. First, they suppose that revision begins only when an essay is nearly ready to be turned in; and second, they think that revision involves only a tidying up of sentence and paragraph structure, word choice, spelling, punctuation, and usage. But as we have mentioned, good writers revise their prose even while they are first producing it. And they stand ready to make not only *editorial* changes, but *conceptual* and *organizational* ones as well.

seeking response   Even if you understand the full importance of revision, however, you face a serious obstacle. Suppose that, with however much struggle, you have completed a draft. How will you be able to know what needs fixing in that draft? If you could put it aside for a week or two, you would see flaws in it that a quick rereading cannot uncover. If, more plausibly, your instructor is willing to look over your draft without assigning it a grade, you will get both encouragement and advice that should point a direction for the rest of your work. But you needn't wait for advice from that official quarter. Do what professional authors and scholars regularly do: consult. A classmate, roommate, or friend may be able to spot problems that will then strike you as glaring and drastic. If your trial reader is unfamiliar with the material discussed, so much the better; you want your essay to make sense as a self-sufficient presentation.

Two cautions, however. First, your trial reader may be off-base on certain points. Some students have come away from a previous English course with a handful of absolute dos and don'ts which, if you took them to heart, could only hamper your effort to address a particular audience and purpose by adopting a calculated voice, tone, and stance. You must be the final judge of your own drafts. And second, be careful not to allow anyone to rewrite part of the paper for you. That would constitute plagiarism (pp. 404–407), the presentation of someone else's work as your own.

redrafting   Let us assume that with or without help, you have noticed at least one major defect in your draft—a weak thesis, a self-contradiction, an inappropriate emphasis on relatively minor points, or an organizational muddle. What do you do next? The answer may seem obvious: you repair the damage where it has been found. But major defects are recognizable as such precisely because they throw the rest of the essay out of kilter. You must reopen the big questions about thesis and structure without losing those parts of your work that are still serviceable.

The following diagram represents, not a universal formula for revision, but a pattern that works well enough for at least one habitual reviser (myself):

MOVE FROM
1. a draft

   to ↓

2. responses

   to ↓

3. a scratch
   sheet or
   two

   to ↓

4. note cards

   to ↓

5. rearranged
   cards

   to ↓

6. a new draft

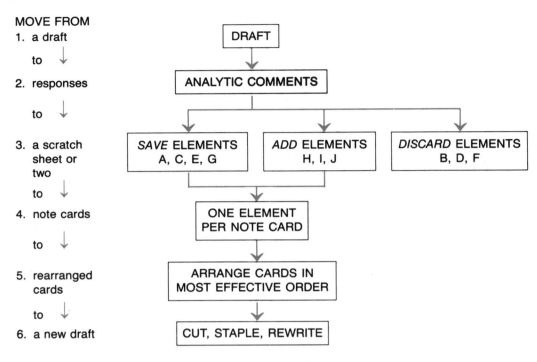

Here you see a method for saving, adding, discarding, and rearranging elements according to a new evaluation of their merits. As soon as (1) your *draft* has been subjected to (2) other readers' *analytic comments* that you find convincing, you can use (3) *full scratch sheets* to assess the stronger, weaker, and missing features of your case. Full pages may serve you better than note cards at that point because you will need room to develop new lines of thought — in effect, to talk back to yourself. But when you have decided which ideas to stress in your next draft, you can find the most effective order for presenting them by (4) *allotting each of them a note card* and (5) *testing various groupings and sequences of cards*. Finally, you can use the cards in your eventual "deck" (6) to *place in sequence the patches of old and new prose* that are now to be included. With a pair of scissors, a stapler, and some room for sorting scraps of paper, you now possess the makings of a better draft.

THREE KINDS OF REVISION

conceptual   One key trait of all reader-based prose is a *resolved position* on the writer's part. However much the writer may have been fishing for ideas while composing the first or second draft, the reader can expect to find, in the finished copy, one and only one thesis controlling all that is asserted. Thus, if you want to offer pros and cons, you must not appear to be first siding with one faction and then with the other. Instead, the idea is to take a position that reflects the relative weight of the favorable and unfavorable considerations. The best guarantee of having such a controlling overview is a carefully framed thesis statement (pp. 100–103). But because sentence-by-sentence composing can and often should lead to new ideas, you must read through your completed draft to be sure it makes the desired impression.

Do not hesitate to alter or even reverse the thesis of your essay if you become more swayed by objections than by supporting points. Such a shift of direction is a sign not of indecisiveness but of respect for evidence. Real indecisiveness, indeed, often sets in at the point where a radical rethinking of the thesis is called for. Many an episode of writer's block is brought about by a reluctant and unacknowledged loss of sympathy for the original thesis. Wanting to cling to material already developed but finding no way to make it convincing, the writer falls into a state that feels like boredom and fatigue but is really frustration.

Hard as it is to believe, at such a moment the most efficient as well as the fairest thing to do is to reassess the thesis and prepare for extensive rewriting. Why most efficient? First, many more unproductive and troubled hours lie ahead of the writer who has lost confidence in the case being made. And second, along with a restoration of purpose comes a clearer sense of structure. Passages, for example, that looked weak as positive evidence may be salvaged as discussions of contrary points to be conceded or refuted. Conceptual revision, though it is usually the most drastic and painful kind, may prove in some instances to be the emergency treatment that saves the patient, your essay.

You should be prepared to make less sweeping conceptual changes as well. Have you exaggerated your claims? Do you need to supply more evidence or answer more objections? If so, you should make the necessary improvements as early as possible so that you can write your final draft with full knowledge of where you are taking your reader.

organizational We have already seen (pp. 103–105) that a sound organization is necessarily reader-based. That is, it addresses the reader's natural questions in the likely order of their occurrence, from *What is this essay about?* through *On what grounds should I believe this thesis?* If you have planned carefully and have made no significant conceptual changes, the organization implicit in your thesis statement will serve you well. But do not be surprised if what looked clear in a thesis statement or outline no longer stands out properly in a draft. Your thesis statement, for example, has not told you how to apportion your points between paragraphs or blocks of paragraphs. Now you must check the draft to see if major ideas have really been given major emphasis. And as a corollary, you should be ready to condense or move passages that preoccupied you in the writing but would keep a reader from concentrating on more important elements.

Needless to say, the point that should stand out most clearly is your thesis. Did you wait to unveil it until you attracted the reader's interest and identified the topic? Does it occupy a prominent place in a prominent paragraph? Is there any chance that your reader will mistake a secondary point for the main one? Moving or eliminating that competing point would be one means of resolving the difficulty without having to declare flatly *And now for my thesis. . . .*

Other organizational problems may need work if you have allowed yourself to improvise. *Digressions,* or passages that stray from the issue at hand, should be removed, though apparent digressions— passages that first look tangential but then turn out to be relevant— can be effective if you remain in control of your reader's expectations. Watch too for *redundancy* (needless repetition), especially in its most common form, restatement of the thesis. If you highlight the thesis properly when it is announced, there should be no need to pound it into your reader's head. Again, check for *lengthy, unanalyzed quotations* which pad your essay without advancing your explanation or argument. Finally, see if you have omitted anything your reader needs to know—for instance, a principle of physics or astronomy, the rules of a little-known game, or the plot of an unassigned novel. Here, as elsewhere, the key to successful revision is to "play reader" and probe for sources of puzzlement or dissatisfaction.

editorial   Though editorial revision is not always the most important kind, it does cover the greatest number of problems. They range from such finicky matters as footnote form to such broad ones as the striking of an appropriate voice, tone, and stance. In every case, proper revision flows from putting the reader's convenience ahead of your own:

FEATURE	REVISE FOR	HELPS READER TO
voice, tone, stance	appropriateness to audience and purpose	appreciate context and point of view
paragraphs	unity, emphasis, development	see relations between major and minor points
sentences	pointedness, efficiency, variety of structure	follow ideas, avoid tedium
words	precise meaning, vividness where appropriate, freedom from formulaic and tactless language	get clear information, avoid jarring effects

grammar, usage, punctuation, spelling, other conventions	conformity with standard written practice	concentrate on substance of essay
citation form	fullness, exactness, consistency	have access to secondary information

Although most of these matters remain to be discussed in later chapters, you can already see the common thread—namely, reader-based consideration—that connects all the kinds of editorial revising. In extreme cases the necessary changes can actually rescue sentences and paragraphs from incoherence, as when a subject and predicate have failed to connect in meaning (pp. 281–282) or when the second half of a draft paragraph unravels what the first half has put together. More often, editorial revision gives the reader immediate access to meanings that would have been apparent after some extra and annoying work of interpretation, as when the writer has used pronouns whose antecedents can only be surmised (see pp. 289–290). One by one, such improvements look small, but taken together they make a huge difference in winning the reader's good will.

Although most instructors have no great love of the infamous red pencil, a student who has not brought problems of standard expression under control may get back essays that look as if they had contracted scarlet fever:

Once people [have gone to the trouble of
acquiring the capacity to treat everyone] as Wdy
equals, they can work with others for the
Chop Exagg common good. A great example is how the Los Pred
Sp Angeles area handled it's pollution problem.
Everyone was aware of the stifling smog. But the
majority of these people were willing only to Ref
complain. One group of citizens, however ^ came up P
with a creative plan for carpooling. Providing DM
an incentive, one lane of freeway was set aside ¶ Unity
Wdy for cars carrying three or more people. [But
after a short period of time,] the committment Sp
was abandoned. [Because of the godawful traffic Colloq
Frag jams in the other lanes.] It was a promising Ref

Pass   idea, but most people <u>are made</u> [less upset by   *Comp*

Rep   smog so that] they actually prefer it to <u>traffic</u>

jams in freeway lanes.   *& Unity*

The symbols in the margins of this made-up paragraph are typical shorthand forms for noting problems and requesting specific kinds of revision. (For a fuller list of symbols, see the two pages inside the back cover of this book.) If the student dealt with the criticisms one by one, the diagnoses and remedies would be these:

SYMBOL	PROBLEM AND SOLUTION	UNREVISED VERSION	REVISION
Wdy	the expression is wordy; make it more concise	Once people have gone to the trouble of acquiring the capacity to treat everyone as equals	Once people can recognize others as equals
		after a short period of time	soon
Exagg	the expression is overstated; tone it down	A great example	One example
Pred	faulty predication; do away with the mismatch between subject and predicate	One example is how . . .	One example is the handling . . . ; *or* Consider, for example, how Los Angeles handled . . .
Sp	spelling error; look the word up and spell it correctly	it's committment	its commitment
Chop	several plain, brief sentences in a row; introduce variety of structure	A great example is how Los Angeles . . . willing to complain.	Consider, for example, how Los Angeles handled its pollution problem. Even though everyone was aware of the stifling smog, few people were willing at first to do anything more than complain.

Ref	pronouns or demonstratives lack clear, explicitly stated antecedents; make the reference clear	these people It was a promising idea	residents The carpooling plan was a promising idea
P	punctuation error; correct it	One group of citizens, however came up with	One group of citizens, however, came up with
DM	dangling modifier; supply an agent to perform the action	Providing an incentive, one lane of freeway was set aside	Providing an incentive, county officials set aside
Colloq	the expression falls beneath the level of diction appropriate to this paper; find a middle-level substitute	godawful	serious
Frag	sentence fragment; rewrite or combine to form a grammatically complete sentence	Because of serious traffic jams in the other lanes.	But because of serious traffic jams in the other lanes, the commitment was soon abandoned.
Pass	unnecessary use of passive voice; shift to active voice	most people are made less upset	most people would rather
Comp	faulty comparison; match the compared terms or completely recast the expression	most people are made less upset by smog so that	most people prefer smog to traffic jams; *or* most people find smog less offensive than traffic jams
Rep	this expression repeats an earlier one; rephrase it	traffic jams in the other lanes . . . traffic jams in freeway lanes	. . . most people prefer lung congestion to traffic congestion

But one further symbol, *# Unity* , should be considered before any of these others, for it suggests that some completely new sentences are called for. Note that the writer began by asserting that *people can work for the common good,* but then he went on to illustrate a nearly opposite point—that *most people cannot put the public interest before their immediate convenience.* Until that contradiction is resolved, no amount of tinkering can make the paragraph effective. Thus the writer now faces a crucial choice: either muster support for the original point or change that point to conform with the traffic example.

If you were in this writer's shoes, how could you tell which option to prefer? The answer is: Ask yourself which idea shows more regard for real experience, the initial one or the one that surfaced in the drafting process. It is really no contest. *Working with others for the common good* is a limp concept, as wishful and unprovocative as a "Smile" button. The conflict between selfish private habits and the common good is a more "realistic" consideration, one that could place on view the writer's ability to face facts. He should skip the moralizing, then, and rethink his whole thesis. His eventual, radically improved paragraph might look like this:

> When selfish private habits and the common good come into conflict, the outcome is likely to be all too predictable. Take a recent example from Los Angeles, where everyone's health would be safeguarded by a significant reduction in automobile exhausts. Acting on the suggestion of a citizens' group, county officials tried to promote carpooling by setting aside one lane of each freeway for cars carrying three or more people. If it had worked, this plan would have enabled everyone to breathe more easily. The plan had to be dropped, however, when so few people cooperated that motorists refusing to share rides were hopelessly clogging the remaining lanes. Forced to choose between lung congestion and traffic congestion, Los Angelenos will take lung congestion every time.

EXERCISES

3. Show one of your drafts to a classmate, friend, or roommate, and ask for an evaluation of strong and weak points. Return to the draft, and see where you agree and disagree with your helper. Then submit two or three paragraphs explaining what, if anything, you have learned from this seeking out of criticism. Were the criticisms always justified? Did friendship interfere with frankness? Do you expect to make use of such "peer judgment" in the future?

4. Think of the three kinds of revision—conceptual, organizational, and editorial—in relation to your own work as a writer. Submit two or three paragraphs explaining which kind(s) of revision is (are) most necessary for you. Offer specific illustrations from your previously submitted work.

BEGINNINGS, TRANSITIONS, ENDINGS

Let us turn now to three key aspects of a successful essay that always need attention after the first-draft stage: *catching the reader's interest, fitting paragraphs together,* and *ending strongly.*

Arousing Curiosity in the First Paragraph

Ideally, the first draft of your essay will not only convince your readers that your thesis is correct but also persuade them to take an interest in it. In practice, however, effective openings tend to be largely the fruit of revision. Neither your opening nor your closing remarks should concern you very much in an early draft. When revising, you can read through the main body of your draft and look for clues to a rewritten opening that will make a more decisive and attention-seizing impression.

leading to the topic or thesis   A good introduction customarily accomplishes three things: it catches the reader's interest; it establishes the voice, tone, and stance of the essay; and — usually but not always — it reveals the one central matter that is going to be addressed. Only rarely does a shrewd essayist begin by blurting out the thesis and immediately defending it. The standard function of an introduction is to *move toward* disclosure of the thesis in a way that makes the reader want to come along.

by means of a "funnel opener" . . .   Perhaps the most frequently used device for introducing a topic or thesis is the **funnel opener**. As the name implies, a funnel opener begins with an assertion covering a broader area than the topic will; this gives the reader a wide perspective and a context for understanding the actual topic when it is stated. Then, in perhaps two or three subsequent sentences, the funnel paragraph narrows to the topic or thesis, which is usually revealed just as the paragraph ends. The following example is typical:

> Only a few politicians have taken a craftsman's pride in self-expression, and fewer still — Caesar, Lord Clarendon, Winston Churchill, De Gaulle — have been equally successful in politics and authorship. Of these, Churchill may be the most interesting, for he was not only among the most voluminous of writers, but also commented freely on the art of writing. He was, in fact, a writer before becoming a politician.[3]

By the end of this paragraph we know that the topic will be Churchill's writing, but we arrive at that knowledge by sliding down the funnel:

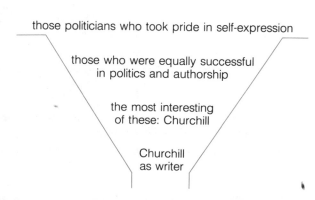

those politicians who took pride in self-expression

those who were equally successful
in politics and authorship

the most interesting
of these: Churchill

Churchill
as writer

You should certainly try your hand at some funnel paragraphs and keep this structure in your repertoire. Instead of waiting tensely for some thunderclap of inspiration, you can call on the funnel opener to get you easily moving toward the substance of your essay. At the same time, you should be aware that this device often makes a mechanical effect. Instead of invariably nudging your reader down the funnel, be alert for opportunities to try the riskier but more arresting **baited opener.**

...or a "baited opener"

A baited opener is an introduction that not only saves its main idea for last, but also teases a reader by keeping its early sentences— in some cases all of its sentences—"out of context." Those offbeat sentences, precisely because they appear from nowhere, draw readers forward and make them want to learn what the missing context is.

Here are two student examples:

> When a man who has had autonomy all his life—a man who has chosen where he would live, how he would dress, what he would do for a living, and what he would eat—becomes the victim of an advancing terminal illness, he is carted away to mandatory hospitalization. Before long he is reduced to a prostrate and puling infant, dependent on the doctors and nurses who govern his life. They puncture him with needles, rig him with tubes, and feed him what and when they see fit.

The paragraph arouses sympathy and interest without indicating whether this will be a narrative essay about one terminally ill man or a general discussion of how such people are treated.

> I can remember when I first saw her in Mr. Ripetto's French class. Of all the students crowded into that room, my eyes fell immediately upon her. Everyone else seemed to fit into some stereotype of the high-school student, but she was aloof and strong; I could see it right away. She sat there alone, yet without any anxiety about being alone. I knew I wanted to meet her, and I was sure that, if we ever got together, she would recognize me as someone of her own kind.

At the end of this paragraph the two characters are still indistinct, but we want to learn more about them. Note how the unidentified pronouns *her* and *she* draw us forward, creating an interest that will be sustained in later paragraphs.

Baited openers work especially well when the writer has a surprise to spring:

> Natasha Crowe, a close acquaintance of mine, recently received an unsolicited invitation from Joanne Black, senior vice president of the American Express Co.'s Card Division. "Quite frankly," the letter

began, "the American Express Card is not for everyone. And not everyone who applies for Card membership is approved." Tasha (as she is affectionately called) ignored the letter. A few weeks later she received a follow-up offer from a different vice president, Scott P. Marks Jr. "Quite frankly," Mr. Marks reminded her, "not everyone is invited to apply for the American Express Card. And rarer still are those who receive a personal invitation the second time."

Despite the honor, Tasha has continued to disregard this and similar invitations she has lately been receiving. For one thing, she has no job. Her savings are minimal. Her credit history is essentially a vacuum and therefore her credit rating, I'd imagine, is lousy. She doesn't even speak English. She's my cat, and I love her.[4]

avoiding the deadly opener   An experienced reader can usually tell after two or three sentences whether the writer has command of the topic and is capable of making it attractive. Whatever else you do, never slip your reader one of the following classic sleeping pills:

1. *The solemn platitude:*

   x Conservation is a very important topic now that everyone is so interested in ecology.

   Ask yourself if *you* would continue reading an essay that began with such a colorless sentence.

2. *The unneeded dictionary definition:*

   x The poem I have been asked to analyze is about lying. What is lying? According to *Webster's Eighth New College Dictionary,* to lie is "1: to make an untrue statement with intent to deceive; 2: to create a false or misleading impression."

   Ask yourself if your reader is actually in the dark about the meaning of the word you are tempted to define. *Lie* obviously fails that test.

3. *Restatement of the assignment, usually with an unenthusiastic declaration of enthusiasm:*

   x It is interesting to study editorials in order to see whether they contain "loaded" language.

   If you are actually interested — and no one would believe it from this sentence — you would do well to *show* interest by beginning with a real statement.

4. *The "little me" apology:*

x After just eighteen years on this earth, I doubt that I have acquired enough experience to say very much about the purpose of a college education.

Is this going to whet your reader's appetite for the points that follow?

sharpening the first sentence If your first paragraph is the most important one, its first sentence is your most important sentence as well. When that sentence betrays boredom or confusion, your chances of gaining the reader's sympathy plummet. If it is crisp and tight and energetic, its momentum can carry you through the next few sentences at least. This is why some people take pains to make that first sentence *epigrammatic*—pointed and memorable. Thus one writer begins a review of a book about Jewish immigrants by declaring:

• The first generation tries to retain as much as possible, the second to forget, the third to remember.[5]

Another wittily begins an essay on divorce:

• There was a time when a woman customarily had a baby after one year of marriage; now she has a book after one year of divorce.[6]

And a student writer advocating gun control begins:

• Thousands of people in this country could make an overwhelming case for the banning of handguns, except for one inconvenient fact: they aren't so much *in* the country as *under* it, abruptly sent to their graves with no chance to protest or dissuade. Arguing with a gun nut may be futile, but have you ever tried arguing with a gun?

As this last example shows, the epigrammatic sentence need not be the very first one; the point is to get a decisive start.

Linking Paragraphs

One risk of writing from an outline is that you may approach each paragraph or block of paragraphs as an independent unit corresponding to a heading in the outline. That is an adequate way to start out, but you may need to revise for continuity—a connectedness not only of logic but of rhetorical signals as well.

Later (pp. 165–170) we will see how paragraphs can be stitched together internally by means of such signals. For now, the important point is to note whether enough of your draft paragraphs begin with indications of linkage to the paragraphs just above them so that a reader feels both a continuity of discussion and a logical relation to the previous idea. Such relations are immediately conveyed by conjunctions like *but* or *yet* and by sentence adverbs like *thus, furthermore, however,* and *nevertheless.* And they become even sharper in paragraphs whose first sentence refers directly to a point made in the previous sentence: *These problems, however . . . ; Nevertheless, there are reasons to doubt that argument;* etc.

In one published essay, for example, some of the paragraphs begin as follows:

- *But* at present these happy prospects are heavily overcast. . . .
- I shall not end on *this* negative note; *but* it is necessary. . . .
- *But* we are in the midst of other explosions . . . that will be just as fatal as long as they go on *in the present fashion.* . . .
- *Closer* comparisons make *our own* achievements seem *even more* destitute. . . .
- Some of *this* attitude is doubtless left over from pioneer days.
- *I have of course intentionally, and doubtless grossly, caricatured the life of the representative American today.* . . .[7]

The emphasized parts of these sentences, including all of the last one, depend for their full meaning on points that concluded the paragraphs above them. Thus, though in each instance readers are aware that a new idea is being announced, they also know that a line of development is being carried forward.

enumeration One formal but often helpful way of linking paragraphs is to enumerate points that have been forecast in an earlier sentence. If you assert, for example, that there are three reasons for rejecting one proposal or four factors that must be borne in mind, you can begin the following paragraphs with *First, . . . , Second, . . . ,* and so on.

the transitional paragraph If you find yourself, in a first draft, devoting a substantial paragraph to maneuvering from one part of your essay to the next, think twice about it. You don't want to retain paragraphs that merely communicate your organizational worry:

x We have now seen that the first part of the question posed at the beginning of this essay cannot be easily answered, and that, specifically, two serious considerations stand in our way. The first of those considerations has now been dealt with, though not perhaps as fully as some readers might prefer. It is time now to go on to the second point, after which we can return to our original question with a better sense of our true options.

What this really says is: *Please bear with me as I try to get through that cumbersome outline of mine.*

From time to time, however, you may want to devote a brief paragraph to announcing a major shift of direction. Do so concisely, with a minimum of distraction from the sequence of ideas:

- But how can such violations of human rights be swept under the rug? Unfortunately, as we will see, the method is simple and practically foolproof.

the paragraph block   A relatively long, well-organized essay typically develops, not merely paragraph by paragraph, but in groups of paragraphs that address major points. Within each of these **paragraph blocks**, one paragraph will usually state the leading idea and the others will modify or develop it. A writer working, for example, from the "rent control" outline on page 108 might decide to introduce Part III, the heart of the argument, with a "theme" paragraph marking a sharp break in the essay:

> Such is the promise that adovcates of rent control offer to students who are weary of expensive housing and long trips to campus. If the promise could be even partially realized, it might be worth giving rent control another try. Unfortunately, there is no reason to think that another experiment would work better than all previous ones. However bad the present housing crisis is, you can be sure that rent control would make it worse.

Then four paragraphs, covering points A through D in the outline, would follow, making a single paragraph block about the disappointing results of rent control.

Ending Strongly

Nobody knows why, but human beings have a persistent need for a sense of completion. They want to feel that a piece of writing, at its end, is truly finished and not just stopped like some toy soldier that needs rewinding. What is more, they like to anticipate, through a revealing change in tone or intensity or generality of reference, when the end is about to occur.

taking a wider view   Just as you can lead to your thesis by beginning on a more general plane, so you can end by looking beyond that thesis, which has now been firmly established. Thus, for example, in a paper defending the thesis that unilateral disarmament is a dangerous and unwise policy, a student writer concluded as follows:

> There is no reason to expect, then, that the world would be safer if we laid down our arms. On the contrary, we could do nothing more foolhardy. *We must look to other means of ensuring our security and that of the nations we have agreed to protect.*

The sentence we have emphasized "escapes" the thesis, posing a goal for some future investigation. That gesture is rhetorically useful as a sign that the thesis has now been made convincing.

the clinching statement   Remember that the final position of any structure—sentence, paragraph, or whole essay—is naturally emphatic. To take advantage of that fact, withhold writing your conclusion until you have found material that bears reemphasizing or expanding. Look especially for striking quotations or stories that are full of significance. If necessary, cut the quotation or story from the body of your essay so that you can use it where it will have maximum impact, at the end:

> Robert M. Hutchins has described the editors of *Britannica 3* as pioneers. After they had established their design "the question became one of execution . . . there were no models to imitate and no horrible examples to shun." One of these deficiencies has been made good by *Britannica 3* itself: they have their horrible example now.[8]

> Heisenberg once likened the role of the scientist to that of Columbus, "who had the courage to leave behind him all inhabited land, in the almost insane hope of finding land again on the other side of the sea." Heisenberg's journey was a long one, and the land he discovered one of the richest in all of science.[9]

linking the last paragraph to the first   Remember, too, that your concluding paragraph can bear some evident, possibly dramatic, relation to your introductory one. If you already have a sound first paragraph and are groping for a last one, reread that opener to see if it doesn't contain some hint that you can now develop more amply. Here, for instance, is the conclusion of a student essay that began by asking whether Mahatma Gandhi was nothing more than a religious fanatic:

> Gandhi's arguments reveal an underlying shrewdness. Far from betraying the dogmas of a fanatic, they are at once moral and cunningly practical. His genius, it seems, consisted in an unparalleled knack for doing right—and, what isn't quite the same, for doing the right thing. It is hard to come up with another figure in history who so brilliantly combined an instinct for politics with the marks of what we call, for lack of a better name, holiness.

Notice how the writer has put his opening question into storage until it can be answered decisively, with a pleasing finality, in the closing lines of his essay.

avoiding the deadly conclusion   To see whether your draft ending needs revising, check it against the following four rules:

1. Don't merely repeat your thesis.
2. Don't embark on a completely new topic.
3. Don't pretend to have proven more than you have.
4. Don't apologize or bring your thesis into doubt.

The reason for these cautions is that readers come away from an essay with the last paragraph ringing in their ears. If you end by sounding bored or distracted or untrustworthy or hesitant, you are encouraging readers to discount everything you have worked so hard to establish. You want to give the impression that things are falling in place. Do so without compromising your position, but also without making preposterous claims for its significance.

EXERCISES

5. Look through the essays you have already written for this or any other course, and find a first paragraph that you would now regard as a "deadly opener" (pp. 127–128). If you cannot find one, choose the weakest opening paragraph you have handy. Copy and submit it along with a revised version that leads toward your thesis in an engaging way.

6. Suppose you have been asked to write an essay about one accident in a nuclear generating plant. Ask yourself how nuclear accidents differ from other kinds. Then write a *funnel opener* (p. 125) for your essay, beginning with a consideration of massive accidents in general and concluding with mention of the case treated in the rest of your (imaginary) essay.

7. Write an alternative first paragraph for the essay contemplated in Exercise 6, this time using a *baited opener* (p. 126).

8. Look through a completed essay, either for your present course or for another, and check the relation between the last sentence of each paragraph and the first sentence of the next one. Did you always make that relation apparent with your language? Revise where necessary. When you are satisfied that all your sets of last-and-first sentences make for easy and logical transitions, copy those sentences, numbering each set of two, and hand them in.

9. Think of a point you would like to make about any topic. Write out that point in one sentence, and then ask yourself how you could best support it. Write at least two sentences that would help establish your main idea. You need not submit any of these sentences. Using them as a starting point, however, do submit a three-paragraph block (p. 130) in which the first paragraph *states* your idea and the other two *support* it.

10. Repeat the procedure of Exercise 5, this time using a *concluding* paragraph that strikes you as relatively ineffective. Use your revised paragraph to *expand upon* — not to repeat — the thesis of your essay, and try to make your language vivid and pointed.

11. Think of a story or quotation that has impressed you, and ask yourself what point it could be used to illustrate. Then write the concluding paragraph of an imagined essay, putting that quotation or story to effective use.

CHOOSING A TITLE

Do not bother thinking of a title until you have finished at least one draft, and be ready to change titles as your later drafts change emphasis. If you begin with a title, it will probably indicate little more than the subject matter treated in your essay. Replace it later with a title expressing your *view of* that subject matter or at least posing the question that is answered by your thesis. Thus, asked to write about revision, you shouldn't remain satisfied with "Revision" or "Revising College Essays"; such toneless titles suggest that you have no thesis at all. Instead, try something like "The Agony of Revision," "Revision as Discovery," or "Is an Essay Ever Really Finished?" Each of those versions tells the reader that you have found something definite to say.

If your essay contains significant quotations, either from real people or from a literary work, be alert to possible sources of titles in the quoted language. One freshman student, for example, began a prize-winning essay about *Hamlet* with the following paragraph:

> While showing Guildenstern how to play the recorder, Hamlet remarks that it is "as easy as lying" (III.ii.343). In a sense, much of the play's meaning is expressed in this line. Almost every character in *Hamlet* is to some extent living a lie: hiding thoughts, playing a role, trying to deceive another character. Claudius conceals his crime; Hamlet feigns madness; private schemes prevail. In the end, Hamlet may even be deceiving himself, forcing himself into the role of avenger when he may not actually fit.

For a title the writer chose "As Easy as Lying"—a phrase that stirred curiosity and hinted at her possession of a well-considered, original thesis.

For the form of titles see pages 359–360, 364.

A CHECKLIST FOR REVISION

Since you cannot always count on having a friendly critic available, you yourself will need to test your drafts against common standards of reader-based prose. The following twenty questions form a checklist that you can consult as soon as you have finished a draft or two. Running through the questions, you ought to be able to pinpoint remaining problems and to locate the relevant discussions of them elsewhere in this book.

A Checklist for Revision

1. Does my title indicate that I have a point to make (p. 133)?
2. Do I have a clear, properly limited, and interesting thesis (pp. 96–98)?
3. Have I adequately supported my thesis (pp. 69–73)?
4. Have I dealt with probable objections to my thesis (pp. 66–68)?
5. Is my thesis conspicuous enough?
6. Are my voice, tone, and stance appropriate to my audience and purpose (pp. 11–14)?
7. Are my paragraphs unified, emphatic, and fully developed (pp. 150–174)?
8. Do all of my paragraphs help to build the reader's confidence in my thesis (pp. 118–120)?
9. Does my first paragraph attract the reader's interest (pp. 124–128)?
10. Have I made clear and helpful transitions between paragraphs (pp. 128–130)?
11. Does my last paragraph give enough sense of completion (pp. 130–132)?
12. Are my sentences pointed and efficient (pp. 177–197)?
13. Do my sentences show enough variety of structure (pp. 198–203)?
14. Do all of my words mean what I think they mean (pp. 212–216)?
15. Is my diction free of clichés, jargon, euphemisms, needless abstraction, and mixed metaphor (pp. 225–234)?
16. Are all of my words correctly spelled (pp. 344–356)?
17. Have I kept to standard idiomatic written usage (pp. 278–308)?
18. Have I followed correct form for punctuation and other conventions (pp. 310–343, 358–370)?
19. If I have quoted long passages, have I kept my own ideas in the foreground?
20. If I have included other people's words or ideas, have I cited them properly (pp. 407–427)?

EXERCISE

12. In preparing an assigned essay pause after completing a draft, and run through the "Checklist for Revision," using the page references to look up any unclear points. Evaluate and revise your draft accordingly, keeping notes on the changes you are making at this stage. Then submit a paragraph or two explaining what weak features of your draft became apparent to you in the light of the checklist.

THE FINAL COPY

No matter how many changes you make between drafts, the essay you eventually submit should look unscarred, or nearly so. It should also meet certain technical requirements of form. The following advice reflects general practice and should be followed whenever your instructor does not specify something different:

1. Type your essay if possible, using standard-sized (8½" × 11") unlined white paper of ordinary weight, not onionskin. If you must write longhand, choose paper with widely spaced lines or write on every other line. Type with an unfaded black ribbon, or write in dark ink. Use only one side of the paper.

2. If you are asked to supply a thesis statement and/or an outline, put them on a separate page along with your name, the course number, your instructor's name, the date of submission, and the title of your essay. Repeat the title on your first page of text.

3. If you are not supplying a thesis statement or outline, omit a title page and put your name, the course number, and the date of submission on four double-spaced lines at the upper right corner of your first page, above your title. Skip four lines between your title and the beginning of your text.

4. Allow 1" margins on all four sides of each page of your main text. Your right margins need not be even. In a handwritten essay, be sure to leave as much marginal space as in a typewritten one.

5. Leave the first page of text (and notes and bibliography, if any) unnumbered, but put unpunctuated Arabic numerals (2, 3, 4) in the upper right corners of subsequent pages.

6. Double-space your whole paper, including any extracted quotations (p. 335) and endnotes (p. 410), but not including footnotes (p. 411), which should be single-spaced.

7. Indent the first line of each paragraph by five type-spaces or, in a handwritten essay, about an inch. Do not skip extra lines between paragraphs. Indent extracted quotations (p. 335) by ten spaces.

8. For citation form, see pages 410–427.

9. Retype any pages on which you had to make more than a few last-minute changes. Otherwise, type those changes or write them clearly in ink, using the following conventions:

    a. Remove unwanted letters with a diagonal slash:
        indigestio̸n

    b. Remove unwanted words by running a line through them:
        ~~nasty~~

c. Replace a letter by putting the new letter above your slash:

compo/ition (with "s" above the slash)

d. Replace words by putting the new word above your canceled one:

~~please every~~ writer (writer above canceled "reader")

e. Add words or letters by putting a caret (∧) at the point of insertion and placing the extra words or letters above it:

notable
Another ∧ feature of this device

f. Separate words or letters by placing a vertical line between them: steel and|iron

g. Close up separated letters with a curved line connecting them from above: hic‿cup

h. Transpose (reverse) letters or words with a curved enclosing line: Al⁀cie, ⁀Carroll Lewis⁀

i. Indicate a paragraph break by inserting the paragraph symbol before the first word of the new paragraph:
¶ Transitions, too, have a certain importance.

j. Run two paragraphs together by connecting them with an arrow and writing *No ¶* in the margin:
She has found a way of turning "nothing"
time into pleasure or learning.
No¶ Isn't that better than having some trivial
chitchat on the sidewalk?

10. Carefully proofread your final copy, looking especially for typing errors. Check all quotations against your notes or, better, against the printed passages.

11. Make sure you have assembled your pages in order. Fasten them with a paper clip or, second best, with a staple.

12. Make a carbon copy of your essay or duplicate it, and retain the copy until you get the original back. Keep the graded original at least until the course is over. These steps will protect you if your instructor should mislay an essay or misrecord a grade.

ONE ESSAY FROM START TO FINISH

A freshman student, asked to save her notes and drafts for her instructor's study of the composing process, found herself with a week and a half in which to write a 1,000-word essay on any topic within the subject area "Technology and the Quality of Life." She knew that her topic would have to be narrower than that. In her earliest notes she mulled over several possibilities:

Computers . . . too broad. Subject doesn't seem to fascinate me anyway.

Cordless phones: nothing here? So you can take the phone into the kitchen without tripping over the cord. That's nice, but so what?

VCR's: Betamax etc. OK in theory—no real ideas yet.

Portable headsets—maybe something here? The world is getting divided into people who do and don't live inside those things.

Robots in factories?

Janet liked the idea of writing about tape recorders that can be carried in a pocket and played through earphones, but she didn't yet know *why* she liked it or what she wanted to say about it. To explore her trial topic, she began with reporter's questions (p. 94), seeing if any of the answers would lead her further:

Who? Joggers, bicyclists, misc. pedestrians, students crossing campus. . . . Mostly middle-class.

What? Walkman, etc.

When? Any waking hours. . . . Addiction?

Where? Buses, streets, workplaces, running trails, elevators, lavatories— where *not*? Urban only?

How? Made possible by micro-miniaturization, I guess.

Why? Love of music? I wonder. Are they just counteracting boredom? Sound junkies? *Tune out the world!*

Already Janet was beginning to crystallize her attitude toward portable headsets. She felt it was time to draw out further thoughts through a session of freewriting (pp. 87–89):

People looking like space creatures; bugs; glazed eyes. Turtles inside their shells? But be fair: they're getting technically great sound quality. Run longer without boredom, blot out ugly street sounds—well, why not? Sights too; life goes by like a movie. Except here the music *is* the movie, i.e. the main thing, instead of being background. Social danger here? Definitely a *physical* danger: get run over, mugged etc. Maybe it's not so good in less obvious ways, too. Shrinking into yourself: trend of the 80's? These people look peaceful, but what have they got (besides some money for toys)? Another fix that they may not be able to do without. (But this is getting a bit too moralistic, maybe? Anyway, general problem: technological marvels bring new fun but make us less able to be *really* calm when *really* alone. Also, no improvement in the stuff people want to hear.

Having gone this far, Janet was reasonably sure she would keep her tentative topic, but now she had to decide what *kind* of essay to write:

> Argument or explanation? What would an argument be—that headsets should be banned? I distrust them, but *that's* too strong. So—no policy issue here. OK, explanation, but what kind? Maybe cause & effect: show where the fad came from and what it may do to us.

Her next step was, therefore, to make lists of causes and effects:

> Causes:
>   technological advances
>   outgrowth of stereo boxes
>   general conditioning to an electronic environment
>   retreat from public world—cult of privacy?
>
> Effects:
>   physical danger? (maybe too trivial)
>   restlessness *without* sets—no real peace
>   more shrinking into oneself
>   less tolerance for disturbance, diversity—just play *your* already known
>   program
>   loss of sympathy with others? political indifference?

Looking over these lists, Janet realized two things: that she was much more interested in the effects of stereo headsets than in their causes and that all the effects she had named were negative. Her essay, then, was beginning to take shape as an explanation of the negative social effects of the headsets. But now she had to consider her reader, who might regard her as a spoilsport and a fanatic if she took a doomsday approach to a harmless-looking appliance. Thus, as a last exercise before attempting a thesis statement, Janet tried to moderate her stance by listing as many "pluses" as she could find:

Pluses:
   great quality
   soothing
   convenient
   no noise for others—not a nuisance
   tool for learning—e.g. a language
   run farther, skate to rhythm, ski without fear?

She was determined to work at least some of those positive qualities into her essay, preferably at a point early enough to stave off doubts about her open-mindedness.

In her first stab at a thesis statement, Janet came up with this:

TRIAL THESIS STATEMENT:

Although we can at least be thankful that portable headphone sets are quiet, they are a perfect symbol of a society that has become dependent on artificial sources of calm, out of touch with reality, and indifferent to other people's problems.

That statement had the degree of complexity Janet needed for a 1,000-word paper, but it left her uneasy. The "although" clause seemed like a throwaway remark rather than a real concession; the sweeping condemnation of all American society looked excessive; and there was something awkward about accusing a *society* of being indifferent to *other people's* problems. In a second version Janet scaled down her claims and tried to sound fairer:

REVISED THESIS STATEMENT:

Although portable headphone sets are undoubtedly convenient and pleasurable, they raise disturbing questions about many Americans' dependency on artificial sources of calm, decreased contact with reality, and shrinkage of concern for others.

Since the point about "shrinkage of concern" was the one that mattered most to Janet, she kept it in the last (most emphatic) position.

Because her essay was to be only a few pages long, Janet thought she could make do with a casual scratch outline (pp. 105–106):

1. Introduce headsets as topic.
2. Admit appeal.
3. No immediate threat to anybody.
4. But (thesis here) three disturbing implications (name them).
5. #1: Dependency for calm.
6. #2: Loss of reality.
7. #3: Shrinkage of concern for others.

8. Conclusion: Though more a symptom than a cause of isolation, sets fit all too well with trend of the times.

As things turned out, Janet found no need to revise this plan. But because she was worried about making her case too one-sided, she devoted two paragraphs instead of one to the positive appeal of the headsets.

At last it was time to draft the essay itself. In its earliest version, this was her opening paragraph (already somewhat revised for conciseness):

> When I stop to think about technology and the quality of life, several interesting possibilities come to mind. Personal computers, of course, are revolutionizing the world in many ways. Robots in industry are giving us more reliable products at the same time that they are throwing many potential consumers out of work. In the field of entertainment, we are deluged with video games and special-effects extravaganzas from Hollywood. But if I had to choose one piece of technology to sum up the quality of our times—a none too flattering symbol for the eighties—I think I would take those portable headsets that one sees everywhere in the street today.

Shown this paragraph, Janet's roommate commented that it would do in a pinch but that she didn't feel particularly motivated to keep reading. Janet had created a classic "funnel opener" (p. 125), but she had also come close to a "deadly opener" (p. 127) as well—the kind that lamely calls an assignment "interesting" instead of showing interest in it. Her revised introduction, Janet decided, would be a "baited opener" (p. 126)—a vivid image of somebody cruising down the sidewalk under earphones. (See p. 141 for the final version.)

As for editorial revisions, Janet worked chiefly on problems her instructor had spotted in earlier papers. For example:

PROBLEM	ORIGINAL	REVISED
exaggerated language, sarcasm	No doubt it is glorious to be surrounded by one's favorite music (however awful) all day. . . .	No doubt it is pleasant to be surrounded by one's favorite music all day. . . .
comma faults	The quality of sound, as I discovered when I once borrowed a set for thirty seconds is extraordinary. People who should know, claim that the reproduc-	[add comma after *seconds*; remove comma after *know*]
faulty parallelism	tion is as faithful as an expensive home stereo	. . . as faithful as that of an expensive . . .

And since she knew that her main writer-based tendency was word-iness, Janet worked to tighten her phrasing throughout the essay. For example:

FIRST DRAFT	REVISED
But what worries me the most about the people who wear headphones is their indifference to other people—an indifference that probably has some political effects, too. Even when he or she is doing something as active as running or skiing, the person who is wearing the speakers has retreated within a cozy space that is shut off from the real-life situations and needs of other people. The same holds true if the headset if being worn on a city street. Perhaps the street is full of old people, or sick people, or crazy people. It wouldn't matter who they are—workers, people out on strike, immigrants, or whoever. It would be as if they weren't there at all. For all that the headset wearer knows or cares, World War III could be starting!	What worries me most about the headphone wearers is their social—and therefore also political—in-difference. Even when running or skiing, the person sandwiched be-tween the speakers has retreated within a cozy space, insulated from the claims of other people and their problems. That space remains just as private on a city street, where no one—not the old or the sick or the crazy, not workers or strikers or im-migrants or beggars—can interrupt the programmed mood. If the city is decaying, if depression or race war is just around the corner, what does it matter? One can always raise the volume if the world's troubles ap-proach too near.

As for a title, Janet had expected to use either "Personal Conven-ience versus Social Concern" or "Stereo Headsets: Symbol of the In-different Eighties." The second seemed better because it was more definite, but neither of them sounded especially lively. Reading through a draft, Janet ran across something more promising, the phrase "head tripper." What about "The New Head Trippers" for a title? It might whet the reader's interest, set an informal tone, hint at Janet's disapproval of the stereo fad, and refer punningly both to headgear and to portability.

Here is Janet's essay as submitted:

Janet Stein

English 1A, sec. 2

Mr. Peterson

THE NEW HEAD TRIPPERS

Most of us by now have had the experience of
coming across a friend or acquaintance dreamily
tuned in to a stereo headset as she weaves through
a crowd of pedestrians. We are glad to recognize
Sally, as I will call her; we slow down, smile,
and prepare a greeting. But Sally, though she is
looking our way, sees nothing at all. She is on
automatic pilot, avoiding the other walkers by a
kind of radar that never requires her eyes to focus.
And suddenly we change our mind about saying hello
to her. To take Sally away from her tapes--assuming
we could get her attention at all--would be as in-
trusive as waking her with a midnight phone call or
dropping in to share her dinner. We pass by, disap-
pointed and vaguely bothered.

And perhaps vaguely envious as well. For, unless
we happen to have a headset of our own, we can only
imagine how agreeable it must be for Sally to occupy

2

a movable cocoon of rock music or Beethoven or language
lessons. Sally has missed out on a small personal
encounter, but so what? She has found a way of turning "nothing" time into pleasure or learning. Isn't
that better than having some trivial chitchat on the
sidewalk?

Let us admit it: those little tape players are
a marvel. The quality of sound, as I discovered when
I once borrowed a set for thirty seconds, is extraordinary. People who should know claim that the reproduction is as faithful as that of an expensive
home stereo. In fact, if you want sheer music without
distraction or irrelevant noise, you might do better
to play tapes on your headset than to attend the
finest live concert.

Though Sally may risk being run over in the
intersection, she is not threatening or endangering
anyone else. Indeed, she makes a favorable contrast
with the brash kid who climbs aboard a bus with his
giant hand-held stereo box turned all the way up.
He may be looking for trouble; at the very least he
is trying to impose his music on a captive audience.
But Sally is the very picture of somebody minding her

3

own business. Why, then, is there something unsettling
about watching her electronic trance?

I can only answer for myself. For all I know, I
may be the only person in the world to find this latest
wonder of technology a little scary. But even very
enjoyable novelties can have negative consequences for
the society as a whole. Many informed experts now
consider television, for all its obvious benefits, to
be such a mixed blessing, and video games may offer a
less debatable example. Surely there is something a
little flabby and weird about a mass passion for
shooting down little figures of spaceships that appear
on idiotically beeping screens. To me, the tiny
stereos look like a similar development. In particular, I am worried about three implications of the
headset vogue: a growing dependency on artificial
means of staying calm, decreased contact with reality,
and a corresponding shrinkage of concern for other
people.

First, the matter of dependency. No doubt it
is pleasant to be surrounded by one's favorite music
all day, but I wonder if the experience isn't addic-
tive. To be constantly under the earphones in the

4

midst of other activities seems rather like having to
pop "happy pills" to keep one's sanity or good temper.
What becomes of the headset junkies when they are
stranded without their fix? I suspect that they are
left more fidgety than they were before Sony or Sanyo
came to their aid. The possibility is worth looking
into, anyway.

Second, as you could tell from seeing her glazed
expression, Sally is not exactly alert to new experience. In a literal sense she has become a head tripper, tuning out whatever may be fresh or unpredictable
in her environment while she strolls to the beat of
tapes that are totally, soothingly familiar. She is
turning life into a movie with background music--but
there is a revealing difference. In the movies, the
music builds appropriate excitement or emotion for a
significant action. For Sally, in contrast, the music
is the action; reality will get through to her only
when it is compatible with her mental Muzak.

But what worries me most about the headphone
wearers is their social--and therefore political--
indifference. Even when running or skiing, the person
sandwiched between the speakers has retreated within

5

a cozy space, insulated from the claims of other people
and their problems. That space remains just as private
on a city street, where no one--not the old or the sick
or the crazy, not workers or strikers or immigrants or
beggars--can interrupt the programmed mood. If the
city is decaying, if depression or race war is just
around the corner, what does it matter? One can always
raise the volume if the world's troubles approach too
near.

Of course I am overdramatizing here; we are not
yet a nation of callous zombies. Furthermore, for all
I know, the movable cocoon may be more a symptom than
a cause of isolation. Let me admit the point but still
insist that even as symbolism, the image of the music-
ally tranquilized citizen, aloof from everything except
that steady tapping on the cranium, tells us something
unsettling about the times we live in. Not long ago,
the latest toy was CB radio--a means of <u>communicating</u>,
even when there was nothing much to say. If the
eighties are to be the self-absorbed era of the head
tripper, those who wear the sets are not the only ones
who will want to put the whole decade out of mind as
soon as it is over.

NOTES

[1]Samuel L. Clemens, *Mark Twain's Notebook*, ed. Albert B. Paine (New York: Harper, 1935), p. 380.

[2]Linda Flower, "Writer-Based Prose: A Cognitive Basis for Problems in Writing," *College English*, 41 (1979), 19–37. The discussion below adapts and expands on Flower's ideas.

[3]Manfred Weidhorn, "Blood, Toil, Tears, and 8,000,000 Words: Churchill Writing," *Columbia Forum*, Spring 1975, p. 19.

[4]Steven J. Marcus, "How to Court a Cat," *Newsweek*, 22 Mar. 1982, p. 13.

[5]Theodore Solotaroff, rev. of *World of Our Fathers*, by Irving Howe, *New York Times Book Review*, 1 Feb. 1976, p. 1.

[6]Sonya O'Sullivan, "Single Life in a Double Bed," *Harper's*, Nov. 1975, p. 45.

[7]Joseph Wood Krutch, *The Forgotten Peninsula: A Naturalist in Baja California* (1961; rpt. New York: Apollo), p. 177.

[8]Samuel McCracken, "The Scandal of 'Britannica 3,'" *Commentary*, Feb. 1976, p. 68.

[9]Peter Gwynne with Anthony Collins, "The Quantum Mechanic," *Newsweek*, 16 Feb. 1976, p. 90.

PART III
UNITS OF EXPRESSION

7

PARAGRAPHS

WHAT MAKES A PARAGRAPH?

The largest and perhaps the most important unit of meaning in every essay is the paragraph. Although each sentence conveys a thought, an essay is not a sequence of, say, fifty thoughts; it is rather a development of one central point through certain steps. Those steps are, or ought to be, paragraphs. The sentences within an effective paragraph support and extend one another in various ways, serving a single unfolding idea, or **theme**.

In one sense nothing could be easier than to form paragraphs; every now and then you simply indent the first word of a sentence by five letter-spaces. If those indentions do not correspond to real breaks in thought, however, you will be throwing away one of your best means of making yourself understood. All readers sense that a new paragraph signifies a conspicuous shift either of subject, idea, emphasis, speaker, time, place, or level of generality. When your indentions fail to match those shifts, you are making things unnecessarily hard for your reader.

Though you may not be aware of it yet, you as a reader already

150

hold some strong and sensible views about the proper makings of a paragraph. You will not have much trouble, for example, recognizing what is wrong with each of the three following efforts, which we will call antiparagraphs:

x A. Computers are getting cheaper all the time. A volcanic eruption in Mexico disturbed the weather two years ago. Spaghetti is not as fattening as people think. How much longer will it be before the Yankees fire their manager again?

x B. Spanish is my favorite language. Of all languages known to me, it is the one I like best. In a ranking of the languages of my acquaintance, Spanish would finish a strong first. All others would find lower places in the order, thanks to the fact that the place of honor would be occupied by Spanish, the language that pleases me most of all.

x C. The idea of a "flat tax" to replace the graduated income tax will, if adopted, be the salvation of our treasury and our national peace of mind. How many citizen-hours of hateful sweating over tax forms will be spared! How simple and fair it will be to eliminate all loopholes and insist that everyone pay at the same rate! The only losers will be parasitic tax lawyers and accountants. But since I want to become a parasitic tax lawyer myself, I have just decided that I oppose the flat tax.

Antiparagraph A reminds us that we expect a paragraph to be *about something*—one central idea that we can identify without having to flip a coin. When every sentence has equal emphasis and no sentence connects logically to the others, we sense that whatever else we may be reading, it isn't a paragraph. Note, by the way, that coherence is more than a matter of throwing in *signs* of connection. To add *moreovers* and *thuses* to antiparagraph A would only change its effect from disjointed to insane.

Antiparagraph B corrects the defect in A with a vengeance but does nothing *except* state a central idea—over and over. Reading antiparagraph B, we remember that a paragraph generally *develops* or *leads to* an idea. In short, it must go somewhere. Later (pp. 153–160) we will study three classic ways of fulfilling that requirement.

Finally, antiparagraph C, with its startling reversal at the end, reminds us that a paragraph should have a *consistent point of view*. That point of view need not be revealed at the outset—indeed, sometimes there are excellent reasons for delay—but a paragraph must never contradict itself. Readers expect it to be a unit in the service of a total rhetorical structure. Once a paragraph sets out on its purposeful march, then, none of its sentences should be guilty of mutiny or desertion.

It may be helpful to think of a paragraph as a mini-essay. Like the full essay, a paragraph of explanation or argument

1. presents one main idea;
2. conveys thoughts that are connected both by natural association and by rhetorical signals;
3. reveals its main idea in a conspicuous, emphatic way, usually but not always toward the start;
4. usually supports or illustrates that idea;
5. may also deal with objections or limitations to that idea, but without allowing the objections to prevail; and
6. may begin or end expansively, taking a wider view of the subject.

To start seeing how paragraphs typically work, study the following example:

1. Walt Whitman's "A Noiseless Patient Spider" is built on a comparison of the poet's soul to a spider. 2. Both of them, he says, stand isolated, sending something from inside themselves into the surrounding empty space; in their obviously different ways they are both reaching for *connection*. 3. Whitman does not say what the spiritual connection may be, except that his soul hopes to find "the spheres to connect" the "measureless oceans of space" out there. 4. He is vague—but so is the unknown realm toward which he yearns.

theme sentence

The heart of this paragraph is its opening sentence, which reveals its theme or main idea. We will call such a statement the **theme sentence**, and we will expect to find a theme sentence in every well-formed paragraph of explanation or argument. Here sentence 1 provides a controlling idea—that Whitman's poem is built on a comparison of the poet's soul to a spider—and the paragraph gains its coherence from the purposeful development of that idea in sentences 2, 3, and 4. Though paragraphs can follow other patterns (pp. 156–160), they usually resemble this one in giving special prominence to one statement and using the other sentences to introduce, address, or develop the theme found there.

As for their functions, paragraphs can be put to every rhetorical use found in whole essays or parts of essays. Specifically, a paragraph can

catch the reader's interest
announce a topic
divide a topic
illustrate a topic
announce a thesis
support a thesis
handle objections to a thesis

define a term
describe a scene
tell a story
identify a problem
solve a problem
make a transition
analyze a process
analyze a text
compare and contrast
draw an analogy
show causes or effects
call for action
recapitulate and emphasize

1. Taking any topics except those used in the "antiparagraphs" on page 151, write three anti-paragraphs of your own, illustrating the three defects of *lack of focus, restatement of the same idea,* and *lack of a consistent point of view.* Submit your antiparagraphs along with revised versions that remove the defect in each case.

2. Write out a theme sentence for a paragraph on any topic. Follow it with two or three sentences that develop, explain, or illustrate the theme. Number all the sentences. Beneath your paragraph, briefly explain each sentence's function (e.g., "Sentence 4 gives an example of the idea proposed in sentence 3").

3. If a paragraph can be regarded as a mini-essay (p. 152), you ought to be able to boil down an essay to paragraph size. Try that experiment with an essay you have already read for this course. Your paragraph should have as its theme sentence a statement of the essay's thesis, and your other sentences should cover the author's most important supporting points.

PATTERNS OF DEVELOPMENT

Nearly all the printed advice usually given to paragraph writers pertains to one kind of development, which we will call *direct.* In a direct paragraph the theme sentence comes at or near the beginning and the remaining sentences are guided by it. Make no mistake: it is essential to master that pattern. In practice, however, all capable writers feel at home not with one pattern but with three. We will treat those patterns—the *direct,* the *pivoting,* and the *suspended*—in order of their increasing flexibility and difficulty.

The Direct Pattern

When you skim an article to get the gist of it, which sentences do you read? In all likelihood you read the first sentence of every paragraph and, when dissatisfied, the second one. You know intuitively that the theme sentences of most paragraphs occupy one of those positions. When they do, the paragraph is committed to a **direct pattern**, whereby the later sentences will support and perhaps also place limitations on an early sentence that states the theme. Even if the theme sentence comes third, the paragraph can still show the characteristic features of the direct pattern.

theme sentence first   Most well-organized paragraphs begin with a theme sentence:

> There is a paradox about the South Seas that every visitor immediately discovers. Tropical shores symbolize man's harmony with a kind and bountiful nature. Natives escape the common vexations of modern life by simply relaxing. They reach into palms for coconuts, into the sea for fish, and into calabashes for poi. But when the tranquilized tourist reaches Hawaii, the paradise of the Pacific, he finds the most expensive resort in the world and a tourist industry that will relieve him of his traveler's checks with a speed and ease that would bring a smile to the lips of King Kamehameha.[1]

Here the theme sentence announces a *paradox*—that is, a seeming contradiction—and the rest of the paragraph consists of supporting or explanatory sentences that develop the two halves of that paradox, harmonious nature and commercial exploitation. The result is extreme clarity: the structure of the paragraph fulfills the promise given in the theme sentence, and the reader feels guided by that structure at each moment.

theme sentence delayed   When a theme sentence within the direct pattern does not come first, it usually comes second, after an introductory sentence that prepares for a shift of emphasis:

introductory sentence
theme sentence

supporting sentences

> The statistics, then, paint a depressing picture. Yet if we set aside the government reports and take the trouble to interview farm workers one by one, we find an astounding degree of confidence in the future. The workers are already thinking a generation ahead. Even if they have little expectation of improving their own lives, most of them are convinced that their children will begin to participate meaningfully in the American dream.

And sometimes, still within the direct pattern, you will find a theme sentence coming third, after *two* sentences that prepare for a new idea. The following student paragraph is representative:

introductory sentences { Such a calamity should be avoided at all cost. But what if the very act of predicting an earthquake caused more chaos than the earthquake itself?

theme sentence { The existing evidence suggests that immediate earthquake predictions, when released to the public, would have tremendous social consequences.

supporting sentences { People fleeing the cities would create traffic jams of monumental proportions. The work hours lost would be considerable. Looting of abandoned homes and businesses would surely ensue. And suppose the prediction turned out to be false? Who, then, would be held accountable for the loss of business income, the loss of looted property, and the shaking of people's confidence in the future of the area? All these consequences should be weighed against the merits of alerting people to the likelihood that an earthquake may be on the way.

If a paragraph is sufficiently long, then, it can show a direct pattern of development even when the theme sentence comes neither first nor second. The essential feature of the direct pattern is that the theme sentence comes *relatively* early, so that we have the main point in mind when limiting or supporting considerations are introduced.

Note that a direct paragraph, just like an essay whose thesis is stated near the outset, can comfortably include **limiting** considerations — those that "go against" the theme. In the following student paragraph, for example, the writer can afford to offer a "con" remark, which is placed strategically between the theme sentence and two final sentences of support for that statement:

theme sentence { The "greenhouse effect," whereby the temperature of the atmosphere rises with the increased burning of hydrocarbons, may have devastating consequences for our planet within a generation or two.

limiting sentence { Similar scares, it is true, have come and gone without leaving any lasting mark.

supporting sentences { Yet there is an important difference this time. We know a good deal more about the greenhouse effect and its likely results than we knew, say, about invasions from outer space or mutations from atomic bomb tests. The greenhouse effect is already under way, and there are very slender grounds for thinking it will be reversed or even slowed without a more sudden cataclysm such as all-out nuclear war.

Direct paragraphs, then, can follow two models, one including and one omitting limiting sentences:

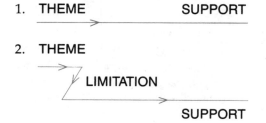

These models bypass some variants (pp. 154–155), but they show the heart of the matter, which is that direct paragraphs *eventually* supply supporting points to make the theme believable.

The Pivoting Pattern

Many effective paragraphs not only delay the theme sentence, but begin by "going against it" with one or more limiting sentences. Such paragraphs work by pivoting decisively from the limiting considerations to the theme, which then dominates any remaining sentences.

Thus a scheme of the **pivoting** paragraph would look like this:

LIMITATION

THEME   [SUPPORT]

The brackets around "Support" indicate that a pivoting paragraph *can* end with its theme sentence. More commonly, though, the theme sentence is supported by one or more following sentences.

Why should you bother to master the pivoting pattern? There are several reasons. In the first place, that pattern is suited to showing your reader that you have considered objections to your theme; by placing the objections first, you give them a fair hearing. Then, too, a successfully executed pivot requires, and therefore exhibits, a relatively high degree of control; your reader sees that you were secure enough about your theme to delay revealing it. Thus an occasional pivoting paragraph identifies you not only as a writer who is capable of various "moves," but also as someone who has passed beyond the first-draft stage of grasping at ideas and clinging to them for dear life. Indeed, the best time to think about devising some pivoting paragraphs may be after you have finished a draft, when you actually possess the degree of control that this pattern demands.

Since the pivoting paragraph operates by taking a sharp turn, it customarily announces that turn with a signal word, alerting the reader to the paragraph's new and conclusive direction. Notice how the following student paragraph, taken from an essay quoted earlier (p. 131), pivots neatly on the word *But* in sentence 2:

limiting sentence { 1. When we think of Gandhi fasting, plastering mud poultices on his belly, and testing his vow of continence by sharing a bed with his grand-niece, we can easily regard him as an eccentric who happened to be politically lucky. 2. BUT the links between his private fads and his

pivot to the theme sentence { political methods turn out to be quite logical. 3. Gandhi's pursuit of

supporting
sentences

> personal rigors helped him to achieve a rare degree of discipline, and that discipline allowed him to approach political crises with extraordinary courage. 4. The example of his self-control, furthermore, was contagious; it is doubtful that a more worldly man could have led millions of his countrymen to adopt the tactic of nonviolent resistance.

Similarly, the classic pivoting signal *however* shows us that the third sentence of the following paragraph is making a reversal of emphasis:

> Health experts always seem to be telling Americans what *not* to eat. Cholesterol, salt and sugar are but a few of the dietary no-no's that threaten to make dinnertime about as pleasurable as an hour of push-ups. In a report last week on the role of nutrition in cancer, HOWEVER, a blue-ribbon committee of the National Academy of Sciences offered a carrot—as well as oranges, tomatoes and cantaloupes—along with the usual admonitory stick. While some foods appear to promote cancer and should be avoided, said the panel, other comestibles may actually help ward off the disease.[2]

A pivoting paragraph can get along without a "turn signal" word if other language makes the turn sufficiently clear—for example, *That is no longer the case* or *Such is the theory, at any rate.* In general, though, the farther you venture from a straightforward theme-first pattern, the more important it is to guide your reader with directional markers.

The pivoting pattern is especially common in paragraphs of comparison and contrast (pp. 52–53). As we have observed, the first part of such a paragraph usually dwells on resemblances, and then a somewhat more emphatic part dwells on differences. The following student paragraph is typical:

resemblances

theme sentence

differences

> 1. Tillie Olsen's short stories, "Hey Sailor, What Ship?" and "O Yes," both chronicle the disintegration of a close relationship. 2. In both stories, a friendship falls apart when one or both parties find it more trying to sustain the friendship than to let it go. 3. The underlying causes of strain, however, are quite different in the two cases. 4. In "Hey Sailor . . ." a change in Whitey's character leads to his falling out with his family, but in "O Yes" external forces—social pressures—tear Carol and Parry apart.

Note once again how a key signal word, *however*, alerts us to the pivoting movement.

The Suspended Pattern

We have seen that a *direct* paragraph offers an early theme sentence, so that a reader knows what idea will be supported (and perhaps limited) as the paragraph proceeds. A *pivoting* paragraph, in contrast, delays the theme sentence until at least one limiting consideration has been addressed. In both models the paragraph's theme exercises a powerful organizing control. The longer a theme sentence is delayed, however, the more opportunity a writer has to do something other than support or limit the theme. And this is sometimes an advantage, for paragraphs have more uses than mere position taking.

Look, for instance, at this distinctly uncombative narrative paragraph:

> Shortly after dawn, at the Saint-Antoine produce market in the ancient French city of Lyons, a white pickup truck screeches around a corner, double-parks impatiently and disgorges a rugged man wearing a rumpled windbreaker. As if by prearranged signal, prize raspberries, dewy spinach and pristine baby carrots suddenly emerge from hiding places below the trestle tables where they've been saved for inspection by this very special customer. *"Viens ici, Paul,"* shouts a fruit vendor. "I've got some melons you won't believe." Slicing a sample in half, the man in the windbreaker rejects the melons and some string beans as well ("too fat"). But thirty-five minutes later, he has sniffed, nibbled, pinched, prodded, and fondled his way through the choicest fruits and vegetables, loaded fifteen crates of produce into his van and hummed off toward his next quarry: plump chickens from Bresse, Charolais beef and fresh red mullet. Paul Bocuse, the most visible, the most influential —and possibly the best—chef in the world, has begun another working day.[3]

Here the theme sentence comes last, as it also might in certain pivoting paragraphs. But in this case there is no pivot to be found—no reversal of poles between initial limiting sentences and the theme. Indeed, strictly speaking, the paragraph contains neither limiting nor supporting sentences. Rather, it proceeds through narrative development—one event succeeds another—to a climactic theme sentence in which Paul Bocuse's identity is revealed. This is a **suspended** paragraph, one that builds to a climax or conclusion by some means other than a sharp reversal of direction.

Sometimes, as in the "jogging" paragraph on page 57 or in the following student paragraph, the theme sentence at the end follows logically from all the sentences ahead of it:

> In the early fourteenth century, Northern Europe was subjected to a terrible famine. Meanwhile, economic instability caused whole kingdoms

to go bankrupt. Then in 1348–50 the worst plague in history ravaged the Continent, killing perhaps half the population. It is little wonder, therefore, that this was a period of profound social and political unrest; the supposedly stable order of feudalism had proved helpless to cope with various forms of disaster.

theme sentence

But even when a suspended paragraph turns out to have been constructed as evidence ————→ conclusion, it does not "read" that way. How are we to know that the early sentences are evidence for a point that has not yet been made? As you can see from the "Bocuse" example (p. 158), the suspended paragraph moves from *discussion* to theme, maintaining the reader's sentence-by-sentence interest while leading to a statement that brings things together at last:

DISCUSSION   THEME

If you wondered whether you should trouble yourself to master the pivoting paragraph, you probably regard suspended paragraphs as an arty luxury. As it happens, however, the suspended pattern has a workaday usefulness: it is ideal for both *introductory* and *concluding* paragraphs (pp. 125–128, 130–132). An introductory paragraph that ends with its theme sentence—a sentence revealing either the topic or the thesis of the paper—can gradually entice a reader into becoming interested in that topic or thesis. At a moment of maximum reluctance on the reader's part to become involved, you can put suspense to work for you. And a suspended concluding paragraph allows you to end your paper with a "punch line"—an excellent tactic if you have saved one strong point for your last paragraph. In addition, suspended paragraphs in any part of an essay redouble that sense of pleasurable drama, risk taking, and control that we found in deftly handled pivoting paragraphs.

Note, finally, that the crucial trait of a suspended paragraph is not that the theme sentence comes exactly last, but that the reader gets caught up in a discussion whose point is being deliberately held back. In the following suspended paragraph, for example, the theme sentence comes second to last:

Linus Pauling has one of those faces that photographers love because it does their work for them. In moments of repose, it has that dreamy quality that Einstein's had—hair rising in eccentric silver wisps, periwinkle eyes that often glance inward during the conversation at some abstract law of motion or of matter. It would be tempting to see it as the Face of Science, except that Pauling is also a man of action. At 77, he

discussion

theme sentence {

final remark {

has a schedule that would exhaust a man half his age. Last month major trips to Scotland and Cuba were sandwiched into a calendar of speaking engagements and scientific conferences booked as far in advance as a star rock group's. Wherever he goes, and whatever else he does, however, he is an ambassador of vitamin C. It is a subject never far from his mind.[4]

Perhaps it has occurred to you that the three patterns of paragraph development correspond to three patterns of essay structure. The direct paragraph resembles an essay that quickly reveals its thesis and then defends it, sometimes with a treatment of opposing considerations as well. The pivoting paragraph is like an essay that starts out with opposing considerations but then turns to its thesis. And the suspended paragraph corresponds to the essay, rarely seen, that saves its thesis for the end, where it turns out to be the upshot of all that has been said. Each pattern, when skillfully executed, delivers a form of satisfaction that the others lack.

EXERCISES

4. Submit a _direct_ paragraph on any topic you have not treated in previous exercises. Your paragraph should consist of an opening theme sentence followed by three or more sentences of support.

5. Look over the paragraph you wrote for Exercise 4. Then submit (a) one or two introductory sentences that could precede the theme sentence and (b) one or two limiting sentences (pp. 155–157). Indicate where you would place the limiting sentences in the original paragraph.

6. Reusing as many sentences as you please from Exercises 4 and 5, submit a _pivoting_ paragraph on the same topic. Use a "turn signal" word (p. 156) to indicate where your paragraph is pivoting toward its theme, and underline that word. Beneath your paragraph, write a full sentence that would perform the same function as the signal word.

7. Think of resemblances and differences between two of your recent teachers. Then write a pivoting paragraph of about six sentences comparing and contrasting those teachers (see p. 157).

8. Write a two- or three-paragraph analysis of the following paragraph, showing what effects the writer has gained from use of a _suspended_ pattern:

> Knowing that it is possible to see too much, most doormen in New York have developed an extraordinary sense of selective vision: they know what to see and what to ignore, when to be curious and when to be indolent; they are most often standing indoors, unaware, when there are accidents or arguments in front of their buildings; and they are usually in the street seeking taxicabs when burglars are escaping through the lobby. Although a doorman may disapprove of bribery and adultery, his back is invariably turned when the superintendent is handing money to the fire inspector or when a tenant whose wife is away escorts a young woman into the elevator—which is not to accuse the doorman of hypocrisy or cowardice but merely to suggest that his instinct

for uninvolvement is very strong, and to speculate that doormen have perhaps learned through experience that nothing is to be gained by serving as a material witness to life's unseemly sights or to the madness of the city. This being so, it was not surprising that on the night when the Mafia chief, Joseph Bonanno, was grabbed by two gunmen in front of a luxury apartment house on Park Avenue near Thirty-sixth Street, shortly after midnight on a rainy Tuesday in October, the doorman was standing in the lobby talking to the elevator man and saw nothing.[5]

9. Think of someone you know or would like to know, and write a suspended paragraph which, like the "Paul Bocuse" paragraph on page 158, reveals that person's identity at the end, after taking your reader through an action or sequence of actions characteristic of that person.

10. Submit a suspended paragraph which, like the "fourteenth century" paragraph on pp. 158–159, offers supporting sentences that lead to the theme sentence as a conclusion to be drawn from them.

UNITY

Because they dread seeing pot-luck paragraphs that lack any theme at all, teachers of composition have been known to take an extremely strict view of paragraph unity. Every paragraph, they declare, must begin with a theme sentence, and every following sentence must be (a) less general in scope and (b) subordinate in meaning. But a writer who sticks to this formula, like a ball carrier who can only plow straight ahead, will soon become too predictable to gain much ground. Although unity is essential, you should not allow it to become an excuse for writing inflexible paragraphs.

Options within Unity

Specifically, you can deviate from the plainest paragraph model in three ways:

1. *You can move the theme sentence to other positions* (pp. 154–160).

2. *You can begin with a more general sentence than the theme sentence.* Consider the following student paragraph:

1. For one reason or another, much of Alaska is all but impassable by land. 2. Thus the airplane will probably remain the most serviceable of far-north vehicles. 3. Though clearing small airstrips can be difficult, it is child's play compared to cutting major roads through the icebound major ranges. 4. And it would be hard to picture more efficient transportation to and from Alaska's abundant lakes than small planes equipped with pontoons.

If the theme sentence here is number 2, then number 1 is a "narrowing" introductory sentence, guiding the reader toward the theme. As we saw in an earlier chapter (pp. 125–127), such narrowing is a customary way of beginning an essay.

3. *You can end expansively.* Just as the last paragraph of an essay can take a broader perspective, looking beyond an already established thesis (pp. 130–131), so the last sentence of a paragraph can expand upon a fully supported theme. Look at the way this student paragraph ends:

theme sentence { Nobody had a good word for the 1970s while they lasted, but the passage of a few years has begun to make things look mellower. The

supporting sentences { country was at peace during most of those years. The famous gasoline shortages were a nuisance but not exactly a tragedy, and the Iranian hostage affair can no longer be considered an earthshaking crisis. As for double-digit inflation, it appears quite bearable compared to the 11%

expansive final remark { unemployment of more recent times. Sooner or later, we might conclude, every decade becomes the good old days—even the forgettable Seventies.

Here the opening theme sentence deals only with the 1970s, while the "expansive final" sentence extends the paragraph's horizon to include *every decade*. The theme sentence, then, is not the most general one, as purists would expect it to be. But unity has not been violated; the writer has "earned" a broad parting reflection by keeping the rest of his paragraph nicely together.

Tests for Unity

Given the flexibility shown by any number of acceptable paragraphs, unity comes down to a *yes* answer to all three of the following questions:

does the paragraph avoid contradictions? The most obvious and drastic disunity occurs when, as in antiparagraph C (p. 151), a paragraph "changes its mind." Note that such contradiction is very different from merely *including material that limits the theme.* Compare:

A. The seepage of dioxin into a community's water supply always terrifies everyone once it has been discovered. Citizens naturally expect the Environmental Protection Agency and the guilty industry to remove the source of risk as soon as possible. Unfortunately, however, this chemical is so incredibly toxic in small doses that decades may pass before the threat to public health is truly over.

x B. The seepage of dioxin into a community's water supply always terrifies everyone once it has been discovered. Citizens naturally expect the Environmental Protection Agency and the guilty industry to remove the source of risk as soon as possible. Yet many people react to the crisis calmly, refusing to worry about cancer, birth defects, and other proven results of contact with dioxin.

Both of these paragraphs end with a theme sentence that "goes against" the preceding two sentences. In A, however, there is no contradiction; the writer simply turns from one aspect of the dioxin problem (citizens' demand for a speedy solution) to a more serious aspect (long-term toxicity). In B, on the contrary, the writer says two *incompatible* things: that everyone is alarmed and that some people are not alarmed. Paragraph A pivots adroitly toward its theme sentence; paragraph B falls to pieces through self-contradiction.

does the paragraph avoid digression? A paragraph that shows strong internal continuity (pp. 165–170), hooking each new sentence into the one before it, can cover a good deal of ground without appearing disunified. Every sentence, however, should bear *some* relation to the theme — either introducing it, stating it, elaborating it, asking a question about it, supporting it, limiting it, or reflecting about it. A sentence that does none of those things is a **digression** — an irrelevant statement. Just one digression within a paragraph is enough to sabotage its unity.

Suppose, for example, paragraph A on dioxin contained this sentence: *The threat posed by dioxin was not fully appreciated fifteen years ago.* Even though that remark deals with the subject matter of the paragraph, dioxin, it amounts to a digression, for it has no bearing on the paragraph's *theme:* dioxin can remain hazardous for decades. In a revised version the digressive sentence would have to be removed.

does the theme have the last word? If it is sometimes useful to include statements that limit or oppose a paragraph's theme, it is never wise to *end* the paragraph with such a sentence. Final positions are naturally emphatic. If your last sentence subtracts something from the paragraph's thematic thrust, you will sound indecisive or uncomfortable and the paragraph will not cohere as a rhetorical structure. Compare:

x A. One reason for the recent popularity of Hollywood autobiographies is surely the decline of serious fiction about important, glamorous people. We know that readers crave intimacy with the great, and we also know that modern novelists have ignored that craving. What people no longer get from fiction, they now seek in true confessions from Tinseltown. Of course, other factors must be at work as well; literary fads are never produced by single causes.

B. One reason for the recent popularity of Hollywood autobiographies is surely the decline of serious fiction about important, glamorous people. Of course, other factors must be at work as well; literary fads are never produced by single causes. But we do know that readers crave intimacy with the great, and we also know that modern novelists have ignored that craving. What people no longer get from fiction, they now seek in true confessions from Tinseltown.

Notice that these paragraphs say the same thing but leave the reader with different impressions. Paragraph A trails off weakly, as if the writer were having second thoughts about the theme. Paragraph B gets its limiting sentence about *other factors* into a safely unemphatic position and then ends strongly, reinforcing the theme that was stated in the opening sentence.

---

11. Suppose you have been writing an essay about the difficulties people face when they try to write essays. You have just ended a paragraph with this sentence: *Writing provides rich confirmation of Murphy's Law: "If anything can go wrong, it will."* Your next paragraph will supply an example from your own experience as a student writer. Submit that paragraph, including (a) a theme sentence stating what your experience taught you and (b) several supporting sentences describing that experience. (If you have no relevant story to tell, make one up.)

12. Submit both an *introductory* sentence and an *"expansive final"* sentence (p. 162) that could be added at the beginning and end of the paragraph you wrote for Exercise 11.

13. Find the *digressive* sentence (p. 163) that has been inserted into the following paragraph. Submit an explanation of why that sentence interferes with paragraph unity.

> In 1886 Grinnell suggested in the pages of *Forest and Stream* that concerned men and women create an organization for the protection of wild birds and their eggs, its administration to be undertaken by the magazine's staff. Grinnell did not have to grope to name this organization. He had grown up near the home that the great bird painter, John James Audubon, had left to his wife and children at his death. As a boy Grinnell had played in an old loft cluttered with stacks of the red muslin-bound copies of the *Ornithological Biography* and boxes of bird skins brought back by Audubon from his expeditions. He had attended a school for small boys conducted by Lucy Audubon nearby. All his life he would remain an avid reader. Grinnell quite naturally called the new organization the Audubon Society.[6]

14. Choosing any topic not already used in this sequence of exercises, write three paragraphs that suffer respectively from *contradiction* (pp. 162–163), *digression* (p. 163), and *failure to give the theme the last word* (pp. 163–164). Submit the three faulty paragraphs along with a fourth, adequately unified, paragraph on the same theme. Label the four paragraphs to leave no doubt about the effect you intend in each case ("Contradictory," etc.).

CONTINUITY

As you have gathered by now, each sentence of a paragraph should fit snugly with the one before it. Such linkage is **continuity**, or the felt connection between all the sentences of a paragraph.

Maintaining a degree of continuity is not really hard. You need only reread the sentence you have just written and ask yourself, "All right, what follows from this?" What follows may be

1. a question (or a further question);
2. an answer (if the sentence above is a question);
3. support or illustration of the point just made;
4. a limitation or objection to the point just made;
5. further support or illustration of an earlier point, or further limitation or objection to an earlier point;
6. a transition; or
7. a conclusion or reflection appropriate either to the sentence above or to the whole theme of the paragraph.

With all these options to choose from, you can always find a way of moving forward, giving your reader that sense of developed thought that distinguishes a paragraph from an array of baldly isolated statements.

If, for example, the most recent sentence in your draft reads *The economic heart of America has been shifting toward the Sunbelt,* your next sentence might be any of the following:

- But how much longer will this trend continue? [Question]

- The recent history of Buffalo, New York, is a case in point. [Illustration]

- It may be, however, that the country also has a quite different kind of heart —one that is not so easily moved. [Limitation]

- Without forgetting that trend, let us turn now to less obvious but possibly more important developments. [Transition]

- If so, it can only be a matter of time before the moral or spiritual heart of the country is similarly displaced. [Reflection]

Signs of Continuity

For a bare minimum of continuity within a paragraph, the idea of each sentence must be somehow related to the idea of the previous one. But a reader-based paragraph (pp. 114–115) does more than show continuity when analyzed for its logic; it does so on a first reading, without obliging the reader to pause and puzzle out hidden connections. To that end you need to supply some plain *signs* of relation to foregoing sentences, alerting your reader that a train of thought is being begun, developed, challenged, or completed.

signal words   The most important signs of continuity are words indicating exactly how a statement in one sentence relates to the statement it follows. The possible types of relation, along with examples of each type, are these:

CONSEQUENCE:
• therefore, then, thus, hence, accordingly, as a result

LIKENESS:
• likewise, similarly

CONTRAST:
• but, however, nevertheless, on the contrary, on the other hand, yet

AMPLIFICATION:
• and, again, in addition, further, furthermore, moreover, also, too

EXAMPLE:
• for instance, for example

CONCESSION:
• to be sure, granted, of course, it is true

INSISTENCE:
• indeed, in fact, yes, no

SEQUENCE:
• first, second, finally

RESTATEMENT:
• that is, in other words, in simpler terms, to put it differently

RECAPITULATION:
• in conclusion, all in all, to summarize, altogether

TIME OR PLACE:
• afterward, later, earlier, formerly, elsewhere, here, there, hitherto, subsequently, at the same time, simultaneously, above, below, farther on, this time, so far, until now

Such signals need not appear in every sentence, but they are always useful and sometimes essential. Look back, for example, to the "fourteenth century" paragraph on pages 158–159. Its suspended structure would be too confusing without the key signals *meanwhile,* *then,* and *therefore.* And we have already seen that pivoting paragraphs usually dare to veer away from their true theme only because a clue such as *but* or *however* can be counted on to show where the major emphasis falls.

Other signal words show continuity not by specifying what kind of relation one sentence has to its predecessors, but simply by indicating that something already treated is still under discussion. They make sense only when taken as references to people, things, or ideas mentioned above:

PRONOUNS:
- Ordinary people know little about the causes of inflation. What *they* do know is that they must earn more every year to buy the same goods and services.

DEMONSTRATIVE ADJECTIVES:
- *The Scarlet Letter* was first shown in April 1979. *That* production was among the best ever developed for American television.

REPEATED WORDS AND PHRASES:
- We should conserve fossil fuels on behalf of our descendants as well as ourselves. Those *descendants* will curse us if we leave them without abundant sources of light and heat.

IMPLIED REPETITIONS:
- Some fifty Americans were trapped in the embassy when the revolution broke out. *Six more* managed to scramble onto the last helicopter that was permitted to land on the roof.

One key word, repeated several times, can do much to knit a paragraph together. Thus in the following paragraph the name *Ottawa* (capitalized here for emphasis) is artfully plucked out from other names:

Perhaps a visitor cannot truly understand the country until he has traveled from the genteel poverty of the Atlantic coast with its picturesque fishing villages and stiff towns through the Frenchness of sophisticated Quebec cities and rural landscapes, past the vigorous bustling Ontario municipalities and industrial vistas, over mile after mile of wheat fields between prairie settlements into the lush and spacious beauty of British Columbia; but he must also visit OTTAWA and the House of Commons. OTTAWA the stuffy, with its dull-looking houses, its blistering summer heat, its gray rainy afternoons; OTTAWA the beautiful, on a snowy day when the government buildings stand tall and protective, warmly solid above the white landscape; on a sunny spring afternoon with the cool river winding below, and people moving easily through the clean streets, purposeful but not pushed. Even during the morning and evening traffic rushes, OTTAWA seems to remain sane.[7]

In the first sentence *Ottawa* belatedly emerges as the key name among several; it gains importance by being weighted singly against all the "travelogue" references before the semicolon. In the second sentence (or independent sentence fragment) the name is used insistently and fondly. And the author exploits this effect in her final sentence, using the name yet again to reinforce her idea that Ottawa stands apart from the rest of Canada.

sentence patterns A further means of making the sentences of a paragraph flow together is to give them some variety of structure. In particular, avoid an unbroken string of choppy sentences, each consisting of one statement unmarked by pauses (see pp. 198–199).

Within certain limits, however, you can show continuity by *repeating* a sentence pattern. Those limits are that (a) only parts of paragraphs, not whole paragraphs, lend themselves comfortably to such effects and (b) the sentences so linked must be parallel in meaning. When you want to make their association emphatic, you can give them the same form.

In this paragraph, for instance, the writer expresses her reservations about the nuclear arms race by asking two sets of three questions each:

OK. *But where is this train going? Is it ever going to stop? And doesn't every extra mile and every new load of weapons we take on increase the chance that something will go wrong?* It is the open-ended quality of the argument Haig espouses—an argument, incidentally, that pretty much represents the traditional American policy over the years—that is its main defect. *What are we headed for? An MX missile in every garage? An SS-18 in every dacha?*[8]

Here each of the two passages in italics is knit together by the question form of its three sentences. Less obviously, the sets of questions "call" to *each other* across the declarative sentence that separates them. That sentence is psychologically important, as you can tell by rereading the paragraph without it. Then you get six questions in a row, and the writer's intended effect—a worried impatience—degenerates into nagging. Thus the real paragraph's success as continuous, readable discourse depends *both* on its parallel features and on the relief it offers from them.

A similar combination of likeness and difference of structure lends continuity to this paragraph by a critic of urban planning:

But look what we have built with the first several billions: Low-income projects that become worse centers of delinquency, vandalism and general social hopelessness than the slums they were supposed to replace. Middle-income housing projects which are truly marvels of dullness and regimentation, sealed against any buoyancy or vitality of city life. Luxury housing projects that mitigate their inanity, or try to, with a vapid vulgarity. Cultural centers that are unable to support a good bookstore. Civic centers that are avoided by everyone but bums, who have fewer choices of loitering place than others. Commercial centers that are lackluster imitations of standardized suburban chain-store shopping. Promenades that go from no place to nowhere and have no promenaders. Expressways that eviscerate great cities. This is not the rebuilding of cities. This is the sacking of cities.[9]

The body of this paragraph consists of independent sentence fragments (p. 279), each of which takes its sense from the writer's opening words: *But look what we have built.* . . . An entirely different parallelism of structure brings the paragraph to its emphatic end: *This is not the rebuilding of cities. This is the sacking of cities.* This writer, too, has risked annoying us with relentless hammer blows, but her shifting to a second variety of patterning leaves her in control of our response.

unbroken sequences   Finally, continuity is served by keeping together sentences that all bear the same general relation to the paragraph's theme. To simplify, let us reduce all such relations to support and limitation. Sentences that support the theme by either restating it, offering evidence for it, illustrating it, or expanding upon it belong in an uninterrupted sequence. So do all sentences that limit the theme by showing what it does *not* cover or by casting doubt on it.

Continuity is especially threatened by two sets of limiting sentences within a paragraph. To see why, examine the following draft of a pivoting paragraph:

limitation { ˣ Not many people would want to endure the lonely hours, the aches and pains, and the probable injuries awaiting anyone who trains seriously for a

theme { marathon race. The pride, however, that comes from finishing one's first marathon makes all the struggle seem worthwhile. But is it really worth-

limitation { while? What does running twenty-six miles in glorified underwear have to do with real life? For veteran marathoners, however, long-distance racing *is*

support { real life, while all other claims on their time are distractions or nuisances.

Here the direction established by the theme is pro-marathon, but that direction is opposed twice in the course of the paragraph, and both the "pro" and the "con" sentences are interrupted. Thus we are bounced from one side to the other without gettting the satisfaction of a decisive turn. Compare:

limitation { Not many people would want to endure the lonely hours, the aches and pains, and the probable injuries awaiting anyone who trains seriously for a marathon race. Is all the effort worthwhile? More than once, no doubt, exhausted beginners must ask themselves what running twenty-six miles in

theme { glorified underwear has to do with real life. Yet the pride that comes from finishing one's first marathon makes all the struggle seem worthwhile. And

support { for veteran marathoners, long-distance running *is* real life, while all other claims on their time are distractions or nuisances.

Now the paragraph's shuffling between pros and cons has been replaced by *one* definitive pivot on the signal word *Yet*. One such turn per paragraph is the maximum you should allow yourself. To observe that rule, simply make sure that all of your supporting and limiting sentences remain within their own portion of the paragraph —with the limiting sentences first to keep them from "having the last word."

EXERCISES

15. Write out a sentence stating an idea about any topic. Then, on separate lines, write five numbered sentences, *each* of which could be the next sentence following that one in a paragraph. (Your numbered sentences are not meant to form a sequence; they are five alternative ways of maintaining continuity with the first sentence.) Give your five numbered sentences the form of (1) a question, (2) a supporting point or illustration, (3) a limitation or objection, (4) a transition, and (5) a conclusion or reflection. (See p. 165.)

16. Take (or write) a paragraph of your own on any topic and revise it until you are satisfied that it shows adequate continuity from sentence to sentence. Number the sentences. Submit your paragraph along with a sentence-by-sentence explanation of its elements of continuity (e.g., "Sentence 3: *furthermore* shows that another supporting statement will be added to the one in sentence 2").

17. Revise the following paragraph for continuity, adding signal words (pp. 166–168) to show relations between sentences:

Most people hesitate to enter photo contests because they are sure that professionals will take all the prizes. Professional photographers are barred from most photo contests. When professional photographers are permitted to enter photo contests, they hardly ever win the top prizes. There is no reason for a competent amateur photographer to feel handicapped in competing against professionals.

18. Choosing any topic, submit a paragraph which, like the "Ottawa" paragraph on pages 167–168, gains continuity from the repetition of a key word or phrase.

19. Choosing any topic, submit a paragraph which, like the "arms race" paragraph on page 168, gains continuity from asking one or more strings of questions.

20. Choosing any topic, submit a paragraph which, like the "urban renewal" paragraph on page 169, gains continuity from reuse of the same structure in sentences or independent sentence fragments.

21. Write a brief analysis of the effectiveness or ineffectiveness of the order of sentences in the following paragraph. If you believe the order could be made more effective, rewrite the paragraph, keeping nearly all the same language but changing words as needed to bring out relations between supporting and limiting remarks.

> 1. Some of the most haunting music of our century was composed by the eccentric Parisian Erik Satie. 2. Once you have acquired a taste for his fanciful and melancholy works, you will find it hard to keep them out of your head. 3. But not everyone can take Satie seriously; his modesty makes him appear trivial compared, say, to the bold and colorful Stravinsky.

22. Being as specific as possible about the writer's language, submit a discussion of the elements of continuity in the following paragraph:

> 1. Royalty and riots; riots and royalty. 2. There seems almost a symbiotic correlation between pomp and desperation in Britain these days. 3. In the space of twenty-four of the most memorable hours in recent British history, for example, the grindingly poor Toxteth district of Liverpool was seared by violence yet again. 4. Dozens of people were injured and an innocent bystander named David Moore was killed by the British police. 5. The next morning the British government—in the midst of the worst economic crisis the country has known since the Depression—dispensed some $2 million on the nuptials of the Prince and Princess of Wales. 6. The photographs of Moore's mangled body made the newspapers in London, but the day was dominated by the captivating smile of Lady Diana Spencer.[10]

LENGTH

There is no single "right" size for all paragraphs. In newspaper reporting, where the purpose is to communicate nuggets of information with a minimum of analysis, paragraphs consist of one, two, or three sentences at the most. Paragraphs of dialogue also tend to be short; most writers indent for every change of speaker. So, too, scientific and technical journals favor relatively brief paragraphs that present facts and figures with little rhetorical development. And essayists vary considerably among themselves, both in their preference for short or long typical paragraphs and in the paragraph sizes they use within a given essay.

Within that variability, however, some norms are apparent. Competent essayists generally write paragraphs consisting of at least three or four sentences, and very few devote a full typewritten, double-spaced page (or about 250 words) to a typical paragraph. These limits have their roots in reader psychology. A succession of long paragraphs taxes the memory, making a reader work too hard to retain the thread of connection between one theme sentence and the next. Very short paragraphs, like very short sentences, would seem to be easily grasped. Monotony, however, is always annoying and finally intolerable. If you hurry along from one brief paragraph to the next, never modifying or extending your blunt assertions, readers will gather that you are not much interested in what you are saying—and they won't be, either.

expanding the choppy paragraph If you realize that you have a tendency to write brief, stark paragraphs in which the theme sentence is paired with just one supporting or limiting sentence, you can correct that tendency by rereading your theme sentences and asking *where they might lead, what questions might be asked about the terms they contain,* and *what objections might be raised against them.* The answers to those questions can become supporting and limiting sentences that will flesh out the stark skeletons of your paragraphs.

One student, for example, usually wrote paragraphs like these:

THEME SENTENCE   SUPPORTING SENTENCE
x Man is a highly social animal. He has always lived within organized groups.

LIMITING SENTENCE
Early man must have been too occupied with bare survival to concern

THEME SENTENCE
himself with moral codes. But as man became more secure, morality arose.

When he recognized how emaciated his paragraphs were, the student at first decided simply to combine them, two by two. That made a more complex effect, but it also caused confusion: which was the real theme sentence of the new, combined, paragraph? Eventually he saw that he needed one clearly dominant sentence in each paragraph and that he must ask himself questions about that sentence so as to generate an adequate set of related sentences. Thus, in revising the essay quoted above, he decided that he had been struggling toward the theme *Morality arose when man became relatively secure.* Asking himself three questions—*What do I mean by morality? What is relative security? How certain can I be that my statement about prehistory is true?*—he came up with a single adequately developed paragraph:

At some point, presumably, early man ceased to be governed primarily by instinct and bound himself to morality, or socially determined rules of permitted and forbidden conduct. When did that change occur? Unfortunately, we have no way of knowing for sure. It seems reasonable to suppose, however, that our ancestors began to exchange instinct for morality when they had gained a minimal control over natural threats to survival—predators, extremes of weather, and the like—and could turn some of their attention to threats posed by one another.

Note that this suspended paragraph is more complex both in sentence structure and in development of thought than the two paragraphs it replaced. Just as undeveloped thoughts and choppy sentences go hand in hand, so do adequately developed thoughts and sentences showing a pleasing variety of structure.

surgery for the bloated paragraph If a paragraph in your first draft seems to ramble endlessly, seek out its theme sentence. If you can't find one, start over. Otherwise, mark the sentence and then review all of the following sentences to see whether they are truly relevant to the theme. Eliminate those that are not, and then see what you have left. If you are lucky, you will find that you have simply written two complete paragraphs without marking the break between them. When you do divide a draft paragraph in two, however, check to make sure that each of your new paragraphs is tightly organized and adequately developed.

Many draft paragraphs start out purposefully but bloat as the writer gets absorbed in details. The following student example illustrates this gradual loss of control:

limiting sentence
theme sentence
supporting sentences

x 1. If a person feels guilty about something, the obvious thing to do is to get that guilt out in the open. 2. But many people take a different approach, one that only makes matters worse: they try to stifle their bad feelings by means of depressants or stimulants such as alcohol, methedrine, or marijuana. 3. A friend of mine in high school felt guilty about getting low grades. 4. Her solution was to stay high nearly all the time. 5. But of course that made her get even lower grades and it thus redoubled her guilt, so she had even more bad feelings to hide in smoke. 6. I tried to talk to her about her problems, but she was already too depressed to allow anyone to get through to her. 7. Finally, she left school. 8. I lost touch with her, and I never did learn whether she straightened herself out. 9. I think that people like her deserve a lot of pity, because if she hadn't been so sensitive in the first place, she wouldn't have had the guilt feelings that sent her into a tailspin. 10. People who just don't care are sometimes better off.

This begins as a competent pivoting paragraph, contrasting two approaches to the problem of handling guilty feelings and providing an example of the second, self-defeating, approach. The momentum, however, begins to drag as the writer shifts attention to herself in sentence 6, and the paragraph falls apart completely at sentence 9, which escapes the control of the theme sentence, number 2. Revising for economy and relevance, the student decided to do without the sentences about herself and her compassionate attitude:

limiting sentence { If a person feels guilty about something, the obvious thing to do is to get that guilt out in the open. But many people take a different approach

theme sentence { —one that only makes matters worse. They try to stifle their bad feelings with stimulants or depressants such as alcohol, methedrine, or marijuana. Thus a friend of mine in high school, feeling guilty about

supporting sentences { her low grades, tried to stay high nearly all the time. The result was that she got even worse grades, felt guiltier still, smoked even more dope, and eventually dropped out of school. Her supposed remedy had become a major part of her problem.

After establishing a middle-sized paragraph as your norm, you can depart from that norm with good effect. A reader who comes across a somewhat longer paragraph will know that a particularly complex point is being developed. Occasionally you can insert a very short paragraph—a sentence or two, or even a purposeful sentence fragment—to make a major transition, a challenge, an emphatic statement, or a summary. The emphasis comes precisely from the contrast between such a paragraph and the more developed ones surrounding it.

EXERCISES

23. Write out a theme sentence for a paragraph on any topic you have not treated in a previous exercise. Beneath that sentence, write out answers to the three questions that can usually lead to a remedy for choppy paragraph structure: (a) Where does the theme sentence lead? (b) What questions might be asked about the terms it contains? (c) What objections might be raised? Then, using some of the material you have developed, write an adequately full paragraph on your chosen topic, using either a direct, a pivoting, or a suspended pattern (pp. 153–160).

24. Look through the readings assigned for this course, or any other prose you may have handy, until you find a paragraph that, in your opinion, goes on too long to be readily grasped by a reader. Rewrite the paragraph to make it more compact and comprehensible, and submit your version with the original—or with a page reference if you found the original in an assigned text. Be sure that the material you omit is not essential support for the theme sentence.

NOTES

[1]Timothy E. Head, *Going Native in Hawaii: A Poor Man's Guide to Paradise* (Rutland, Vt.: Charles E. Tuttle, 1965), p. 7.

[2]Matt Clark and Mary Hager, "A Green Pepper a Day," *Newsweek,* 28 June 1982, p. 83.

[3]"Food: The New Wave," *Newsweek,* 11 Aug. 1975, p. 50.

[4]Peter Collier, "The Old Man and the C," *New West,* 24 Apr. 1978, p. 21.

⁵Gay Talese, *Honor Thy Father* (1971; rpt. Greenwich, Conn.: Fawcett-Crest, 1972), p. 16.

⁶Adapted from Carl W. Buchheister and Frank Graham, Jr., "From the Swamps and Back: A Concise and Candid History of the Audubon Movement," *Audubon*, Jan. 1973, p. 7.

⁷Edith Iglauer, "The Strangers Next Door," *Atlantic*, July 1973, p. 90.

⁸Meg Greenfield, "The Terrible Vs. the Thinkable," *Newsweek*, 19 Apr. 1982, p. 108.

⁹Jane Jacobs, *The Death and Life of Great American Cities* (New York: Vintage, 1961), p. 4.

¹⁰T. D. Allman, "Pomp and Desperation," *Harper's*, Nov. 1981, p. 14.

8

SENTENCES

All the virtues of strong paragraphs—clarity of main idea, emphatic placement of that idea, adequate support for it, variety of structure from one paragraph to another—apply to sentences as well. Indeed, just as the paragraph can be regarded as a mini-essay, so the sentence resembles a condensed paragraph, with major and minor elements that ought to be easily discernible:

	ESSAY		PARAGRAPH		SENTENCE
MAJOR	Thesis	=	Theme	=	Assertion
MINOR	Supporting Paragraphs		Supporting Sentences		Modifying Clauses and Phrases

On each level—essay, paragraph, sentence—your chief purpose in redrafting should be to highlight the main element and to see that it is adequately backed by elements that are clearly subordinate to it.

This chapter assumes that you can already write complete sentences that make a grammatically coherent statement (pp. 279–282), and it takes for granted your ability to tell the difference between active and passive verbs (pp. 249–251), phrases and clauses and in-dependent and subordinate clauses (pp. 272–273). If you feel uncertain about any of those matters, a little review may be advisable before you read on. But since you have already succeeded in getting countless sentences onto paper, we will start our discussion not with the blank page but with draft sentences that a student writer might plausibly want to improve.

Our keynote will be revision in the direction of readability, or the ease with which a reader can grasp your intended meaning. As we will see, the kinds of revision that can make a sentence more readable are also those that can make it memorable. Specifically, we will cover four kinds of sentence improvement that can help you

1. make distinct, readily graspable assertions;
2. distinguish between main and subordinate elements;
3. match related elements; and
4. vary your patterns of development.

DISTINCT ASSERTION

Recognize Your Main Assertion

Since your chief concern in writing any sentence is to communicate an idea, the logical starting point for revision is to locate that idea and see if it has been stated as clearly as possible. Some sentences—those with two or more independent clauses (p. 272) joined by words like *and* or *but*—will prove to have more than one main assertion, but every sentence that makes a statement will contain at least one. The mere act of isolating it from other elements can often bring a problem of fuzzy meaning to light and point the way to a solution.

The following sentences illustrate main assertions with and without relation to other elements. The main assertions are italicized:

1. *The professional basketball season now runs from September through the end of May.*

   The whole sentence is a main assertion.

2. *The players are always tired,* and *they find it hard to take every game seriously.*

   The sentence makes two statements that receive equal emphasis. Both are main assertions.

3. *So many teams make the playoffs,* furthermore, *that first-place finishes within a division are scarcely important.*

Here one word, *furthermore*, stands apart from the main assertion, relating it to a previous statement. Although *furthermore* plays a useful role in the sentence, it does not change the point being made.

4. Although basketball, as many people claim, may have replaced baseball as the national pastime, *we might do better to pass a little more time between seasons.*

The main assertion—the one that could stand by itself—does not begin until after the word *pastime.*

EXERCISES

1. Locate and submit the main assertion(s) of each of the following sentences:

    A.   All over the world, airline safety has become a major issue.
    B.   People are wondering whether jumbo jets are as safe as their defenders claim.
    C.   Crashes caused by pilot error are just as tragic, but those resulting from defects in design and maintenance are even more unsettling to the public.
    D.   Whoever is to blame, however, confidence in air travel has been shaken, at least for a while.
    E.   One recent passenger at a ticket counter, asked if he would be smoking, replied, "That depends on the way you land."

2. Type out or photocopy any paragraph of your own prose, written for this or any other course. Underline all the main assertions, and submit the paragraph.

Align Your Meaning with Grammatically Important Words

When you come back to a draft sentence and begin looking for ways to improve it, you should put yourself in your reader's place and ask if the main assertion makes total sense. Your reader wants above all to get the point—to take in the main assertion without difficulty. Isolate your assertion and study it with fresh, doubting eyes, as if you didn't yet know what the writer had in mind. Does the point become immediately clear? If not, the reason is probably that you have not yet put the essential parts of your idea into the grammatically strongest elements.

Those elements are generally a *subject* and a *verb,* usually linked to either a *direct object* or a *complement* (pp. 242–243):

       SUBJECT   VERB
• The *committee exists.*

       SUBJECT   VERB
• The *committee meets* on Tuesdays.

SUBJECT   VERB   DIRECT OBJECT
- The *committee is drafting* a *report.*

SUBJECT   VERB   COMPLEMENT
- The *committee is* an official *body.*

SUBJECT   VERB COMPLEMENT
- The *committee seems prepared.*

When you have made an indistinct assertion, you will often find that the grammatically strong elements of your sentence convey very little information about the action or state you wanted to get across. Consider, for example, this "correct" but unimpressive statement:

x The departure of the fleet is thought to be necessarily conditional on the weather.

Here the essential grammatical elements are a subject and verb, *The departure . . . is thought.* This is scanty information; we must root around elsewhere in the sentence to get the full idea. That idea is that bad weather—here tucked into an unemphatic prepositional phrase, *on the weather*—may delay the fleet's departure. To make the assertion distinct we can get *weather* into a subject position and re-place the wishy-washy construction *is thought to be* with a verb that transmits action to an object:

- Bad weather may keep the fleet at anchor.

Notice that we now have three grammatically strong elements—a subject, verb, and direct object—that do carry significant meaning: *Bad weather may keep the fleet. . . .*

detecting an indistinct assertion   You can look for certain classic signs of trouble as soon as you have completed a draft. Be especially ready to revise a sentence if you notice that its main assertion

six danger signals

1. has as its verb a form of the colorless, inert *to be* (*is, are, was, were, had been,* etc.);
2. conveys action through a noun rather than a verb (*there was a meeting* instead of *they met*);
3. has its verb in the passive voice (pp. 181–182);
4. begins with one of the delaying formulas *it is, it was,* etc. (*It was the butler who was suspected of being the murderer*);
5. contains one or more *that* or *what* clauses, suggesting a displacement of your main idea to a grammatically minor part of the assertion; or
6. seems to go on and on without interruption, requiring an effort of memory to keep it together (*It is what she recalled from childhood about the begonia gardens that were cultivated in Capitola that drew her to return to that part of the coastline one summer after another*).

Of these six danger signals, the last one *always* calls for revision; you never want your reader to work overtime to understand you. As for the other five, they are simply warning flags. You can write acceptable sentences using the verb *to be* instead of an action verb, using the passive voice for special emphasis, beginning with *it is* or *there is*, or including clauses beginning with *that* or *what*. Authorities who forbid any use of these elements are overruling the normal practice of professional writers. But when you *have* made an indistinct assertion, it will probably show more than one of the features we have named; and you can make your assertion more distinct simply by replacing those features. In moving a main idea into a main position or in choosing an active verb to express an action, you are sharpening your reader's focus on the heart of your meaning.

Here are some further misalignments of grammar and meaning, followed by suggestions for improvement:

x The lack of information that he sought from the evidence squelched the desired future of the inquiry all along.

> Here the subject, verb, and direct object are *lack, squelched,* and *future.* Can a *lack,* which is an absence, be said to have *squelched* a *future*? For that matter, can anyone *seek* a *lack*? From a reader's point of view the sentence is absurd. The writer must have meant to say something like *His indifference to evidence doomed the inquiry from the start.* (The unrevised sentence shows faulty predication; see pp. 281–291.)

x The thing the novelist seems to say is that the human race is lacking in what is needed to keep from being deceived.

> This whole sentence is a main assertion whose subject and verb are the uninformative *thing is.* The writer wants to present a novelist's view of humanity, but he has not yet aligned that purpose with the grammatical heart of his assertion. Compare:

• Human beings, the novelist seems to say, necessarily deceive themselves.

> Now the main assertion is shorter and more easily grasped; it is clearly set off from a secondary part of the sentence; and the key grammatical elements, subject–verb–direct object, bear the chief burden of meaning: *Human beings deceive themselves.*

x There is no reason to suspect that there is much difference between what he wrote in his last years and what he felt when it was not so easy for him to be candid in his thirties.

> Thanks to its *there is* constructions, this sentence is clogged and listless. Once again the usually strong positions are occupied by uncommunicative words, and we must hunt through the rest of the sentence for the information we need. Compare:

• His statements in his last years probably express ideas he already held, but was censoring, in his thirties.

> Now the subject–verb–object combination is *statements express ideas*; grammar and meaning are properly aligned.

x She made a negative decision with regard to her membership in the party.

> Vague terms of connection like *with regard to* often indicate an indistinct statement. Here we can locate the problem by asking what action the woman took. The answer is that she *decided* something. The difference between *she decided* and *she made a decision* may seem trivial, but *she made a decision* subtracts energy from the statement and calls forth the awkward *with regard to*. A forthright assertion would be best: *She decided to resign from the party.*

x At the present time, the realities of nuclear terror are such that countries that possess equal power find, when they oppose each other, that the weapons that carry the most force are precisely the weapons that they cannot use.

> This is potentially a fine sentence, but its several *thats* displace the main idea, forcing us to dig it out of a long assertion. Try:

• In this age of nuclear terror, equal adversaries are equally powerless to use their strongest weapons.

> Here thirty-eight words have been compressed into sixteen, and a slack, cud-chewing sentence has become tight and balanced (*equal adversaries are equally powerless*). Notice, yet again, how the grammatical core of the sentence is no longer empty of meaning: not *realities are such* but *adversaries are powerless*. Strong, message-bearing elements of thought have been moved into naturally prominent positions, where they belong.

x The consequences of a thermonuclear war could not be escaped by any country in the world.

> The statement is clear enough, and its key words are informative: *consequences could not be escaped*. But one essential element, the country that cannot escape, takes a minor role in the sentence. Why not get it into the subject position?

• No country in the world could escape the consequences of a thermonuclear war.

> Once again, the revision provides a meaty subject–verb–direct object combination: *country could escape consequences*.

reliance on the active voice   This last example illustrates the desirability, not only of choosing verbs that show action, but also of putting those verbs in the active voice (pp. 249–251). An **active verb** like *could escape* shows that the grammatical subject is doing the acting, and it allows an alignment of the direct object with the receiver of the verb's action. A **passive verb** like *could be escaped* eliminates the possibility of having a direct object, and it either pushes the performer of action into a delayed and minor sentence element *(by any country)* or suppresses any mention of that performer. Thus, unless you have a good reason for de-emphasizing the performer of action, you should put your verb in the active voice.

This means that every time you find a passive verb in a draft sentence, you should ask whether you intended to give the receiver of action more emphasis than the performer. If your sentence is *The chili dog was eaten by Max,* you will certainly want to change it to *Max ate the chili dog.* But if your sentence is *Max was taken to the emergency room,* you have properly de-emphasized the performer of action—perhaps some anonymous hospital orderly—in favor of poor Max, the center of concern.

In scientific writing, which often stresses impersonal, repeatable procedures rather than the individuals who followed those procedures in an experiment, passive verbs are common. In essay prose, however, habitual use of the passive makes a needlessly dry and evasive effect:

x It *is believed* by the candidate that a ceiling *must be placed* on the budget by Congress.
x Their motives *were applauded* by us, but their wisdom *was doubted.*

Note how the substitution of active forms saves words and imparts vividness:

- The candidate *believes* that Congress *must place* a ceiling on the budget.
- We *applauded* their motives but *doubted* their wisdom.

EXERCISES

3. Type out or photocopy the following student paragraph, whose main assertions are printed in italics. Above the grammatically essential elements of those assertions, write letters indicating the subject *(S)*, the verb *(V)*, and any direct object *(DO)* or complement *(C)*.

Our society has always prided itself on having an impersonal, unemotional system of justice. Supposedly, *we imprison criminals not to take revenge on them but to "rehabilitate" them under safe conditions. Prisons,* however, *do not rehabilitate;* if anything, *they are training schools for further crime.* If, knowing this, *we leave people in prisons anyway, we evidently do care about revenge. Perhaps the state as a collective body has no vengeful feelings,* but *its individual members demand punishment,* not rehabilitation.

4. The passage used in Exercise 3 shows a good alignment of meaning and grammatically strong elements. To get a better feeling for the difference between distinct and indistinct assertion, rewrite that passage to make it *less* distinct. The "six danger signals" on page 179 will give you clues for committing this mischief.

5. Go over your own written work (papers or drafts) for this or any other course, looking for insufficiently distinct assertions. Revise five sentences to make them more distinct, and submit the original sentences and the revised versions together.

6. Although you would generally do well to shift passive verbs to the active voice (not *it was done by them,* but *they did it*), we have seen that you can resort to the passive when you want to focus on the receiver of action rather than the performer: *the full moon was widely believed to cause insanity.* Study the passive verbs in each of the following sentences. Indicate which sentences use the passive voice justifiably, and rewrite the others to cast the verbs in the active voice.

> A. The defendant was brought to trial after a delay of eleven months.
> B. The ball was kicked out of bounds by Biff on his own four yard line.
> C. Novosibirsk has been called the most important city in Siberia.
> D. Pollution of lakes and rivers is deeply resented by the typical Minnesotan.
> E. The Declaration of Independence was called by Thomas Jefferson "the holy bond of our union."

7. The following paragraph, adapted from a competent student paper, has been doctored to *prevent* a vivid alignment of subjects, verbs, and direct objects with performers of action, actions, and receivers of action. Submit a revised version in which every main assertion is as distinct as you can make it.

> It is within the graveyard that Hamlet's final revelations about mortality are made. The function of the graveyard setting is operative in several ways. First, Hamlet's continuing confrontation with death receives highly dramatic emphasis here. Second, the digging up of buried motives, which has been a concern of Hamlet's from the beginning, is related to the literal digging of a grave. The buried skulls which are unearthed by the gravedigger are like the secrets toward which Hamlet's investigative efforts have been directed. Finally, Hamlet's final realization of his earthly limits is appropriate to a setting in which an abundance of anonymous bones is evident.

8. Here is a draft paragraph containing assertions that could be made more distinct. Submit a revised version, numbering your sentences to correspond with those below.

> 1. It is generally recognized that most colleges were subjected to a backlash of academic intensity after the political turmoil of the late sixties. 2. There was a desire for restoration of academic standards on the part of faculty members, students showed a concern for the acquisition of preprofessional training, and cost effectiveness was uppermost in the minds of administrators. 3. Now, however, a period of second thoughts appears to have arrived. 4. Whether or not the era of activism can be said to be over, there is a general realization that college life should make provision for something more than a professional union card. 5. What has happened is that the courses required by many colleges have actually been reduced in number in the interest of allowing time for attendance at public lectures and concerts, good conversation, and even physical and spiritual recuperation from the daily grind of classes.

9. Each of the following sentences needs improvement on grounds of insufficiently distinct assertion. To see the problem in each case, find the grammatically essential elements and ask how well they fit together. In addition, check the length of each main assertion. When you

are sure you see what the problem is, rewrite the sentence to align main elements of meaning with main elements of grammar. In most instances you will have to write a shorter main assertion, demoting some parts of the original assertion to secondary positions. As a sample, suppose this were the original sentence:

x Instructions are contained in this book for the identification of specific dialect features that teachers should know about if they want to understand their students' problems with the writing of standard English.

A sound revision might be:

• By showing how to identify specific dialect features, this book can help teachers to understand their students' problems in writing standard English.

Note that the main assertion of the new sentence extends only from *this book* to the end.

A. The rise in the price of oil drilled in conventional wells is a major inspiration for a renewed consideration of the development of new techniques for the extraction of what is known as tar sand crude oil.
B. High hopes for the future of this technology are causing a hopeful mood among many petroleum engineers.
C. The tar sand oil is so heavy that it cannot be pumped and instead must be strip-mined with the sand and then subjected to a process of treatment whereby the oil and sand are separated by hot water, steam, and air.
D. There are reasons to believe that the objections of environmentalists rather than technical difficulties will postpone development of this resource.
E. A choice must be made between goals of oil production to be maintained if the world is not to run out of vital energy supplies and the understandable reluctance felt by many people to permit the devastating if perhaps temporary damage caused by strip mining.

SUBORDINATION

The first thing to do with any draft sentence, then, is to see if you can make its main assertion more distinct. In doing so, you will usually find yourself **subordinating**, or placing certain elements in secondary positions. To make one element clearly minor is, of course, to concentrate attention on another element which has now become primary.

Subordinate elements can be either (1) single words, (2) phrases, or (3) subordinate clauses:

1. *single words:*

• That proposal, *however,* was soundly defeated.

2. *phrases,* or clusters of words lacking a subject-verb combination:

- *In view of the fuel shortage,* we must cut back on unnecessary travel.

3. *subordinate clauses,* or clusters of words that do contain a subject-verb combination but do not form an independent statement:

- The telephone company, *which has enjoyed a near monopoly on phone appliances,* is now being challenged in the open marketplace.

Subordinate to Highlight Your Main Assertion

Wherever one of your ideas in a sentence is less important than another, you should place it within a subordinate structure. Thus, if your draft sentence says *The government collects billions of dollars in taxes, and it must meet many obligations,* you should ask yourself whether you really want those two remarks to have equal importance. If not, you must choose which one to emphasize. Suppose you decided that the first statement is the more important one. Then you would want to show that importance by demoting the other statement to a subordinate status:

SUBORDINATE ELEMENT
- The government collects billions of dollars in taxes *to meet its obligations.*

Or, more emphatically:

SUBORDINATE ELEMENT
- *To meet its obligations,* the government collects billions of dollars in taxes.

Any element of thought can be made either primary or subordinate, depending on your intended emphasis. When you do make an element subordinate, however, it will usually fit into one of the following (left-column) categories. Note how the right-column sentences are more precisely focused than those in the middle column, sparing us the trouble of deciding which is the main idea:

	WITHOUT SUBORDINATION	WITH SUBORDINATION
Time	The earthquake struck, and then everyone panicked.	Everyone panicked *when the earthquake struck.*
Place	William Penn founded a city of brotherly love. He chose the juncture of the Delaware and Schuylkill rivers.	*Where the Schuylkill River joins the Delaware,* William Penn founded a city of brotherly love.

Cause	She was terrified of large groups, and debating was not for her.	*Because she was terrified of large groups,* she decided against being a debater.
Concession	He claimed to despise Vermont. He went there every summer.	*Although he claimed to despise Vermont,* he went there every summer.
Condition	She probably won't be able to afford a waterbed. The marked retail prices are just too high.	*Unless she can get a discount,* she probably won't be able to afford a waterbed.
Exception	The grass is dangerously dry this year. Of course I am not referring to watered lawns.	*Except for watered lawns,* the grass is dangerously dry this year.
Purpose	The Raiders moved to Los Angeles. They hoped to find bigger profits there.	The Raiders moved to Los Angeles *in search of bigger profits.*
Description	The late Edward Steichen showed his reverence for life in arranging the famous exhibit "The Family of Man," and he was a pioneer photographer himself.	The late Edward Steichen, *himself a pioneer photographer,* showed his reverence for life in arranging the famous exhibit "The Family of Man."

free versus bound subordinate elements   Note, in the right column above, that all but two of the italicized subordinate elements are set apart from the main assertions by commas. They are "free" in the sense of standing alone. By contrast, the sentences *Everyone panicked when the earthquake struck* and *The Raiders moved to Los Angeles in search of bigger profits* contain *bound* subordinate elements; that is, they are tied together with the main assertions. Here are some further contrasts:

BOUND	FREE
The Germany *that he remembered with horror* had greatly changed.	Germany, *which he remembered with horror,* had greatly changed.
Germany was now inclined toward neutralism *instead of being fiercely militaristic.*	*Instead of being fiercely militaristic,* Germany was now inclined toward neutralism.
Hitler had vanished from the scene *along with everything he stood for.*	*Along with everything he stood for,* Hitler had vanished from the scene.

This distinction turns out to be a valuable one. When you find an awkward main assertion in a draft, you may discover that it already contains much *bound* subordination:

bound
subordinate
elements

x Nuclear power is an energy source *whose enormous risks to health and safety are out of scale in importance with the fact that it accounts for less than 5 percent of energy production in the United States.*

Here a main assertion has been glued tight to eight subordinate elements: two subordinate clauses *(whose enormous risks . . . , that it accounts for . . .)* and six prepositional phrases *(to health and safety, of scale, in importance, with the fact, of energy production, in the United States)*. The result is an unnecessarily heavy demand on the reader's patience; the sentence offers no resting place and no clear sign of its logical structure. Compare:

free subordinate
element

• *Although nuclear power accounts for less than 5 percent of our energy production,* it poses enormous risks to health and safety.

Subordination does lead to clarity in this revision, for the subordinate clause has been set apart from the main assertion. We thus gain two crucial advantages: the main assertion now takes up only eight words, and the *Although* construction immediately tells us what the sentence's logic will be (*although* x, *nevertheless* y).

When you find a lengthy, labored main assertion in a draft, then, look for ways of shortening it by turning bound subordinate elements into free ones:

BOUND:

x The censorship *that is not directly exercised by a sponsor when a program is being produced* may be exercised *in many instances by the producers themselves.*

FREE:

• *Even when a sponsor does not directly censor a program,* the producers often censor themselves.

Note the importance of the comma after *program,* leaving the reader in no doubt about where the main assertion begins.

position of free subordinate elements   One important feature of free subordinate elements is that they can be moved without a radical loss of meaning. The *Even when . . .* clause above, for example, could have been placed at the end of its sentence. How can you tell where a free element would make the best effect? If you don't trust your ear, you can apply one of the following three principles:

1. *If a free element explains or places conditions on a main assertion, you should usually put it first, so that it can affect your reader's understanding of the assertion:*

- *Unless scientists come up with a better explanation,* we will have to lend our belief to this one.
- *Although he finished the test in time,* he missed many of the answers.
- *Because he becomes nervous whenever he isn't listening to music,* he wears earphones while he works.

In first-draft prose, main assertions tend to come first, with limiting or explanatory elements dragging behind. Get those elements into early positions; they will show that you have the entire logic of the sentence under control. And since last positions tend to be naturally emphatic, you can generally make a stronger effect by putting your main assertion after your free subordinate element. That is why the second "government" sentence on page 185 is more emphatic than the first.

2. *If a free element merely adds something to a main assertion, you can put that element last:*

- Her smile disguised her fierce competitiveness, *a trait revealed to very few of her early comrades.*
- His life revolved around his mother, *who never ceased making unreasonable demands.*

In both sentences the free element is a further reflection rather than a reason or limitation that we should have in mind when we get to the main assertion.

3. *If a free element pertains to only one part of the main assertion, you can place it right after that part:*

- Cézanne's colors, *earthy as his native Provence,* are not adequately conveyed by reproductions.
- They gave me, *a complete newcomer,* more attention than I deserved.

Since each of the italicized modifiers pertains to only one word (*colors, me*) within the main assertion, both modifiers are put in an interrupting position.

Avoid Vague Subordination

Certain routine expressions tend to make a subordinate element too imprecise or cumbersome to be useful. In rereading your drafts, watch especially for tags like *in terms of, with regard to,* and *being as.* Such umbrella language fails to specify what the subordinate relation is to the main assertion. More often than not you can solve the problem by doing without the whole empty construction:

x *In terms of swimming,* she was unbeatable.
• She was an unbeatable swimmer.

x *Being as it was noon,* everyone took a lunch break.
• Everyone took a lunch break at noon.

x He felt quite sympathetic *with regard to their position.*
• He felt quite sympathetic to their position.

> Note that *in regards to* or *with regards to* would be not just vague but incorrect as well.

Other potentially vague subordinators include *with, as, as to, in the area of, in connection with, in the framework of, along the lines of,* and *as far as.* For example:

x *With all that he says about the natives,* I believe he has misrepresented them.
• I believe he has altogether misrepresented the natives.

x *As far as finals,* I hope to take all of them in the first two days of Exam Week.

> To be correct in usage the writer would have to say *As far as finals are concerned, . . .* But unless there is some special reason for singling out finals, it would be preferable to write

• I hope to take all of my finals in the first two days of Exam Week.

> Note that one vague-looking formula is used so commonly by good writers that it can be considered acceptable: *as for,* when meant to address the last of several previously mentioned items:

• As for the alleged bribery, it is a figment of the district attorney's imagination.

> This use of *as for* escapes vagueness because its context has been supplied by an earlier sentence.

> Subordination, as you can see, is not an absolute goal or a cure-all. In revising, check to see (a) that a subordinate construction is clearly required by your meaning and (b) that the relation between the main and subordinate elements is a definite one.

EXERCISES

10. Combine each pair of sentences below to form two new sentences using subordination. First subordinate element 1 to element 2 and then vice versa. Be prepared to explain the difference in emphasis between your sentences in each new pair.

    A. 1. Unemployment is beginning to look like a permanent problem in America.

        2. Every student wants assurance that a job will be waiting after graduation.

    B. 1. Postage rates are discouragingly high.

        2. There are few real alternatives to using the mails.

    C. 1. Hang gliding is growing in popularity.

        2. It will never catch on in Kansas.

    D. 1. I am an avid sports fan.

        2. I do not intend to watch next Sunday's underwater tug of war between the Miami Dolphins and a team of alligators.

    E. 1. The alligators will do all they can to win the prize.

        2. It is hard to imagine what the alligators would do with $500,000.

11. Each of the following sentences uses the coordinating conjunction *and* inappropriately, allowing a subordinate meaning to be lost. Rewrite the sentences, using a *free element* (p. 186) to bring out a single main assertion in each case.

    A. He is going to apply for the job, and he doesn't have a chance.

    B. She hopes to quit work early today, and she wants to get to the mountains ahead of the weekend traffic.

    C. Farmers want the price of corn to rise this year, and otherwise many of them will be driven out of business.

    D. There has been very little snow this year, and most of the ski resorts are closed.

    E. Most species of American animals have recently been declining in population, and the sea otter is one exception to the rule.

12. Each of the following sentences consists of a single main assertion clogged with *bound* subordinate elements (pp. 186–187). Submit revised versions using *free* subordination to simplify the main assertions. Do not feel obliged to cover every last bit of information in the original sentences.

    For example:

    ORIGINAL:

    x Any time that an accident that involves a spill of toxic substances occurs is a time that could reasonably cause alarm to everyone who lives in the area that surrounds the scene where the accident occurred.

    REVISION:

    • Whenever a spill of toxic substances occurs, everyone in the surrounding area has cause for alarm.

    A. It is an interesting fact that in America the statistics show that for every adult member of the population there is approximately one automobile.

    B. The use of these 130 million vehicles results every day in the consumption of 5.5 million barrels of gasoline coming partly from domestic sources while the rest is made up from foreign ones.

    C. Standards for the fuel economy of new cars that the government put into effect for domestic auto makers beginning in 1978 have brought about a steady rise in the number of miles per gallon of new cars in each year since that date.

D. The total consumption of oil in the United States is now less by 3.5 million barrels of oil a day than it was at the time that the new fuel economy standards were passed.

E. Yet it is unfortunately true that the advantage in terms of reduction of dependence on foreign sources of oil has been largely offset by the fact that the domestic production of oil has been declining at about the same rate as the decline in the demand for gasoline.

13. Review the three points of advice about placement of free subordinate elements (p. 188). Then submit three sentences illustrating those points in turn. Your sentences may be about any topic except those used in the examples on page 188.

14. Each of the following sentences shows vague subordination (pp. 188–189). Submit revised versions that eliminate the problem.

A. In the framework of chocolate consumption, the British probably take first place.

B. Regarding the weather, it has been unusually mild in recent weeks.

C. She left nothing to be desired in terms of her eagerness to learn.

D. As far as ethics, that is a subject of very little interest to them.

E. With reference to the obligations facing him this semester, volunteer work would seem to be out of the question.

15. The following passage lacks adequate subordination. Rewrite it, combining sentences and indicating subordinate relations.

> Hippocrates used garlic as a pharmaceutical. He used it to treat different diseases, and so did other early doctors. They believed that a plant or herb had a very penetrating odor so it must have a lot of therapeutic value. Tuberculosis and leprosy are not at all alike but garlic was used to treat both of them. There was a Roman naturalist named Pliny. He listed sixty-one diseases; garlic was supposed to cure them all. And he added the information that garlic has very powerful properties and you can tell this because serpents and scorpions are driven away by the very smell of it.[1]

16. In earlier papers or in a draft you have been preparing, find three sentences that now strike you as lacking adequate subordination or as using subordination awkwardly. Submit those sentences along with three revised versions that clear up the problem.

MATCHING

We have seen that you can usually improve sentence clarity by getting your grammar aligned with your meaning. Now we can extend that point to cover two or more elements within a sentence. When those elements are parallel in meaning, it is good to show their relation by making them grammatically alike. That is the principle of **matching**, which can eliminate extra words while making your meaning emphatically clear.

To appreciate these advantages, compare two passages expressing the same information:

A. Animals think *of* things. They also think *at* things. Men think primarily *about* things. Words are symbols that may be combined in a thousand ways. They can also be varied in the same number of ways. This can be said of pictures as well. The same holds true for memory images.

B. Animals think, but they think *of* and *at* things; men think primarily *about* things. Words, pictures, and memory images are symbols that may be combined and varied in a thousand ways.[2]

Passage A, a classically choppy paragraph, takes seven sentences and fifty-one words to say what passage B says in two sentences and thirty-one words. In passage B seven main assertions are condensed to four, with a corresponding gain in understanding. And the key to this concentration is matching—of paired clauses *(Animals think, but they think . . .)*, of conspicuously equal halves of a sentence marked by a semicolon, of nouns in a series *(Words, pictures, and memory images)*, and of verb forms *(combined and varied)*. Passage B inspires confidence in the writer's control; we feel that she could not have packed her sentences with so much matching structure if she hadn't known exactly what she wanted to say.

Matching would seem to be opposite in spirit to subordination, for matching *associates* where subordination *differentiates*. In practice, however, much effective matching occurs *within* subordinate structures—for example, within free elements that follow a main assertion:

MAIN ASSERTION
• A life such as his tests our sense of purpose, making us wonder *why the*

MATCHING ELEMENT #1   MATCHING ELEMENT #2
unfortunate child was born, what possible joy he could bring to his parents,

MATCHING ELEMENT #3
and *whether so much suffering could ever be repaid,* even in an afterlife.

Notice that this long and complex sentence is readily understandable, thanks to a concise initial assertion and a tight alignment, or grammatical **parallelism**, among three matching elements outside that assertion. Each italicized element bears exactly the same grammatical relation to one other word, *wonder*. (All three are *objects* of that *infinitive*; see p. 268.)

Pair Two Elements That Belong Together

Most instances of matching involve two items that are conspicuously equivalent in emphasis. The following table shows how such items can be matched, with or without *conjunctions* or joining words such as *and* and *or:*

PATTERN	EXAMPLE
x and y	*x* *y* She was tired of *waiting* and *worrying*.
x or y	If he had continued that life, he would have *x* *y* faced death *in the electric chair* or *at the hands of the mob*.
x, y	*x* He strode away, *the money in his hand*, *y* *a grin on his face*.
x:y	*x* *y* He had *what he wanted: enough cash to buy a new life*.
x;y	*x* *y* *He wanted security; she wanted good times*.

As you can see from these few examples, matching can involve units as small as single words (*waiting* and *worrying*) or as large as whole statements (*he wanted security* and *she wanted good times*).

anticipatory patterns   In the sentences above, each *y* element comes as a mild surprise; we see that a matching structure is in progress only when we reach the second item. Other matching formulas, however, *anticipate* both items by beginning with a "tip-off" word:

PATTERN	EXAMPLE
both x and y	*x* *y* Both *guerrillas* and *loyalists* pose a threat to the safety of reporters covering foreign revo- lutions.
either x or y	*x* Either *reporters should be recognized as y neutrals* or *they should not be sent into combat zones*.
neither x nor y	*x* Neither *the competition of networks* nor *the y ambition of reporters* justifies this recklessness.

whether x or y	Reporters must wonder, when they wake up each morning in a foreign city, whether they *x* will be *gunned down by the loyalists* or *y* *kidnapped by the guerrillas.*
more (less) x than y	*x* It is more important, after all, *to spare the lives* *y* *of journalists* than *to get one more interview with the typical freedom fighter.*
not x but y	*x* It is not *the greed of the networks*, however, *y* but *the changed nature of warfare* that most endangers the lives of reporters.
not only x but also y	Now reporters covering a guerrilla war find *x* it hard, not only *to distinguish "friendly" from "unfriendly" elements*, but also *to convince* *y* *each side that they are not working for the other one.*
so x that y	*x* Such reporting has become so *risky*, in *y* fact, that *few knowledgeable journalists volunteer to undertake it.*

Note, in these anticipatory examples, how the first word of the matching formula prepares us for the rest. As soon as we read *both* or *either* or *so*, we know what kind of logical pattern has begun, and this certainty enables us to process complex paired elements without difficulty. Anticipatory matching, then, always constitutes a gain in readability—provided that the grammar and punctuation of your sentence make the intended structure clear (pp. 295–299).

Note too that paired items do not always have to be equally important. When the pattern is *more (less) x than y, not x but y, not only x but also y,* or *so x that y,* one item clearly dominates the other. The pairing in such cases succeeds not because the items are equivalent but because they are covered by a single mental operation.

To see how anticipatory matching can aid a reader, let us compare some imaginary first-draft prose with a finished version:

A. He swore a lot. He would swear at absolutely anybody. For him, it was just the natural thing to do. The people who worked for him probably thought he was angry at them all the time, but it wasn't necessarily true. A man like that could have been just making conversation without being angry at all, for all they knew.

B. He swore so often and so indiscriminately that his employees were sometimes not sure whether he was angry at them or merely making conversation.[3]

Passage A uses more words to make more assertions, yet it never lets us see where it is headed. The better version uses two anticipatory structures—*so x and so y that z* and *whether he was x or y*—to pull elements of thought into alignment without squandering whole sentences on them.

balance   When a sentence uses emphatic repetition to achieve matching, it shows **balance**. A balanced sentence usually does two things: (1) it repeats a grammatical pattern, and (2) it repeats certain words so as to highlight key differences. Thus the two halves of *He wanted security; she wanted good times* use the same subject-verb-object pattern and the same verb, *wanted*, in order to contrast *he* with *she* and *security* with *good times*.

You can see the ingredients of balance in the following **aphorisms**, or memorable sentences expressing very general assertions:

- What is *written without effort* is in general *read without pleasure*. (Samuel Johnson)
- We must indeed *all hang together*, or, most assuredly, we will *all hang separately*. (Benjamin Franklin)
- Democracy substitutes *election by the incompetent many* for *appointment by the corrupt few*. (George Bernard Shaw)

Notice in each instance how the writer has used identical sentence functions to make us confront essential differences: *written/read, effort/pleasure, together/separately, election/appointment, incompetent/corrupt, many/few*.

Because balanced sentences are always emphatic and often rather commanding in tone, a series of them would make an unpleasant impression. Now and then, however, as you are revising for matching, you may find a chance to create a balanced effect. The trick is to notice elements of sameness and contrast in your draft sentence and to rearrange your grammar so that those elements occupy identical structural positions.

Thus:

DRAFT SENTENCE:

* Love of country is admirable, but I think that it is more important today to love the human species as a whole.

BALANCED VERSION:

* Love of country is a virtue, but love of the human species is a necessity.

The first sentence is adequately formed, but it still reads like an idea in the making, the transcript of a thought process. The second, radically concise, sentence uses balance to convey authority and finality.

Make Your Series Consistent and Climactic

One indispensable form of matching is the **series** of coordinated items, three or more elements in a parallel sequence. A series tells your reader that the several items it contains share a logical relation to some other part of the sentence. You can place a series anywhere —within a main assertion, in elements preceding or following it—so long as the items really belong together:

> X   Y   Z
> * *Declining enrollments, obsolete audio equipment,* and *hostility from the administration* have hurt the language departments.

This says that *x, y,* and *z* are comparable factors, each making its contribution to the effect named. Such a condensed, immediately clear statement might replace as many as three rambling sentences in a draft paragraph.

order within a series   Although the parts of a series must be alike in form, they may have different degrees of importance or impact. Since the final position is by far the most emphatic one, that is where the climactic item should go:

> * He was prepared to risk everything—*his comfort, his livelihood, even his life.*
>
> If you try to put *his life* into either of the other positions in the series, you will see how vital a climactic order is.

Because a series *condenses* ideas, reducing them to matched items governed by a single word or phrase, there is always a risk that certain parts of the series won't fit. In assembling a series, you must be careful to see that the items really belong together, that you have kept them properly separate from one another, and that you have clearly shown where the series ends (see pp. 316, 327). In addition, you should ask whether you have placed the items in an emphatic and logically consistent order. You do not want to write, for example, x *She gathers pears, apples, and assorted fruits;* the third category, *fruits,* overlaps with the first two. Nor should you toss in items of markedly different importance:

x Travelers in this part of the country fall in love with *the fields of waving grain, the infinite sky, and the deluxe jumboburgers.*

Such effects of anticlimax are good for a laugh, but embarrassing if the laugh is unexpected.

optional forms   As the last example shows, you do not always have to put *and* or *or* before the last member of a series. Omitting the conjunction can give the series an air of urgency or importance:

• A moment's *distraction, hesitation, impatience* can spell doom for an aerialist.

Again, if you want to make a crowded or overwhelmed effect, you can omit the commas and put coordinating conjunctions between all members of the series:

• No sooner does one international crisis fade from the headlines than a new one arrives, *an Angola or Nicaragua or Lebanon or El Salvador* to keep us on edge.

You can even combine both of these variations within one sentence, if your meaning allows it:

• *The growing national debt, the annual trade deficit, the default of international loans* —these are sources of continual *anxiety and doubt and wishful thinking* in Washington these days.

EXERCISES

17. Study the following passage, and submit a paragraph or two explaining its use of matched effects. Be specific about the writer's language, and try to relate your findings to his apparent attitude or purpose.

> Riffling through the pages of the new magazines devoted to running, one could conclude from the advertisements that there are more kinds of running shoes now on the market in America than there are feet. But this is not to speak of such auxiliary items as special arch supports, heel protectors, insoles; nor of fog-repellents for glasses, or skin lube to prevent chafing under the arms, or runner's mittens; nor of warm-up suits, singlets, socks, and shorts (one manufacturer sells shorts that he advertises as "almost like running nude"). Then there are metric conversion scales, chronographs and stopwatches, wallets that attach to running shoes, pouches to fit on the back of shorts. One of my favorite items is a "jogging stick," comparable to a military swagger stick, to be carried along while running and to be used, apparently, for beating off dogs, muggers, perhaps smokers.[4]

18. Looking through earlier papers or a draft that you have been working on, find a paragraph of your own prose that now strikes you as lacking in the conciseness that matching structures can provide. Type out or photocopy that paragraph, and submit it along with a revised version that *is* concise and rich in matching. In the revised version, underline all the words that, like the terms marked by *x*'s and *y*'s on pages 193–194, constitute the matched items.

19. Using any paper or draft, find three of your own sentences that you can revise to achieve the effect of *balance* (pp. 195–196). Submit both the original and the revised versions.

20. For each item, compose a sentence that places the three terms in a series. Be sure to choose the most emphatic, climactic order of arrangement for those terms:

    A. courage   cheerfulness   patience
    B. the neighborhood   the county   the city
    C. grade school   college   high school
    D. terrors   worries   fears
    E. an inconvenience   an outrage   a disturbance

21. Submit three sentences containing series. In the first, omit a conjunction before the final item in the series. In the second, join all items in the series with conjunctions, not commas. And in the third, include two series, using *both* of the devices practiced in the first two sentences. (See p. 197.) Beneath each of your three sentences, briefly explain why the optional form or forms you are illustrating suit the idea or mood of this particular statement.

VARIETY

Although you have revised your sentences one by one, they are going to be read together in paragraph-sized sequences. You too, therefore, should read them that way, checking to see that they sound comfortable in one another's company. If they seem abrupt and awkward, the problem may be partly an insufficient continuity of thought. But sentences can be related in thought and still feel unrelated because they are too alike in structure. This is especially true of an unbroken sequence of **choppy sentences** – brief, plain statements lacking any internal pauses. What you want instead is an easy play between relatively plain sentences and those that do contain pauses.

Include Significant Pauses

One extremely simple sentence, nestled among more complex ones, can be effectively emphatic, but several of them together make a kindergarten impression. The following passage shows extreme monotony:

> x The high snow in the Wasatch Mountains is light and dry. You can't make a snowball out of it. This is Utah powder. It makes for some of the West's

greatest skiing. The numerous slopes are regularly groomed. The snow crunches under your skis. It forgives your rusty technique. It gives gently under your fall. There is deep, new powder in the back bowls. You float up and over the ground. Plumes of white mist curl around your waist like smoke.

Here every sentence consists entirely of a brief main assertion. The passage goes almost nowhere in little jerks, like a stalled snowmobile being nudged by its starter motor. Now compare the actual published text:

- The snow that falls high in the Wasatch Mountains is so light and dry that you can't make a snowball out of it. This is Utah powder, and it makes for some of the West's greatest skiing. On the numerous slopes that are regularly groomed, the snow crunches under your skis, forgiving if your technique is rusty, giving gently if you fall. On the deep new powder of the back bowls, you float up and over the ground, plumes of white mist curling around your waist like smoke.[5]

These four sentences contain more words than the eleven above—their average length is twenty-two words instead of seven—yet their message is more comprehensible, and certainly more pleasant to take in, than exactly the same message delivered in Dick-and-Jane sentences. Why? Since the words used are almost identical, the difference in effect must be entirely due to sentence variety. Three features are especially noteworthy:

1. The second passage requires us to deal with only five main assertions, not eleven.
2. The second passage, therefore, spares us the bothersome work of deciding which among the eleven assertions are the important ones.
3. The five assertions, because they are not all bunched together, allow us some "breathing space" between emphatic statements and a sense of increasing freedom as we progress.

To illustrate this last point, we can italicize the main assertions and study the sentences one by one:

1. *The snow that falls high in the Wasatch Mountains is so light and dry that you can't make a snowball out of it.*

   The entire first sentence is a main assertion. Although it contains two subordinate clauses (both beginning with *that*), the efficiently completed *so . . . that* matching structure keeps it concise and straightforward in effect.

2. *This is Utah powder, and it makes for some of the West's greatest skiing.*

Straightforwardness is still the desired effect, achieved this time by two matched assertions separated only by a comma and a conjunction.

3. On the numerous slopes that are regularly groomed, *the snow crunches under your skis,* forgiving if your technique is rusty, giving gently if you fall.

Now that the theme sentence (number 2; see p. 152) has appeared, the paragraph can become more expansive, vividly illustrating the already mentioned point that Utah powder *makes for some of the West's greatest skiing.* In sentence 3 the main assertion, in a departure from sentences 1 and 2, is delayed and cushioned on both sides by free subordinate elements (pp. 186–187).

4. On the deep new powder of the back bowls, *you float up and over the ground,* plumes of white mist curling around your waist like smoke.

The final sentence is closely matched in structure to sentence 3. Yet the effect is not monotonous, for the pairing helps us grasp the subordination of both sentences to sentence 2, the theme sentence of the paragraph.

Can you feel the effect of the abundant free elements in sentences 3 and 4? They are supportive, elaborative, evocative. If sentences 1 and 2 get you to Utah, sentences 3 and 4 get you skiing, first with some uncertainty but eventually with a sense of floating in harmony with the gentle snow. Note how the free elements, properly separated from the main assertions by commas, enable those assertions to be concise and muscular: *the snow crunches under your skis; you float up and over the ground.* The directness of those statements helps to explain why the passage, despite its gathering complexity of structure, is readily understood on a quick reading.

Not all pauses are equally useful in providing a feeling of sentence variety. The commas between items in a series (pp. 196–197) have little effect, for those items are all "heading the same way." But even the smallest free element, properly set off by punctuation, makes for a significant pause, for it calls notice to a relation of one part of the sentence to another:

* *Although the bill passed the Senate,* it was defeated in the House.
* *Without hesitating,* the chairman of the board resigned.
* Such a man, *furthermore,* can be expected to cause trouble in the future.

Here we see a measure of complexity supplied by, respectively, a subordinate clause, a modifying phrase, and an isolated sentence adverb (pp. 265–266).

In addition, a pause marked by the comma separating two main assertions works against choppiness:

* The bill passed the Senate, but it was defeated in the House.

See pages 313–316 for the relevant comma rules.

Experiment with Sentence Patterns

Once you feel sure you can defeat choppiness by means of significant pauses, you can begin mastering special sentence patterns that every accomplished writer uses from time to time. The *cumulative sentence, interruption,* the *suspended sentence, inversion,* and the *question* or *exclamation* all hold out a promise of expressiveness beyond the mere communicating of information.

the cumulative sentence A cumulative sentence is one whose main assertion is followed by one or more free subordinate elements. It is called **cumulative** because it accumulates or collects modifying words, phrases, or clauses after the heart of the statement is complete. The following sentences, already encountered in this chapter, are typical:

* Her smile disguised her fierce competitiveness, *a trait revealed to very few of her early comrades.*
* A life such as his tests our sense of purpose, *making us wonder why the unfortunate child was born, what possible joy he could bring to his parents, and whether so much suffering could ever be repaid, even in an afterlife.*
* He was prepared to risk everything—*his comfort, his livelihood, even his life.*
* No sooner does one international crisis fade from the headlines than a new one arrives, *an Angola or Nicaragua or Lebanon or El Salvador to keep us on edge.*

The beauty of the cumulative pattern is that it offers refinement without much risk of confusion. Since the basic structure of the sentence is complete before the end modifiers (italicized above) begin, your reader has a secure grasp of your idea, which you can then elaborate, illustrate, explain, or reflect on. And since much of our speech follows the cumulative model of statement-plus-adjustment, a cumulative sentence on the page can make a pleasantly conversational effect, as if one afterthought had brought the next one into mind.

interruption To give special emphasis to one statement or piece of information, try turning it into an interruption of your sentence:

* The street she lived on—*it was more like an alley than a street*—was so neighborly that she scarcely ever felt alone.

- The hot, moist summer air of Florida—*people call it an instant steambath*—makes an air conditioner a necessity in every home and office.
- A woman of strong opinions—*her last movie grossed $50 million, and she calls it a turkey*—she is not exactly a press agent's dream come true.

As you can gather, dashes are the normal means of punctuating an emphatic interruption. (See pp. 329–332 for the handling of dashes, parentheses, and brackets.)

the false start
In a variation on the interruptive pattern, you can begin your sentence with a lengthy element—for example, a series—and follow it with a dash announcing that the grammatical core of the sentence is about to begin:

- *Going to hairdresser school, marrying the steady boyfriend, having the baby, getting the divorce*—everything in her life seemed to follow some dreary script.

Such a sentence throws the reader off guard by making a false start. We assume at first that the opening element will be the grammatical subject, but we readjust our focus when we see that the true subject will come after the dash. (The first element is actually in apposition to the subject; see p. 243.)

the suspended sentence   If you substantially delay completing the essential structure of your sentence, forcing your reader to wait for the other shoe to drop, you have written a **suspended** (often called **periodic**) sentence. Like a suspended paragraph, it can be an effective means of leading to a climax:

- It appears that their success was due more to the influence of their father, *so dominant in the worlds of business and politics that every door would open at his bidding,* than to any merits of their own.
- The states argued that they had indeed complied, *if compliance can mean making a good-faith effort and collecting all the required data,* with the federal guidelines.
- If you are still unused to the idea of gasohol, you will certainly not be ready to hear that some diesel engines will soon be running on *that most humble and ordinary of products, taken for granted by homemakers and never noticed by auto buffs,* vegetable oil.
- And, what was even more exciting, she felt, too, *as she saw Mr. Ramsay bearing down and retreating, and Mrs. Ramsay sitting with James in the window and the cloud moving and the tree bending,* how life, *from being made up of little separate incidents which one lived one by one,* became curled and whole like a wave which bore one up and threw one down with it, there, with a dash on the beach.[6]

This last example, from Virginia Woolf's novel *To the Lighthouse*, shows that a suspended sentence need not postpone an essential element until the very end; it is the effect of significant delay, of withheld closure, that matters. The italicized elements in all four examples bring about such suspension.

inversion Readers normally expect subjects to come before verbs, but for that very reason you can gain emphasis by occasionally reversing, or **inverting**, that order. The subject becomes more prominent when it is held back:

* In the beginning was *the Word.*
* Most important of all, for the would-be tourist, is a *passport* that has not expired.

Similarly, the element that has been wrenched out of its normal position and placed first gets extra attention:

* *Not until then* had he understood how miserable he was.
* *Never again* will she overlook the threat of an avalanche.

Note that the principle of inversion extends not only to reversed subjects and verbs but to any moving forward of a normally late element:

* *About such a glaring scandal* nothing need be said.

  Here the subject and verb, *nothing* and *need*, are in the usual sequence, but the sentence shows inversion by moving a prepositional phrase from the end to the beginning.

the question or exclamation To show strong feeling, to pinpoint an issue, to challenge your reader, or simply to enliven a string of sentences, you can make use of a strategically placed question or exclamation:

* *What are we to make of such a fuss over the tiny, frigid, wind-blasted Falkland Islands?* Let us begin with the subject of offshore oil. . . .
* . . . and this is all the information released so far. *Does anyone doubt that the congressman has something to hide?*
* *A million tons of TNT!* The power of this bomb was beyond anyone's imagination.
* Once the grizzlies were deprived of garbage, their population declined steeply. *So much for the "back to nature" school of bear management!*

Just as it is good to feel at ease with the sentence patterns reviewed above, it is good to understand that most of them work best when used sparingly. Although a cumulative sentence is almost always welcome, beware of peppering your essays with too many agitated dashes, questions, and exclamations. If you keep returning to relatively calm and straightforward discourse as your norm, readers will have a better appreciation of your occasional emphatic flourishes.

Listen for Sentence Rhythm

Without consciously realizing it, readers will be listening to your prose with what Robert Frost called the audial imagination. There is, as Frost perceived, a "sentence sound," or rather many sentence sounds, whose patterns are deeply fixed in our minds. "You may string words together without a sentence sound to string them on," Frost remarked, "just as you may tie clothes together by the sleeve and stretch them without a clothesline between two trees, but—it is bad for the clothes."[7]

The words in a "sleeve-tied" sentence pull against each other discordantly and oppressively. For instance:

x The subject of rhythm in speech or writing is one of those subjects which deal with complex sets of interrelationships between multiple but not altogether specifiable variables such as rise-fall patterns and the like, which makes it a sea-to-wave and wave-to-wave kind of thing.

There is a near-absence of significant pauses here; we have to plod ahead two or three words at a time, trying not to become dizzy. All the nouns, furthermore, have about the same degree of stress on their accented syllables, and there is no alternation between brief, emphatic phrases and longer ones. Read the sentence aloud and you will hear its monotony.

Now compare this with the actual words of H. W. Fowler:

Rhythmic speech or writing is like waves of the sea, moving onward with alternating rise and fall, connected yet separate, like but different, suggestive of some law, too complex for analysis or statement, controlling the relations between wave and wave, waves and sea, phrase and phrase, phrases and speech.[8]

Although this sentence is elaborate in structure, we grasp it without much difficulty as it proceeds. Fowler's commas are like architectural supports that spare us the necessity of trying to bear the weight of the whole sentence at once. We see that one main clause is going to govern a sequence of phrases that will carry us along *like waves of the sea,* and our voice pauses naturally on accented syllables: *like wáves of the séa, móving ónward.* These long, heavily stressed vowels make a pleasing contrast with harsher, more staccato phrases like *Rhýthmic spéech or wríting.* Fowler has illustrated his principle of complex relationship in the act of naming it—as, for example, in his "like but different" sets of three-word phrases:

• connected yet separate, like but different
• waves and sea, phrase and phrase, phrases and speech

To return from Fowler's example to the first one is like going from navigation to seasickness.

For a different use of "sentence sounds," listen to this paragraph of Peter Matthiessen's about the Kilimanjaro area of east Africa. Matthiessen, in search of "the tree where man was born," comes across Maasai herdsmen at a pool:

> By the water's edge man squatted, worn rags pulled low over his brow against the sun. Manure smell, flies, the stamp and lowing of the herds, the heat. In the shallows a naked dancing boy darted and splashed. Then cloud shadow dimmed the water shine on his round head, and he turned black. In foreboding he paused; the water stilled, and clouds gathered in the water. He picked at his thin body, one-legged in the evanescent pool that will vanish in summer like the haze of green on this burning land.[9]

This prose gains some of its force from a bunching of strongly accented syllables:

- wáter's édge mán squátted, wórn rágs púlled lów
- Manúre sméll, flíes, the stámp and lówing of the hérds, the héat
- a náked dáncing bóy dárted and spláshed
- Thén clóud shádow dímmed the wáter shíne on his roúnd heád, and he túrned bláck
- the wáter stílled, and cloúds gáthered in the wáter
- He pícked at his thín bódy, oñe-légged in the eṽanéscent póol . . .

The jolting rhythm, accentuated by the shackled nouns *Manure smell, cloud shadow,* and *water shine,* is subtly loosened in the final clause, which comes closer to regular meter—that is, to an alternation of accented and unaccented syllables:

- that will vánish in súmmer like the háze of gréen on this búrning lánd.

Thus the paragraph as a whole accumulates tension and releases it like rain after thunder. The controlled uneasiness of Matthiessen's prose matches the vague ominousness of the scene: human life is precarious in this setting, and any change of weather seems to bear a threat of extinction.

The lesson here is that in reading and writing you should use your ear as well as your brain. Although the principles that go to make up a pleasing rhythm are too obscure to be stated as advice, by reading good stylists you can pick up a feeling for graceful and emphatic cadences.

EXERCISES

22. Here are several choppy sentences in a row. Using much of the same language but adding and subtracting where necessary, write a revised version that eliminates the problem of choppiness. You need not keep the same number of sentences.

> Atari was the pioneer in video games. The company ran into serious problems in the early 1980s. The trouble was that the real profits lay in software. Atari had invented the hardware. Any rival company could market programs that could run on Atari's console. Activision, Imagic, and Mattel's Intellivision quickly exploited that advantage. This happened as soon as they realized the opportunity before them. Atari's managers were so used to leading the field that they failed to realize they were being overtaken.

23. Here are five relatively plain sentences. Make each of them *cumulative* (p. 201) by adding end modifiers, and submit the revised versions. In one of your sentences, see how many elements you can add without making the result absurd or impossible to follow.

> A. Much more than transportation is provided by the bicycle.
> B. One virtue we should all treasure is sincerity.
> C. Before visiting Europe you would do well to become better acquainted with your own country.
> D. We find few heroes to admire in the 1980s.
> E What should be the penalty for growing marijuana?

24. Find five relatively plain sentences in your own writing, and submit them along with five expanded versions that have been made *cumulative* (p. 201). If you do not find sentences you can work with, invent them.

25. Submit *interrupted* variations on the five sentences you submitted for Exercise 24. (See pp. 201–202.) You need not include all the material used in those versions.

26. Starting from any five sentences, perhaps including some already used in this sequence of exercises, add the subordinate elements necessary to create five *suspended* sentences (pp. 202–203). You need not submit the versions you began from.

27. Submit five sentences illustrating the principle of *inversion* (p. 203). In each case underline the word or words that you have made more emphatic by means of the inverted structure.

28. Submit five numbered sets of two sentences each. In each pair, include one *question* or *exclamation* (p. 203) that is closely related to the other sentence.

29. Submit a whole paragraph that either begins or ends with a question or exclamation. You may choose any topic.

30. Taking the numbered sentences one by one, analyze all the elements of sentence variety that you find in the following paragraph:

> 1. In desperate fantasy one thinks, at times, of escaping. 2. From childhood there remains a faint memory, nearly lost, of a stream in a Northern forest: a stone dam, a trickling sluice, a hut of some sort where the dam-keeper lives. 3. The loon cries over a lake, the pines stretch endlessly, black against the sky. 4. And then one thinks of *The New York Times* on Sunday, five pounds of newsprint, a million-and-a-half copies a week. 5. How many miles of forest, birds flung from their nests, the work of honey bees wasted, does our Sunday paper, thrown aside between breakfast and lunch, consume?[10]

NOTES

[1]Adapted from Michael Field, *All Manner of Food* (New York: Knopf, 1970), pp. 4–5.

[2]Susanne K. Langer, "The Lord of Creation," *Fortune*, Jan. 1944, p. 140.

[3]Nora Ephron, "Seagrams with Moxie," *New York Times Book Review*, 11 Mar. 1979, p. 13.

[4]Joseph Epstein, "Running and Other Vices," *The American Scholar*, 48 (1979), 156.

[5]"Skiing Utah Powder," *Sunset*, Jan. 1976, p. 39.

[6]Virginia Woolf, *To the Lighthouse* (1927; rpt. New York: Harvest, 1955), p. 73.

[7]Quoted by Lawrence Thompson, *Robert Frost: The Early Years 1874–1915* (New York: Holt, 1966), p. 434.

[8]H. W. Fowler, *A Dictionary of Modern English Usage* (1926; rpt. n.p.: Oxford Univ. Press, 1937), p. 504.

[9]Peter Matthiessen, *The Tree Where Man Was Born* (New York: Dutton, 1972), p. 193.

[10]Jason Epstein, "Living in New York," *New York Review of Books*, 6 Jan. 1966, p. 15.

9

WORDS

If you want words to function effectively within your sentences, you will have to know them well and respect their often subtle differences from one another. Specifically, in revising your drafts you should make sure that your words mean what you think they mean; that they are appropriate to the occasion; that you have been concise; and that your language is as lively as your audience and purpose allow. We will look at these requirements one by one.

MEANING

Keep a Vocabulary List

The best long-range aid to strong **diction** (word choice) is frequent reading of good prose; words become serviceable to your writing only after you have seen them used accurately in other people's sentences. You can speed up the process, however, by systematically working to increase the number of words you have mastered.

the college dictionary   For this purpose it is essential that you own a college dictionary such as *The Random House College Dictionary, Funk and Wagnalls Standard College Dictionary, Webster's New World Dictionary of the American Language, Webster's New Collegiate Dictionary,* or *The American Heritage Dictionary of the English Language*. These dictionaries are large enough to meet all your needs without being too cumbersome to carry around. Once you learn (from the guide at the front) how to interpret your dictionary, it can be a source book for a wide variety of information: not only the spelling, parts of speech, definitions, alternate forms, pronunciation, capitalization, origins, usage levels, and syllable division of words, but also principles of usage, abbreviations, symbols, biographical and given names, places and population figures, weights and measures, and names and locations of colleges. And by scanning definitions and *synonyms*, or words with the same meaning, you can use your dictionary to remind you of alternatives to words you do not want to repeat.

   To see what a college dictionary can and cannot do, look at Random House's entry under *fabulous:*

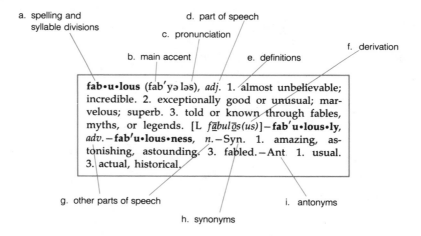

The entry shows, in the following order:

a.   how the word is spelled and the points where syllable divisions occur (*fab-u-lous*);

> *Comment:* The lower-case *f* shows that *fabulous* is not normally capitalized.
> If this word could be spelled correctly in different ways, the less common form would appear in a separate entry with a cross reference to the more common form; thus the entry for *reenforce* merely sends you to *reinforce*. In your writing, use the spelling under which a full definition has been given.
> Syllable division is not completely uniform from one dictionary to

another, but you cannot go wrong by following your dictionary's practice in every case. (You can also spare yourself trouble by not breaking up words at all; a little unevenness in right-hand margins is normal.)

b. where the main accent falls *(fab')*;

> *Comment:* If the word has another strongly stressed syllable, like *hand* in *beforehand*, you would find it marked with a secondary accent: *bi • for'hand'*.

c. how the word is pronounced;

> *Comment:* The pronunciation key at the bottom of every pair of pages reveals, among other things, that ǝ = *a* as in *alone*. (One dictionary's key will differ from another's.) College dictionaries make no attempt to capture regional or nonstandard pronunciations, like *n$\overline{oo}$⁻' cul • ǝr* for *n$\overline{oo}$'kl$\overline{e}$ • ǝr* (nuclear).

d. the part of speech *(adj.* for *adjective)*;

> *Comment:* Some words, like *can* and *wait*, occupy more than one part of speech, depending on the context. Definitions are grouped according to those parts of speech. Transitive verbs (those that take an object — p. 247) are usually listed separately from intransitive verbs (those that take no object — p. 247). Thus Random House gives all the intransitive senses of *wait (v.i.)* before the transitive senses *(v.t.)*, as in *Wait your turn!*

e. three definitions;

> *Comment:* No dictionary lists definitions in the order of their acceptability. The dictionary illustrated here begins with the most common part of speech occupied by a given word and, within each part of speech, offers the most frequently encountered meaning first. Some other dictionaries begin with the earliest meaning and proceed toward the present. The system used in your dictionary is clearly set forth in the prefatory material, which you should read through at least once.

f. the word's derivation from the first three syllables of the Latin word *fabulosus*;

> *Comment:* the derivation or *etymology* of a word is given only if its component parts are not obviously familiar — as they are, for example, in *freeze-dry* and *nearsighted*. Many symbols are used in stating etymologies; look for their explanation in the prefatory material of your dictionary.

g. an adverb and a noun stemming from the main word;

> *Comment: Fabulously* and *fabulousness* are "run-on entries," words formed by adding a suffix (ending) to the main entry.

h. synonyms of definitions 1 and 3;

> *Comment:* In most dictionaries a word with many apparent synonyms is accompanied by a "synonym study" explaining fine differences. Thus, this dictionary's entry for *strength* concludes:

> —**Syn. 4.** STRENGTH, POWER, FORCE, MIGHT suggest capacity to do something. STRENGTH is inherent capacity to manifest energy, to endure, and to resist. POWER is capacity to do work and to act. FORCE is the exercise of power: *One has the power to do something. He exerts force when he does it. He has sufficient strength to complete it.* MIGHT is power or strength in a great degree: *the might of an army.*

> This would be useful information if you were wondering which of the four similar words to use in a sentence. If you looked up *power, force,* or *might,* you would find a cross reference to the synonym study under *strength.*

i. antonyms (words with the opposite meaning) of definitions 1 and 3.

> *Comment:* If you are searching for a word to convey the opposite of a certain term, check its listed antonyms. But if you still are not satisfied, look up the entries for the most promising antonyms and check their synonyms. This will greatly expand your range of choice.

In addition, two typical features of dictionary entries are not illustrated here. If the word has uncommon or dubious *inflected forms*—that is, changes expressing different syntactic functions—the entry will supply them. Such forms include unusual plurals (*louse, lice*); unusual principal parts of verbs (*run, ran, run*—see p. 248); pronoun forms (*I, my, mine,* etc.); and comparative and superlative degrees of adjectives (*good, better, best*—see pp. 263–264). Also, every dictionary offers *restrictive labels* where necessary. Those labels, often abbreviated, indicate the region where a word is used in a given sense (*Southern U.S., Austral., Chiefly Brit.*); a rare or obsolete term or meaning (*Archaic, Obs., Poetic.*); the subject or discipline within which a certain meaning is understood (*Bot., Anat., Law*); and, most important for the writer, the level of usage for words not clearly within standard American English (*Nonstandard, Informal, Slang*).

Beyond its usage labels, your dictionary may offer especially valuable *usage studies* for certain controversial words or meanings, such as *ain't, different from/than,* or *hardly* with negative forms:

> **—Usage.** HARDLY, BARELY, and SCARCELY all have a negative connotation, and the use of any of them with a supplementary negative is considered non-standard, as in *I can't hardly wait* for *I can hardly wait.*

Writers are sometimes advised to use a *thesaurus* (a dictionary of synonyms and antonyms) as a way of avoiding repetitiousness in their prose. But there is a danger here. Synonyms are rarely exact, and the thesaurus will not indicate fine differences of meaning. The risk of inaccuracy or faulty tone is great when you borrow unfamiliar terms. It is important not only to build your vocabulary, but also to keep new words out of your writing until you have seen how other writers use them.

the continuing list   The more familiar you are with the way your dictionary works, the more often you will consult it. Your efforts to build vocabulary, however, will be more efficient if you are willing to take some extra trouble:

1. Whenever someone criticizes your use of a word or you come across an unfamiliar word in your reading, look it up or make a note of it until you can get back to your dictionary.
2. After you have looked it up, write the word and its definition on a note-book page.
3. Every time you add an entry, quickly scan the previous entries to see if you have mastered them yet. Cross out entries that you now consider to be part of your normal working vocabulary.

Avoid Common Confusions of Meaning

Increasing your effective vocabulary is by no means simply a matter of memorizing "big words" that are seldom used. It is much more important that you overcome misunderstandings about ordinary words, some of them as small and essential as *its* and *whose*. You may think it odd at first that such words could make for trouble. The trouble, however, arises not from the words themselves but from their resemblance to quite different words *(it's, who's)*. Then, too, some words look and sound different *(few, little)* but are close enough in meaning to become confused.

When you do confuse one word with another, the readability of your sentence may be drastically reduced, and, what is worse, you will make an impression of carelessness or incompetence. Be alert, then, for the following distinctions that young writers often fail to observe, and take note of any other word pairs that have caused trouble in your previously submitted papers.

accept, except   *Accept* is a verb meaning *take* or *receive. Except* is sometimes a verb meaning *exclude,* but more often a preposition meaning *excluding: I accept everything except that.*

adapt, adopt   To *adapt* something is to *change it for a purpose: He adapted the Constitution to his own ends.* To *adopt* something is to *take control or possession* of it: *He adopted the Constitution as his Bible.*

affect, effect   As a verb, *affect* means to *influence: This affected the outcome.* The verb *effect* means to *bring about: She effected a stunning reversal.* When *effect* is a noun, it means *result: The effect of the treatment was slight.*

all ready, already   The two words *all ready* mean that everything is ready; *already* is an adverb meaning *so early. Already, they are all ready.*

allusion, illusion   An *allusion* is a *passing reference: an allusion to quantum theory.* An *illusion* is *something that deceives by giving a false impression: the illusion of prosperity.* The common error is to use *allusion* for *illusion,* as in x *His supposed power over women was an allusion.*

amount, number   Use *amount* for total quantities that are not being considered as units: *the amount of the debt; a large amount of radiation. Number* is for countable items: *a small number of crabs.* The common error is to use *amount* for *number,* as in x *The amount of people in the hall was extraordinary.*

angry, mad   In serious writing, *mad* doesn't mean *angry* but *insane: She was so angry that she went mad.*

a while, awhile   *While* is a noun, as in *a while ago. Awhile* is an adverb: *I worked awhile.* Do not write x *awhile ago* or x *I worked a while.*

beside, besides   *Beside* means *at the side of; besides* means *in addition to. Besides her father and the groom, no one stood beside Susanna at the altar.*

born, borne   The first has to do with birth, the second with carrying. But note that pregnancy is itself a form of carrying: *She had borne six children.*

compare, contrast   *Compare* means either *make a comparison* or *liken.* To compare something *with* something else is to make a comparison between them; the comparison may show either a resemblance or a difference. To compare something *to* something else is to assert a resemblance between them. To *contrast,* however, is always to emphasize differences: *He contrasted the gentle Athenians with the warlike Spartans.*

complement, compliment   As nouns, *complement* means *something that completes or accompanies,* and *compliment* means *an expression of praise: As a complement to the presentation, she complimented the organizers.*

continual, continuous   *Continual* means *recurring at intervals; continuous* means *uninterrupted. The screaming of ambulance sirens was continual, but the whirring of the fan was continuous.*

convince, persuade   *Convince* means *win agreement; persuade* means *move to action. If I convince you that I am right, I may persuade you to join me.* The common error is to use *convince* for *persuade*, as in ₓ *I convinced him to join.*

disinterested, uninterested   Many writers use both to mean *not interested,* but in doing so they lose the unique meaning of *disinterested* as *impartial: a disinterested umpire.*

doubtful, dubious   Someone who feels doubt is *doubtful;* an outcome or statement may be *dubious. She felt doubtful about the dubious assertion.*

eminent, imminent   *Eminent* means *prominent: He became eminent as an economist. Imminent* means *about to happen: The outbreak of war was imminent.*

enormity, enormousness   The common error is to use *enormity,* which properly means *atrociousness,* in place of *enormousness,* or *of great size:* ₓ *the enormity of his feet.*

every one, everyone   The two words *every one* mean *each one; everyone* means *everybody.* The common error is to substitute *everyone* for *every one,* as in ₓ *Everyone of your arguments is false.*

few, little   *Few,* like *number,* refers to countable items; *little,* like *amount,* refers to total quantities that are not being considered as units. *Few people were on hand, and the speaker aroused little enthusiasm.*

flaunt, flout   To *flaunt* is to *display arrogantly: They flaunted their superior wisdom.* To *flout* is to *defy contemptuously: They flouted all the rules.*

good, well   *You look good tonight* means that you make a pleasant impression; *you look well tonight* means that you do not look sick.

ignorant, stupid   To be *ignorant* of something is not to know it: *Newton was ignorant of relativity.* To be *stupid* is to be mentally incapable of learning: *The main cause of his ignorance was his stupidity.*

imaginary, imaginative   *Imaginary,* meaning *unreal* or *imagined,* is sometimes wrongly displaced by *imaginative,* which should always mean *showing imagination.* Do not write ₓ *I reject that idea as totally imaginative.*

imply, infer   To *imply* is to *leave an implication;* to *infer* is to *take one. She implied that she would stay, but he inferred from her embarrassed manner that she would leave.*

incidence, incident   *Incidence* means *rate of occurrence: the incidence of crime.* An *incident* is *one occurrence.* Do not write ₓ *The crowd dispersed without incidence.*

in to, into   The words *in to* combine direction with purpose: *We went in to do* *some shopping. Into* indicates direction only: *We went into town.* The common error is to use *in to* in sentences like this second one.

it's, its   *It's* is a contraction of the subject-verb combination *it is; its* is a possessive pronoun. Do not write x *Its amusing* or x *it's turn.*

lay, lie   *Lay* usually means *set,* and it always takes an object: *lay it here.* If you mean *repose,* use *lie: lie down.* The common error is x *lay down.* In the past tense, *lay* becomes *laid: They laid it here. Lie* becomes *lay: He lay down.*

many, much   *Many,* like *number* and *few,* refers to countable items; *much,* like *amount* and *little,* refers to total quantities that are not being considered as units. *Many problems make for much difficulty.* The common error is to use *much* for *many,* as in x *There were too much people there.*

oral, verbal   *Oral* means *by mouth; verbal* means *in words,* whether or not the words are spoken. Do not write x *a verbal presentation* unless you have in mind a contrast with some form of communication that doesn't involve words.

persecute, prosecute   To *persecute* is to *single out for mistreatment;* to *prosecute* is to *bring to trial. They persecuted him by prosecuting him on a false charge.*

precede, proceed   To *precede* is to *go ahead of;* to *proceed* is to *go forward. The king preceded his courtiers as they proceeded toward the castle.*

predominant, predominate   *Predominant* is an adjective, *predominate* a verb. Do not write x *a predominate idea.*

prejudice, prejudiced   *Prejudice* is a noun; *prejudiced* is a past participle often used as an adjective. The common error is to use *prejudice* adjectivally: x *He is prejudice.*

rebut, refute   To *rebut* an argument is to *oppose* it; to *refute* an argument is to *disprove* it. The common error is to use *refute* for *rebut:* x *You may be right, but I will refute what you said.*

replace, substitute   *Replace* takes as its object the term being abandoned: *She replaced her large old car with a small new one. Substitute* takes as its object the new item: *She substituted a small new car for her large old one.*

sensual, sensuous   *Sensual* means *carnal, voluptuous,* or *having to do with sex: a sensual magazine. Sensuous* means *pertaining to the senses* or *showing a general receptivity to the senses: Frostbite impaired his sensuous powers.*

set, sit   *Set* usually takes an object: *set the table. Sit* usually takes no object: *She sat down.* The common error is to use *set* for *sit,* as in x *He just sets there all day.*

some time, sometime, sometimes   The two words *some time* mean *a span of time: It took some time to get there. Sometime* means *at an unspecified time: We will have to meet again sometime. Sometimes* means *now and then: We sometimes quarrel.*

usage, use   *Usage* implies custom or convention: *English usage.* When you simply mean *employment, use* is the right word. Do not write x *He discouraged the usage of cocaine.*

who's, whose   *Who's* is a contraction of the subject-verb combination *who is: Who's coming to dinner? Whose* is a possessive pronoun: *Whose turn is it?*

you're, your   *You're* is a contraction of the subject-verb combination *you are: You're all right. Your* is a possessive pronoun: *your virtues.*

Once you realize that you have confused one word with another, you would do well to put both of the words into your vocabulary list, reminding yourself pointedly of the difference between them.

EXERCISES

1. Once your vocabulary list (p. 212) has begun to grow, copy and submit any five entries, including a definition for each word.

2. After consulting your dictionary, use your own words to write brief definitions of both terms in each of the following pairs:

    A. accent, accentuate *(verbs)*
    B. accused, suspected *(adjectives)*
    C. adverse, averse
    D. alternate, alternative *(adjectives)*
    E. barbaric, barbarous
    F. childish, childlike
    G. elemental, elementary
    H. healthful, healthy
    I. infect, infest
    J. possible, feasible

3. Using your dictionary as necessary, explain the chief differences of denotation, or dictionary meaning, between the following paired words:

    A. ample, excessive
    B. avenue, road
    C. cunning, politic
    D. overhear, spy
    E. ecstatic, happy
    F. bold, brash
    G. erotic, lustful
    H. impartial, indifferent
    I. simulate, fake
    J. opponent, enemy

Control Connotations

Knowing the denotations, or dictionary definitions, of the words you use is the major requirement for controlling meaning, but it is not the only one. Words also carry **connotations**—further suggestions or associations—based on the ways in which the words have been habitually used. By and large, you will not find connotations in your dictionary; you have to pick them up from encountering the same words over and over in reading and conversation. As with denotation, you obviously cannot hold yourself accountable for all the connotations of every word you meet. But you *can* ask yourself whether the words you have allowed into your first drafts have connotations that might work against your intended emphasis.

Take, for example, the words *teacher* and *educator*. Because of the contexts in which they most often appear, the words *connote* different things. When we think of a teacher, we immediately see someone in front of a classroom, lecturing and scribbling on the blackboard; a teacher is someone directly engaged with students. The word *educator*, by contrast, has a bureaucratic ring; it calls to mind principals, curriculum coordinators, and theorists of education. If you were writing about dedicated, overworked, underpaid young instructors lacking job security, you would hardly want to call them *educators*; the connotations of the word would be opposing your purpose.

If connotations can only be inferred from wide reading, how can you control them in your essays? The answer is twofold: (1) you can restrict the vocabulary of your essays to words whose connotations you do understand, and (2) you will often find, simply through reflection, that you know more about a word's connotations than you thought you did.

Think about two examples, *complex* versus *complicated* and *workers* versus *employees*. Although the members of each pair are approximate **synonyms**—words with the same meaning—on the denotative level, you probably sense that their connotations differ. Suppose you wanted to characterize the overelaborate language you had found in an instruction manual; would you call it *complex* or *complicated*? I hope you would choose *complicated*, which implies, not just intricacy (as *complex* does) but *needless* intricacy. Or again, if you were criticizing inhuman factory conditions, would you write about *workers* or *employees*? Don't those words have slightly different "flavors" for you? They denote exactly the same people, but *employees* encourages us to see them from a corporate point of view, as people whose identity and livelihood are tied to the company. *Workers*, the better word in this case, suggests people who labor for wages without having much say about the nature of their work and without necessarily feeling any ties to the company.

A word of warning. In discussing control of tone (pp. 16–17, 74–76), we saw that there is such a thing as getting connotations too lopsidedly in your favor. If you weight your language with prejudgments of an issue (pp. 63–65), slandering your opponents and implying that no sane person could disagree with your position, you empty your argument of meaningful substance. Choose words, then, whose connotations accurately express your meaning, not words suggesting an inflexible bias.

Use Words in Established Senses

Many words that everyone now considers "good English" won their respectability only after decades of resistance from offended purists. We cannot say which of today's new terms will be noncontroversial twenty years from now; many of them will certainly have disappeared. As a writer, you have to consider those of your readers who regard new usages with horror. By being conservative in your choice of words, you can avoid arousing automatically negative responses.

Many faddish-sounding words have a common feature: they belong to one part of speech but are being used as another. Sometimes a suffix such as *-wise* or *-type* has been hastily added to turn a noun into an adverb or adjective: *Preferencewise, she was looking for a commuter-type car.* More often, a noun is appropriated as a verb (to *author* a book, to *gift* the newlyweds), a noun or adverb becomes an adjective (a *fun* party, a *together* person), or a verb becomes a noun (a long *quote*, an effective *rewrite*).

The use of nouns as adjectives deserves special mention in the age of bureaucratese. Standard English allows some latitude for such attributive nouns, as they are called, but officials have a way of jamming them together in a confusing heap. A frugal governor, for example, once proposed what he called a *community work experience program demonstration project.* This row of attributive nouns was meant to describe, or perhaps to conceal, a policy of getting welfare mothers to pick up highway litter without receiving any wages.

Prefer Middle Diction

We saw in Chapter 1 (pp. 16–17) that despite the many options a writer faces in choosing a voice, tone, and stance, a "middle way" generally suits the audience and purpose of a college essay. That is, you can usually get the best results by trying to sound straightforward, unpretentious, and engaged in your topic, steering between the extremes of self-display and impersonality. Not surprisingly, one of the main components of the middle way is **middle diction**—language that is neither too casual to express serious concern nor too stiff and pompous to express feeling. Such language appears in the middle column below:

informal	middle	formal
mug	face	visage
kicks	pleasure	gratification
dude	man	individual
threads	clothes	attire
specs	glasses	spectacles
rip off	steal	expropriate
hard-nosed	stubborn	recalcitrant

mixed diction This is not to say that all your words have to come from the same level of diction. *Ironical* writers—those who say one thing while hinting that they mean something quite different—sometimes make droll shifts between formal and informal diction, as in this sentence about New Year's Eve:

> I, as is customary in my household, will remain sequestered, give the servants the night off, perhaps whip up a light quiche, reflect on the vagaries of the year past with a coterie of my more thoughtful associates and then, of course, get smashed out of my melon.[1]

The wild diversity of language in this sentence, from *sequestered* and *vagaries* and *coterie* to *smashed out of my melon*, is of course deliberate; the writer wants us to understand at the end that the whole statement has been a hoax.

Avoid Offensive Language

slurs and stereotypes Since you are writing to convince, not to insult, nothing can be gained from using terms that shock and offend people. Some readers, of course, would not mind obscene words; but neither would they mind the generally acceptable alternatives that you ought to prefer. Extensive use of "dirty language" proves only that you are more interested in sounding tough than in winning agreement to your ideas. Racial slurs like *nigger, honky,* and *wop* and demeaning stereotypes like *pushy Jew* and *dumb Swede* are inexcusable. And sexually biased phrases such as *lady driver, schoolgirl gush, female logic,* and *typical male brutality* mark their user as a prisoner of condescending stereotypes.

sexism: names, titles, . . . Sexism in language has become an especially sensitive topic in recent years. You would be foolish as well as obtuse to include depersonalizing terms like *chick, tomato,* and *broad* in your serious essays; and "humorous" use of such words is rarely funny. Less obviously, you should realize that the word equivalent to *man* is *woman,* not *lady* or *girl* or *gal.* If William Shakespeare is *Shakespeare* in your prose, then Emily Dickinson should be *Dickinson,* not *Miss Dickinson* or *Emily.* And designations such as *authoress* and *lady lawyer* should be avoided for their objectionable hint that genuine, normal authors and lawyers are always men. Even *coed* should be dropped on these grounds; it insinuates that the higher education of women is an afterthought to the real (male) thing.

Yet because the idea of sexism is relatively new, and because different groups have reached different stages of resentment against sex-weighted language, it is not easy to say how far you should go toward purging English of its longstanding favoritism to the male. The title *Ms.,* which does not indicate marital status, is becoming well established as the female counterpart to *Mr.,* and you cannot go wrong by changing *stewardess* to *flight attendant* and *cleaning lady* to *housekeeper. Actress* and *waitress,* on the other hand, have so far resisted all pressure to step aside for genderless words; if you used *actor* and *waiter* to indicate women, readers would be misled or taken aback. Are *mankind, man-made,* and *chairman* offensive? More and more readers believe they are. You can substitute *humanity* for *mankind* and *artificial* for *man-made,* without attracting notice; but *chairperson,* though it is rapidly becoming common, will still bother some readers. Many people find *person*-suffixed words clumsy and self-conscious. Before using one, see if you can find a truly neutral alternative: not *chairperson* but *head,* not *congressperson* but *representative,* not *policeperson* but *officer,* not *weatherperson* but *meteorologist.*

. . . and common gender The sorest of all issues in contemporary usage is that of the so-called *common gender.* Which pronouns should be used when an indefinite person, a "one," is being discussed? Traditionally, that indefinite person has been "male": *he, his, him,* an in *A taxpayer must check his return carefully.* For the centuries in which this practice went unchallenged, the masculine pronouns in such sentences were understood to designate, not actual men, but people of either sex. Today, however, many readers find those words an offensive reminder of second-class citizenship for women. Remedies that have been proposed range from using *he or she* (or *she or he*) for the common gender, to treating singular common words as plural (*A taxpayer must check their return*), to combining masculine and feminine pronouns in forms like *s/he,* to using *she* in one sentence and *he* in the next.

Unfortunately, all of these solutions carry serious drawbacks. Continual repetition of *he or she* is cumbersome and monotonous; most readers would regard *A taxpayer must check their return* as a blunder, not a blow for liberation; pronunciation of *s/he* is uncertain; and the use of *she* and *he* in alternation, though increasingly common, risks confusing the reader by implying that two indefinite persons, a female and a male, are involved:

x A telephone operator cannot afford to lose *her* temper. Some of *his* conversations are routinely taped and reviewed by *his* supervisor. *She* will be in trouble if. . . .

To avoid such awkwardness, follow these guidelines:

1. Use *she* whenever you are sure the indefinite person would be a female (a student in a women's college, for example).
2. Do not use *she* for roles that are "traditionally female" but actually mixed: filing clerks, grade-school teachers, laundry workers, etc. Points 3 through 5 will help you in such cases.
3. Use an occasional *he or she* or *she or he* to indicate an indefinite person. But be sparing with this formula.
4. Avoid the singular whenever your meaning is not affected: *Taxpayers must check their returns.*
5. Omit the pronoun altogether wherever you can do so without awkwardness: not *Everyone needs his or her vacation* but *Everyone needs a vacation.*

EXERCISES

4. Explain whatever differences of *connotation* (pp. 217–218) you find between the following paired words:

   A. stout, fat
   B. express, communicate
   C. hasten, scurry
   D. talented, gifted
   E. investigate, inquire

5. Submit a paragraph of your own prose written for this or any other course. Circle three words whose connotations strike you as appropriate to your precise intention. Then, beneath the paragraph, briefly discuss the connotations of all three words, contrasting them with the connotations of three other words that would have proved less appropriate. (Your rival choices should be "near misses," not wildly implausible terms.)

6. Rewrite the following sentences to eliminate *words not used in established senses* (p. 218) and *sexist implications* (pp. 219–221):

   A. Betsy was enthused to discover that her relating to men problems, along with all her other problems, were covered in Dr. Dollar's new book.
   B. He gifted her with an autographed copy of the work he had authored.
   C. Any reasonable person and his wife or girlfriend could learn something from Dr. Dollar.
   D. Betsy was unsure how literally to interpret the publisher's complete-satisfaction-guaranteed assurance.

E. She didn't know whether to believe Dr. Dollar's assertion that the universe was already pulsating with all the love a chick could wish, but she knew that *Three Easy Steps to Perfection* was a start-to-finish good read.

7. Use your dictionary, if necessary, to help you decide which level of diction (formal, middle, or informal) is illustrated by each of the following words. Whenever you label a word as formal or informal, provide a middle-level equivalent (pp. 218–219):

   A. irritate
   B. hyperbole
   C. birdbrain
   D. groovy
   E. fluoridate
   F. refractory *(adjective)*
   G. indemnify
   H. gal
   I. oafish
   J. resist

8. For each of the following middle-level words; give one formal and one informal equivalent:

   A. friend
   B. understand
   C. smell *(noun)*
   D. clothes
   E. rob
   F. see
   G. idea
   H. change *(verb)*
   I. leave *(verb)*
   J. good

9. Return to the "airplane food" paragraph on page 5, and examine its language. Submit a paragraph or two showing how the writer has achieved her effect in part by controlling levels of diction. Be specific in citing her words.

CONCISENESS

Avoid Redundancy and Circumlocution

Your reader's alertness will depend in large part on the ratio between information and language in your prose. The fewer words you can use without harm to your meaning, the better.

redundancy   A **redundancy** is an expression that conveys the same meaning more than once. Thus *circle around* is redundant because the idea of *around* is already contained in *circle*; *new innovation* says nothing not already apparent in *innovation*; *shuttle back and forth* is a redundancy for *shuttle*; and a *personal friend* is simply a *friend* accompanied by an irrelevant adjective.

Your first drafts, like those of any writer, will almost certainly contain redundancies that you can expose by constantly applying the test *Is this word necessary?* Finding *advance planning* in one of your sentences, you should ask whether *advance* says anything not contained in *planning.* No; so out it goes. *Share in common* fails the same test and should be reduced to *share; deliberate lie* becomes *lie, set of twins* becomes *twins, adequate enough* becomes either *adequate* or *enough,* and so on. The revision makes for a cleaner, more purposeful effect.

circumlocution   All redundancies fall into the broader category of **circumlocutions** —that is, roundabout forms of expression. But some circumlocutions, instead of saying the same thing twice, say next to nothing in a ponderous phrase. Formulas like *in a manner of speaking* and *to make a long story short* are simply ways of sounding deliberate or perhaps of making a short story long.

Some circumlocutions are so brief that they might almost be mistaken for concise phrasing. Yet even the most inconspicuous use of wordiness saps a reader's attention. If you have written *He was of a kindly nature,* pare it to *He was kind,* and your prose will be slightly more energetic. Instead of writing *It was of an unusual character,* try *It was unusual.* Do not surrender at once to cumbersome verb phrases like *give rise to, make contact with,* and *render inoperative;* prefer *arouse, meet,* and *destroy.* And if you mean *because,* do not settle for *due to the fact that.* When five words do the work of one, all five sound anemic.

To develop an aversion to circumlocutions, you might try to use as much padding as you can in one gruesome paragraph. For example:

> As far as the wolf was concerned, Little Red Riding Hood was basically a person who was acting, rightly or wrongly, on the hypothesis that by dint of exhibiting a tendency to girlish charm, so to speak, she might play a leading role in militating against being devoured. The contributing factors, by and large, that entered the area of concern that indicated a less sanguine conclusion had the effect, frankly speaking, of rendering inconsequential whatever ambitions the diminutive lass might have possessed in terms of establishing truly positive relations with a beast who was one of such a disputatious and unpredictable nature. It stood to reason that with respect to a simple-type female along the lines of herself, and with a viewpoint toward clarifying for a certainty the premises that might take effect should the wolf succeed in giving grounds for apprehension, Little Red Riding Hood felt strongly impelled toward the posing of a query serving the purpose of allowing the wolf to give expression to his intentions in a forthright manner and to the fullest extent. In this instance, however, things soon came to the point that further speculation either pro or con, as the case may have been, was reduced to zero—as, to make a long story short, was our heroine herself.

Prune Intensifiers

In conversation most of us use **intensifiers**—"fortifying" words like *absolutely, basically, certainly, definitely, incredibly, intensely, just, of course, perfectly, positively, quite, really, simply,* and *very*—without pausing to worry about their meaning, if any. These terms bolster our morale as we pick our way through a maze of half-formed ideas; their actual sense is *maybe* or *I hope.* Our friends have to forgive us for talking this way, so that they in turn can be forgiven. But written prose is expected to convey fully developed thoughts, and readers are impatient with writers who include intensifiers just for their re-assuring sound. If you mean *very* you can write it without apology, but first make sure you do mean it; most of the intensifiers in a typi-cal first draft deserve to be pruned.

While we are talking, we do not hunt for adjectives to express the exact degree of our enthusiasm or dismay. We veer toward the ex-tremes of *fantastic, terrific, sensational, fabulous,* and *awful, horrible, ter-rible, dreadful.* In print these words are often doubly inaccurate: they misrepresent the author's true mood and they violate their own proper meaning. Something *fantastic* should have to do with fan-tasy; *dreadful* means "inspiring dread." Do not, in a serious essay, write *I am awfully glad* or *It was terribly thoughtful of him to come* —unless the one who came was Dracula.

Put Statements in Positive Form

Negative ideas are just as legitimate as positive ones; you may have to point out that something did not happen or that an argument leaves you unconvinced. But the negative modifiers *no* and *not* sometimes make for wordiness and a slight loss of readability. If you write *We are not in agreement,* you are asking your reader to go through two steps, first to conceive of agreement and then to negate that conception. If, instead, you write *We disagree,* you have saved three words and simplified the mental operation. The gain is small, but good writing results from a sum of small gains.

Of course you need not develop a phobia against every use of *no* or *not.* Observe, however, that negatively worded sentences tend to be slightly less emphatic than positive ones. Compare:

NEGATIVE	POSITIVE
She did not do well on the test.	She did poorly on the test.
He was not convicted.	He was acquitted.
They have no respect for rationing.	They despise rationing.

EXERCISES

10. Type out or photocopy a paragraph of your own prose that now strikes you as containing several redundancies, circumlocutions, and/or needless intensifiers. Underline the wordy expressions, and submit the paragraph along with a concise revised version.

11. Go back to the "Little Red Riding Hood" paragraph on page 223, and write a similar paragraph about any other well-known story, packing every line with roundabout expressions. Submit your paragraph along with a concise version containing the same information.

12. Without reversing the meaning of these negatively framed sentences, make them more concise and emphatic by rewriting them, replacing all *not* constructions with stronger words:

   A. It is not unlikely that Biff will try to return his own kickoff.
   B. A person who does not go into cities when it is not necessary will not experience some fine pleasures.
   C. The Easter Bunny did not like hearing himself described as a basket case.
   D. He did not agree with the mental-health experts who did not approve of hiding painted eggs in gardens.
   E. Few of his critics, he suspected, were not subject to little quirks of their own that didn't harm anyone.

LIVELINESS

Certain kinds of writing, we have seen, call for prose that conveys facts neutrally, drawing as little attention to itself as possible (pp. 5–6). In a typical "English essay," however, you want your language to sparkle. It should contain concrete and vivid terms; it should avoid stale phrases; it should show imagination as well as sober logic; and its "sound effects" should reinforce your meaning, not interfere with it.

Revise toward Concreteness

You have already been introduced to the difference between *concrete* and *abstract* language (p. 23). Concrete words convey observable things or properties like *classroom* and *smoky*, whereas abstract words convey intangible ideas like *education* and *pollution*. Of course there are gradations between the extremes: a *university* is more concrete than *education* but less so than a *classroom*, which is a distinct physical place. The more concrete the term, the more vivid it will be to a reader. Thus it is a sound idea to strive for concreteness wherever possible.

Here, for example, are two versions of a student paragraph. In drafting the first, the writer was evidently thinking of himself as a social-science major. When asked to revise for an essay audience, he looked for ways of turning abstract statements into concrete ones:

A.   Lasting trauma from early stress is probably causally related to two fac-
     tors: heritability of susceptibility and the age at which the stress occurs.
     In infant rhesus monkeys, certain members of the experimental popula-
     tion prove more susceptible to permanent disturbance than others; herit-
     ability is thus an indicated factor. Furthermore, the entire population
     yields a finding of greater vulnerability when administration of stress oc-
     curs between the precise ages of two and seven months. Such a finding
     suggests that among humans, too, a period of maximum vulnerability
     may obtain.

B.   A recent study of rhesus monkeys may offer us some clues to the way
     people react—and sometimes don't react—to early stress. Baby monkeys
     who have been put into solitary cages tend to become feisty and to stay
     that way. We might have expected as much. But some monkeys, oddly,
     act normal again almost as soon as they have rejoined their fellows; it
     seems that they have inherited a resistance to trauma. Furthermore, the
     most aggressive monkeys turn out to be those who were isolated within
     a precise period, between the ages of two and seven months. If these
     findings carry over to humans, we can see why it is risky to generalize
     about the effects of *all* early stress. What matters may not be whether
     you suffered in infancy, but who your parents were and exactly when
     your ordeal occurred.

Neither of these paragraphs abounds in concrete language, but the *relative* concreteness of passage B helps to explain why it is easier to grasp and more pleasurable to read. Note that weighty, awkward abstractions like *heritability of susceptibility* have disappeared and that we now see *Baby monkeys . . . in solitary cages*, not a *population* that has undergone *administration of stress*.

Accomplished writers do not shrink from abstract language, how-ever, when they want to get from the mere fact of a thing to its sig-nificance. Turn back, for example, to the paragraph on yo-yoing on page 49. Should we criticize its author for relying on the abstract terms *pleasure, dramatization, laws, geometric purity, enactment of theo-rems, idea, energy, momentum,* and *nothing*? His paragraph succeeds because he has been able to show precisely how his intellect was en-gaged by the abstract properties of a childhood toy. The effect he achieves is very different from that of a writer who typically *hides* his meaning behind abstractions. Such a writer, given the same theme, might have foggily invoked *the illustration of various physical laws by the component elements of toys, the discipline of mastery of diverse tech-*

niques, and combined intellectual and aesthetic satisfactions, without describing the activity itself.

Avoid Formulaic Language

Writers struggling with elusive ideas in a first draft cannot afford to be finicky about the language they scribble out. Almost inevitably, some of that language will consist of **formulaic** (ready-made) expressions: *clichés* or *jargon* or *euphemisms*. These are phrases that pop into mind because they have been seen and heard everywhere. And that is just why they should be eliminated in a later draft; language that has been used to cover any number of vague meanings cannot pinpoint your particular meaning in a lively way.

clichés   **Clichés** are conventional expressions that have lost their vividness through overuse. When someone writes *off the wall* or *the bottom line,* no reader sees a wall or a line. And as soon as the first part of the formula has appeared, the rest of it is numbingly predictable. The reader who sees *nuclear* knows that *holocaust* will follow; what is *foreseeable* must of course be the *future;* a *mixture* is *heady,* praise is *unstinted,* and so on. The resultant prose—*to be brutally frank*—is a *far cry* from being a *sure winner* in the *minds and hearts* of readers *from every walk of life.*

We all use clichés when speaking, and few of our listeners seem to mind. But writers who habitually resort to clichés—who describe money as *filthy lucre,* whose indifference to language comes *from the bottom of their hearts* and whose meaning is lost *like a needle in a haystack*—end by sounding careless and lazy. And they do not improve matters by bracing their clichés with quotation marks or by inserting *so to speak* or *as the saying goes,* as if to assure us that they, too, know a cliché when they spot one.

It is fairly easy, in the process of revision, to catch gross clichés such as *bring home the bacon, conspicuous by its absence, eat one's cake and have it too,* and *a miss is as good as a mile.* More insidious are harmless-looking pairs of "inseparable" adjectives and nouns (*supreme moment, vicious circle, vital role*) and the pat phrases that lend pseudo-importance to a statement (*it stands to reason, far be it from me, in a very real sense, in the last analysis*). Such handy expressions are *a snare and a delusion,* for they are *part and parcel* of recognizably weak prose.

jargon   Technical terms have technical uses, and you need not apologize for them if the technical meaning is the one you must have. There are important differences between *liquidity* and *cash, ego* and *self, kinship structure* and *family, bankrupt* and *poor, metabolic* and *digestive.* Technical terms become jargon only when ordinary terms would have conveyed all that was meant. Then vividness inevitably suffers, for the jargon term, precisely because of its restricted meaning, fails to convey the writer's *general* idea. If, for example, you write *My kinship structure extends from coast to coast,* you have not only made a pretentious borrowing from anthropology, you have also clouded your meaning; a *kinship structure* is an abstract relationship, not a totality of actual relatives. The same kind of blurring would occur if you wrote *ecosystem* when you simply meant *area,* or *goal-oriented* for *purposeful,* or *reinforcement schedule* for *inducements.* To trade clarity for a pompously learned air is a poor bargain.

Popular academic fields such as sociology and psychology have contributed much to contemporary jargon, for their subject matter is close to everyday affairs. Thus users of **sociologese**, hoping to sound scientific, not only write *sociological* when they mean *social* but also use *upwardly mobile* for *ambitious* and *parameters* for *borders.* Instead of seeing a *resemblance* between two things, they place those things *on a continuum,* draw a *correlation* between them, or call one *a function of* the other. In their world people do not do things but indulge in *behaviors,* taking *orientation* from *peer groups.*

As for users of **psychologese**, they think that every pattern is a *syndrome,* that vanity shows *a large ego,* that hostility means *getting rid of aggressions,* and that a strong interest in anything amounts to an *obsession* or *fixation.* In sad people they detect a *death wish*; in happy ones, *manic tendencies.* But they themselves, luckily, are *adjusted,* although they do face the *trauma* of coping with their many *paranoid* friends.

Advertising, journalism, business, and bureaucracy also exert warping effects on diction. If you find yourself writing about *pay hikes* and *slayers*; if your writing is full of *probes, vows, tolls, blazes, slates,* and *boosts*; if you feel possessed by the urge to say *inks the contract, gets the nod,* and *OK's the pact,* then you have a desperate case of **journalese**. **Bureaucratese**, in contrast, shows up in *breakthroughs, dialogue, decision-making process, viable, massive* (meaning "not small"), *maximize, finalize, priorities, profiles, counterproductive,* and so on. And now we have **computerese** as well: *input, software, readout, on-line, user-friendly,* and novel verbs like *access* and *interface.* All such language can be put to good comic or ironic use, but when you find it appearing uninvited in your drafts, reach for the *delete* key.

For a choice sample of bureaucratese, look at these paragraphs about graduate education:

> It is reasonable to assume that graduate education in the United States developed on undergraduate college campuses because its presence was somehow synergistic with respect to the higher education enterprise. The most important factor was probably the presence of a cadre of scholars engaged in the learning pursuit, both with neophytes and on their own. In addition, libraries, laboratories, and skilled artisans were available.

For half a century or more, the whole clearly exceeded the sum of the parts, whether considered from the viewpoint of quality, cost effectiveness, or a combination of both. Now, however, the proliferation of graduate programs on the individual campus, the increase in the number of campuses providing graduate education, the current oversupply of these graduates, and the seeming inflexibility of many people with advanced degrees calls into question the synergism argument in favor of graduate education on the country's campuses.[2]

Note the redundancy in this passage (*campus* and *campuses* occur three times in one sentence), the abstractions, the unnecessarily fancy words (*synergistic, cadre, neophytes*), the use of nouns in place of adjectives (*the higher education enterprise, the learning pursuit, the synergism argument*), and the impersonal tone. Nothing is happening here; no one is doing anything to anybody. Instead we have ghostly states: a factor was a presence, libraries were available, the whole exceeded the sum, the proliferation calls into question the synergism. . . . The ratio of noise to information is so high that you probably had some difficulty concentrating on the writer's ideas.

euphemism Once you have armed yourself against bureaucratese, you will already be somewhat on guard against *euphemism*, the substituting of vague or "nice" expressions for more direct ones. This work of prettification often has commercial or political motives behind it—a wish to sell a product, appease a faction, or make a harsh policy appear mild. Thus cemeteries become *memory gardens*; unemployment becomes *human resources development*; concentration camps are *relocation centers*; statements discovered to be false are called *inoperative* now that they have been *clarified* (retracted); and a major accident in a nuclear plant is demoted to an *episode*, perhaps in the hope that we will all be here to tune in for tomorrow's episode. The user of deliberate euphemism fears vividness above all. "Continued driving with a failed bearing," said a letter recalling certain defective cars, "could result in a disengagement of the axle shaft and adversely affect vehicle control." Just *how* inconvenienced a driver would be when the rear axle dropped onto the road, the concocters of the letter preferred not to say.

You, however, do want your prose to be concrete and informative; you cannot afford to leave the impression that you have something to hide. Do not give in to the advertiser's lingo and write *discomfort* for *pain* or *wetness* for *sweat*. Call a rape a *rape*, not an *assault*; don't write *The victim's skull was fractured, but tests proved she had not been assaulted.* The seeming dignity and delicacy implied by euphemisms often comes across as squeamishness or insincerity. Without going to the opposite extreme and dealing in blunt obscenities, you should generally prefer a forthright term to its euphemism.

Sharpen Your Figurative Language

If you think about your topic imaginatively as well as rationally, your mind will be continually likening the material before you to other things. We have already seen that comparison and contrast and analogy are ways of putting such thinking to extended rhetorical use (pp. 52–53, 54–55). But even on the level of single words and phrases you can heighten interest and lend clarity by stating one thing in terms of another.

metaphor versus simile

Two **figures of speech**, or special effects of language, should be of special concern to you as an apprentice writer: **metaphor** and **simile**. Both are ways of drawing a likeness, but a metaphor omits acknowledgment that a comparison is being made:

METAPHOR:
* George's hedgeclipper mind gives a suburban sameness to everything it touches.

> George's mind is compared to hedgeclippers, but without either of the open terms of comparison, *like* or *as*.

SIMILE:
* Like a patio rotisserie, George's mind always keeps turning at the same slow rate, no matter what is impaled on it.

> George's mind is explicitly (openly) compared to a rotisserie.

In theory, a metaphor is a more radical figure of speech than a simile, for it asserts an identity (George's mind *is* a hedgeclipper). But in practice, one kind of figure can be as striking as the other. What counts is not the choice between metaphor and simile but the suitability of the **image**, or word picture, to your intended meaning.

Student writers differ greatly in the degree to which they "think in metaphors." Some find their first drafts already teeming with images that need only a little refining to become a delight to the reader. Others, literal-minded by disposition or training, are satisfied when they have weeded out formulaic language and achieved a good measure of concreteness. Understandably, they have chosen to put plain communication first. To insist that they sprinkle their papers with conspicuous figures of speech would be like asking an intermediate swimming class to concentrate on perfecting the racing turn.

When an image does come to mind, you will want to think through its implications to see if they fit with your idea. Typically, the drawbacks to one image will send you on a trial-and-error search for a more appropriate one. To illustrate, let me show how I arrived at the figure that ends the paragraph above this one. *To insist that they sprinkle their papers with figures of speech would be like*—what?

FIRST TRY:

x painting a rally stripe on a delivery truck.

> COMMENT: Good for capturing the flashy, unnecessary effect of adorn-
> ing something that just does the job. But is a student paper really like a
> delivery truck? How? The comparison is strained. Maybe I should see if
> the paper can be likened to a car that isn't running smoothly.

SECOND TRY:

x painting a rally stripe on a car that needs a tune-up.

> COMMENT: This won't do. A car that needs a tune-up used to run per-
> fectly, but the barely adequate paper may represent a best-ever effort. I
> see that I need a figure expressing *learning*, not falling away from some-
> thing already achieved.

THIRD TRY:

x putting a toddler on water skis.

> COMMENT: No good. Student readers will justly resent being com-
> pared to babies. Find a learning situation closer to the college level.

FOURTH TRY:

• asking an intermediate swimming class to concentrate on perfecting the racing turn.

> COMMENT: Somewhat duller than the first try, but the connotations
> are all right. Presumably, some members of the intermediate class will
> get to be racers. This is also the only one of my four figures that conveys
> a too-advanced demand that interferes with the learning experience.
> OK, this one will do.

When an image works well for you, it usually shows more than
one kind of appropriateness to the thing or idea being characterized.
Thus, the simile about the racing turn not only captures the idea of a
premature demand, but also fits reasonably well with a college student's experience. The two images about George's mind, similarly,
suggest his suburban background as well as his conformism. Or
again, a critic once hit upon an ideal image to express the mixture of
confused thought and flowery language that she found in a notably
vain middle-aged author. Norman Mailer, she wrote with expert
malice, *combs metaphors over the bald spots on his theory.*[3]

the extended *figure of speech* If you do have a suitable image, you may find
that it is not altogether self-explanatory. Without running the image
into the ground, you can sometimes add a sentence or two that clari-
fies its implications. Thus a student writer *extended* her simile:

For me, the idea of going on for an advanced degree is like that of row-ing across the ocean. Perhaps I could do it and perhaps I couldn't. But what, I wonder, is waiting for me on the other side, and isn't there some faster and safer way of getting there? Until I know the answers to these questions, I intend to keep my feet planted on familiar soil.

So, too, a professional author added a clarifying sentence of elabora-tion to a striking simile:

This generation thinks—and this is its thought of thoughts—that noth-ing faithful, vulnerable, fragile can be durable or have any true power. Death waits for these things as a cement floor waits for a dropping light bulb. The brittle shell of glass loses its tiny vacuum with a burst, and that is that.[4]

In either of these passages one further sentence might have pro-duced tedium. Both of them go on just long enough to give us full access to the thought behind the image.

mixed metaphor We have seen that you ought to test a figure of speech for ap-propriateness before including it in the final draft of an essay. In addition, you should also check to see that you have *carried through* each image, completing the figure in a self-consistent way. If you lose control, you may end with the embarrassing effect of **mixed metaphor**, whereby the implications of one image clash with those of a neighboring one. Compare:

A.   Technology has given Goliath a club so heavy he cannot lift it. And it has given every David a sling: mass communications.[5]

B.   The American landscape is littered with the hulks of federal social pro-grams—launched amid noisy trumpetry from on high—which have sub-sequently been dismembered, truncated for lack of funds, or strangled by the problems they set out to conquer.[6]

Passage A concisely and emphatically summarizes the writer's thesis, and its two sentences—one for Goliath, one for David—are com-pletely integrated: no mixed metaphor here. But passage B, begin-ning with an image of a landscape covered with junk, is gradually invaded by contradictions. Federal social programs, first likened to ships that were *launched* and are now *hulks*, are littering the whole *American landscape*. Ships in Kansas? And is a ship *dismembered*, much less *strangled*? The writer seems to have forgotten that the im-age in view is an inanimate object. Does a ship, furthermore, *set out to conquer problems*? The whole sentence has an air of empty, con-fused grandeur.

Perhaps you feel that you can avoid mixed metaphors by shunning figurative language altogether. But things are not so simple. Many ordinary terms and nearly all clichés (p. 227) are "dead metaphors"—that is, they contain the latent implication of an image but are not usually intended to evoke it. When clichés are used in close succession, they revive each other and become mischievously vivid:

x The community should *vomit up* this moral *question mark*.
x *Climbing to the heights* of oratory, the candidate *tackled* the issue.
x Either we *get a handle* on these problems or we are all *going down the drain*.
x You can't *sit on your hands* if a recession is developing, because *you don't know where the bottom is*.
x This was a report on *the population of the U.S. broken down by age and sex*.[7]

Certain people, such as the late movie producer Sam Goldwyn, have such a genius for inappropriate figures that they can create an effect of mixed metaphor with a single cliché:

x This atom bomb is really dynamite.
x An oral agreement isn't worth the paper it's written on.
x A man who goes to a psychiatrist should have his head examined.

Others, wary of mixed metaphor but unsure of a remedy, abandon their cliché-images halfway through:

x I would like to rattle all the skeletons in the current controversy.
x He had no intention of providing grist for that debate.

If you are going to *rattle skeletons* at all, they have to be in a *closet*; and *grist for the mill*, lame enough as a whole cliché, is not improved by being left incomplete.

Figurative language, then, is as tricky as it is useful. When you intend an abstract meaning, you have to make sure that your dead metaphors stay good and dead. And when you do wish to be figurative, see whether you are getting the necessary vividness and consistency. If not, go back to literal statement; it is better to make plain assertions than to litter your verbal landscape with those strangled hulks.

Watch for Sound Patterns

Knowing that repeated sounds draw attention, you can sometimes use them deliberately, as Mark Twain did in referring to

• the *calm confidence* of a *Christian* with four aces,

or as Thomas Paine did in writing

- These are the *times* that *try* men's souls,

or as Theodore Roosevelt did in advising his countrymen to

- *Speak softly* and carry a big *stick.*

In these examples the "poetic" quality goes along with a studied effort to make a concisely emphatic statement.

Unless you are after some such effect, however, beware of making your reader conscious of rhymes *(the side of the hide)* or alliteration *(pursuing particular purposes)* or repeated syllables *(apart from the apartment).* These snatches of poetry usually result from an unconscious attraction that words already chosen exert on subsequent choices. Having written *the degradation,* you automatically write *of the nation* because the *-ation* sound is in your head. You may have to read your first draft aloud, attending to its sound and not its sense, in order to find where you have lapsed into jingling.

Abstract Latinate words—the ones that usually end in *-al, -ity, -ation,* or *-otion* — are especially apt to make for redundancy of sound. It is worth the pains to rewrite, for example, if you find bunched words like *functional, essential, occupational,* and *institutional* or *equality, opportunity, parity,* and *mobility.*

Finally, watch for clusters of prepositions that stand out annoyingly:

x A lot *of* people *of* different points *of* view were there.
x They learned a lesson *from* her conclusions *from* the incident.

Compare:

- Many people holding different points of view were there.
- Her conclusions from the incident taught them a lesson.

EXERCISES

13. Make the following sentences more vivid by substituting *concrete* language where it is appropriate (pp. 225–226):

   A. He attended scheduled sessions at the institution of higher learning with unfailing regularity.
   B. Daytime serial dramatic programs had her undivided concentration.
   C. The small rodents are of lasting interest to cats, who would never willingly forgo an opportunity for the pursuit and seizure of same.
   D. In northern regions, conspicuous display of emotions on the part of members of the populace is rather the exception than the rule.

E. Loss of control of one's sense of reality has come to be recognized by courts of law as a factor tending to favor the acquittal of a defendant who was afflicted in that manner.

14. Professor X describes himself as follows in a classified advertisement:

> Sophisticated, debonair college prof., 35, recently divorced, with liberal values and classical tastes, seeks broadminded female companion for travel and cultural pursuits. Knowledge of vintage wines and modern verse desirable. Send photo. Box 307, NYR.

What do you think Professor X is really like? Write a paragraph describing him vividly, and then underline all the *concrete diction* you have used.

15. Submit a paragraph which, like the "yo-yoing" passage on page 49, discusses a favorite activity of yours (perhaps a sport or pastime). Include some specific details and some general comments. Underneath your paragraph, list at least three *concrete* and three *abstract* terms you have used.

16. Rewrite the following sentences to eliminate any needless *clichés* (p. 227) or *euphemisms* (p. 229):

A. The departed one is now receiving visitors in the adjacent chamber, prior to journeying to his final resting place in the memory garden.
B. Biff expects the game to be a very physical contest, with both teams pulling out all the stops to bring home the bacon.
C. Repair of defective underground wastewater conveyance devices constituted his mode of employment.
D. The chairman of the board has declared that certain facilities, along with their attendant personnel, will be granted an indefinite respite from utilization in view of demand slackness throughout the consumer sector.
E. For Clifford, the bottom line was flashing on a concept that would be far out but not so off the wall that the Hollywood heavies would get uptight about shelling out big bucks for the movie rights.
F. Crazy Hoarse made no bones about his dissatisfaction; he put his foot down and said, straight from the shoulder, that a little million-dollar contract dispute with Acne Records shouldn't nip in the bud his hopes of having "Should I Hug Ya or Mug Ya?" played in every home from sea to shining sea.

17. With classmates or friends, draw up a list of clichés supplementing those mentioned on page 227. Then submit five sentences in which you call attention to the clichés by treating them literally.
   Examples:

   • She will *string him along* until he agrees to *tie the knot.*

   • Never trust ventriloquists; they *talk out of both sides of their mouth.*

18. Here is a fictitious letter making fun of a certain "official" style. Pick out several examples of *jargon* (pp. 227–229), and comment in writing on the way they convey or disguise meaning:

Dear Miss Dodds:

Thank you for your letter deploring the 14,000 fish deaths apparently related to thermal outflow into Long Island Sound from our nuclear power facility at Squaw Point. While the blame for this regrettable incident might most properly be ascribed to the fish, which swam closer to the Connecticut shore than is their normal habit, we believe that the ultimate solution must be found in terms of "the human element." Specifically, it is a task of public education in this era when customer demand for power markedly exceeds the deliverability capability of the electrical segment of the energy usage industry.

Do you ever stop to think, Miss Dodds, where the power comes from when you flick on your air-conditioner, your hair dryer, your cake mixer, your vacuum cleaner, and the myriad other appliances that enable you to live in "the lap of luxury" vs. the meager subsistence standard enjoyed by most of the peoples of the world? Until the American housewife is willing to go back to the egg beater and the broom, the utilities industry cannot be made the scapegoat for occasional episodes of ecological incompatibility.

Many consumers today advocate "zero growth" and a turning back of the clock to a simpler agrarian past. Quite frankly, if the rural American of 1900 had been as counter-oriented to the ongoing thrust of technology as certain romantic elements are in 1973, the outhouse would never have been supplanted by the flush toilet.

Very truly yours,
NORMAN R. HOWELL
Vice President for Consumer Relations
AFFILIATED UTILITIES COMPANY[8]

If you like, comment freely on other *euphemistic* aspects of the letter.

19. Look through your own prose—earlier papers or drafts—until you find five examples of *cliché, jargon,* and/or *euphemism.* Copy the guilty sentences, and submit them with revised versions. If your own writing doesn't yield five examples, make up the difference from any published source.

20. The following classic paragraph by George Orwell deals with euphemism in political language. Write a paragraph of your own about this passage, showing how it embodies or exemplifies its author's belief in the need for vivid diction.

In our time, political speech and writing are largely the defence of the indefensible. Things like the continuance of British rule in India, the Russian purges and deportations, the dropping of the atom bomb on Japan can indeed be defended, but only by arguments which are too brutal for most people to face, and which do not square with the professed aims of political parties. Thus political language has to consist largely of euphemism, question-begging, and sheer cloudy vagueness. Defenceless villages are bombarded from the air, the inhabitants driven out into the countryside, the cattle machine-gunned, the huts set on fire with incendiary bullets: this is called *pacification.* Millions of peasants are robbed of their farms and sent trudging along the roads with no more than they can carry: this is called *transfer of population* or *rectification of frontiers.* People are imprisoned for years without trial, or shot in the back of the neck or sent to die of scurvy in Arctic lumber camps: this is called *elimination of unreliable elements.* Such phraseology is needed if one wants to name things without calling up mental pictures of them.[9]

21. List all the figures of speech you find in the following passage, and briefly discuss the relation of each image to the one preceding it. Do you find any problems of *mixed metaphor* (pp. 232–233) here? If so, explain.

Academics, it has been said before, are very much like people who drive their cars by looking through their rear-view mirrors. Looking backward does offer certain satisfactions and provides splendid intellectual vistas, but it hardly brings into focus the best view of the road ahead. Academics may seem to bemoan the fact that the federals now hold the cards, and that they must do their bidding, however reluctantly. But the facts would appear to be otherwise: it is the federals who are at least trying to game-plan an extremely delicate future, while most academics remain on the sidelines, seized by fits of moral indignation about the felt deprivation of their intellectual autonomy. It would rarely occur to them that the federal planners would like nothing better than a showing of academia's own imaginative initiatives and social vision, if only they would gird themselves for that sort of resolve.[10]

22. Look through your own prose—earlier papers or drafts—until you find five examples of figurative language. Copy the complete sentence in each instance, and submit it with a brief comment on the appropriateness or inappropriateness of the image you chose. If you now think a different image would have served better, present and justify that image. If your own writing doesn't yield five examples, make up the difference from any published source.

23. Submit five sentences in which patterns of repeated sound cause an unwelcome distraction. (Do not choose your rhyming terms from those mentioned on pp. 233–234). Circle the words or syllables at fault. Then add five revised sentences that eliminate the problem. If you find that one of your revised sentences contains *positive* "sound effects," lending emphasis to your meaning, circle the language that produces the effect.

NOTES

[1]John L. Wasserman, "A Three-Ounce Dress and Other Favorites," *San Francisco Chronicle*, 31 Dec. 1977, p. 28.

[2]Norman Hackerman, "The Future of Graduate Education, If Any," *Science*, 175 (1972), 475.

[3]Cynthia Buchanan, cited by John Leonard in *Private Lives in the Imperial City* (New York: Random House, 1979), p. 49.

[4]Saul Bellow, *Herzog* (1964; rpt. New York: Viking, 1967), p. 290.

[5]Lewis M. Branscomb, "Taming Technology," *Science*, 171 (1971), 973.

[6]Constance Holden, "Community Mental Health Centers: Storefront Therapy and More," *Science*, 174 (1971), 1221.

[7]Cited by Wilson Follett, *Modern American Usage*, ed. Jacques Barzun (New York: Hill and Wang, 1966), p. 344.

[8]William Zinsser, "Frankly, Miss Dodds," *Atlantic*, Apr. 1973, p. 94.

[9]George Orwell, "Politics and the English Language," in *A Collection of Essays* (Garden City, N.Y.: Anchor, 1954), pp. 172–73.

[10]G[eorge] W. B.[onham], "The Decline of Initiative," *Change*, Apr. 1973, p. 16.

PART IV

CONVENTIONS

10

A REVIEW
OF GRAMMAR

Writers who want their prose to be effective—and who doesn't?—
must obviously use the language in ways that other people consider
"correct English." A personal style, with its own characteristic vocabulary and patterns of phrasing, cannot afford to stray very far from
the *usage*, or accepted contemporary practices, of **standard written
English**, the kind of writing people expect to find in nearly all public
communication. Acceptable usage in turn rests on a foundation of
general English grammar—the formal, relatively stable features that
distinguish the whole language from others.

In theory, then, we all share a common grammar, but as writers
we must additionally follow certain practices of usage that are more
debatable. For example, "grammar" supposedly requires us all to
form past tenses and the plurals of nouns in the same way, but we
can choose whether or not to accept such niceties of usage as the
ban on split infinitives (p. 292) and the distinction between *disinterested* and *uninterested* (p. 214).

dialect . . . In practice, this separation immediately dissolves. The fact is that in
most **dialects**, or group practices of speaking, some of the supposedly

fundamental rules of grammar are ignored. In Black American English, for example, *he say* and *I be trying* are perfectly acceptable; and more Americans probably say *she don't dance* and *I don't want no potatoes* than *she doesn't dance* and *I don't want any potatoes.*

. . . versus grapholect   If we concentrate only on the *written* language, however, order is restored. Despite its many dialects, English has only one **grapholect**, or set of principles for correct *writing* of the language. That grapholect, standard written English, is quite uniform both in its grammar and in its principles of usage. There will always be fine points on which experts disagree, but standard written English (henceforth *standard English*) became more or less fixed in its rules almost two centuries ago, and in every generation it has become more conservative and predictable. Whatever your speaking dialect may be, therefore, you have just one grapholect to learn. And that grapholect encompasses both "grammar" and "usage" as the two terms are usually understood.

diagnosing errors   Many fine writers have mastered the standard grapholect simply by reading other writers. But suppose you happen to make a good many mistakes in forming plurals and possessives, getting subjects and verbs to agree, matching pronouns with antecedents, and so on. In that case, your reading alone has not sufficed; now you need to troubleshoot, deliberately mastering whatever principles you failed to pick up through intuition. For that purpose you need to study *both* grammar and usage. You cannot understand the rules of usage unless you are familiar with a minimum of grammatical terminology.

Look, for example, at the following chart:

SAMPLE SENTENCE	ERROR	RELEVANT GRAMMATICAL CONCEPTS
Having decided to stay home.	sentence fragment (pp. 279–280)	subject, verb, independent clause (pp. 242, 272)
Hastily brushing her hair, the concert was only an hour away.	dangling modifier (pp. 293–294)	modifier, modified term, proper relation between them (pp. 263–266)
They divided the prize between her and I.	wrong pronoun case for *I* (pp. 287–288)	pronoun, object of preposition, objective case (pp. 256, 260)
He stayed home, whereas, I left immediately.	inappropriate comma after *whereas*	subordinating conjunction versus sentence adverb (pp. 265–266)
Miners, who go underground without proper equipment, are risking their lives.	inappropriate commas after *miners* and *equipment*	restrictive versus nonrestrictive element (p. 276)

If you write sentences like those in the left column, your instructor will tell you what kinds of errors they contain (middle column). But that information will help you in future cases only if you can recognize the grammatical concepts named in the right column. You have to know, for example, that a sentence normally contains a subject and a verb in an independent clause, and you must be able to tell that *Having decided to stay home* contains neither a subject nor a verb and is therefore not a clause at all. As soon as you can thus analyze the grammatical components of your draft sentences, you can diagnose and correct your errors without guesswork and without waiting for your instructor's advice.

SENTENCE ELEMENTS

The building blocks of all statements are **sentence elements**—functional parts that can be supplied by single words or groups of words.

subjects and verbs   Except in commands *(Beware!)* and exclamations *(Ouch!)*, every sentence is expected to include at least one subject and at least one verb:

- *Biff kicks.*
  (S V)

- *Biff is angry.*
  (S V)

A **subject** tells who or what the statement is about. *Biff* is doing the kicking; *He* is the one who is angry. A **verb** conveys the action performed by the subject or the state of the subject. What does Biff do? He *kicks*. What is his state? He *is* angry.

implied subject   A sentence like *Beware!* is said to have an **implied subject**, namely, *You.*

simple versus complete subject   In the sentence *The hot-tempered Biff is angry*, the **simple subject** is *Biff*; the **complete subject** is *The hot-tempered Biff*. The same distinction applies to other sentence elements as well.

subject and predicate   Each complete sentence can be regarded as consisting of a subject and a **predicate**: what the sentence is about (subject) and what is said about that thing (predicate). The subject, in this use of the term, is always the complete subject (above). Similarly, the predicate is the verb plus all of the words—objects and modifiers—that belong with it:

| SUBJECT | PREDICATE |

- *A man like Biff, left to himself, is likely to develop some fairly strange ideas.*

direct objects

$$\overset{\text{S}\quad\text{V}\qquad\text{D OBJ}}{\text{Biff kicks the quarterback.}}$$

• *Biff kicks the quarterback.*

The verb takes a **direct object**, something that the subject acts upon through the activity of the verb.

indirect objects

$$\overset{\text{S}\quad\text{V}\qquad\text{IND OBJ}\qquad\text{D OBJ}}{}$$

• *Biff gives the referee an argument.*

A sentence containing a direct object may also have an **indirect object**, the being, thing, or idea for whom or which or to whom or which the action of the verb is done. (Note that when *for* or *to* is actually used, we have a prepositional phrase instead of an indirect object: *for Biff; to the referee.* See p. 260.)

complements: predicate noun, predicate adjective

$$\overset{\text{S}\quad\text{V}\quad\text{COMPL}\quad\text{S}\qquad\text{V}\quad\text{COMPL}}{}$$

• *Biff is a sore loser. He has become bitter.*

Now the verb, instead of sending an action from subject to object, connects the subject to a **complement**—an element in the predicate that helps to identify the subject (Biff as a sore loser) or describe the subject (Biff as bitter). We will see that the two major types of complements, illustrated here, are respectively a *predicate noun* and a *predicate adjective*.

objective complements

$$\overset{\text{S}\qquad\text{V D OBJ}\quad\text{OBJ COMPL}}{}$$

• *They call Biff a sore loser.*

The word *Biff* has become a direct object, but once again it has *sore loser* as a complement. The complement of a direct object is called an **objective complement**.

modifiers

$$\overset{\text{M}\quad\text{M}\qquad\text{M}\qquad\text{S}\qquad\text{M}\qquad\text{V}\quad\text{M}\qquad\text{M}\qquad\text{M}\quad\text{D OBJ}}{}$$

• *The angry, vengeful fans energetically toss their dangerously heavy bottles.*

The sentence is crammed with **modifiers,** or elements that limit or describe other elements. We will see that the single-word modifiers here belong to different parts of speech: an article (*The*), three adjectives (*angry, vengeful, heavy*), two adverbs (*energetically, dangerously*), and a possessive pronoun (*their*).

appositives

$$\overset{\text{M}\qquad\text{M}\qquad\text{S}\quad\text{APP M}\quad\text{M}\qquad\text{V}\quad\text{M}\quad\text{M}\quad\text{D OBJ}\qquad\text{APP}}{}$$

• *The terrified referee Jones no longer scorns a gentler sport, badminton.*

In this sentence *Jones* and *badminton*, though they may look at first like modifiers, are really **appositives**—elements whose function is to identify the preceding element. Whereas a modifier limits the modified word, an appositive is equivalent ("stands in apposition") to the element it follows. You can test for an appositive by trying to substitute it for that element: *The terrified Jones no longer scorns badminton.* That makes sense; *Jones* and *badminton* are confirmed as appositives in the original sentence.

connectives

```
             CON   M    S   CON M    S    V CON   V   MOD D OBJ
```
 • *Neither the coaches nor the players aid and comfort the referee.*

Essential elements, the subject and the verb, are now compound, consisting of more than one item. They must be linked by **connectives**: *Neither . . . nor, and.*

These are the functioning parts of sentences, then: subjects, verbs, objects, complements, modifiers, appositives, and connectives. If you can recognize them where they appear, you have made a significant start toward comprehending English grammar—and toward ensuring that your own sentence elements will work together efficiently. The rest of this chapter will examine the three types of units that can serve as or within sentence elements: words in their various parts of speech, phrases, and subordinate clauses.

EXERCISE

1. The italicized words in the following passage cannot be found in any dictionary. Nevertheless, each of them functions here as a *sentence element*—a subject, verb, direct object, indirect object, complement, modifier, appositive, or connective. List the sentence element of each numbered word:

Much needless *fragdoodle* [1] is written on the subject of threnkies. Are not *threnkies* [2] shy and harmless *fridclumpers* [3]? Unlike the fruit fly, a much less restrained *aerotomane* [4], the threnky *unsnops* [5] his or her *yumyodels* [6] quite *rendly* [7]. In this manner the whole *cosmonopoly* [8] acquires a good *unctuation* [9]. Why, then, do some people call threnkies repulsive *ickles* [10]? Perhaps the nimble and *ambitendile* [11] threnky gives certain insecure *corsetchokers* [12] an acute *neuromaly* [13]. By criticizing threnkies, they merely *splot* [14] their own *parsonecherous* [15] *phlegmotility* [16]. The threnky, a simple and innocent *thumpzinger* [17] *pok* [18] there ever was one, has outlasted many *crunchuglies* [19] in its million-year history, and will *mence* [20] be here when its human detractors are extinct.

PARTS OF SPEECH

Sentence elements, we have seen, identify functions within a sentence. Some of those functions can be served by words of different types, or **parts of speech**. A subject, for example, may be either a noun *(Biff)* or a pronoun *(he)*.

In general, a word's part of speech is the type named in a dictionary entry for that word. Thus, if the dictionary says **and·i·ron** (and′ ī ərn), *n.*, you know by the *n.* that *andiron* is a noun. But since some words have more than one part of speech, you must look to see how a word is being used in the sentence before you. Sometimes, in fact, the sentence will leave the dictionary behind. Thus, although the dictionary will tell you that *skateboard* is always a noun, in the sentence *They skateboard well* it has been made into a verb.

Full definitions of the parts of speech would have to include the kind of meaning a part of speech conveys; its inflectional features or changed forms, if any; and a list of all the sentence positions it can occupy. As a writer, however, you are probably more interested in recognition and effective use than in formal classification. The following definitions will therefore concentrate on essentials.

Verbs

The heart of any sentence is its main **verb**, the word or set of words that tells what is going on:

        V
- You *are* a bore.

          V
- You *have exhausted* all my patience.

      V
- I *am leaving* now.

    V   V
- I *will* never again *listen* to your Folkways record, *Termite Mounds of Somaliland.*

tests for a verb Though the exact meaning of the concept *verb* is hard to pin down, the three tests of *meaning, inflection,* and *position* allow you to spot the verb or verbs in any sentence.

meaning 1. If you can locate the subject, you can find the verb by spotting the word that either *sets up the characterization* of the subject or *transmits the action* of the subject to an object. Thus, in the first example above, which word sets up the characterization of *You* as a *bore*? The answer is the verb *are*. And in the second example, which word or words transmit the action from the subject *You* to the direct object *patience*? The answer is *have exhausted*—the verb, or, since it consists of more than one word, the **verb phrase**. A verb, then, either (a) establishes a bridge between the subject and the subject's condition or identity or (b) tells what the subject does. Note that the verb itself is never a thing or idea, nor can it **modify** (limit) another word.

inflection   2. Verbs show **inflection** (altered form) for different *voices* (active or passive) and *tenses* or times:

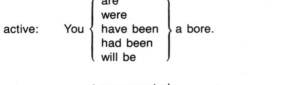

active: You { are / were / have been / had been / will be } a bore.

passive: You { are resented / were resented / have been resented / had been resented / will be resented } for your indifference to Wanda.

Some verbs remain uninflected in certain forms: *They always beat* (present) *us, just as they beat* (past) *us yesterday.*

position   3. Because a verb is not a thing, it cannot occupy substantive (nounlike) positions in a sentence. Thus *iron*, which might be either a verb or a noun, is not a verb in these sentences:

- The iron is hot.
- He had a stomach of iron.

But it is a verb in *They iron their underwear.* In that sentence, only a verb could occupy the position between the subject *They* and the direct object *their underwear.* Again:

- She *is singing.*
- *Is singing* offensive?

The same two words appear in both sentences, but they constitute a verb only in the first, where they follow an apparent subject. Only a verb could fill the first sentence slot; only a nounlike element could be the middle word in the second one. In the second sentence the verb is simply *Is,* standing where we would expect to find it in a question. *Singing* turns out to be the subject of that verb.

In the following passage the verbs are marked with *V:*

"I *have decided*^{V} to become a guru," *declared*^{V} Norbert. "Many years of study and self-denial *will be involved*,^{V} but the world *stands*^{V} in need of my services. Once certified as an adept, I *will bestow*^{V} advice upon everyone seeking enlightenment. People *will come*^{V} to know me as 'Norbert the Purified One of Daly City.'"

Note here that *become, certified, seeking,* and *know,* which resemble verbs, fail the tests of function and position. In this passage they are actually *verbals* (pp. 268–271) of different kinds.

A verb is the most complex, sensitively "tuned" part of speech. To appreciate all the communicative features of a given verb, you must observe not only its meaning, but also its *transitive, intransitive,* or *linking* function; its *person, number,* and *tense;* its *voice;* and its *mood.*

transitive, intransitive, and linking verbs   A verb appearing in any clause is either transitive, intransitive, or linking. A **transitive verb** transmits an action to a direct object:

>   S   TRANS V   D OBJ
> * Norbert *burned* the incense.

An **intransitive verb** expresses an action or state without reference to an object or complement:

>   S   INTRANS V
> * The incense *burned.*

A **linking verb**, like a transitive one, establishes a relation between the subject and part of the predicate. Instead of transmitting an effect, however, a linking verb allows the subject to be identified or modified by a complement. Where the subject is *identified,* the complement is a **predicate noun**:

>   S   LV   PRED N
> * Norbert *is* a *fanatic.*

Where the subject is *modified,* the complement is a **predicate adjective**:

>   S   LV PRED ADJ
> * Norbert *is fanatical.*

By far the most frequently used linking verb is *to be* in its various forms. Other linking verbs include *act, appear, become, feel, grow, look, loom, prove, remain, seem, smell, sound, taste,* and *turn.* Note, however, that you cannot be sure you are reading a linking verb—or, for that matter, a transitive or intransitive one—without checking its relation to other words in the sentence. *Grew,* for instance, is by turns transitive, intransitive, and linking in these three sentences:

    S   TRANS V D OBJ
- Norbert *grew*   lotuses in his window box.

    S INTRANS V
- He   *grew*   in spiritual strength.

      S   LV   PRED ADJ
- Wanda *grew* impatient with his holy ways.

person and number   Verbs "agree" in person and number with their subjects—even when the subjects are implied, as in [*You*] *Come!* English uses three "persons," according to whether someone is speaking (**first person**: *I, we*), being spoken to (**second person**: *you*), or being spoken about (**third person**: *he, she, they*). The "numbers" are **singular** (*I, you, he, she, it*) and **plural** (*we, you, they*). English verbs show little inflection for person and number, but the changes that do exist are important. *He go,* for example, strikes most readers as ungrammatical, since the standard third-person singular form of *go* is *goes.*

tenses   The **tense** of a verb is the time it expresses. All tenses are based on one or more of the following forms of a verb:

the base or simple infinitive (without *to*):
    I go, she goes
the present participle:
    I am going, she is going
the past form:
    I went, she went
the past participle:
    I have gone, she had gone
and various forms of the verbs *be* and *have:*
    I have gone, she is going, I have been going, she will have been going

principal parts   The base infinitive, past form, and past participle of a verb are known as its **principal parts**: *go, went, gone.*

    The most commonly recognized tenses are:

present (action happening now): *meditates*
present progressive (action ongoing in the present): *is meditating*
present perfect (past action regarded from the present): *has meditated*

present perfect progressive (past action continued into the present):
    has been meditating
past (completed action): *meditated*
past progressive (action that was ongoing in a previous time): *was meditating*
past perfect (action completed before another past time): *had meditated*
past perfect progressive (ongoing action completed before another past time):
    had been meditating
future (action to take place later): *will meditate*
future progressive (continued action to take place later): *will be meditating*
future perfect (action regarded as completed at a later time): *will have
    meditated*
future perfect progressive (continued action regarded as completed before a
    later time): *will have been meditating*

irregular verbs   Perhaps the hardest problem in tense formation is getting the right
past participle of **irregular verbs**—that is, verbs that do not simply
add *-d* or *-ed* to form both the past tense and the past participle.
Irregular verbs change more radically:

infinitive (base)	past tense	past participle
be	was	been
begin	began	begun
choose	chose	chosen
go	went	gone
lie	lay	lain
speak	spoke	spoken
throw	threw	thrown

The list could go on for many pages. When you hesitate between
two forms, consult your dictionary, which gives the full principal
parts of all irregular verbs.

voice   The **voice** of a verb indicates whether the subject performs (is **active**
in) or receives (is **passive** to) the action of the verb.

ACTIVE VOICE:
• Frankie *shot* Johnny.

PASSIVE VOICE:
• Johnny *was shot* by Frankie.

Observe that in these two sentences the actual performer of the action, *Frankie*, is the same. But only in the first sentence is *Frankie* the
grammatical subject of the verb. In the second sentence the subject is
Johnny, who is *acted upon* by the passive verb *was shot*. One peculiarity

of the passive voice, you may notice, is that it can allow the performer of the action to go unmentioned: *Johnny was shot*.

Here are the active forms of a regular verb, *walk*, and an irregular verb, *go*. Of the twelve possible tenses, the eight most common ones are illustrated:

ACTIVE VOICE			
tense	person		
	I	*he, she, it*	*we, you (sing./pl.), they*
Present	walk	walks	walk
	go	goes	go
Present Progressive	am walking	is walking	are walking
	am going	is going	are going
Present Perfect	have walked	has walked	have walked
	have gone	has gone	have gone
Past	walked	walked	walked
	went	went	went
Past Progressive	was walking	was walking	were walking
	was going	was going	were going
Past Perfect	had walked	had walked	had walked
	had gone	had gone	had gone
Future	will (shall) walk	will walk	will (shall) walk
	will (shall) go	will go	will (shall) go
Future Perfect	will (shall) have walked	will have walked	will (shall) have walked
	will (shall) have gone	will have gone	will (shall) have gone

And here are the passive forms of a regular verb, *shock*, and an irregular verb, *take*, in the same eight tenses:

PASSIVE VOICE			
tense	person		
	I	*he, she, it*	*we, you (sing./pl.), they*
Present	am shocked	is shocked	are shocked
	am taken	is taken	are taken
Present Progressive	am being shocked	is being shocked	are being shocked
	am being taken	is being taken	are being taken
Present Perfect	have been shocked	has been shocked	have been shocked
	have been taken	has been taken	have been taken
Past	was shocked	was shocked	were shocked
	was taken	was taken	were taken

Past Progressive	was being shocked	was being shocked	were being shocked
	was being taken	was being taken	were being taken
Past Perfect	had been shocked	had been shocked	had been shocked
	had been taken	had been taken	had been taken
Future	will (shall) be shocked	will be shocked	will (shall) be shocked
	will (shall) be taken	will be taken	will (shall) be taken
Future Perfect	will (shall) have been shocked	will have been shocked	will (shall) have been shocked
	will (shall) have been taken	will have been taken	will (shall) have been taken

Where you see a choice between *will* and *shall,* you should use *will* unless you want to make an unusually formal effect.

mood   English verbs show certain other changes of form to indicate the **mood** or manner of a clause. If the clause is meant to be a statement

indicative   or a question—by far the most common kinds of expression—its verb is in the **indicative mood**:

INDICATIVE:
- I *ate* a banana.
- *Did* you *eat* a banana?

imperative   The **imperative mood** is used for giving commands or directions, whether or not the subject is named:

IMPERATIVE:
- You *eat* that banana!
- *Eat* that banana!

subjunctive   And for a variety of other, less common, uses, the **subjunctive mood** is called for:

SUBJUNCTIVE:
- If I *ate* the banana . . .
- If I *were to eat* the banana . . .

When should the subjunctive be used? Although at one time it was common in daily usage, the subjunctive now survives only in limited kinds of statements:

1. Certain formulas such as:

- as it were
- be it known

- be that as it may
- come what may
- God bless you
- heaven forbid
- long live the Queen
- the devil take it
- the taxpayers be damned

2. *That* clauses expressing requirements or recommendations:

- The IRS requires that everyone *submit* a return by April 15.

3. *Lest* clauses:

- Lest it *be thought* that I am neglectful of my duties. . . .

4. Impossible or unlikely conditions:

- If I *were* on the moon now, I would tidy up the junk that has been strewn there.
- *Had he taken* that plane, he would be dead today.

> Note that the writer of the first sentence is not on the moon and that the person mentioned in the second sentence did not take the plane. The subjunctive constructions *If I were* and *Had he taken* show us these facts.

For uses 1–3 and for all verbs but *be*, the subjunctive forms are the same as the indicative ones, except that the third-person singular form loses its *-s* or *-es.* Thus:

	indicative	imperative	subjunctive
I	like		like
you	like	like	like
he, she, it	likes		**like**
we	like		like
you	like	like	like
they	like		like

Thus the one difference would show up in a sentence such as *I demand that he like me* —in contrast, say, to the indicative *I know that he likes me.*

For use 4, impossible or unlikely conditions, present and past verbs are made subjunctive as follows:

	indicative	subjunctive
present: past:	like liked	liked: If she liked me had liked: If she had liked me; had she liked me

Be is made subjunctive as follows. For all present situations, use *were* or *be:*

If $\left\{\begin{array}{l} \text{I} \\ \text{you} \\ \text{he, she, it} \\ \text{we} \\ \text{you} \\ \text{they} \end{array}\right\}$ *were* here   Lest $\left\{\begin{array}{l} \text{I} \\ \text{you} \\ \text{he, she, it} \\ \text{we} \\ \text{you} \\ \text{they} \end{array}\right\}$ *be* here

For all past situations, use *had been:*

If $\left\{\begin{array}{l} \text{I} \\ \text{you} \\ \text{he, she, it} \\ \text{we} \\ \text{you} \\ \text{they} \end{array}\right\}$ *had been* there

Analysis of verbs is further complicated by the existence of two special kinds of verbs, *auxiliaries* and *merged verbs.*

auxiliaries Certain words are called **auxiliaries** because they combine with, or "help," other verb forms. Unlike other verbs, the auxiliaries remain unchanged in form; but inserted before inflected verbs, they produce important changes in emphasis, obligation, and degree of likelihood. When used in that position, the following words are considered auxiliaries: *can, could, dare, do, may, might, must, need, ought, should,* and *would.* Note that a verb form immediately following an auxiliary is always a simple or base infinitive (lacking *to*): *could throw, must imagine:*

* He *could* throw harder.
* He *must* throw harder.
* He *should* throw harder.

merged verbs A verb form combined with what would usually be a preposition is sometimes called a **merged verb**: *check out, cave in,* and so on. Note that merged verbs can easily be confused with verbs *followed by* a preposition. Compare:

MERGED V
- He *looked up* the number.

PREP   OBJ PREP
- He looked *up the elevator shaft.*

Or again:

MERGED V
- She *turned on* the switch.

PREP OBJ PREP
- She turned *on Norbert* in anger.

The first sentence in each pair contains a merged verb: *looked up, turned on.* In the other sentences, *up* and *on* are prepositions taking the objects *elevator shaft* and *Norbert.* You can tell the difference either by observing the unity of meaning in a merged verb—in the first sentence *look* is incomplete without *up*—or by noting a difference in voice stress. In the merged verbs *look up* and *turn on*, the words *up* and *on* receive more stress than they do when used as prepositions.

Nouns

tests for nouns   The traditional definition of a noun, while not completely ade-
meaning   quate, provides a good start toward recognition of nouns in sentences: a **noun** is the name of a person, place, or thing. The "thing" can be an idea as well as a physical object. Thus *Harry, man, car, lemon, fraud,* and *Sing Sing* are all nouns.

position   A noun can occupy any sentence position where a "person, place, or thing" could be plausibly inserted. It can serve as:

a subject (p. 242)
a direct object (p. 243)
an indirect object (p. 243)
a subject complement (p. 243)
an objective complement (p. 243)
an appositive (p. 243)
an object of a preposition (p. 260)
a subject of an infinitive (p. 268)
an object or complement of an infinitive (p. 268)
an object of a participle (p. 270)
a subject of a gerund (p. 271)
an object of a gerund (p. 271)
part of an absolute phrase (p. 273)
a possessive (*Harry's*)
a term in direct address (What do you plead, *Harry?*)
an adjectival (attributive) noun (the *dictionary* meaning, a *Florida* sunset)

On the whole, the substance denoted by a noun is one that acts or is acted on, or one about which something is said.

inflection   Nouns are also identifiable by their **inflections**, or changes of form. With some exceptions, they can be made both plural and possessive. This distinguishes them from all other parts of speech except pronouns (*she, they*); but while pronouns have a further inflection for case (*she, her; who, whom*), nouns do not.

Nouns are usually made plural by the addition of *-s* or *-es*:

singular	plural
defect	two *defects*
shock absorber	three *shock absorbers*
toothless *clutch*	toothless *clutches*

But quite a few nouns, like *child (children), thief (thieves),* and *deer (deer),* form irregular plurals; see pages 348–350 for details.

Nouns usually become possessive by the addition of *-'s*, but there are exceptions; see pages 350–352. Note that "possession" does not always mean ownership; the possessive form is also used for other relations, as in *a hard day's work, the country's beauty.* All possessives can be thought of as substitutes for an *of* construction: *the delights of the evening; the evening's delights.* But the process is not always reversible: you would not want to turn *the futility of it all* into *the all of its futility.*

The most common error in writing nouns is the mixing up of plural and possessive forms. You must carefully observe the difference:

singular	plural	singular possessive	plural possessive
temple	temples	temple's	temples'
priest	priests	priest's	priests'
contribution	contributions	contribution's	contributions'

In the following passage, all nouns are marked by *N*:

Harry^N has an *answer*^N for everything. If a *customer*^N complains that his newly purchased *used*^N *car*^N won't run, *Harry*^N says, "Think of what you're saving on *gas.*^N" If the *customer*^N says he has had to convert the *car*^N into a *garage*^N *playhouse*^N for his *children's*^N *recreation,*^N *Harry*^N replies, "*Convertibles*^N are hard to find these *days.*^N" And if the *customer*^N protests that he thought he was getting a *luxury model,*^N *Harry*^N tells him, "Your *dreamboat*^N just sits under the *house*^N *week*^N after *week.*^N Now, that's what I call a *luxury.*^N"

Note that *garage* in *garage playhouse* and *luxury* in *luxury model* are *attributive nouns*—that is, nouns serving the function of adjectives. But in such fixed combinations the whole term *garage playhouse* or *luxury model* can be counted as a single noun.

Pronouns

Some, but not all, pronouns meet the old definition of a pronoun as *a word taking the place of a noun*. Pronouns serve so many functions, yet are so limited in number, that the best means of recognition is simply to memorize them. Even so, it is useful to know the types of pronouns and to understand their different grammatical features.

personal pronouns   The **personal pronouns** stand for beings and objects. They consist of all the case forms of *I, you, he, she, it, we,* and *they*—the words traditionally used in showing the tense forms of verbs (*I went, you went,* and so on). English has three **cases** to indicate different sentence functions: the **subjective case** (*I, we, they,* etc.), the **objective case** (*me, us, them,* etc.), and the **possessive case** (*my, mine; our, ours; their, theirs;* etc.). Among all words in the language, only personal pronouns and the relative pronoun *who* show inflection for all three cases. Nouns, you remember, do not change their form to show objective functions.

case

SUBJECTIVE:
- The *boy* went home. ⎱ subject of verb
- *He* went home. ⎰
- He was the *boy.* ⎱ complement
- The boy was *he.* ⎰

OBJECTIVE:
- They punished the boy. ⎱ direct object of verb
- They punished *him.* ⎰
- They taught the *boy* a lesson. ⎱ indirect object of verb
- They taught *him* a lesson. ⎰
- They taught it to the *boy.* ⎱ object of preposition
- They taught it to *him.* ⎰
- They wanted the *boy* to go. ⎱ subject of infinitive
- They wanted *him* to go. ⎰

POSSESSIVE:
- the *boy's* hat ⎱ possession of noun
- *his* hat ⎰
- the *boy's* departing ⎱ subject of gerund
- *his* departing ⎰

Here are all the personal pronouns aligned by person, case, and number:

SINGULAR			
	subjective	objective	possessive
First Person	I	me	my, mine
Second Person	you	you	your, yours
Third Person	he	him	his
	she	her	her, hers
	it	it	its

PLURAL			
First Person	we	us	our, ours
Second Person	you	you	your, yours
Third Person	they	them	their, theirs

Note especially the spelling of the **second possessive** forms: not *This kite is your's* but *This kite is yours;* not *The victory was their's* but *The victory was theirs.*

intensive and reflexive pronouns These are *myself, yourself, himself, herself, itself, oneself, ourselves, yourselves, themselves* (never *theirself* or *theirselves*). These derivatives of the personal pronouns are used either for emphasis (**intensive**) or for indicating that the subject of a verb is also its object (**reflexive**).

INTENSIVE:
• She *herself* will drive the truck.
• For *myself*, I want no part of it.

REFLEXIVE:
• He admires *himself* unreservedly.
• We have done *ourselves* very little good.

Note that an intensive pronoun is nothing more than an emphatic way of supplementing or replacing a personal pronoun. A reflexive pronoun, by contrast, always serves as a direct or indirect object (p. 243), and thus it cannot be omitted or altered without completely changing the meaning of the sentence. In the reflexive examples above, *himself* and *ourselves* are essential parts of their sentences; you would never find intensive pronouns occupying those positions.

reciprocal pronouns These express mutual relation: *each other, each other's, one another, one another's.* Although they always refer to at least two parties, they are always singular in form:

RIGHT:
* Wanda and Norbert compared *each other's* defects.

WRONG:
x Wanda and Norbert compared *each others'* defects.

Although some writers reserve *each other('s)* for two parties and *one another('s)* for more than two parties, the terms are really interchangeable.

indefinite pronouns   An **indefinite pronoun** leaves unspecified the person or thing it refers to. The indefinite pronouns are:

all	both	everything	nobody	several
another	each	few	none	some
any	each one	many	no one	somebody
anybody	either	most	nothing	someone
anyone	everybody	much	one	something
anything	everyone	neither	other	such

Some of the indefinite pronouns can become possessive, but none of them can be inflected in any other way. They are considered indefinite pronouns only when they are not used as modifiers. *Any* is an indefinite pronoun in *any of you,* but it is an adjective in *any coat.*

demonstrative pronouns   *This, that, these,* and *those* are called **demonstratives** because they single out (or "demonstrate") what they refer to:

* *These* are the good old days.
* I don't recognize *this* as your work.

Used adjectivally, these same words are called **demonstrative adjectives**:

* *These* days are the best we will ever see.
* *This* sculpture, consisting of a stack of soup cans on top of a motorcycle, is a powerful social statement.

relative pronouns   The **relative pronouns** are *who, whom, that,* and *which.* They introduce **relative clauses**—that is, adjectival subordinate clauses, relating the information they contain to an earlier sentence element, called an **antecedent**:

   ANT REL PRO   REL CLAUSE
* *Tom, who* is glad to have a working wife, never misses an episode of "One Life to Live."

three conditions
for relative
pronouns

Since *who, whom, that,* and *which* have other possible uses, you must apply a three-part test to see if one of them is really serving as a relative pronoun. It must:

a. introduce a subordinate clause (or follow a preposition that does so: *of whom you speak),*
b. serve a nounlike function, and
c. have an antecedent word or phrase in the same sentence.

Thus, in our example, *who* (a) introduces the subordinate clause *who is glad to have a working wife,* (b) serves a nounlike function as the subject of the verb *is,* and (c) has an antecedent, *Tom.*

indefinite
relative
pronoun

Some grammarians, however, also recognize an **indefinite relative pronoun** in sentences like these, in which the leading pronoun has no antecedent and the subordinate clause is not adjectival:

* He knows *who* he is.
* You are *what* you eat.

relative
adjective and
adverb

Note, incidentally, that some relative clauses are introduced by words other than pronouns:

* That was the time *when* he was needed.
* I know the woman *whose* dog is wearing the mink cape.

In these sentences *when* and *whose* could be called a **relative adverb** and a **relative adjective**, respectively.

In relative clauses whose relative pronoun would serve as a direct object, that pronoun is often omitted:

* This modernistic Studebaker is the car [*that*] Bobo stole from Harry's lot.

interrogative pronouns *Who, whom, whose, which,* and *what,* when they introduce a question, are considered **interrogative** ("questioning") **pronouns**:

INT PRO
* *Who* could have predicted that Tom would put a set in every room?

Note that *whose, which,* and *what,* if followed by a noun, are not pronouns but adjectives. Further, some interrogative forms, such as *why* and *when,* are considered either adverbs or conjunctions but not pronouns, since they do not fill noun positions in their clauses. When *whose* introduces a question but is followed by a noun (*Whose idea was that?*), it is called an **interrogative adjective**.

Prepositions

Prepositions are rather shadowy words, hard to define but usually easy to recognize in a sentence. While they have no characteristic endings and no inflected forms, they always appear in the same kind of construction, a **prepositional phrase**. Though a prepositional phrase may contain various modifiers, its heart is a preposition and the **object of the preposition**:

> PREP   OBJ PREP
> - *without* much *fondness*
>
> PREP   OBJ PREP
> - *for* the finer *points*
>
> PREP OBJ PREP
> - *of grammar*

The most common objects of prepositions are nouns and pronouns, but other nounlike constructions can also serve:

> PREP   OBJ PREP
> - *about* the *deciding*
>
> PREP   OBJ PREP
> - *of   what people like*

In these last examples the two objects are a gerund (p. 271), *deciding*, and a noun clause (p. 274), *what people like*.

A word commonly recognized as a preposition (*by, for, of, onto, to, without*, etc.) is not truly prepositional in a given sentence unless it has an object. Note how the presence or absence of an object affects the parts of speech marked in these examples:

> PREP   OBJ PREP
> - He looked *under* the *bridge.*
>
> ADV
> - He dived *under.*
>
> PREP   OBJ PREP
> - *Apart from* his *shyness,* nothing obstructed his career.
>
> ADV
> - He stood *apart.*

Some prepositions are **compound**, or composed of more than one word: *by means of, in front of, on account of, with respect to*, etc.

Conjunctions

Conjunctions are uninflected words that serve to connect other words, phrases, or clauses. Like prepositions, they express relationship. Indeed, certain words—*after, before, but, for, than,* and *since*—can be either prepositions or conjunctions, depending on the words they join. Thus:

CONJ
* *Before* you leave, please give me your credit cards.

PREP OBJ PREP
* She will leave *before noon.*

CONJ
* She wanted to stay, *but* I said no.

PREP   OBJ PREP
* Everyone *but* her *lawyer* agreed with my decision.

In addition, various conjunctions share their form with adjectives, adverbs, and even pronouns:

PRO
* *That* is certain.

ADJ
* *That* idea is true.

CONJ
* I hope *that* she agrees.

Only in the last sentence is *that* a conjunction, joining two clauses. Again:

ADJ
* *Either* alternative would be fine.

PRO
* Go ahead and choose *either.*

ADV
* I won't, *either.*

CONJ
* *Either* you go or I do.

The *either . . . or* formula joins two clauses, *you go* and *I do.*

The moral is that when you recognize a word as one that might be a conjunction, you cannot be sure until you have made certain it has a connective function. The connected elements can be single words, phrases, clauses, or even whole sentences:

CONJ
* There may be difficulties ahead. *But* it is time to make a decision.

Since conjunctions are most likely to be confused with prepositions and adverbs, look to see if the word at issue takes an object or modifies another word. If it does either, it is not a conjunction.

types of conjunctions All conjunctions are either coordinating, subordinating, or correlative:

memorize

coordinating conjunctions			
and	or		
but	so		
for	yet		
nor			

subordinating conjunctions			
after	because	so (that)	when
although	before	than	whenever
as	how	that	where
as if	if	though	wherever
as long as	in order that	till	while *(etc.)*
as soon as	provided (that)	unless	
as though	since	until	

correlative conjunctions
both . . . and
either . . . or
neither . . . nor
not . . . but
not only . . . but also
whether . . . or

The difference in function between coordinating and subordinating conjunctions is important to a writer aiming at precise statement (see pp. 184–189). **Coordinating conjunctions** are meant to join *logically comparable* elements, without turning one element into a modifier of the other:

The night is young, { and you're so beautiful.
but you aren't.
or perhaps it isn't. }

A **subordinating conjunction,** by contrast, joins *logically distinct* elements, one of which supports, explains, or subtracts something from the other:

Although
Because
If } this is true, you are mistaken.
Provided
Since
Unless

Each of these subordinating conjunctions introduces a subordinate or dependent clause, modifying the main statement *you are mistaken*. Note that the subordinate clause is not necessarily less important in meaning than the independent one; but it is grammatically subordinate, in that it could not stand alone as a sentence.

Adjectives

Among the parts of speech, adjectives and adverbs are the chief modifiers—that is, words whose function is to limit or describe other words. **Adjectives** modify nouns, pronouns, and other nounlike elements:

ADJ   N
• a *happy* viewer

ADJ PRO
• *lucky* you!

ADJ   GER (p. 271)
• his *outrageous* lying

Adjectives usually precede the words they modify, as in these examples, but a **predicate adjective** comes later: *The wind is strong.*

comparison of adjectives   Most adjectives can be compared, or changed to show three *degrees* of coverage. The base form of an adjective is in the **positive degree**: *thin*. The **comparative degree** puts the modified word *beyond* one or more items: *thinner* (than she is; than everybody). And the **superlative degree** unmistakably puts the modified word beyond *all* rivals within its group: *thinnest* (of all).

The comparative and superlative degrees of adjectives are formed in several ways:

1. For one-syllable adjectives, add -*er* and -*est* to the root of the positive form: *wide, wider, widest* (but *less wide, least wide*).
2. For one- or two-syllable adjectives ending in -*y*, change the -*y* to -*i* and add -*er* and -*est*: *dry, drier, driest; lazy, lazier, laziest* (but *less lazy, least lazy*).
3. For all other adjectives of two or more syllables, put *more* and *most* or *less* and *least* before the positive form: *stupid, more stupid, most stupid; incredible, more incredible, most incredible.*
4. For certain "irregular" adjectives, supply the inflected forms shown in your dictionary. For example:

positive degree	comparative degree	superlative degree
bad	worse	worst
good	better	best
far	farther, further	farthest, furthest
little	littler, less, lesser	littlest, least
many, some, much	more	most

Some words usually listed as adjectives cannot be compared at all: adjectival *numbers* (*five* horses) and the pronounlike *demonstrative adjectives* (*those* horses). Nouns serving as adjectives (*horse* lovers) are called **attributive nouns**.

Adverbs

Adverbs are words that modify either verbs, adjectives, other adverbs, prepositions, infinitives, participles, phrases, clauses, or whole sentences. They typically express manner (*pleasantly*), degree (*very*), frequency (*seldom*), time (*now*), place (*there*), affirmation (*certainly*), negation (*not*), qualification (*however*), and logical relationship (*therefore*). While adjectives answer questions like *what kind* (*brown*) and *how many* (*few*), adverbs pose or answer questions like *how*, *when*, *where*, *why*, and *how often*.

Most single-word adverbs end in *-ly*, but some important ones do not:

ahead
down
therefore
well *(etc.)*

Some adverbs are identical in form to adjectives:

better	late	much
close	loud	slow
fast	more	tight *(etc.)*

Thus you often have to distinguish an adverb from an adjective by its function alone. Remember: if a word that looks like an adverb is not modifying a nounlike element, it *is* an adverb.

ADV
• He played *well.*

    The adverb modifies the verb *played.*

ADV ADJ
• He was a *much better* player than Ralph.

    Here *better* modifies the noun *player*, and *much* modifies *better.*

ADV   ADV
• You are someone who buys *cheap* and sells *dear.*

    The adverbs modify *buys* and *sells.*

ADV   ADJ
* He didn't want to go *slow* in that *slow* traffic.

The first *slow* is an adverb modifying the infinitive *to go;* the second is an adjective modifying the noun *traffic.*

To see whether a certain word is an adjective or an adverb, simply try putting *a* or *the* before it. If the resulting expression sounds like English, the word is an adjective. Thus, in the last example above, *the slow traffic* would make enough sense to prove that *slow* is an adjective when it appears before *traffic;* and the absurdity of *go a slow* or *go the slow* proves that the same word cannot be an adjective in *go slow.* If the word stands alone, as in *His driving was slow,* you must rearrange the sentence to apply the test. *The slow driving* sounds like normal English; hence *slow* is a predicate adjective in *His driving was slow.*

comparison of adverbs   Like adjectives, adverbs can be compared: *quickly, more quickly, most quickly.* Note that the *-ly* ending on most adverbs prevents them from being inflected when they are compared: not *sadlier* and *sadliest* but *more sadly* and *most sadly.* But some adverbs do have one-syllable forms *(hard, fast),* and they *are* inflected: He tried *harder;* She ran *fastest* of all.

For the sentence positions an adverb can occupy, see pages 291–292.

sentence adverbs   Certain adverbs, known as **sentence adverbs**, look so much like conjunctions that they are also known by the name *conjunctive adverbs.* Their function is both to modify a phrase or statement and to indicate its logical relation to a previous one:

SENT ADV
* There was nothing more to be done; *furthermore,* there was still a chance that the medicine would take effect.

SENT ADV
* You could not blame her for being superstitious; luck, *indeed,* appeared to be her greatest asset.

sentence adverbs			
again	furthermore	moreover	then
also	hence	nevertheless	therefore
besides	however	nonetheless	thus
consequently	indeed	otherwise	
further	likewise	similarly	

Since sentence adverbs "feel like" conjunctions, inexperienced writers sometimes punctuate them as if they really were conjunctions:

SENT ADV
x She is leaving, *however* I am staying.

Such punctuation makes a classic *comma splice* (pp. 314–315). If you recognize a sentence adverb for what it is, you will always set it apart from surrounding structures:

SENT ADV
• She is leaving; *however,* I am staying.

The comma after *however* indicates that this word, like all sentence adverbs, modifies the whole preceding statement.

transitional expressions   Phrases like *for instance, in fact, in other words, on the contrary, on the other hand, that is,* and *to be sure* function exactly like sentence adverbs. They too indicate a relation between two statements but must not be punctuated as if they were true conjunctions:

TRANS EXPRN
x There is much to be said for working a three-day week; *on the other hand* the reduced pay limits what can be done with the extra free time.

Since *on the other hand* modifies the whole preceding statement, a comma after *hand* is called for.

Interjections

Interjections are certain familiar words that stand apart from other constructions to command attention or show strong feeling: *ah, damn, gosh, hurrah, O, oh, ouch, shh,* etc.

Note that an interjection is not the same thing as an *exclamation.* An exclamation is an outburst—an emphatic statement, not a part of speech. Though in fact an exclamation may consist of or contain an interjection, there is no necessary tie between the two. *O Henrietta Tittle, your hair is like peanut brittle* contains an interjection (the poetical *O*), but it is not an exclamation; *Drop dead!* is an exclamation, but it contains only an imperative verb and an adjective.

Articles

The indicators (or "determiners") immediately preceding nouns, but showing none of the inflectional features of adjectives, are called **articles.** Articles are divided into *definite (the)* and *indefinite (a, an);* those three words compose the entire list. A **definite article** precedes the word for a specific item, whether singular or plural: *the report, the misstatements.* Sometimes a definite article precedes a modifier, as in *The bigger they are, the harder they fall.* An **indefinite article** precedes a general category, always singular, or a singular item not previously identified: *a report is due; an hour has passed; an idea of mine.*

A is used before consonant sounds, *an* before vowel sounds. When an initial *h* sound is distinctly pronounced, as in *historical,* many writers prefer to introduce it with *a: a historical inquiry,* not *an historical inquiry. An historical,* however, is not considered incorrect.

Expletives

In certain uses the words *it* and *there* serve the special function of introducing a postponed subject:

    EXPL   S
- *There* are eleven *oranges* left in the bin.

    EXPL   S
- *It* was clear *that the police had to be called.*

In this anticipatory role *it* and *there* are called **expletives**.

EXERCISES

2. List the parts of speech of the twenty italicized words in Exercise 1 on page 244.

3. Name the parts of speech of all the words in this sentence:

  1   2   3   4   5   6 7   8   9 10   11
  "Hey, Bessie," shouted Max disbelievingly as he stared at the modern
   12   13 14   15   16   17 18   19   20
  painting, "tell me what squashed that poor guy's face."

4. Consider the following one-word sentence: *Choose!*

    A. Do you regard *Choose!* as a complete sentence? Why, or why not? (See p. 242.)
    B. Name the *person, tense, voice,* and *mood* of that verb (pp. 248–253).
    C. Write a brief sentence using the same verb in a *different* person, tense, voice, and mood.
    D. Identify the person, tense, voice, and mood of the verb in your sentence.
    E. What part of speech is each word in your sentence?

5. Write a brief analysis of the grammatical difference between the italicized words in each of the following pairs of sentences:

    A. 1. He charged *up* the field.
        2. He charged *up* the battery.
    B. 1. She bought a pot of *honey.*
        2. She bought a *honey* pot.
    C. 1. They tried *harder.*
        2. It was *harder* than they expected.

D. 1. *This* is absurd.
   2. *This* idea is absurd.
E. 1. Norbert *himself* believes in immortality.
   2. Norbert believes *himself* to be immortal.

VERBALS

Certain words look like verbs, are used in the formation of some verb tenses (is *bringing*, had *done*), but never function as whole verbs by themselves. These **verbals**—namely, *infinitives, participles,* and *gerunds*—serve as equivalents to nouns, adjectives, or adverbs.

Infinitives

The base forms of verbs, customarily preceded by *to*, are called **infinitives:** *to love, to reconsider.* Within sentences, infinitives resemble verbs in that they can have *subjects, objects,* and *complements:*

SUBJECT:

                S INF   INF
- Norbert asked *her to concentrate* on the One.

OBJECT:

                                INF OBJ INF
- He was no longer concerned *to gratify her.*

COMPLEMENT:

            S INF   INF   COMPL INF
- He wanted *her to become enlightened.*
            INF   COMPL INF
- He wanted *to be* her *instructor.*

Note that both subjects and objects of infinitives, when they are pronouns, take the objective case form. You may wonder why this one kind of "subject" is always objective in case. The answer is that every subject of an infinitive is also an object (direct or indirect) of a preceding verb: *asked her to concentrate.* In the rare instance when the complement of an infinitive is a pronoun, it belongs in the objective case:

                COMPL INF
- She was glad not to be *him.*

Infinitives can correspond to several tenses and appear in either the active or the passive voice:

active voice	passive voice
to reconsider	to be reconsidered
to be reconsidering	
to have reconsidered	to have been reconsidered
to have been reconsidering	

The following sentences illustrate typical functions served by in-finitives or by the phrases they appear in:

NOUN FUNCTION:

INF

• *To err* is human.

The infinitive is the subject of the verb *is*.

INF

• Forgetting *to pay* taxes on time can be costly.

The infinitive phrase *to pay taxes on time* is the object of a ger-und, *Forgetting*. (The complete subject of the sentence is *Forget-ting to pay taxes on time.*)

ADJECTIVE FUNCTION:

INF

• That was a meal *to remember.*

The infinitive modifies a noun, *meal.*

INF

• The hour *to gorge* themselves had arrived for Max and Bessie.

The infinitive phrase *to gorge themselves* modifies the noun *hour.*

ADVERB FUNCTION:

INF

• They were eager *to start.*

The infinitive modifies a predicate adjective, *eager.*

INF

• They chewed the celery too noisily *to hear* the waiter's questions.

The infinitive phrase *to hear the waiter's questions* modifies an adverb, *too.*

Infinitives become harder to spot when the telltale *to* is omitted:

INF
* Everyone heard Max *tell* the waiter that "some jerk must have dropped an old piece of bread in this onion soup."

Only the base-verb form of *tell* and its typical infinitive position reveal that it is an infinitive here.

Such **simple** or **base infinitives** are most usually found after auxiliaries: *should go, dare suggest, do know,* etc. In that capacity they are not verbals but parts of the verb phrase.

Participles

Participles are verbal forms used in the formation of certain tenses (pp. 249–251). They are true verbals, however, only when used as adjectives. In that capacity they can appear singly *(disrobing)* or in **participial phrases** including objects *(savagely disrobing the lamb chops)*. They show several forms indicating tense and voice:

active voice	passive voice
shooting	being shot
shot	
having shot	having been shot

Since participles resemble gerunds, certain tense forms of verbs, and even an occasional noun, they must be recognized by their adjectival function:

PART   GER   N
* A person *owning* no property won't have much luck in *getting* the *credit rating*

PART   GER
needed for *borrowing* money.

Here *owning, getting, rating, needed,* and *borrowing* all look like participles, but only *owning* and *needed* serve the necessary adjectival function. The participial phrase *owning no property* modifies the noun *person,* and the past participle *needed* modifies the compound noun *credit rating.*

Participles normally appear immediately before or after the words they modify: *the needed credit rating; the credit rating needed.* The same is true of participial phrases: *owning no property, a person . . .; a person owning no property.* When a participle or participial phrase does not clearly modify a nearby nounlike element, it usually becomes subject to criticism as a *misrelated* or a *dangling modifier* (see pp. 292–293). An exception is made for *absolute* constructions (pp. 273, 294).

Gerunds

Gerunds look just like participles, but they or their gerund phrases are *used only as nouns:*

     GER
* *Meditating* is Norbert's favorite activity.

    The gerund serves as the subject of the verb *is.*

        GER
* He loves *còntemplating* the fact that all of nature worships him.

    The gerund begins a **gerund phrase** containing an object of the gerund *(fact)* and a modifying clause. The entire gerund phrase is the direct object of the verb *loves.* (He loves what? *Contemplating the fact that* etc.)

          GER
* Norbert is weary of *having striven.*

    The gerund is the object of the preposition *of.*

    Gerunds and participles alike can take objects. Thus, if you see a phrase like *achieving perfection,* you can expect that the *-ing* word is either a participle or a gerund; only its function in the sentence will tell you which it is. But the nounlike character of gerunds does give them some identifying features. Like nouns, they can be preceded by articles: *an achieving, the achieving.* If an *-ing* word is or can be preceded by an article, it is not a participle. And like nouns, gerunds can be preceded by possessive forms, called the subject of the gerund: *Norbert's achieving perfection; his losing selfhood.* When you have trouble deciding whether a certain word is a participle or a gerund, try inserting a possessive form before it. If the sentence still makes any grammatical sense at all, the word is a gerund:

     GER
* [her] *Debating* with Norbert is futile.

     PART
x [her] *Debating* with Norbert, Wanda drowned out his chants.

EXERCISE

6. List all the *verbals* you find in the following sentences, and identify each one as either an *infinitive, a participle,* or a *gerund:*

   A. Having nothing better to do, Biff began choking his tackling dummy.
   B. He really wanted to take a nap on the Astroturf.
   C. Having won the big game while he was wearing his lucky socks, he decided never to put them in the laundry again.
   D. Roaring crowds made the only kind of music Biff liked to hear.
   E. Biff's teammates soon learned to refrain from borrowing his socks.

PHRASES AND CLAUSES

Familiarity with the parts of speech can help you tell which words in a sentence are its sentence elements, or main functioning parts. But as we have already seen, sentence elements can also be formed by larger groupings of words, namely *phrases* and *clauses.*

Phrase versus Clause

A **phrase** is a cluster of words, not containing a subject-predicate combination, that functions as a single part of speech. Thus, in the sentence *A trip around the world would be expensive,* you can see that *around the world* is a phrase because (a) it forms a single cluster of words, or unit of meaning, (b) it contains no subject-predicate combination, and (c) it functions as a single part of speech—an adjective modifying *trip.*

A **clause**, by contrast, is a cluster of words containing a subject and a predicate. Thus the whole sentence *A trip around the world would be expensive* is a clause; its (complete) subject is *A trip around the world* and its predicate is *would be expensive.*

Independent versus Subordinate Clause

It is essential to recognize the difference between *independent* clauses —those that could form complete sentences by themselves—and *subordinate* (or *dependent*) clauses, which cannot stand alone:

INDEPENDENT CLAUSE:
* He resented staying at home.

SUBORDINATE CLAUSE:
* Although he resented staying at home, . . .

When you find a subordinate clause in a piece of writing, you automatically look for an independent one to accompany it. You read —though you may sometimes fail to write—with a comprehension that a sentence normally contains at least one independent clause, and you know that independent clauses never begin with subordinating words like *when* and *although*.

Phrases and Clauses as Sentence Elements

Think of a simple noun phrase such as *the ball*. In a sentence like *Biff drops the ball*, it is clear that the phrase serves as the direct object of the verb *drops*. So, too, whenever you come across a prepositional phrase, an infinitive phrase, a gerund phrase, a participial phrase, or an absolute phrase, you can expect it to be serving as a sentence element:

- She worked $\begin{cases} \text{M} \\ \text{slowly.} \\ \quad\text{M} \\ \textit{at a leisurely pace.} \end{cases}$

    A *prepositional phrase, at a leisurely pace,* is functioning as a *modifier* here—an alternative to an adverb, *slowly.*

- $\left.\begin{array}{l} \text{S} \\ \text{Illness} \\ \quad\text{S} \\ \textit{To be ill} \end{array}\right\}$ is always a nuisance.

    An *infinitive phrase* serves as a *subject,* just as the single noun *illness* does.

- She disliked $\begin{cases} \text{D OBJ} \\ \text{haste.} \\ \qquad\text{D OBJ} \\ \textit{hurrying here and there.} \end{cases}$

    A *gerund phrase* becomes a *direct object.*

- $\left.\begin{array}{l} \text{Toothless people} \\ \\ \text{People } \textit{lacking teeth} \end{array}\right\}$ smile less than others.

    A *participial phrase* does the work of a *modifier* (an adjective) in this case.

- He rose from the negotiating table $\begin{cases} \quad\text{M} \\ \text{wearily.} \\ \qquad\qquad\text{M} \\ \textit{, his weary look a sign of discouragement.} \end{cases}$

    An **absolute phrase**—one modifying an entire statement—acts like an adverb, *wearily.*

subordinate clauses as sentence elements By definition, independent clauses cannot serve as sentence elements; they are whole statements in themselves. Every subordinate clause, however, functions in one of the roles that phrases, too, perform.

noun clauses . . . Some subordinate clauses are known as **noun clauses**, since they can serve nounlike functions within a sentence:

> SUB CLAUSE AS S
>
> • *What you tell the committee* will be leaked to the press.

What you tell the committee is clearly a subordinate clause, since it contains a subject *(you)* and a predicate *(tell the committee what)* but is incomplete by itself. The whole clause serves as the subject of the verb *will be leaked*. A noun clause, it functions like a single-word subject such as *Testimony*.

> SUB CLAUSE AS D OBJ
>
> • The press always discovers *what you tell the committee.*

Our same noun clause is now the direct object of the verb *discovers.*

> SUB CLAUSE AS IND OBJ
>
> • The staff gives *what you tell the committee* a very critical reading.

The familiar noun clause is now performing the work of an indirect object. The staff gives a very critical reading *to* something, namely *what you tell the committee.*

> SUB CLAUSE AS OBJ PREP
>
> • Could you give us a general idea of *what you tell the committee* each day?

This time the whole noun clause serves as the object of the preposition *of.*

> SUB CLAUSE AS COMPL
>
> • The crucial thing is not what you actually did but *what you tell the committee.*

Now the clause has become the complement of the subject *thing: The thing is x.*

> SUB CLAUSE AS APP
>
> • Your testimony, *what you tell the committee,* could get us all in trouble.

Finally, the same clause stands in apposition to a noun subject, *testimony.*

adjectival clauses . . .   Just as a noun clause can act as any sentence element normally filled by a noun, so adjectival and adverbial clauses can act as modifiers. An **adjectival clause** does what an adjective would do; it modifies a noun, pronoun, or other nounlike element.

Here are some representative adjectival (or relative) clauses:

SUB CLAUSE AS ADJ
* Wratto, *who can make an entire poem out of zip codes,* deserves to be taken seriously by the critics.

> The adjectival clause modifies the subject *Wratto,* just as *Clever* would in the sentence *Clever Wratto deserves to be taken seriously.* Note that adjectival clauses characteristically follow the words they modify.

SUB CLAUSE AS ADJ
* He is the bard *that America has been seeking.*

> The whole clause modifies *bard,* a predicate noun.

. . . *adverbial clauses*   An **adverbial clause** acts like a single adverb, modifying a verb, an adjective, another adverb, a preposition, an infinitive, a participle, a phrase, another clause, or the rest of the sentence. In short, it can modify anything but nounlike elements:

SUB CLAUSE AS ADV
* *Because you have never answered my letter,* Fannie Farmer, I am now corresponding with Betty Crocker.

> The adverbial clause tells why something has happened; it modifies the verb *am corresponding.*

SUB CLAUSE AS ADV
* *However famous you may be as a sculptor,* that is an abominable snowman.

> The adverbial clause is equivalent to a sentence adverb (p. 265) such as *nevertheless.*

SUB CLAUSE AS ADV
* I want it to melt *as soon as it can.*

> This adverbial clause modifies an infinitive, *to melt.* Note that both clauses and phrases can be imbedded within larger structures that function as sentence elements.

elliptical clauses   Note that some subordinate clauses are incomplete or **elliptical:**

ELL CLAUSE
* Few months are as pleasant in North Dakota *as May.*

> The verb *is* is implied after *May.*

We will see in the next chapter that when an elliptical clause contains a pronoun, the only way to determine the right case form for that pronoun may be to supply the missing verb and then decide what sentence element the pronoun is serving (p. 288). Once again, then, your best hope for making correct choices of usage lies in a secure grasp of grammar.

Restrictive versus Nonrestrictive Elements

One tricky but essential distinction between subordinate elements, whether they be clauses, phrases, or single words, is the difference between restrictive and nonrestrictive functions. A **restrictive element**, as the name implies, serves to restrict—that is, to establish the identity of—the term it modifies:

RESTR CLAUSE
- People *who can't climb as well as monkeys* should stay out of trees.

The restrictive clause *identifies* the word it refers to, *people*, showing us that only certain people are meant.

A **nonrestrictive element**, which should always be set off by commas, provides information about the term it modifies, but does not identify it:

NONRESTR CLAUSE
- People, *who can't climb as well as monkeys*, should stay out of trees.

The commas show that all people are meant.

EXERCISES

7. Ten *phrases* and *clauses* are italicized in the following passage. Name the kind of phrase or clause in each instance. Phrases will be either *prepositional, infinitive, participial,* or *gerund;* clauses will be either *independent* or *subordinate,* and, if subordinate, either *nounlike (nominal), adjectival,* or *adverbial.*

*Interviewed after practice,*¹ Biff offered his opinion that *on any given Saturday*² one team would usually beat another. "Of course," he added, "they do have *to be playing each other*³ on that day. Am I right?" (*Although Biff is all business on the field,*⁵ he has a great sense of humor.) *What he meant*⁶ was that the better team is the one *that puts the most points up there on the old scoreboard.*⁷ "I just think that *getting into the end zone*⁸ is really an important part of the game," Biff said. "You can talk all you want about blocking, blitzing, and praying, but heck, I think the team *with the biggest score*⁹ at the end is the one *you should bet on.*¹⁰"

8. Write five sentences, each containing one subordinate clause. Try to make the five subordinate clauses as similar as possible in content, repeating words whenever you can. But give those clauses five different functions:

   A. a noun clause used as a subject;
   B. a noun clause used as a direct object;
   C. an adjectival clause modifying a subject;
   D. an adjectival clause modifying a direct object;
   E. an adverbial clause modifying the main verb of the sentence.

9. Write three pairs of sentences in which the same words form a *restrictive* element in the first sentence and a *nonrestrictive* element in the second (p. 276). Briefly indicate the difference of meaning in each case.

Our review of grammar has covered some fairly subtle distinctions, some of which may be hard to grasp at first. Do not worry; as a writer, you will find that a handful of concepts hold the key to improvement in usage (Chapter 11) and punctuation (Chapter 12). Those concepts are:

---

1. the sentence elements (pp. 242–244)
2. tense forms of verbs (pp. 248–251)
3. possessive forms of singular and plural nouns (p. 255)
4. the relation between a relative pronoun and its antecedent (pp. 258–259)
5. comparison of adjectives (p. 263)
6. sentence adverbs versus conjunctions (pp. 265–266)
7. the relation between participles and the words they modify (pp. 270–271)
8. use of the possessive in subjects of gerunds (p. 271)
9. the difference between phrases and clauses (p. 272)
10. the difference between independent and subordinate clauses (pp. 272–273)
11. the difference between restrictive and nonrestrictive elements (p. 276).

Having read through this chapter once, go back and sharpen your understanding of these eleven points; they will help you to make practical use of all the advice offered in the next two chapters.

11
PROBLEMS OF USAGE

We have seen that the barest description of English *grammar*—the formal, relatively stable features that distinguish the whole language from others—necessarily involves us in choices of *usage,* or accepted practices within standard written English (p. 241). To be "grammatical" is already to be using "good English," or following the rules of the standard grapholect.

Yet usage is a wider and more complicated territory than grammar. For usage often involves a choice between two forms that are equally "grammatical," such as *He saw that picture of Priscilla* and *He saw that picture of Priscilla's.* Both are proper English sentences, but only one would successfully convey your meaning in a given instance. What is acceptable in speech, furthermore, might look wrong when written down. No grammatical rule can remove all doubt from the choice between writing *I know whom you mean* and *I know who you mean.* The first sentence might sound too stuffy in speech; the second, too informal for an essay. Questions of usage shade into questions of the voice, tone, and stance you want to strike for a given audience and type of essay (pp. 11–14).

Nonetheless, certain broad principles of usage cover most of the problems you are likely to encounter:

1. Write complete sentences (below).
2. Match your subjects and predicates (p. 281).
3. Make your subjects and verbs agree in number (p. 283).
4. Match pronouns with their antecedents (p. 289).
5. Watch for misrelated and dangling modifiers (p. 292).
6. Make most subjects of gerunds possessive in case (p. 294).
7. Give parallel structure to elements that are parallel in meaning (p. 295).
8. Compare only those terms that can be considered together (p. 299).
9. Place your verbs and verbals in consistent sequences (p. 303).
10. Avoid double negatives (p. 308).

COMPLETE SENTENCES

A **sentence** is a group of words that can stand alone because it is understood to constitute a complete thought. It normally requires a *subject* and a *verb* in at least one *independent clause:*

<pre>
   S   V
• She goes.
  ‾‾‾‾‾‾‾‾‾
  IND CLAUSE
</pre>

sentence fragments: independent vs. unacceptable   In the context of a preceding or following sentence, an **independent sentence fragment** is allowable:

<pre>
                                      IND FRAG
• Whose stereo will be thrown overboard? Certainly not mine!
</pre>

<pre>
              IND FRAG
  ‾‾‾‾‾‾‾‾‾‾‾‾‾‾‾‾‾‾‾‾‾‾‾‾‾‾‾‾‾‾
• And now for a closer look at the small intestine.
</pre>

Such constructions are spared from sounding ungrammatical by the fact that they function as complete sentences. That is, readers perceive them as independent units, stating something, even though some of the ordinary makings of a statement are not there. The lack of a subject and verb makes for a calculated informality or an effect of transition from one point to the next. See, for example, the sequences of deliberate fragments in the "Banyan Street" passage on page 37 and the "urban planning" passage on page 169.

In many cases, however, sentence fragments are created by mistake. This is most clearly apparent when the fragment reads like a *continuation* of the sentence before it:

UNACCEPTABLE FRAG

x He found himself unable to proceed to Vancouver. *Having forgotten his raincoat.*

The fragment is a participial phrase modifying *He* in the sentence before. The best correction would be to put it before the modified word: *Having forgotten his raincoat, he found himself unable to proceed to Vancouver.*

x In Clifford's best seller the talking sparrows decide to fly to the very top
UNACCEPTABLE FRAG
of the sky. *Because they understand that every sparrow must strive to realize his or her most soaring dreams.*

The second "sentence" contains two sets of subjects and verbs, but the subordinating conjunction *Because* reveals that the whole construction is a subordinate clause. The fragment would be acceptable if the preceding sentence were a question such as *Why?* As it stands, however, it looks like a broken-off piece of one larger sentence. Try *In Clifford's best seller the talking sparrows, understanding that . . . dreams, decide . . . sky.*

Some writers try to justify haphazard sentence fragments by arguing that their meaning is easy to decipher. But this misses the point. Readers cannot simultaneously piece together an intended statement and be swayed by its aptness. By making sure that each of your sentences contains an independent idea, you work *with* your reader's expectations instead of awkwardly pushing against them.

For the related problem of *run-on* sentences, see page 314.

EXERCISE

1. Each of the following numbered items contains a sentence fragment. Even though they lack the usual makings of a sentence, some of the fragments are of the independent variety that readers generally accept. Others would be perceived as unacceptable or unintentional sentence fragments. Write a brief evaluation of each of the five fragments. Explain what causes you to regard each one as independent or unacceptable. For the unacceptable ones, make the revisions necessary to form complete sentences.

   A. This stock is selling at a price below its book value. What a bargain!
   B. Its price-earnings ratio is 1:0. Which is hard to beat.
   C. The market for laser death rays is expected to become firmer in the 1980's. Unless the peaceniks get control of the White House again.
   D. Why do you suppose it is listed as an under-the-counter stock? To attract the small investor, perhaps?
   E. Many people would kill for a chance to buy some shares. If they don't get killed first.
   F. Although he happens to be in jail at the moment. The chairman of the board has high hopes for General Catastrophe.

PREDICATION

Predication—saying something about something—is the essence of all statement. Every complete sentence hinges on one of the three fundamental predicates: an intransitive verb *(turned)*, a transitive verb and its direct object *(turned the knob)*, or a linking verb and its complement *(turned traitor, turned blue)*. To work properly, of course, a hinge must be securely attached at both sides. If a subject and predicate are incompatible in meaning or structure, the sentence, instead of moving freely like a well-hinged door, becomes annoyingly jammed in its frame.

mixed construction   The most extreme instances of faulty predication show **mixed construction**, whereby a sentence commits itself to one subject but then abandons it for another:

x An old man, he should watch his step in the bathtub.

The reader has every reason to think that *old man* will be the subject of the main verb. After the comma, however, the writer offers a new subject-predicate combination, leaving the *old man* grammatically stranded. The moral is to follow through on your commitments: *An old man should watch his step in the bathtub.*

Note that a deliberate "false start" (p. 202), though it resembles a mixed construction, is allowable if its shift of emphasis serves a rhetorical purpose.

mismatches between agents and actions   More commonly, a sentence showing faulty predication aligns one subject with one verb in a way that strains our sense of possibility. Take a mild example: *The meaning of the book deals with happiness.* The idea is easy enough to grasp, but something is amiss with the predication. A *meaning* is said to *deal with* something. To do that, a meaning would have to be an *agent*, someone or something capable of action. In this case the agent could be the author or even the book itself, conceived as an extension of the author's intent:

- Clifford deals with happiness.
- The book deals with happiness.

But *meaning* is not a subject of the same sort as *Clifford* or *book*. It is an abstraction—a concept, not an agent. If you wanted to keep *meaning* as the subject, you would have to couple it with a linking verb and a complement:

S   LV   PRED ADJ

- The *meaning* of the book *becomes* more *obvious* with each rereading.

S   LV   ADJECTIVAL PHRASE AS COMPL

- The *meaning* of the book *is easy to determine.*

S   LV   NOUN CLAUSE AS COMPL

- The *meaning* of the book *is that happiness lies within the reach of every courageous sparrow.*

In each of these examples the subject is not represented as doing anything. Rather, it is being described or characterized. Every time you write a clause, you are choosing to treat the subject either as a performer of action or as something to be characterized. Where the subject cannot plausibly fill its assigned role, as in *The meaning deals with . . .* , a fuzzy and unsatisfying effect results.

As commonly used by composition instructors, "faulty predication" goes beyond mismatches of subjects and verbs. Sometimes the problem occurs entirely *within* the predicate of a sentence:

x Those sadistic dog trainers have changed the qualities that made the dog "man's best friend" into a demon.

> Here the subject *(dog trainers),* transitive verb *(have changed),* and direct object *(qualities)* go together, but the rest of the predicate falls apart. How can abstract *qualities* be changed into *a demon?* Compare:

- Those sadistic dog trainers have changed man's best friend into a demon.

Faulty predication is likely to result when a writer hurries past the actual words in a sentence, believing that the idea behind them is clear. Often it is. But readers must take in sentences before they can digest ideas, and a sentence whose parts are not smoothly matched may be rejected before its content has been understood at all.

Even when a subject-predicate combination makes adequate grammatical sense, you still need to check it for *distinctness of assertion;* see pages 177–182.

EXERCISE

2. Correct any instances of faulty predication in these sentences:

    A. The reason Crazy Hoarse is a star is because he listens carefully to his research staff.

    B. He is always changing the wording of his lyrics into a song with greater appeal.

    C. His latest musical idea treats thirteen-year-old would-be lovers with special sympathy.

D. Purchases made by thirteen-year-old would-be lovers, it has been learned, buy more popular records than all other groups combined.

E. Crazy Hoarse's definition of success is when a person has three gold records about being broke, lonely, and out of luck.

AGREEMENT OF SUBJECT AND VERB

In standard English, verbs are supposed to agree in number with their subjects: singular subject, singular verb; plural subject, plural verb. The rule is clear, but applying it can sometimes be tricky. Here are the main sources of doubt.

Collective Nouns

A **collective noun** is singular in form but possibly plural in meaning, since it refers to a *collection* of members: *administration, army, audience, band, class, committee, crowd, faculty, family, fleet, government, public, team,* etc. Because such words are technically singular, you should usually make the verb singular:

- The orchestra *is playing* better now that the conductor is sober.
- A strong, united faculty *is needed* to stand firm against the erosion of parking privileges.
- In Priscilla's opinion the middle class *is* altogether too middle-class.

words like majority   But certain "numerical" collective words, such as *majority, minority, plurality, mass,* and *number,* take either a singular or a plural verb according to what is being discussed, the *totality* (singular) or the *items* (plural) that make it up. Thus:

TOTALITY (singular):
- The Democratic majority *is composed* of workers and shirkers.
- The mass of the two particles *was* difficult to measure.

SEPARATE ITEMS (plural):
- The majority of Democrats *are* staunchly opposed to local blackouts of the Game of the Week.
- The mass of men *lead* lives of quiet desperation.

Quantities

When the subject of a verb is a plural quantity such as *twenty-six miles,* ask yourself whether it is meant as a unit (singular) or as a number of items (plural):

AS A UNIT (singular):
* Twenty-six miles *is* the length of the race.

AS A NUMBER OF ITEMS (plural):
* Twenty-six difficult miles *lie* ahead of her.

mathematical relations   When adding or multiplying, you can use either a singular or a plural verb:

* One and one *is* [*are*] two.
* Eleven times three *is* [*are*] thirty-three.

In multiplication, the singular is more common. But the plural is required when a multiplication is expressed without *times*:

* Eleven threes *are* thirty-three.

Use the singular for all subtraction and division:

* Sixty minus forty *is* [*leaves*] twenty.
* Six divided by three *is* two.

Troublesome Terms

each; either; neither   As pronoun subjects, these words are always singular, even when followed by a plural construction such as *of them*:

      S   V
* *Each* of them *has* her own way of doing things.

      S   V
* *Either* of those purple skateboards *is* good enough for me.

      S   V
* *Neither* of Clifford's novels *has been reviewed* in the zoology journals.

    In the three sentences, *them, skateboards,* and *novels* are objects of prepositions, not true plural subjects.

Note that *each* sometimes appears in *apposition to* a plural subject (p. 243). In this role it means *apiece* and does not affect the number of the verb:

      S   APP V
* *They each have* their own favorite chapters to cry over.

none   The number of *none* should be determined by its meaning within a given sentence. If you mean *none* in the sense of *not a single one*, make the verb singular:

> S   V
> • *None* among us *is* likely to agree with Stanley's proposal to smash racism by blowing up Kentucky Fried Chicken.

But if you mean *all are not,* you can use a plural verb:

> S   V
> • *None* of us *are* enthusiastic about Operation Fingerlicker.

In doubtful cases you would do well to stick to the singular verb, preferred by purists.

or; either . . . or; neither . . . nor   When these conjunctions link the parts of a compound subject, the verb should be governed, not by the sum of the parts, but only by the *nearest* (the last) item in that subject. Thus, if the last item is singular, the verb too should be singular:

>   LAST ITEM IN S
> • Neither apple pie nor her cat posters nor her neglected *guppy collection*
> V
> *holds* the slightest interest for Priscilla any more.

It is always preferable, however, to avoid such awkward conflicts of number. Try *Priscilla no longer has the slightest interest in her apple pie, her cat posters, and her neglected guppy collection.*

along with; as well as; in addition to; together with   These and other compound prepositions (p. 260) should not be mistaken for *conjunctions.* In other words, they do not make a singular subject plural:

>   S
> • Stanley's *mimeograph machine,* along with his bullhorn and spray paint,
> V
> *gives* him a sense of comradeship with working people everywhere.

> The prepositional phrase *along with his bullhorn and spray paint* does not affect the number of the verb.

Subject Following Verb

When a subject comes after its verb, make sure you do not allow an earlier noun to control the number of the verb. That error occurs here:

> x Immediately after the light rains of early November have dampened the
>   V   S
> woods *come* the *time* when Melody can be found gathering certain prized mushrooms.

> The writer has mistaken *woods,* the direct object of *have dampened,* for the subject of *come.* The verb must be *comes,* in agreement with the singular subject *time.*

Subjects Consisting of Phrases or Clauses

Even if it contains plural items, a phrase or clause acting as a subject takes a singular verb:

> PHRASE AS S   V
> • *Having the numbers of several bail bondsmen is* useful in an emergency.
>
> NOUN CLAUSE AS S   V
> • *That none of his customers wanted to buy a matching fleet of De Sotos was* a disagreeable surprise for Harry.

Subject Pronouns with Plural Antecedents

When a subject like *who, which,* or *that* introduces a relative clause (p. 258), you should make the verb in that clause agree in number with the antecedent (p. 258) of the subject pronoun—that is, with the earlier word that the pronoun stands for:

> ANT   S PRO V
> • *Math problems, which are* her specialty, give her no trouble at all.

The singular complement, *specialty,* would tempt many writers to say **x** *which is her specialty.* Ignore the complement and be guided by the antecedent.

it is + *plural subject as antecedent*   Consider this imperfect sentence:

> x It is the vegetables that makes Max feel queasy.

Here the writer has felt required to make the second verb agree with a singular antecedent, *It.* But *It* in this sentence is an expletive (p. 267), not a pronoun. Its function is simply to anticipate the true subject, *vegetables.* And since *vegetables* is also the antecedent of the relative pronoun *that,* the verb in the relative clause should agree with it: *make.*

EXERCISE

3. For each sentence, choose the verb form that makes for subject-verb agreement:

 A. It is their own secret vices that *(allows, allow)* people to tolerate the vices of others.
 B. Neither of them *(remembers, remember)* who ran for President against Harry Truman.
 C. Above the wealthiest section of Rio *(stands, stand)* some of the world's most miserable slums.
 D. Baseball, along with all other sports, *(strikes, strike)* Priscilla as utterly meaningless.
 E. There *(is, are)* four candidates in this election.

F. A number of people *(dislikes, dislike)* mushroom pizza.
G. Each of them *(is, are)* equally certain of being right.
H. Any idea for improving this company's profits *(is, are)* welcome.
I. A majority of votes *(is, are)* all you need to be elected.
J. Neither age nor illness *(prevents, prevent)* her from laughing at the world's follies.

PRONOUN PROBLEMS

Shift of Person

When you refer to a general "third person" in one part of a sentence, beware of shifting back to the personal *you:*

x A good song lends comfort to *people,* so that *you* feel less alone.

You would be appropriate only if the first part of the sentence had laid the groundwork for it: *A good song comforts you,* . . . . If you leave the first part of the sentence unchanged, *you* must become *they.*

Choice of Case

overcorrection The choice between subjective *(she)* and objective *(her)* case forms of pronouns causes misery for many writers. Knowing that uneducated speakers tend to use objective forms where standard English calls for subjective ones (x *Him and me are friends*), they automatically "overcorrect" in certain situations:

        D OBJ   D OBJ
x They appointed *she* and *I* to a subcommittee.

As direct objects, the pronouns must be *her* and *me.* Nothing should be changed by the fact that there are two direct objects instead of one.

Similarly, do not allow the case of a pronoun to be determined by a following appositive (p. 243):

        OBJ PREP   APP
x Parking is a tragic dilemma for *we* professors.

Since you would not write *for we,* do not write *for we professors.*

Observe that the way to decide between two pronoun forms is not to choose the one that sounds like "better English" but to see which grammatical function is being performed. If you identify a pronoun as a direct or indirect object, an object of a preposition, a subject of an infinitive (*gave her to understand*), an object of an infinitive (*to meet her*), or a complement of an infinitive (*to be her*), make it objective in case.

pronoun complements   In speech, pronoun complements are often heard in the objective case (*That's him; It's them*). In standard English writing, the same policy would raise some eyebrows, Should you, then, write *That is he* and *It is they*? Perhaps—if you do not mind sounding like a fussy purist. It would be better to duck the problem: *He is the one; I meant them; etc.*

<u>*who versus whom*</u>   Most worries over pronoun case have to do with the relative and interrogative forms *who* and *whom*. The advice already given suggests that (1) you should not use one form where the other is strictly correct, and (2) you should not use either of them if the "right" form sounds like a forced attempt at "good English."

1. Wherever you find yourself using *who* as the *subject of a clause*, go ahead and do so—even though the whole clause may have an objective function in its sentence:

    s
• Stanley had no doubt about *who* would be elected Minister of Defense.

    The whole clause *who would be elected Minister of Defense* is the object of the preposition *about*. But *who*, as a pronoun *within* that clause, must remain subjective; it is the subject of the verb *would be elected*. Remember that case is always determined by the function within the clause, not by the function *of* the clause.

2. Wherever the "correct" form makes a strained effect, recast the whole sentence. Thus, if *Whom did you see there?* sounds overformal, do not write *Who did you see there?* Find an alternative: *Who was it? Who was there? Who was it that you saw? etc.*

pronoun following <u>than or as</u>   After *than* or *as*, a pronoun can be either subjective or objective in case, depending on the intended meaning. To see the function—and therefore the case—of the pronoun, supply any missing parts of the clause:

• Biff tackled Otto harder than [he did] me.
• He is stronger than I [am].
• He is as tall as they [are].

Since the "right" choices in such elliptical clauses (p. 275) often sound strained, however, you may prefer to include the missing sentence elements: *He is stronger than I am*, and so on.

Pronoun Reference

Personal, relative, demonstrative, and some indefinite pronouns usually stand in relation to *antecedents*—words for which they are substitutes. **Pronoun reference** has to do with the two key relations between a pronoun and its antecedent. First, is the antecedent immediately recognizable? And second, does the pronoun agree with its antecedent in number and person?

identification of antecedent As a rule, the **antecedent** of a pronoun is a noun or nounlike element in the same sentence or the one just before. Sometimes a personal pronoun, such as *she* or *they*, is so clearly identified that it can appear in several sentences in a row without repetition of the antecedent. A whole paragraph without an antecedent, however, would exhaust your pronoun credit; the first sentence in a paragraph is an especially important place to remind readers of a continuing antecedent.

An antecedent ought to be explicitly stated, even when the reader could supply it. The following sentences do not measure up:

                                                    PRO
x The peanut jar was empty, but Bobo was tired of nibbling *them* anyway.

> There are no *peanuts* here to serve as the antecedent of *them*.

x He was opposed to gun control because he felt that every citizen should
        PRO
have *one* in case the cops staged a surprise raid.

> The word *gun* appears in the sentence, but only as an attributive (adjectival) noun. A phrase like *control of guns* would put things right.

Even when an explicit antecedent is present, make sure it can be easily spotted. If a reader has to study the context in order to see which of two nounlike elements is the antecedent, the sentence should be clarified:

              ANT?   ANT?   PRO
x Because Biff now loved *Suzie* better than *Alice*, he made *her* return his souvenir faceguard.

> After some reflection, a reader might see that *Alice* must be the intended antecedent. But why not make the meaning clear at once? Try *he made Alice return* etc., or rewrite the sentence: *Because he had decided to split up with Alice, Biff made her return* etc.

vague this When revising, check your drafts for sentences beginning with the demonstrative pronoun *this: This means that. . . .* When *this* refers to the whole previous statement rather than to a specific part of it, the sentence can be confusing. Force yourself to be more definite by changing demonstrative pronouns to demonstrative *adjectives: This opinion . . .; This turn of events. . . .*

ambiguous which Similarly, when you find a clause beginning with the relative pronoun *which,* check to see whether it refers to a preceding *word* or to a *whole statement.* Many *which*'s in draft sentences prove to be fatally ambiguous:

x The plane was grounded by a strike, which is what we had expected all along.

> What was expected, the strike or the grounding of the plane? Once you decide, you can make the sentence clear:

• As we had expected, the plane was grounded by a strike.

agreement with antecedent Personal pronouns agree with their antecedents in *number* and *person,* but not necessarily in case. Shifts of number or person, although often heard in speech, should be avoided in writing:

```
                        ANT                           PRO
```
x Melody learned that if a *clerk* has a hang-loose attitude, *they* will get fired from the lingerie department.

> The plural pronoun *they* disagrees in number with the singular antecedent *clerk.* Although it gets around a sometimes awkward choice between *he* and *she* (see pp. 220–221), it does so at the expense of accepted usage. Try instead:

• Melody learned that a clerk who has a hang-loose attitude will etc.

that versus which Once you have grasped the difference between restrictive and nonrestrictive elements (p. 276), you can sharpen the distinction by keeping *which* for nonrestrictive uses:

```
                    NONRESTR EL
```
• Melody's hair, *which* had not been cut in years, came in handy as a towel.

```
                                    RESTR EL
```
• She admired the trouble *that* her friends took to dye their hair orange and green.

> *Which* would be allowable in the second sentence, but *that* leaves no doubt about the restrictive (defining) role of the clause it introduces.

EXERCISES

4. Some or all of the following sentences show either an unacceptable shift of person (p. 287) or a wrong choice of case (pp. 287–288). For each item, explain why the handling of pronouns is correct or incorrect.

    A. If a person gets upset easily, you shouldn't play golf.

    B. It is hard for we Americans to realize how rapidly the balance of power is shifting.

    C. Whom could you trust with the keys to a gas station these days?

    D. For success in business, much depends on who you know.

    E. The customs officers gave her and we to understand that we would be thoroughly searched.

5. Some or all of the following sentences show faulty pronoun reference (pp. 289–290). For each item, explain why the handling of pronouns is correct or incorrect. Submit a correct version of each sentence that you find faulty.

    A. I want to drum some statistics into your heads which are concrete.

    B. His father always told him what to do, but sometimes he wasn't familiar enough with the facts.

    C. Although she was worried at first, it diminished after a while.

    D. A woman who turns in their friend to the police isn't going to be very popular.

    E. If your goldfish won't eat its food, feed it to the canary.

MODIFIERS

Emphatic Placement of Adverbs

The position you assign an adverb can significantly affect the meaning of your sentence. Compare:

- *Only* I can understand your argument. [No one else can.]
- I can *only* understand your argument. [I can't agree with it.]
- I can understand *only* your argument. [But not your motives; *or* The arguments of others mystify me.]

Although most adverbs belong immediately before the words they modify, emphasis and sentence rhythm may sometimes dictate other positions if there is no danger of ambiguity. The placement of sentence adverbs (p. 265) like *therefore* and *however* is especially flexible. Unlike other adverbs, sentence adverbs place a stress on the words that immediately precede them:

- I, *however*, refuse to comply. [I contrast myself with others.]
- I refuse, *however*, to comply. [My refusal is emphatic.]

In the initial and final positions, sentence adverbs are less emphatic:

* *However,* I refuse to comply.
* I refuse to comply, *however.*

The final position is the least emphatic of all.

Misrelated Modifiers

A misrelated modifier is one with a flawed relation to the term it modifies. Either the modified term is hard to identify, or the modifier unnecessarily interrupts another construction, or there is too much distance between the modifier and what it modifies.

squinting modifiers   Guard against trapping a modifier between two sentence elements that might compete to serve as the modified term. This becomes a **squinting modifier**—one that seems to be looking in two directions at once:

SQ MOD
x How Harry silenced the transmission *completely* amazes me.

Does *completely* modify *silenced* or *amazes*? In saying the sentence aloud, a speaker would control the meaning by pauses and stresses, as you can see if you speak each of the possible versions in turn. Again:

SQ MOD
x Priscilla was confident *on Tuesday* she would receive a divine signal.

Was she confident on Tuesday, or would she receive the signal on Tuesday? A timely *that,* placed either before or after *on Tuesday,* would make everything clear.

split infinitives   Much nail-biting over adverbs can be traced to the overrated taboo of the **split infinitive**, an infinitive containing an adverb between *to* and the next verb form: *to thoroughly understand.* Most writers would now indulge in an occasional split infinitive, but only where every alternative position for the adverb would make for even more awkwardness:

* Harry always made it a point to *clearly* state that his cars carried a twenty-minute, thirty-mile guarantee.

A writer in terror of splitting an infinitive might have written *clearly to state* or *to state clearly.* But the trouble with these alternatives, especially the first, is that they would have called attention to the writer's discomfort. It is better to split and have done with it than to sound overfastidious.

Although opinion is divided about the importance of avoiding split infinitives, everyone agrees that adverbial constructions of more than one word make an ugly effect in the split-infinitive position: x *I want to soberly and patiently analyze the problem.* Rephrase: *I want to analyze the problem soberly and patiently* or *I want to make a sober and patient analysis. . . .*

hidden modified terms Modifiers should come immediately before or after the words they modify. Do not allow other nounlike elements to stand where a reader would expect to find the modified term:

$$\overset{\text{M}}{\overbrace{\hspace{5cm}}}$$

MODIFIED TERM

x *Head of the Fingerlickers from the start,* they naturally looked to *Stanley* for ideological guidance.

> The pronoun *they* stands where the modified term ought to be. Possible revision: *All the Fingerlickers looked to Stanley, their leader from the start, for ideological guidance.*

Again:

$$\overset{\text{M}}{\overbrace{\hspace{6cm}}}$$

x *Thinking that a Snoopy sweat shirt would win Priscilla over,* it only re-
MODIFIED TERM
mained for *Philo* to choose an appropriate greeting card.

> Here the anticipatory pronoun *it* stands where the modified term ought to be. Revise: *Thinking . . . over, Philo turned his attention to the choice of an appropriate greeting card.*

Dangling Modifiers

If the modified term is altogether absent, the modifier is called **dangling**. These faulty sentences illustrate the problem:

$$\overset{\text{M}}{\overbrace{\hspace{4cm}}}$$

x *Embracing the astonished Priscilla,* a rash erupted behind Philo's left knee.

> The possessive form *Philo's* cannot serve as the modified term; its function is adjectival, and one adjectival element cannot modify another. Revise: *Embracing* etc., *Philo felt a rash erupting* etc.

$$\overset{\text{M}}{\overbrace{\hspace{3cm}}}$$

x *Anticipating every taste,* it was decided to advertise the car as "an oversexed, pulse-quickening respecter of environmental quality."

> Nobody is doing the anticipating here. Try *Anticipating* etc., *the agency executives decided* etc.

Note that *absolute phrases* (p. 273) look like misrelated or dangling modifiers, but are not held accountable to the usual requirement of having a nearby modified term:

ABS PHRASE
- *Generally speaking,* Melody's memory is rather smoky.

ABS PHRASE
- *The Gauls having been defeated,* Caesar sat down to practice his declensions.

EXERCISE

6. Some or all of the following sentences contain misrelated or dangling modifiers. For each item, explain why the handling of modifiers is correct or incorrect. Submit a correct version of each sentence that you find faulty.

    A. He knew by Friday he would soon be free.
    B. Before going to bed, the false teeth should be removed for maximum comfort.
    C. If you want to quickly, safely, and pleasantly make your way through the dense jungle at Disneyland, a native guide is necessary.
    D. His coach, though he was still very inexperienced, believed he detected some athletic promise in the eight-foot Elbows Lodgepole.
    E. He paid the penalty for his crimes in prison.

POSSESSIVES

Care is required for the correct formation of ordinary possessives (pp. 350–352). In addition, problems arise over *double possessives* and *subjects of gerunds.*

Double Possessives

The possessive or genitive relation is usually indicated by either an -'s inflection (*Lindbergh's*) or an *of* construction (*of Lindbergh*). Sometimes, however, the two forms can be meaningfully combined. Observe the difference between these sentences:

- She remained unmoved by any thought $\begin{cases} \text{of Philo.} \\ \text{of Philo's.} \end{cases}$

These are two distinct statements. The top one deals with a thought *about* Philo; the bottom one, with a thought *proposed by* Philo—it is *his.*

Note that although some grammarians frown on double possessives, everyone uses them with pronouns: *a peculiarity of hers; that nasty habit of his.* You can use them just as easily with nouns: *a book-keeping trick of Harry's; that sawed-off shotgun of Bobo's.*

Subjects of Gerunds and Gerund Phrases

The subject of a gerund (p. 271) is usually written in the possessive case:

>   S GER GER
> * Biff didn't know why everyone laughed at *his saying* he would like to be an astronaut and see all those steroids going by.

But the rule is hard to apply in many instances. For example, if the gerund's subject is separated from the gerund by other words, that subject goes in the objective case instead of the possessive:

>   S GER   GER
> * People were surprised at *him,* a veteran speaker on many campuses, *having* no ready reply when Stanley seized the microphone and called him an irrelevant murderer.

Again, when the subject of a gerund is an abstract or inanimate noun, it can appear in a nonpossessive form:

>   S GER   GER
> * We cannot ignore the danger of *catastrophe striking* again.

EXERCISE

7. Correct any mistaken use (or absence) of possessives in the following sentences:

    A. That plan of Stanley is one that even his closest friends can't endorse.
    B. He being there came as a shock to everyone.
    C. Philo didn't enjoy thinking of Priscilla's, his beloved's, spurning him.
    D. They all rejected that idea of the Senator's.
    E. Stanley leaving town was suspiciously hasty.

PARALLELISM

Closely matched parts of a sentence (pp. 191–197) are said to be *parallel*. Parallelism shows, not necessarily that the items have equal importance, but that they fit within one mental operation. Thus, if your matching structure is *either x or y, not x but y,* or *not only x but y as well,* you are telling your reader to consider one item in close relation to another. Likewise, a parallel *series* indicates that all the included items share the same logical relation to another element in the sentence: *The causes of erosion are x, y, and z.*

Potentially valuable as it is, parallelism can become a handicap if your grammar and punctuation fail to keep the included items in alignment. Watch for the following common problems.

Inconsistent Parallelism

The elements you match in a parallel construction ought to be of the same kind—verbs aligned with verbs, nouns with other nouns or nounlike elements, objects of prepositions with other objects of prepositions, and so forth. This sentence fails the test:

x   y

x Melody was both habitually *late* to work and a sound *sleeper* on the job.

> The sentence awkwardly matches an adjective and a noun. Grammatically like elements—*late* and *sleepy*, or *latecomer* and *sleeper*—are needed for adequate alignment.

The same principle applies to items within a series. Compare:

x Fido's whole ambition in life was *to eat, to play,* and *sleeping.*
• Fido's whole ambition in life was *to eat, to play,* and *to sleep.*

> In the first sentence, two infinitives are awkwardly matched with a gerund. In the second, the three infinitives form a grammatically consistent parallelism.

Again:

x In this modern success story, the hero decides to *give up* making sand candles, *leave* his commune, and *goes* to New York to become an IBM executive.

> The verb *decides* and the infinitive marker *to* prepare us for a parallelism of three infinitives: *decides to x, y, and z.* Instead, the "z" turns out to be a verb. Change *goes* to *go.* Or, if *goes* conveys what you mean, take it out of the parallel series:

• . . . the hero decides to give up making sand candles and leave his commune. Eventually, he goes to New York etc.

Note that if you begin repeating any word within a series, you should do so consistently until the series ends:

• He never misses *his* sandals, *his* yogurt, *his* goat, and *his* compost heap.

Once the second *his* appears, the writer is committed to supplying the other two.

• The hope of the world, he now realizes, must lie *in* software, *in* semiconductors, and *in* systems analysis.

The second *in* makes the third one necessary. Note that *in software, semiconductors, and systems analysis* would be equally right.

not . . . neither In *not . . . neither* constructions, make sure the first negation does not warp the meaning of the second one:

x The Marquis de Sade was not an agreeable man, and neither are his novels.

The complement *man* makes the sentence appear to say that the novels were not an agreeable man. Compare:

• The Marquis de Sade was not agreeable, and neither are his novels.

compound verbs Beware also of compound verbs involving a change of tense:

x Melody *can,* and indeed *has been, hitchhiking* in both directions at once.

The way to check such sentences is to read them without the interruption: *Melody can hitchhiking* etc. If you want to save the present form of the sentence, write *Melody can hitchhike, and indeed has been hitchhiking, in both* etc. But that sounds clumsy. A better solution is to get rid of the compound verb: *Melody has been hitchhiking* etc.

Invaded Parallelism

Many parallel constructions go awry because a sentence element preceding the construction, and therefore standing outside it, is allowed to invade it toward the end. For example:

x They serve *as* either fire roads or *as* hiking trails.

The intended pattern here is *as either x or y;* the second *as* has wrongly invaded the construction. To revise, either drop the second *as* or begin the parallelism earlier:

• They serve either as fire roads or as hiking trails.

Now the pattern is *either as x or as y;* the second *as* is justified because it matches an element within the construction, not outside it.

not only . . . but also   When you undertake the useful but tricky *not only . . . but also* pattern, you must be especially careful to see where in your sentence the parallelism begins. A sentence function preceding *not only* should not be duplicated *within* the parallel construction. To illustrate, let us consider three ways of handling a subject *(S)*, a verb *(V)*, and a direct object *(DO):*

PATTERN	EXAMPLE
1. not only S V DO, but also S V DO	• Not only does *he broaden* his *outlook*, but *he* also *broadens* his *waistline*.
2. S not only V DO, but also V DO	• He not only *broadens* his *outlook*, but also *broadens* his *waistline*.
3. S V not only DO, but also DO	• He broadens not only his *outlook*, but also his *waistline*.

Although the last of these sentences is preferable on grounds of conciseness, all three are correctly formed. Compare:

x He not only *broadens* his *outlook*, but *he* also *broadens* his *waistline*.

> The excluded subject, *he*, wrongly finds its way into the parallel construction.

x He broadens not only his *outlook*, but *he* also *broadens* his *waistline*.

> Here the invasion is more drastic; an unwanted subject and verb ruin the intended parallelism of two direct objects.

Note that some parallel formulas do allow for a duplication of sentence functions: *She was less concerned about x than she was about y; He is not so much x as he is y;* etc. The "extra" subject-verb combinations *(she was; he is)* are not invasions, but optional aids to clarity.

Incomplete Parallelism

Just as you should not insert elements that belong outside your parallel construction, so you must follow through with a pattern once begun. Suppose, in the last set of examples, we had tried this version:

$$\overset{S}{} \quad \overset{V}{} \quad \overset{DO}{} \quad \overset{DO}{}$$

x Not only does *he broaden* his *outlook,* but also his *waistline.*

The inclusion of essential sentence elements—a subject, a verb, and a direct object—within the first part of the construction leads us to expect comparable elements in the other part. Instead, we find only a direct object. Although it is easy enough to understand, the parallelism is faulty on grounds of incompleteness.

parallel <u>*that*</u> *clauses* When you place whole clauses in parallelism, you must guard against allowing the parallel effect to lapse prematurely. The danger is greatest when the first of two items is a *that* clause:

x He wrote that *he already disliked British rule,* but *at the same time he was glad to learn about parliamentary government.*

A second *that* is needed before the "*y*" element to show its parallelism with the "*x*" element. As the sentence stands, the "*y*" element reads like an independent clause—a new statement rather than a second part of what *he wrote.*

EXERCISE

8. The following sentences show faulty handling of parallel structure. Submit correct versions in each case.

   A. He is not an outstanding swimmer, and neither is his running.
   B. Harry told his angry customer that the car was indeed loaded with options, just as he had claimed, and one option was whether or not to start on cold mornings.
   C. George couldn't remember whether Susan had asked him to buy low-fat milk, condensed milk, defatted, reconstituted, or evaporated milk.
   D. Stanley writes leaflets, makes underground broadcasts, tape recordings, and paints warnings on police-station walls.
   E. Not only is he skilled in sabotage, but in psychological warfare as well.

COMPARISONS

Comparative words like *more, better,* and *least,* indicating a ranking of two or more related items, bring with them a special set of problems. When you find such words in a draft, look to see if you have courted one of the following kinds of trouble.

Missing Term

At least two terms should be explicitly present if a comparison is to be made. This point seems obvious, but it is blurred by the influence of advertising style: *Get 23 percent less emphysema!* It is true that some normal expressions contain incomplete comparisons: *I feel better today, It is best for you to leave, You have been most helpful,* etc. No one would regard these sentences as wrong; the comparative word is being used merely as an intensifier (*most* = "very"). The problem sentences are those in which we wait for the second shoe to drop:

x Biff learned that it was *more* important for a pro athlete to be able to shave in front of a TV crew without snickering.

More important than what? Once this information has been promised by the comparative word *more,* it ought to be supplied.

Comparing the Incomparable

Do not allow your language to imply a comparative relation between items of completely different types:

x y
x The *accuracy* of Bobo's shooting was greater than his *tax return.*

The sentence appears to compare *accuracy* to a *tax return.* Revise: *greater than that of his tax return.*

Comparison of Absolutes

Words like *complete, equal, infinite, perfect,* and *unique* are sometimes called *absolutes;* that is, they are regarded as not lending themselves to qualification. If something is not altogether unique, it is not unique at all. But does this mean that such words should never be modified or compared? When you look at sentences one by one, you find that matters are not so simple. Thus the comparison of *perfect* sounds normal enough in this sentence:

• Our purpose in founding this institute in Zurich is to form a *more perfect* Jungian.

Or again:

• The inclusion of his early letters to Santa Claus makes this the *most complete* edition of Dickens ever published.

But compare:

x The sands of Lake Havasu City are *less infinite* than those of the Sahara.

Here the dictionary meaning of *infinite* is being violated; the word cannot be applied to any number or size smaller than the greatest. *Perfect* and *complete*, by contrast, have secondary meanings of *excellent* and *thorough*, and in those senses they can be modified.

Faulty Suspended Comparison

Suspended (delayed) comparisons often end in a tangle:

x Melody likes total strangers *as much,* if not *more than,* her closest friends.

The problem here, as in many suspended comparisons, is that the last part of the comparison fits with only one of the two elements that lead to it. *More than her closest friends* makes sense, but *as much her closest friends* does not. To be technically right, the suspended comparison would have to say *as much as, if not more than, her closest friends.* But why not do away with the clumsy suspended formula altogether? Try *She likes total strangers at least as much as her closest friends.*

Use of <u>Like</u> for <u>As</u>

Properly speaking, *like* is usually a preposition introducing a prepositional phrase, and *as* is usually a conjunction introducing a subordinate clause:

PREP
* <u>*Like* General MacArthur,</u> Melody was very fond of wading.
　　　　PREP PHRASE

CONJ
* <u>*As* the *Maine* goes,</u> so goes the nation.
　　SUB CLAUSE

Both words have other functions as well, but in written prose, *like* should not crowd out this particular function of *as:* x *Like the Maine goes, ...*

When in doubt, remember that *like* usually compares *things or people* (Melody and General MacArthur) while *as* usually compares *actions or states* (the *Maine* goes; the nation goes). In short, look for a following verb. When you find a draft sentence saying *like the poet writes* or *like I insisted above,* change *like* to *as.*

Inconsistent Comparison

Since comparing is a form of matching, it is not surprising that comparisons run into problems of faulty parallelism. Many a comparison begins acceptably but fails to carry through:

   x Stanley said the dean *was more like* a Gestapo officer, *rather than* a liberal administrator.

> The right formula is *more like x than y.* The comma and the extra word *rather* interrupt that formula, making the first part of the comparison read like an independent statement.

Again:

   x No sooner had I left when my typewriter was stolen.

> The right formula is *no sooner . . . than.*

   x She was not so much selfish, but rather impulsive.

> *Not so much* must be completed by an element starting with *as: She was not so much selfish as impulsive* or *She was not so much selfish as she was impulsive.*

Misuse of the Superlative

When comparing only two things, do not use the superlative degree of an adjective *(most, least,* etc.):

   x Sluggo and Bobo had a playful little fight to see who would pick up the check. Bobo, the survivor, proved the *strongest* of the two.

> Change *strongest* to *stronger,* the comparative form of the adjective.

> Many readers object to the "gushy" use of superlatives when no comparison is intended:

   x Biff has the *oddest* complexion since he started taking those shots.

EXERCISE

9. Each of the following sentences contains a faulty comparison. Submit a corrected version in each case.

    A. The chemical structure of smog is entirely different from cigarette smoke.
    B. Heating systems for neocolonial-Elizabethan tract houses are harder to install than large apartment buildings.
    C. Melody wears the sweetest smile all day long.
    D. She is more totally carefree now than ever before.
    E. The store manager couldn't believe that a salesperson would rather lean out the window and wave at passers-by instead of tending to business.
    F. Like he told Melody, he had started his own career in underwear.

G. At least as much, if not more than, his fellow clerks, he had always tried to keep his eye on the bottom line.
H. Between Melody and himself, he was clearly the most dedicated to making a sale.
I. Looking forward to her vacation was Melody's most favorite way of occupying her mind.
J. The manager thought she would do better to wait on the customers rather than asking them for spare change.

SEQUENCE OF TENSES

The first verb in a sentence establishes a time frame for the rest of that sentence, affecting the tense of any later verb, infinitive, participle, or gerund. A reader will be jarred if one of those later forms unexpectedly drops out of the frame:

> PAST   PRESENT
> x When he *phoned* her, she *tells* him to leave her alone.

The second verb must be *told,* to conform with the past frame established by *phoned.*

Although this principle looks clear enough, applying it consistently can become difficult in certain cases:

Verbs

past perspective on a prior time   If your main verb is in the past tense and you want to relate it to a still earlier time, the verb expressing that earlier time should be in the *past perfect* tense:

> PAST   PAST PERFECT
> • Philo *discovered* that he *had made* a mistake in giving Priscilla a pink teddy bear.

past perspective on a later time   If your main verb is in the past tense and you want to look forward from that time to a later one, use the auxiliary *would* plus the base (infinitive) form of the verb:

> PAST   AUX BASE V
> • He *knew* that he *would have* some explaining to do.

action to be completed before a future time   If your sentence looks forward to a time when a certain action will have been completed, combine the present and future perfect tenses:

               PRESENT   FUTURE PERFECT
- When Philo *sees* her next week, she *will have exchanged* the teddy bear for tickets to the harpsichord recital.

hypothetical conditions   Some sentences describe what would be true or would have been true in certain imagined circumstances. For circumstances imagined *as present,* use the present subjunctive (p. 251) in the "condition" clause and *would* plus a base verb form in the "consequence" clause:

         PRES SUBJV   AUX BASE V
- If Philo *phoned* Priscilla now, he *would get* an icy reception.
        CONDITION CLAUSE   CONSEQUENCE CLAUSE

For circumstances imagined as *past,* use the past subjunctive (p. 253) in the "condition" clause and *would have* plus a past participle in the "consequence" clause:

         PAST SUBJV   AUX   PAST PART
- If he *had phoned* her then, he *would have gotten* an icy reception.
        CONDITION CLAUSE   CONSEQUENCE CLAUSE

Note that you can use an alternative subjunctive form for present hypothetical conditions: *If he were to phone* etc. But for past hypothetical conditions, stay with the subjunctive form that is identical to the past perfect:

         PAST SUBJV   AUX   PAST PART
- If he *had called,* she *would have said,* "Priscilla is not at home. This is her teddy bear speaking. Leave your message at the sound of the tone."

A common mistake is to allow *would* to enter both clauses: **x** *If he would have called, she would have said* etc. Remember that *would* always belongs with the consequence, not the condition.

indirect discourse   Reporting what was said, instead of directly quoting it, is known as **indirect discourse**. Observe what happens to tenses in shifting from quotation to indirect discourse:

	quotation	indirect discourse
present verb in quotation	"I find it difficult to remember your name," she said.	She said that she *found* it difficult to remember his name.
past verb in quotation	"Your interest in bowling gave cause for alarm," she revealed.	She revealed that his interest in bowling *had given* cause for alarm.
present perfect verb in quotation	She protested, "I have never encouraged your crude advances."	She protested that she *had* never *encouraged* his crude advances.

past perfect verb in quotation	"Until then," she reflected, "I had never known how barbarous a male could be."	She reflected that until then she *had* never *known* how barbarous a male could be.
future verb in quotation	She added, "You will do better to bestow your 'date,' as you choose to call it, for the 'demolition derby' on some companion more keenly appreciative of such cultural gatherings than myself."	She added that he *would do* better to bestow his so-called "date" etc.

In short, indirect discourse

> makes a *present* verb *past;*
> makes a *past* or *present perfect* verb *past perfect;*
> leaves a *past perfect* verb *past perfect;* and
> turns a *future* verb into *would* plus a base (infinitive) form.

You can deduce other tense changes in indirect discourse from these basic ones; *will have refused* becomes *would have refused, has been refusing* becomes *had been refusing,* etc.

discussion of literature   Although most literary works are narrated in the past tense (*Mike poured Brett a triple martini*), you should shift the action to the present tense when you write about it: not *poured* but *pours.* In other words, treat the action of the story, novel, poem, or play as if it were unfolding in a continuous present time.

You may be tempted to break this rule when you are quoting as well as summarizing the literary work, for the quotations are likely to contain verbs in the past tense. Do not allow such past forms to influence your own verbs, as this writer does:

> PRESENT
> x Lawrence *describes* Cecilia as "a big dark-complexioned, pug-faced young
> PAST   PAST
> woman who very rarely *spoke* . . ." When she *did* speak, however, her
> PAST
> words *were* sharp enough to kill her aunt Pauline.

Everything is fine here until the second sentence, where the writer, confused by the past *spoke* in his quotation from Lawrence, shifts his own verbs to the past tense. Correct: *When she does speak, however, her words are sharp enough. . . .*

Note also that there can be tense sequences within the reporting of the action. A certain event in the plot *follows* certain developments and *anticipates* others that you may want to mention. In such a case, use the present tense for the action being immediately discussed, and the past and future for the preceding and following times:

PAST   PAST
• When Dimmesdale *wrote* the sermon he *believed* he would be setting sail
PAST
secretly for England with Hester on the day after he *delivered* it. By the time
PRESENT   PRESENT
he *enters* the pulpit, however, he has changed his mind. He now *knows* that
FUTURE
after the sermon he *will mount* the scaffold and confess his guilt before the

assembled populace.[1]

Note, finally, that an author has two kinds of relation to his or her completed work. First there is a past, or *historical*, relation, reflecting the fact that the writing and publishing of the work have taken place once and for all:

HISTORICAL RELATION:
• Hawthorne wrote the novel feverishly.
• He published it in 1850.

Second, a quite different, *continuing*, relation also exists. No matter how long ago it was written, the work addresses us in an unfolding present as we read it. Thus, when you are discussing what the author "says to us" through the work, you should use the present tense:

CONTINUING RELATION:
• Hawthorne *gives* us little insight into his hero's mind.
• He *does* everything he can to heighten the suspense.

Verbals

The tenses of infinitives, participles, and gerunds must be changed to show different relations to the indicated time of action.

infinitives No matter what tense the controlling verb is in, use a *present* infinitive to show action *at the same time as*, or *later than*, the indicated time:

SAME TIME:
PRES INF
• Bobo tried *to read* the obituaries every day.

LATER TIME:
PRES INF
• He hopes *to offer* protection to wealthy widows.

Use a *past* infinitive to show action *earlier than* the indicated time:

EARLIER TIME:

PAST INF
* Bobo expected the police *to have become* more cooperative than they had so far.

participles and gerunds Whatever the tense of the controlling verb, use *present* participles and gerunds to show action *at the same time as* the indicated time:

SAME TIME:

PRES PART
* *Expressing* her outlook on life, Priscilla asserted that she would rather be a snob than a slob.

PRES GER
* *Displaying* her emotions in public had never been one of her aims.

Use *past* participles and gerunds to show action *earlier than* the indicated time:

EARLIER TIME:

PAST PART
* *Having entitled* her essay "Some Things Are Surely Less Vulgar than Others," she began to worry about the scarcity of good examples.

PAST GER
* *Having written* a high-school paper on "Good Citizenship" didn't help her a bit with this project.

EXERCISE

10. Some or all of the following sentences show mistaken uses of tense, either in verbs or in verbals. Indicate which sentences you find correct, and submit revised versions of the others.

    A. He knew she stopped smoking five years before.
    B. She had wanted to have quit even earlier.
    C. Forster publishes *A Passage to India* in 1924.
    D. At the beginning of the novel, Aziz has no idea that he will be the defendant in a notorious trial.
    E. If I would have known Marilyn Monroe, I would have treated her respectfully.
    F. She had always wanted to be named Mother of the Year, but she was not altogether pleased when the quintuplets had been born.
    G. "I warned you before," said the hero of the novel, "and now you are going to be sorry."

H. Going to a good high school was of considerable use to her in college.
I. She will have completed the paper by next Tuesday.
J. We concluded by saying that we have never had such a thoroughly enjoyable time.

DOUBLE NEGATIVES

Although they were accepted for centuries as imparting extra emphasis to denials, double negatives are now regarded as canceling those denials and forming roundabout affirmations. Thus, *I don't intend to tell you nothing* would be read either as a nonstandard sentence or as a confusing way of saying *I intend to tell you something.*

Certain phrases that are fairly common in speech are widely disapproved in writing:

negatives with shouldn't wonder, wouldn't be surprised, etc. In a sentence like *I shouldn't wonder if it didn't rain*, the negative sense is unnecessarily doubled and thus made doubtful. *Didn't rain* should be *rained.*

cannot help but Many readers would consider this a double negative, since *not* and *but* are separate forms of denial. You can satisfy everyone by changing *cannot help but wonder,* for example, to *cannot help wondering.*

can't hardly; can't scarcely, etc. Since a negative sense is already contained in *hardly* and *scarcely*, the verb should be left in affirmative form: *Bobo can hardly wait to get his finger on the trigger.*

doubt but what; no doubt but that Both *doubt* and *but* have a negative force; thus in combination they make a double negative. In every case where *doubt but what* or *no doubt but that* comes to mind, try *doubt that:*

- I don't doubt that fleas and mosquitoes will one day inherit the earth.
- There is no doubt that this is so.

EXERCISE

11. Submit five correctly formed sentences using, in turn, each of the following phrases:

    A. shouldn't wonder
    B. wouldn't be surprised

C.   cannot help
D.   can hardly
E.   doubt that

NOTE

[1]Henry Nash Smith, "Some Patterns of Transcendence in Hawthorne and Howells," *English Studies Today*, 6 (1975), 437.

12

PUNCTUATION

The ideal of correct punctuation may appear at first to be a very small matter. No one, after all, is likely to exclaim that you punctuate like an angel or to single out your brackets and quotation marks for special praise. In writing, however, small matters count; that is, they count against you if you botch them. After you have decided just what to write and have gotten it down in pointed, well-formed phrases and clauses, one little comma or dash in the wrong place can sabotage your sentence. Punctuation marks are like railroad switches. Their job is the inconspicuous one of allowing sentences to go where a writer intends; if they are noticed at all, it is because something has just plunged off the track.

Punctuation, it is sometimes said, is a writer's way of trying to substitute for pauses in speech. That may be so, but marks of punctuation can be much more exact and revealing than pauses. Often we cannot tell whether a speaker has finished a sentence at all, much less how its parts are related. But by using such subtly graded devices as commas, parentheses, brackets, dashes, colons, semicolons, and periods, writers can offer us a total, continuing grasp of their logic and emphasis. Even when, as sometimes happens, writers "listen" for a pause to tell whether punctuation is called for, they must still decide which of several marks to choose. Only an understanding of the unique function of each punctuation mark can resolve such questions.

Some of the dos and don'ts of punctuation are rather complex, but you should not allow them to distract you from the main general principles. If you master the following five rules, you will be able to avoid the mistakes that occur most frequently.

---

1. Do not separate *parts* of sentences as if they were full sentences (below), or punctuate two sentences as one (p. 314).
2. Join independent clauses *either* with a comma and a coordinating conjunction (p. 313) *or* with a semicolon (p. 327).
3. Use commas to separate items in a series (p. 316), introductory modifying clauses and phrases (p. 317), and nonrestrictive elements, including those which are parenthetical (pp. 319, 320).
4. Do not insert needless punctuation between main sentence elements, compound elements, or terms of comparison and preference (p. 321).
5. Use the same marks at both ends of parenthetical elements (p. 320).

PERIOD •

End of Sentence

A period signifies a full stop, not a pause. The normal place for a period is at the end of a complete sentence—one containing at least one independent clause. Independent sentence fragments (p. 279) can also end with periods:

• Did Betsy want to become a gardener? *Yes, Ava Gardner.*

Beware, however, of writing unacceptable sentence fragments, those that clearly belong within the preceding sentence:

x Biff wanted to sell his talents to the highest bidder. *Either the AAU or the NCAA.*

For this important difference between independent and unacceptable fragments, review the discussion on pages 279–280.

Indirect Questions

A sentence constituting an indirect question should end with a period, not a question mark:

WRONG:
x He asked me whether I could go?

RIGHT:
• He asked me whether I could go.

Abbreviations

Abbreviations such as *Mr., Dr., Jr.,* and *N.Y.* require periods, but some common abbreviations and acronyms (p. 368) often appear without periods: *UAW, NOW, SST,* etc.

Note that when an abbreviation ends a sentence, one period does the work of two:

• Send the money directly to Lincoln Dollar, M.D.

QUESTION MARK

Direct Questions

Question marks follow direct questions wherever they occur in a sentence:

• Can a camel pass through the eye of a needle?
• I know that many strange things are possible, but can a camel really pass through the eye of a needle?
• It was just fifteen years ago today—remember?—that the camel got stuck in the eye of the needle.
• "Can a needle," asked the surrealist film director when he met the Arab veterinary surgeon, "pass through the eye of a camel?"

Indications of Doubt

A question mark within parentheses expresses doubt:

• Saint Thomas Aquinas, 1225(?)–1274

Some writers unwisely use such question marks as a form of sarcasm:

x The President expects to make four nonpolitical (?) television speeches in the month of October.

> The sentence is momentarily in contradiction with itself. First it offers the "straight" assertion that the speeches will be nonpolitical; then it negates that idea through the parenthetical question. By eliminating the question mark and putting quotation marks around *nonpolitical,* the writer would get the desired effect without inconsistency.

Questions Within Questions

When a sentence asking a question also *contains* a question at the end, one question mark will serve the purpose:

- Why didn't Melody stop to ask herself, "Isn't it strange that I'm the only person in this whole zoo who is trying to feed peanuts to the elephant train?"

EXERCISE

1. Correct any errors in the use of periods and question marks:
   - A. Aunt Sophia was disoriented by the family reunion. Never having played frisbee with thirty-five people before.
   - B. He wondered if I would like to shoot the rapids with his novelist friend?
   - C. I am not sure—will you correct me if I'm wrong—that porpoises are more intelligent than raccoons.
   - D. She wanted her psychiatrist to tell her whether it was possible to get seasick in Iowa?
   - E. His fellow workers at the car wash did not seem very impressed by his Ph.D..

EXCLAMATION POINT

Use exclamation points sparingly to punctuate outbursts or statements requiring extraordinary emphasis:

- "My geodesic dome! My organic greenhouse! My Tolkien collection! When will I ever see them again?"
- Standing in the bread line, he had a moment of revelation. So *this* was what his economics professor had meant by structural unemployment!

Frequent use of exclamation points dulls their effect. Be especially slow to use sarcastic exclamation points in parentheses:

x The General told them on Monday that the battle had to be completely won (!) by Wednesday afternoon.

COMMA

Independent Clauses

When you write two independent clauses in a row, you should separate them either with a semicolon (p. 327) or with a comma and a coordinating conjunction (*and, but, for, nor, or, so, yet*):

- George was lonely at first, but after a while he came to like having the whole house to himself.

Many writers consider the comma optional if the first independent clause is short:

- He ate constantly but he still couldn't get enough food to satisfy his cravings.

   Note, however, that nobody would object to a comma after *constantly*.

When a short independent clause and a following independent clause share the same logical relation to an earlier part of the sentence, you can bring out that connection by dropping the comma:

- George's reliance on prepared foods was total, for Susan had left him and she had taken her cookbooks with her.

   The omission of a comma after *him* helps to show that everything from *for Susan* to the end of the sentence constitutes a single explanation of the first clause.

run-on sentences   Failure to join independent clauses properly results in a **run-on sentence**—that is, the punctuating of two sentences as if they were one. Run-on sentences come in two varieties, either of which can turn your prose into a leaking faucet.

fused sentence   For an all-out, unstoppable flow there is the alarming **fused sentence**, in which the independent clauses run together with no punctuation at all:

| IND CLAUSE | IND CLAUSE |

x George brushed his hair vigorously most of it came off in the poodle-grooming brush.

   A semicolon after *vigorously* would put things right; so, alternatively, would a comma followed by a conjunction:

- George brushed his hair vigorously, but most etc.

comma splice   Fused sentences are usually easy to spot, but student writers tend to have more trouble with the "slow leak" variety of run-on sentence, the comma splice. A **comma splice** occurs when you join two independent clauses with a comma alone, omitting the necessary conjunction:

x George's health was now much improved, his diet was rich in preservatives.

Without a conjunction such as *for* after the comma, the two clauses become separate sentences unnaturally presented as one.

Why are comma splices so troublesome? The answer is that they "sound all right." In speech, any pause is sufficient to keep independent statements apart. To become adequately sensitive to the comma splice you must bear in mind that you are addressing a reader, not a listener. Readers need a clear signal that one statement is completely over before the next one begins. In x *George's health was now much improved, his diet was rich in preservatives,* the comma leaves a reader wondering whether a series is in progress: *George's health was now much improved, his diet was rich in preservatives, and the mirror told him that his pectorals were irresistible.* A full stop after *improved,* or a comma plus a conjunction, would head off any such expectation.

Writers who are properly wary of comma splices may still fall into them if they mistake sentence adverbs for conjunctions (pp. 265–266):

x He turned the oven dial to the "Clean" position, however the dishes seemed dirtier than ever when he took them out.

Here the *however* is meant to function like a coordinating conjunction such as *but* or *yet*. Strictly speaking, though, this is no less a run-on than the sentence about George's health. *However* can never serve as a conjunction; here it is a sentence adverb modifying the whole first statement.

In the example above, a comma after *however* is required to bring out that word's function as a sentence adverb. Yet that improvement leaves the comma splice unrepaired. We need a clearer stop after *position*:

• He turned the oven dial to the "Clean" position; however, the dishes . . .

or:

• He turned the oven dial to the "Clean" position; the dishes, however, seemed . . .

or:

• He turned the oven dial to the "Clean" position, but the dishes . . .

emphatic sequence of clauses You can sometimes omit a coordinating conjunction when presenting several brief, tightly related independent clauses in a sequence:

- He saw the frozen tamale pie, he yearned for it, he stuffed it eagerly into the shopping cart.

> Here the lack of a conjunction before the third clause helps to bring out the rapidity and compulsiveness of the activities described.

reversal of negative emphasis   Similarly, you can join two independent clauses with a comma if the second reverses the negative emphasis of the first:

- That summer Thoreau did not read books, he hoed beans.

> The *not* clause leaves us anticipating a second clause that will tell us what Thoreau did do that summer. The absence of a conjunction brings out the tight, necessary relation between the two statements. Compare:

x Thoreau hoed beans all summer, he did not read books.

> Lacking a "reversal of negative emphasis," this sentence falls into a classic comma splice.

Members of a Series

Use commas to separate items in a series, with a coordinating conjunction before the last item: *x, y, and (or) z.*

- When he felt lonely in the kitchen, he drowned out the silence by turning

  on *the blender,* *the food processor,* and *the garbage disposal.*

omission of final comma   It is also acceptable to omit the final comma, provided you do so consistently; do not mix styles of punctuation. But the *x, y and (or) z* formula may not always allow your meaning to come through clearly. Consider:

x The returning knight had countless tales to tell of *adventure, conquest of hideous monsters* and *helpless damsels in distress.*

> Did he conquer the damsels as well as the monsters? A comma after *monsters* would remove all doubt. If you keep to the traditional *x, y, and (or) z* method, such problems will not arise.

series without commas   If all the members of a series are connected by conjunctions, no commas are needed:

- In his new frame of mind, George began to understand that every man must learn to live alone with *his cable^x television* and *his stereo^y tape deck* and *his video^z recorder.*

Coordinate Modifiers

Coordinate adjectives or adverbs, if not separated by coordinating conjunctions, must be separated by commas:

- George fixed himself a *delicious,^{ADJ} nutritious^{ADJ}* dinner of Gatorade and Chun King Chop Suey.

    Here *delicious* and *nutritious* are coordinate, for they both modify the same noun, *dinner.*

But note that some paired modifiers are not coordinate:

- He wolfed down his *typical^{ADJ} American^{ADJ}* meal.

    Here *American* modifies *meal,* but *typical* does not; it modifies *American meal.* A comma after *typical* would wrongly imply that *typical* and *American* modify the same word.

To determine whether you have a coordinate series, try shifting the order of the terms. Truly coordinate items can be reversed without affecting their meaning: *a nutritious, delicious dinner.* Noncoordinate items look all wrong when reversed: *an American typical meal.*

sandwiched modifier   When a modifier is sandwiched between two parts of the modified term, you can set it off by commas on *both* sides:

- His final, unusually tedious, lecture was poorly received.

    The extra comma after *tedious* tells us that *final* and *unusually tedious* are not coordinate modifiers of *lecture.* Rather, the modified term is *final lecture;* the sentence is an alternative version of *His unusually tedious final lecture was poorly received.* Note the absence of commas in this simpler version.

Modifying Clauses and Phrases

modifier preceding main clause   Modifying clauses and phrases are usually set off by commas if they precede the main clause:

- *After Susan left,* George spent a few evenings reading Dr. Lincoln Dollar's helpful book of advice, *The Aerobic Kama Sutra.*

But you can omit the comma if the clause or phrase is brief and its grammatical distinctness from what follows is clear:

- *When Susan came back* she found George sitting in the lotus posture and eating a Ho-Ho.
- *Until that moment* she hadn't appreciated the spiritual side of his nature.

> Commas after *back* and *moment* would also be correct. When in doubt, supply the comma.

Never omit a comma if the sentence would become even momentarily ambiguous without it:

- *Although Susan begged,* George said that she could go live with Julia Child for all he cared.

> Without the comma, we might think at first that the sentence says *Although Susan begged George. . . .*

modifier following main clause When a modifying clause or phrase follows a main clause, ask whether it *completes the meaning* of that main clause (no comma) or *adds something new* (comma required). In reading the sentence aloud, you can tell a modifier of the first type by the lack of a pause before it:

- An apple a day was all Betsy allowed herself *until the diet was completed.*

> The modifying clause limits the time of the action described in the main clause. Because it affects the meaning of that main clause, we tend to read it without a break.

- She would dip the apple in chocolate *to improve the flavor.*

> The modifying phrase gives us essential information about the purpose of the action described in the main clause. A comma after *chocolate* would obscure this fact.

A clause that adds something new without affecting the meaning of the main clause is preceded by a pause in speech and a comma in writing:

- Betsy's apple a day required great self-control, *for which a few evening milk shakes seemed a fitting reward.*

Notice that the meaning of the main clause is complete with or without the italicized modifier.

Restrictive versus Nonrestrictive Elements

When you are unsure whether to set off a subordinate element that does not come first in its sentence, ask yourself if it is *restrictive* or *nonrestrictive* (p. 276). Restrictive elements, you recall, narrow down the meaning of the terms they refer to; they can do that work only if they are *not* isolated by commas. Nonrestrictive elements, which tell something new about terms that have already been identified, make the desired effect only if they *are* set apart.

restrictive: no commas The following examples show how an absence of commas helps to convey a restrictive or identifying effect:

> RESTR EL
> • The task *to be performed* requires great concentration.

The passive infinitive *to be performed* tells us which task is meant. Commas before and after it would imply that we already knew which task was meant.

> RESTR EL
> • The discipline *that George had recently adopted* was called Transcendental Weight-watching.

A restrictive adjectival clause, identifying the discipline in question, is presented without commas.

nonrestrictive: commas Nonrestrictive, or nonidentifying, elements *should* be set off on both sides by commas (except of course if they come at the beginning or end of a sentence):

> NONRESTR EL
> • The task, *to be performed adequately,* requires great concentration.

It is clear that *The task* has already been identified in a previous sentence. The nonrestrictive modifier tells something further about a known subject.

> NONRESTR EL
> • Transcendental Weight-watching, *which George had adopted as his newest discipline,* struck Betsy as a promising idea.

The subject is fully identified before we reach the nonrestrictive modifying clause, which must therefore be set off by commas.

The importance of setting off nonrestrictive elements at both ends may be brought home by this sentence from a newspaper:

x Noteworthy here are a painted settee and two armchairs, decorated with scrollwork and female figures that belonged to President Monroe.[1]

> *Female figures that belonged to President Monroe?* A comma after *figures* is needed to head off wild ideas about the Chief Executive's leisure pursuits.

Parenthetical Elements

A **parenthetical element** is a word or group of words that interrupts the main flow of a sentence. Thus it is always nonrestrictive. Since it comes between parts of the sentence that belong together in meaning, it must be set off by identical punctuation *at both ends*.

A parenthetical element could be a modifying phrase or clause, a sentence adverb like *moreover*, an appositive (p. 243), a name in direct address (you, *Andrew Marvell*), or an inserted question or exclamation. What makes it parenthetical (as in "parentheses") is that the elements before and after it fit together grammatically:

• A diet, *she believed*, called for strong discipline during the sleeping hours.

> Note that the sentence is perfectly coherent without the parenthetical clause *she believed*.

Extreme breaks such as whole statements, questions, or exclamations demand parentheses, brackets, or dashes, but commas are preferred for milder interruptions:

• Reindeer droppings on the roof, *to be sure*, count as strong evidence for Santa's existence.
• Congress, *it appears*, has little interest in closing tax loopholes.
• You, *George*, have been chosen by the computer to be Betsy's mate.
• The computer, *an antique Univac*, is badly in need of repair.

testing for parenthetical elements To be considered parenthetical, a modifier must meet two conditions: it must be nonrestrictive in meaning and it must come *between* essential parts of a statement. Compare:

• But *without hesitating for a moment*, Betsy enrolled in the biofeedback course.

> The italicized modifier comes before the modified statement has properly begun. A comma after *But* would not be wrong, but it is unneeded. As for the comma after *moment*, see "modifier preceding main clause" (p. 317).

- *No one was surprised when, without hesitating for a moment,* Betsy enrolled in the biofeedback course.

No one was surprised by a certain event, to be identified in the *when* clause. But *after that clause has begun,* we must pause to consider the modifier, which thus becomes a parenthetical interruption. The commas on both sides are necessary.

Conjunctions versus Sentence Adverbs

conjunctions: no comma follows Conjunctions (*and, but, since,* etc.) that are not followed by parenthetical elements should never be followed by commas. Beware, for example, of starting a sentence with a conjunction and comma:

x Yet, even she had no clear idea of what she wanted.

The conjunction is intended to connect, but the comma uncouples it.

sentence adverbs: set off with commas The mistake just illustrated derives from confusing conjunctions with *sentence adverbs* ("conjunctive adverbs"), those words that modify a whole statement by indicating its relation to a previous statement (p. 265). Words like *furthermore, however,* and *moreover,* not being true conjunctions, *should* be set off by commas:

- Her production of alpha waves, *however,* increased whenever she turned her mind to food.

Note that true sentence adverbs can always be moved. Thus, in the example above, *however* could have begun the sentence. If you see that a "joining" word cannot be moved, omit the comma after it.

Unnecessary Separation of Sentence Elements

do not separate Unless you are setting off parenthetical elements, do not allow commas to come between sentence elements such as a subject and its verb, a verb and its object or complement, a subordinating conjunction and the clause it introduces, or a preposition and its object. The following sentences are incorrectly punctuated:

subject
and verb x *Betsy* alone among all her classmates, *had* trouble chanting through the dinner hour.

The wish for a pause after *classmates* should be resisted, since the comma makes a distant subject even harder to connect to its verb. (Note that in this case the writer could treat *alone among all her classmates* as parenthetical, marking it off by commas at both ends.)

verb and direct object

x She *saw* in her mind's eye, the chocolate-covered *apple* that was sitting in the refrigerator.

Again an intervening phrase prompts a comma, and again the logic of connection between main sentence elements demands that the comma be removed.

verb and complement

x Alpha waves *were* to an alarming degree, *deficient* in essential sugars.

Once again, as soon as you decide not to treat an element standing between main sentence elements as parenthetical, you must be sure not to anchor it with a comma at the end.

subordinating conjunction and its clause

x Another problem with biofeedback was *that,* the name reminded her of getting fed.

Some writers might feel a "natural" pause after *that* in such a sentence. Natural or not, it should be left unmarked; the whole subordinate clause *that the name reminded her of getting fed* must be kept together.

preposition and object

x Her thoughts kept returning *to, dripping cakes, aromatic pies, and quarts of non-diet soda.*

When a preposition has several objects, as in this sentence, you may be tempted to "take a deep breath" with a comma after the preposition. By resisting the temptation you can keep the whole prepositional phrase intact as a unit.

compound subject and verb   For further evidence of the way grammatical logic must sometimes contradict "natural" pauses, consider a sentence whose subject is *compound,* or composed of more than one part:

- A delightful drive through the Holland Tunnel, an exquisite hour on the Pulaski Skyway, and a whiff of the fragrant North Jersey marshlands were Gertie's idea of a fine outing.

Although this sentence is correctly punctuated, many writers would be tempted to put a comma after *marshlands.* Keep to the rule—but also try to avoid constructions that put the rule under a strain.

direct object or objective complement first: comma allowed In one unusual situation you *can* separate sentence elements that go together. When a direct object or objective complement (p. 243) *precedes* the subject and verb, you may want to put a comma after it to show that it is not the subject:

D OBJ   S   V

- *That Walt Whitman is nothing less than a cosmos,* few *readers would accept* without question.

> The comma notifies us that the direct object (a noun clause) is ending, and it thus encourages us to look elsewhere for the subject of the sentence.

OBJ COMPL   S   V   D OBJ

- *What she calls happiness, I call slavery.*

> The comma indicates that *What she calls happiness* will not be the subject. It proves to be the complement of the direct object, *slavery.*

Separation of Compound Elements

When you are trying to pair two elements in a sentence by including them within a matching structure, you must not separate them with a comma:

x   *y*

x Both *sodium nitrate,* and *sodium nitrite* have been suspected of causing cancer.

x   *y*

x Sterno has been called *a killer drug by some people,* and *a modest depressant by others.*

x   *y*

x *Either you are wrong about that,* or *I have forgotten everything I knew.*

> The commas in all three sentences block the intended matching effect. Note that the temptation to insert a misleading comma increases with the length of the "*x*" element. Try, then, not to strain the rule; keep your "*x*" elements short enough to be easily grasped without a following pause.

Comparisons and Statements of Preference

When comparing two terms or expressing a preference for one over the other, do not allow commas to come between them. These sentences follow the rule:

- George felt more inclined *to watch the roller derby* than *to brood about his troubles.*

> A comma after *derby*, whether or not you "hear" it as a natural pause, would wrongly interrupt the comparative structure.

- He preferred *the shoving and gouging that he saw on television* to *the subtle nastiness of his wife.*

> He *preferred x to y;* even though the "*x*" element is lengthy, it should not be followed by a comma.

Appositives

In punctuating appositives (p. 243), follow the rule for restrictive and nonrestrictive elements (pp. 319–320). When an appositive is restrictive, *identifying* the term it refers to, you should omit commas before and after it:

- The union leader *John L. Lewis* was not amused by the headline "*Lewis Drops Union Suit.*"

> The two italicized elements identify who this particular union leader was and which headline is being quoted.

Compare:

- A union leader, *a man like John L. Lewis,* led a dangerous life back in those days.

> Here a nonrestrictive appositive gives an *instance* of a leader instead of ruling out everyone but Lewis. The commas are necessary.

Conventional Uses

Commas occur routinely in certain contexts:

numbers of more than four digits Commas should separate every three digits (counting from the right) of a number consisting of more than four digits: *109,368,452.* In four-digit numbers the comma is optional: *6083* and *6,083* are both correct.

No commas separate the digits of years *(2001),* telephone numbers, zip codes, serial numbers, and other figures meant to identify an item or place. Such figures are sometimes divided into segments by hyphens.

dates A comma should separate the day of the month and the year if the month is given first: *July 4, 1934*. If the sentence continues after the date, the year too should be followed by a comma: *July 4, 1934, was the date of her birth*. But if the day is given first, no punctuation is necessary: *She was born on 4 July 1934 in Peralta Hospital*.

When only the month and the year are stated, commas before and after the year are optional. You can write either *July 1934 was the month of her birth* or *July, 1934, was the month of her birth*.

addresses New York, New York
7713 Radnor Road, Bethesda, Md. 20034
Department of Economics, Simon Fraser University, Burnaby, B.C., Canada V5A 1S6

Within a sentence, put commas after as well as before the name of an area that serves to locate a specified place: *Laramie, Wyoming, celebrates its Jubilee Days every July*.

titles and degrees following names As a rule, titles and degrees are set off by commas on both sides:

- Herbert Moroni, Ph.D., was present.
- Adlai Stevenson, III, served on the committee.

But *Adlai Stevenson III* would also be acceptable.

For the use of a comma to introduce a quotation, see pages 335–336.

EXERCISES

2. Correct any comma splices and fused sentences (pp. 314–315) that you find:
   A. Henry James was fond of Italy, in fact, he wrote a whole book about its civilized pleasures.
   B. This surprised Biff he had thought that Henry James spent all his time playing the trumpet.
   C. This book is not illustrated, however its text is very clear.
   D. Dr. Dollar wants to help us through the energy crisis, he is also aware of the recent physical fitness craze.
   E. Many potential readers are just now changing their habits, therefore many of them ought to buy *The Complete Book of Hopping to Your Place of Business*.

3. Some or all of the following sentences show faulty use (or absence) of commas. Write a brief comment about each sentence, explaining *where and why* you would make changes, if any.

    A. Some judges have begun experimenting with a new concept, known as "house arrest."

    B. A convicted criminal, who is not considered dangerous, may be spared a prison sentence.

    C. The criminal however, is not allowed to go completely free.

    D. Instead, he or she is required to stay home although shopping trips are permitted.

    E. This policy spares nonviolent offenders, the degrading and unnecessary experience of being locked away for years.

4. Most or all of the following sentences show faulty use (or absence) of commas. When you find an adequately punctuated sentence, note that it is correct. For all the others, indicate what changes should be made.

    A. Animals, vegetables, and minerals, all get involved in the exciting game of "Twenty Questions."

    B. September 1939 was a bad time to be in Europe.

    C. But without a broad-brimmed hat or an umbrella, no one can go out in this tropical sun.

    D. Airline passengers seem to prefer a safe trip with armed guards, to an unsafe trip without them.

    E. They won't lower the taxes, merely because people complain.

    F. Did you know that, the first baseball game played under electric lights occurred in 1883?

    G. Whether the earthquake was caused by fault slippage, or by excessive drilling, could not be determined.

    H. The nutrition expert voiced some doubts about a generation of American children raised on, "Crazy Cow, Baron Von Redberry, Sir Grapefellow, Count Chocula, and Franken-Berry."

    I. One good reason for moving to San Antonio is that it is the cleanest city in the United States.

    J. Every person, no matter how incompetent he or she may be at everything else is the world's greatest expert at deciphering his or her own handwriting.

    K. The issue of 16 October, 1975 contained some of the finest prose he had ever read.

    L. What Shaw called the most licentious of institutions, other people call holy matrimony.

    M. Statisticians, who are slavishly admired by some people, and criticized as frivolous by others, have discovered that the taste for dill pickles declines after age sixty-five.

    N. Most Americans it seems, suffer from aching feet.

    O. Homemakers agree that soyburgers are the best, low-cost, high-protein, food to serve these days.

    P. A porcupine has approximately 30,000 quills for your information.

    Q. As the press had expected the President announced on Friday that the price of steak, not gold, would henceforth define the value of the dollar.

    R. In a house work is more tedious than in an office.

S. The one mystery, that I can't explain, is why Mick and Bianca had to call it quits.
T. You Gertie are a woman of taste and sensitivity.

SEMICOLON

To Join Independent Statements

Use a semicolon to join independent statements that are closely related. When one statement explains the other, for example, a semicolon allows you to get them both into the same sentence:

- The candidate became somewhat confused in his campaign speech; no one could understand what he meant by "a chicken in every garage."

Although some purists think otherwise, there is nothing wrong with following a semicolon with either a conjunction (*and, but*) or a sentence adverb and a comma (*nevertheless, likewise,*). But it *is* wrong to put an independent statement on one side of a semicolon and a fragment on the other:

x Wratto decided to write a poem about the energy crisis; because he felt tired most of the time.

There is no independent clause after the semicolon.

To Show Main Divisions in a Series

When members of a series are subdivided into parts separated by commas, it may be hard to tell where each member ends and the next begins. The solution is to use semicolons at the *main* points of separation:

- The poem said that lack of energy could keep people out of a lot of trouble; that moving around and doing things, burning calories unnecessarily, makes people forget about important things, such as supporting poetry; and that by sitting perfectly still, just letting the universe run down all by itself, you can actually get *with* the energy crisis and make it beautiful.

The semicolons help to show where each of the three items ends; otherwise the commas would be too confusing. Note that the items *in a series* punctuated by semicolons do not have to constitute independent clauses.

If you pepper your first drafts with semicolons as a way of keeping one thought in mind while struggling with the next, look back to see if the connected statements really belong together. Remember that the basic unit of communication is the one-statement sentence, not a string of statements looped together by semicolons. Abundant semicolons can tax a reader's patience.

COLON

To Introduce a Statement or Figure

A colon marks a formal introduction:

- Once in office, the Mayor devoted all his attention to an urgent priority: getting reelected.

colon versus semicolon　A colon implies a symmetry or equivalence between items on either side. Something is to be presented: this thing. If you do not mean to insist on the equivalence, you may want a semicolon rather than a colon. A semicolon announces development of, or relationship to, what has just been stated; a colon delivers the thing itself in different terms. Use a colon only if you could plausibly insert *namely* or *that is* immediately after it.

Note that a colon is inappropriate when you want to interrupt the main flow of a sentence and then pick it up again. For this function you need dashes or parentheses—marks, that is, that can be closed off at both ends.

Do not allow a colon to wall off sentence elements that belong together, such as a verb and its object, a preposition and its object, or an infinitive and its object:

x The Mayor was soon working harmoniously with: the Police Officers Association, the District Attorney's office, and the Mafia.

The colon wrongly separates the preposition *with* from its three objects. Use a colon only when you have a genuine stopping point: *The Mayor was soon working with three bodies: the Police Officers Association,* etc.

Colons are often used to introduce figures:

- The results of the poll were surprising: 7 percent in favor, 11 percent opposed, 82 percent no opinion.

Other Uses

A colon should be used between hours and minutes in time references, and after the salutation of a business letter:

- 10:15 p.m.
- Dear Mr. Green:

Subtitles of books and articles are also introduced by colons:

- *Hemingway: The Inward Terrain*
- "Windward Oahu: Last Stand Against the Developers?"

For the use of a colon to introduce a quotation, see pages 335–336.

For the use of a colon to introduce a quotation, see pages 335–336.

EXERCISE

5. Correct any errors in the use of colons and semicolons:

   A. A penny saved is a penny earned: but rich people, I have noticed, tend to put their pennies into shrewd investments.
   B. The planning commissioner said that in his judgment the new skyscraper had: "all the earmarks of an eyesore."
   C. Special sunglasses have now been developed for skiers, some of whom suffer acutely from glare; for people who want to wear only one pair of glasses in sun and shade; and for others who, for whatever reason, do not want their fellow citizens to catch sight of their eyes.
   D. The robber asked for only two things; her money and her life.
   E. Biff told his teammates to watch out on the next play for one of the following: a quarterback sneak; a statue of liberty play; or a drop-kick field goal.

DASH ▬

A dash signifies an abrupt break in thought. If the main sentence does not resume after the break, only one dash is used:

- The Senator stood ready to remedy any grievances—for a price.

If the main sentence resumes, a second dash is needed:

- The Senator stood ready—for a price—to remedy any grievances.

Do not allow a comma to substitute for the second dash, and be sure that your sentence would make complete sense if the portion within dashes were omitted. Sentences like this are all too common:

x Although Betsy took up massage—somebody told her it would increase her human potential—but she soon discovered that she was too ticklish.

> The material between dashes has caused the writer to forget the presence of *Although. But* has to be deleted.

A dash can serve as a less formal equivalent to a colon:

- At least Betsy had accumulated some souvenirs—a black eye from Encounter, bruised ribs from Rolfing, and a whiplash from Aikido.

Dashes can be used to mark the beginning and end of a series which might otherwise get confused with the rest of the sentence:

- The people who knew Betsy most intimately—her doctor, her pharmacist, and her lawyer—were eager to know what she would try next.

Dashes are also used to mark the interruption of a sentence in dialogue:

> "Run, Jane, run!" yelled Dick. "I see the principal and he's coming toward us with—"
> "It's too late, Dick, it's too late! The curriculum enrichment consultants have blocked the gate and—"
> "Oh, Jane, oh, Jane, whatever will become of us?"

Do not combine a dash with a comma or a period. A comma and a dash together are redundant; a period and a dash are contradictory.

As a stylistic matter you should be frugal with dashes, or you will make a scatterbrained impression. Do not fall into the careless habit of using the dash as an all-purpose punctuation mark.

PARENTHESES

Parentheses mark a gentler interruption than dashes do. The material enclosed is grammatically parenthetical (p. 320) in both cases, but parentheses have the effect of *subordinating* it, so that the reader is less distracted from the rest of the sentence. Parentheses can be used either to set off incidental information such as numbers, dates, and references or to signal a digression from the main thought:

- Your furniture will be repossessed in thirty (30) days.
- The article appears in *National Geographic*, 149 (1976), 755-85.
- Julia Moore (revered in her lifetime as "the Sweet Singer of Michigan") offered the memorable observation that "Literary is a work very difficult to do."

A parenthesis should not affect the punctuation of the rest of the sentence. If a comma is called for but a parenthesis intervenes, the comma is delivered at the end of the parenthesis:

• After she had tried Primal Jogging and I'm-O.K.-You're-Not O.K. (she still hadn't met any interesting men), Betsy resolved to become a Hatha Backpacker.

Similarly, if no comma would have been required without the parenthetical material, none is required with it:

• Betsy discovered (though not with true surprise) that swarms of mosquitoes were no remedy for loneliness.

When a parenthetical statement is placed between complete sentences, it too should be punctuated as a complete sentence. The end-punctuation comes within the parenthesis, not after it:

• Betsy soaked her feet in the river and reached into her backpack for a book. (It was *Think Your Blisters Away,* by Dr. Lincoln Dollar.) Becoming absorbed in reading, she absent-mindedly swallowed three granola bars, countless handfuls of chocolate chips, and a packet of Bushwack Buster Oyster Purée.

Like dashes, parentheses should be regarded as a stylistic luxury. If your prose is full of them, you will annoy your reader:

x The "King of Swing" (I use quotation marks because in my judgment this was a misnomer from the first) thought he had to have a concert (?) in Carnegie Hall (where else?) before he could be accepted by the mass public.

To read a sentence like this is comparable to being poked in the ribs several times by a drunken jokester.

BRACKETS   [ ]

Brackets, which are often confused with parentheses, have a special function. They set off an insertion of your own words into a quotation:

• "My personal idols," said the forty-four-year-old defendant, "are Jerry [Rubin] and Abbie [Hoffman]."

Note that parentheses in place of brackets would imply a parenthetical remark by the speaker, not by the writer. Brackets are necessary to indicate that the quotation is being interrupted.

The bracketed, italicized word *sic* (Latin 'thus') is used to signal that a peculiarity occurs in the original and therefore is not an error of your own. A misspelling, for instance, could be marked this way:

- "Beachcombbing [*sic*] no longer appeals to me," Melody wired. "Send money."

But do not abuse this device to get a cheap advantage over an opponent:

x The Republican nominee, who describes himself as a "statesman" [*sic*], wouldn't know that World War Three had started if they didn't print it on the sports page.

Try to avoid situations in which parenthetical material occurs *within* parenthetical material, but if you cannot, use brackets for the inner set. The problem arises most often in footnotes:

⁸It may be difficult to imagine why anyone would want to challenge the idea of insanity. (See, however, D. L. Rosenhan, "On Being Sane in Insane Places," *Science*, 179 [1973], 250–58.)

The date would normally have gone into parentheses, but brackets are useful because they distinguish this material from the larger parenthesis.

ELLIPSES ● ● ●

The ellipsis mark, consisting of three periods separated by single spaces, is used to signify that something has been omitted from a quotation. For discussion, see page 337.

Some writers use ellipses in their own prose to indicate that a statement contains further implications that need not be spelled out:

- And thus he came to feel that he had triumphed over the government. How little he knew about the workings of bureaucracy. . . .

Note here that, because the sentence does not resume after the ellipsis, the ellipsis is preceded by a normally placed period.

In general, it is good to avoid the "stylistic" use of ellipses to connect your own sentences or to link elements within them:

x Wratto goes beyond the achievements of Olson and Creeley in many ways. . . . Listing them would probably be too tedious. . . .

x Yogurt improves your morale . . . releases your inhibitions . . . postpones death. . . .

In these examples the ellipses make a vague and lazy effect.

---

6. Correct any errors in the use of dashes, parentheses, brackets, and ellipses:

   A. "We'd better double-team the Doctor (Julius Erving)," the coach advised.
   B. It is simply untrue,—and nothing you can say will convince me—that trees make wind by waggling their branches.
   C. Although some researchers blame LSD use for damage to chromosomes, others (knowing that people who take LSD tend to consume other drugs as well), are now focusing their suspicions on marijuana.
   D. He didn't want to accuse her of being forward with other suitors—after all, women were supposed to be more independent nowadays, but he couldn't help wondering why she had a toll-free telephone number.
   E. Student unrest reached a peak in the late 1960's. (Those were the years of strongest protest against the Vietnam War).
   F. Stanley issued an ultimatum which gave the world twenty-four [24] hours to get out.
   G. "Since I want to try a mountain gig anyway," wrote Melody on her application form—"I might as well pick up some bread being a counciler (sic)."
   H. She enjoyed sitting around the campfire ring . . . watching the smoke rise . . . after everyone else had gone to bed . . . and the fire had gone out.
   I. Melody told the campers in her tent to be careful with matches, (she remembered her own early troubles) especially if they hadn't learned how to roll paper properly.
   J. Every morning—because the camp director insisted on it,—she inspected each bed, but she hardly ever found anything she could use.

APOSTROPHE

Apostrophes are used chiefly in the formation of possessives (pp. 350–352), certain plurals (pp. 348–350), and contractions (*won't, didn't, havin' fun,* etc.). The apostrophe also marks the omission of one or more digits of a number: *the winter of '65.* In dates expressing a span of time, however, the apostrophe is usually dropped: *1847–63.* And when page numbers are shortened, the apostrophe is never used: *pp. 207–91.*

In addition, apostrophes are used to form the past participles of certain verbs derived from nouns:

- Hearns was K.O.'d in the second round.
- Young parents these days are so Spock'd and Gesell'd that they hardly trust their own feelings about how a child should be raised.

In forming contractions, think of the two original words that are being joined. If you recall that *doesn't* comes from *does not*, for example, and that an apostrophe signifies a missing *letter* and not a missing *space*, you will not commit the spelling error *does'nt*.

When you are writing longhand, be sure to leave a break between letters surrounding an apostrophe: write *day's* and *John's*, not *days* and *John's*.

7. Correct any errors in the use or omission of apostrophes:

    A. He is'nt sure what he will do tomorrow.

    B. *Working in the K-9 Corps was a dog's life.*

    C. She had been looking forward to the summer of 82.

    D. Americans suffered greatly in the period 1929–39.

    E. You can find the information on pages 223–'33.

QUOTATION MARKS " "

Quotation marks, which are usually double (" ") in American English, set off direct speech in dialogue, quoted material, certain titles, definitions and translations, and words given certain special emphases. (Single quotation marks are normal in British usage.) Whether single or double, quotation marks must come in pairs. Do not leave your reader wondering where a quotation really begins or ends.

For convenience, we will put together various aspects of quotation form here, going beyond the mere question of when to include quotation marks.

Dialogue

Direct speech in dialogue is usually enclosed in quotation marks:

• "You get away from those chocolate chips right now, you nasty old bear!"

If a character's speech extends for more than a paragraph, put quotation marks at the beginning of each paragraph, but at the end of only the final paragraph. (This is the only exception to the rule that quotation marks must come in pairs.) Begin a new paragraph for each change of speaker.

Incorporated versus Extracted Quotations

short quotations: incorporated   When you are quoting material other than dialogue, you have to be aware that there are two ways of doing so. Short quotations—prose passages of fewer than five typed lines or verse passages of one or two (sometimes three) typed lines—should be placed within quotation marks and incorporated into your main text:

- "Take a loftier view of your blisters," writes Dr. Dollar. "Regard them as so many lucky opportunities to expose the real inner you."
- The poet tells us, "Ain't got my food stamps yet this month, & wonder if / Maybe this is fascism at last."

> The slash, or virgule, in the second example indicates a line ending in quoted poetry. Notice that it is preceded and followed by a space.

longer quotations: extracted   Longer quotations—more than four typed lines of prose or more than two or three lines of verse—should be extracted (set apart), following these rules:

---

1. Separate the passage from your main text by skipping an extra line above and below.
2. In most cases, introduce the passage with a colon.
3. Indent the whole passage ten spaces from your left margin, or somewhat less if the quoted lines of verse are very long.
4. Double-space the passage, treating it just like your main text.
5. Omit the quotation marks you would have added to an incorporated quotation, but reproduce any quotation marks found in the quoted passage itself.
6. In extracting verse, follow the spacing (beginnings and line endings) of the original passage. In extracting prose, indent all lines equally if the passage consists of one paragraph or less. When you extract more than one paragraph of prose, indent the first line of each full paragraph by three extra spaces.

Introducing a Quotation

To decide what punctuation to use when introducing a quotation, disregard any quotation marks you may have added and simply read the quoted matter as an ordinary part of your sentence. If the quotation fits readily into one of your clauses or phrases, do not insert a comma or colon before it:

- Macbeth expresses the depth of his despair when he describes life as "a tale told by an idiot."

A comma or colon after *as* would wrongly separate the preposition *as* from its object *tale*.

But a quotation that does not form part of a phrase or clause in the rest of the sentence should be introduced by either a comma or a colon:

- When asked what he thought of Western civilization, Gandhi smiled and replied, "I think it would be a very good idea."

A colon after *replied* would be equally correct.

Because a colon makes a more formal pause, a greater separation between your own prose and the quoted passage, you should generally introduce *extracted* quotations with a colon. If the extracted passage begins by completing one of your own phrases or clauses, however, you can omit introductory punctuation:

- Macbeth describes life as

                                    a tale
    Told by an idiot, full of sound and fury,
    Signifying nothing.

The same passage could be incorporated as follows:

- Macbeth describes life as "a tale / Told by an idiot, full of sound and fury, / Signifying nothing."

Quotation Marks Within a Quotation

When you incorporate a quoted passage into your own text, you must not only enclose it in quotation marks, but also change any quotation marks that it already contains to *single* marks:

- "The concluding lines of Wratto's 'Ode to Amerika,'" observes Pieper in *The Defenestrated Imagination*, "rest on an ingenious paradox."

In general, quotations-within-quotations require single marks. In the rare case in which a third set of marks must be boxed in, they become double ("'" "'"):

- Orwell's friend Richard Rees informs us that "when Socialists told him that under Socialism there would be no such feeling of being at the mercy of unpredictable and irresponsible powers, he remarked: 'I notice people always say "*under* Socialism." They look forward to being on top—with all the others underneath, being told what is good for them.'"[2]

Omitting Material Within a Quotation

brief omissions Use an ellipsis mark (p. 332) to show that you have omitted a modest amount of material from a quoted passage:

* President Clearance declared that he had "nothing . . . to hide," and that "secrecy in University affairs is . . . contrary to all my principles."

If an ellipsis occurs within a sentence, type three spaced periods preceded and followed by a space, as in the example above. If the ellipsis occurs just after the end of a sentence, retain the end-punctuation of the sentence and then add the ellipsis:

* Clearance was lavish in his praise for the University: "Everything is fine. . . . We're tooled up to turn out a real classy product."

Similarly, use four periods when omitting material that contains a period:

* "I resent the implication that nerve gas is being developed. . . . Besides, every safety precaution has been taken."

longer omissions If you are omitting a whole line or more of verse, or a whole paragraph or more of prose, mark the omission by a complete line of spaced periods:

What have U done fer yr poets O Amerika?
I'm sitting here waiting fer a call from the Nash
Ional Endowment fer the Arts and Humanities.
Is it arty to keep me waiting Amerika?
Is this yr crummy idea of a humanity?

. . . .
How much longer must I borrow & steal?
O Amerika I hold U responsible fer this hole in the seat of my Levis!

quoting sentence fragments When quoting a fragment of a sentence, introduce it with a clause or phrase that fits it into your own sentence structure. In that way you can avoid *beginning* the quotation with an ellipsis:

* Is Wratto referring to his high vocation when he writes that he is "waiting fer a call"?

dialogue Ellipses sometimes occur in dialogue to indicate incomplete or inter-rupted statements or thoughts:

* "You may be right," she said pleadingly, "but I don't really see why you can't . . ."
  "Oh, stop your infernal whining, will you?"

Certain Titles

The titles of essays, poems, articles, stories, chapters, and other units smaller than a whole volume are indicated by quotation marks:

- Joyce's story "The Dead"
- Keats' poem "To Autumn"
- Robert Alter, "The New American Novel," *Commentary,* Nov. 1975, pp. 44–51.

Note that this rule applies only to titles being cited or discussed. When you compose an essay and provide a title for it (p. 133), no quotation marks or italics should be added (except of course for titles mentioned in your title). Except in newspapers, where italics are generally not used, you should underline (to indicate italics) the titles of whole volumes, without including quotation marks (see p. 364). If a poem occupies a whole volume, you should underline it: *Paradise Lost, The Prelude, Paterson.* Names of newspapers, magazines, and journals are also underlined rather than placed in quotation marks:

- Biff felt sure that marijuana would soon be legalized when he spotted an article in *Reader's Digest* called "I Owe My Life to L-Dopa."

Definitions and Translations

When a word or phrase is cited in italics and defined or translated, the definition or translation should be put within quotation marks:

- *Benevolent,* which means "desiring to do good to others," should be kept distinct from *beneficent,* which means "doing good to others."
- The German term for "a little" is *ein wenig.*

When a foreign word is immediately followed by a translation, you can put the translation in single quotation marks without intervening punctuation:

- *ein wenig* 'a little.'
- They call the Fiat 500 *Topolino* 'Little Mouse.'

Special Emphasis

Quotation marks call attention to the words they enclose. Some writers use them in place of italics to indicate that a word is being treated *as* a word, not as the thing it stands for:

- The term "Iron Curtain" was coined by Winston Churchill.

It may be necessary now and then to put a word within quotation marks to show that you do not share a certain attitude:

* Nero's solution to "the Christian problem" also helped to cut the monthly budget for lion food.

Quotation Marks Combined with Other Punctuation

In British usage quotation marks generally go inside other punctuation, but American usage is more complicated. You have to know the following conventions:

1. *Commas* and *periods* should be placed *inside* the closing quotation marks in all circumstances. You do not have to consider whether the comma or period is part of the quotation or whether the quotation is short or long. Just routinely put the comma or period inside the closing quotation marks:

* Quoth the Raven, "Nevermore."
* "Nevermore," quoth the Raven.

2. *Colons* and *semicolons* are just as rigidly placed as commas and periods. They always go *outside* the closing quotation marks:

* "Nevermore": that is what the daffy bird said.
* Once again the bird said "Nevermore"; and I said, "Why do you always have to take such a negative attitude?"

3. *Question marks, exclamation points,* and *dashes* go *either inside or outside* the closing quotation marks, depending on their function. If they are punctuating the quoted material itself, they go *inside:*

* "Is it helpful to sit there all day and nag, nag, nag?"

The same marks go *outside* the closing quotation marks if they are not part of the quotation:

* Do you think the Raven could be taught to say "I'll think it over and let you know in the morning"?

4. When the quotation must end with a question mark or exclamation point and your own sentence calls for a period at that point, the period vanishes:

* Grandpa used to listen to Dan Rather every evening and constantly scream, "Horsefeathers!"

5. Otherwise, the end-punctuation of the quotation makes way for your own punctuation. If the quoted passage, for example, ends with a period but your own sentence does not stop there, you should drop the period and substitute your own punctuation, if any:

- "I wonder why they don't impeach newscasters," said Grandpa.

  The quoted passage would normally end with a period, but the main sentence calls for a comma at that point.

6. In general, a closing quotation mark can be accompanied by only one other mark of punctuation. But an exception can be made for the rare case in which extra punctuation rescues a sentence from ungrammaticality:

- When the Dow-Jones Index fell through 600—the market analysts had the nerve to call it a "technical adjustment"!—Stanley decided to become a revolutionary again.

  The quotation marks, exclamation point, and dash after *adjustment* each serve a necessary function.

7. When a quotation is accompanied by a footnote number, the footnote number should come *after* all other punctuation except a dash that may resume your own part of the sentence:

- Burgess finds "no substance to these charges."[8]
- Burgess finds "no substance to these charges"[8]—and I emphatically agree with him.

8. When a quotation is integrated into your text (without indention) and is followed by a parenthetical citation (pp. 419–420), the parenthesis should come *after* the final quotation marks but *before* a comma or period—even if the comma or period occurs in the quoted passage:

- Dr. Dollar says, "No modern home should be without a queen-sized trampoline" (*Aerobic Kama Sutra*, p. 217).

9. But if the quotation ends with a question mark or an exclamation point, you should include it before the closing quotation marks and add your own punctuation after the parenthesis:

- "Should we in the education industry," Clearance asked, "allow ourselves to lag behind in the vital areas of packaging and promotion?" (*Times* interview, p. 18, col. 2).

10. When, finally, a quotation is indented and set apart from your text, the parenthetical citation follows *all* punctuation and is customarily given either in a footnote or on a separate line:

* I'm just sittin here washing television
  washin telvsn
  wshn t.v.
  (yeah!)
  wshn *tee veeee.*
                      ("Ode to Amerika," ll. 13–17)

Fuller advice about citation is given in Chapter 15 (pp. 404–427).

EXERCISE

8. Correct any errors in the use of quotation marks:

    A. "We want a "G" rating for this movie," said the director, so I'd like you to stab her only in the throat and stomach."
    B. Is it true that the witness said, "I refuse to answer on the grounds that my answer might tend to incinerate me?"
    C. Stanley's most secret communiqués were signed *El Macho* 'the masculine one.'
    D. The poet tells us a good deal about his life when he writes,
        "Counted up Fri. and saw I still got
        Four lids and two caps,
        One lovin' spoonful,
        Three buttons from Southatheborder,
        Some coke but no Pepsi,
        And a bottle of reds.
        O Amerika we can still be friends fer a few more weeks."
    E. Since he hoped to become a dog trainer when his football career was over, Biff was especially eager to read the article in "National Geographic" called *Sikkim.*

SLASH /

A slash (or virgule) is used chiefly to separate alternatives *(the moon and/or the stars; the who/whom controversy)* and to indicate line divisions in brief poetic quotations that are not set apart:

* Wratto informs us that he is "just sittin here washing television / washin telvsn. . . ."

The slash may replace a dash to show a time period covering parts of two successive years:

- Biff had his greatest season in 1983/84, when he endorsed a mouthwash, an athlete's foot ointment, and a home permanent kit.

The slash symbolizes the word "per" in expressions like *km./hr.* (kilometers per hour) and *ft./sec.* (feet per second).

PUNCTUATING BY TYPEWRITER

To see how the punctuation marks are normally typed and spaced, examine the typescript papers on pages 429–445 and 448–456. In addition, note the following points:

1. Place punctuation marks directly next to the punctuated word without leaving a space. The one exception is an ellipsis in the middle of a sentence; leave one space before typing such an ellipsis (`hardly any . . . secrets`).
2. Leave two spaces after each period, question mark, or exclamation point.
3. Leave one space after commas, colons, semicolons, closing parentheses, closing brackets, and closing quotation marks, unless other punctuation immediately follows the mark in question. In that case, put the two marks together without a space between.
4. Leave no space before or after dashes, hyphens, and apostrophes, unless the apostrophe ends a word and is followed by no other punctuation.
5. Dashes come in three lengths, depending on their function. A dash separating numbers is typed as a hyphen: `pp. 132-39`. As the sign of a break in thought, a dash is typed as two hyphens with no space between: `Try it--if you dare`. A dash standing in place of an omitted word should be longer. Use four unspaced hyphens: `He refused to disclose the name of Ms.----`.
6. If your typewriter lacks keys for brackets, improvise by either
   a. typing slashes (/) and completing the sides with underlinings: $\underline{/\ /}$
   b. typing the slashes and adding the lines later in ink; or
   c. leaving blank spaces and doing the brackets entirely in ink.
7. Leave one space after each of the periods making up an ellipsis, but leave two spaces after the last period if you are beginning a new sentence.

8. Do not begin a line with any mark that punctuates a *preceding* word, and do not carry an ellipsis from one line to the next. (See, for example, the faulty Wratto sentence on p. 332.)

NOTES

[1]David Maxfield, "What Nancy Reagan Has Done to the White House," *San Francisco Chronicle,* 23 Dec. 1981, p. 16.

[2]Richard Rees, *George Orwell: Fugitive from the Camp of Victory* (London: Secker and Warburg, 1961), p. 153.

13

SPELLING AND OTHER CONVENTIONS

SPELLING

The Spelling List

Every reader—even one whose own spelling is poor—expects writers to spell correctly and holds it against them if they do not. That, in brief, is why you should check your drafts for misspellings and work to increase the number of words you can spell correctly without having to look them up. If spelling causes you trouble, you cannot afford to label yourself a poor speller and leave it at that; you need to develop some habits that will eliminate the wrong choices one by one.

The first such habit is, of course, that of using your college dictionary (p. 209) whenever you are in doubt about the form of a word you want to use. (If you like, you can wait to do this until you have finished a draft.) Second, as you read other people's writing, take note of words whose spelling seems odd to you. And third, just as you are doing for new *meanings* (pp. 208–212), keep a continuing *spelling list,* including not only the words you have already misspelled in papers, but also words whose spelling troubles you when you meet them in printed texts.

Treat your spelling list like your vocabulary list, adding and removing entries from one day to the next. You would also do well to look through your current list before rereading the final drafts of your papers; that will help you to notice and remove misspellings.

As with vocabulary, the most serious misspellings are not those that would eliminate you from the finals of a spelling bee, but slips with ordinary words. If you have been making such slips with some regularity, you may not be able to cure them simply by noting the correct versions. Add a middle column to your spelling list, using it to distinguish the word from another one, to remind yourself of a rule, or to jog your memory with a catchy phrase. For example:

misspelling	remember	correct spelling
seperate	not like *desperate*	sep*a*rate
alot	one word is not a lot	a lot
hypocracy	not like *democracy*	hypocr*i*sy
heighth	get the *h* out of here!	height
concieve	*i* before *e* except after *c*	conc*ei*ve
mispell	don't *miss* this one	mis*s*pell
fiting	say it out loud!	fit*t*ing
beautyful	*y* misspell it?	beaut*i*ful
wierd	a weird exception to *i* before *e*	w*ei*rd
goverment	govern + ment	gover*n*ment
complection	*x* marks the spots	comple*x*ion

Common Errors

Certain words are so commonly misspelled in student writing that you should review them right now, beginning your spelling list with the words you do not yet firmly command. In addition to the items in the list above, consider these:

absence
accommodate
acknowledgment
across
actually
address
adolescence, adolescent
advice (noun), advise (verb)
aggravate, aggravated,
  aggravating

aggress, aggressive,
  aggression
aging
all right
allege
altar (of a church), alter
  (change)
altogether
always
analysis, analyses (plural)

analyze
apparent
appearance
appreciate, appreciation
aquatic
arctic
argument
assassin, assassination
assistant, assistance
athlete, athletic, athletics

attendance
bachelor
balloon
beggar
benefit, benefited, benefiting
besiege
biased
bigoted
breadth *(width)*, breath (noun), breathe (verb)
Britain
bureau
bureaucracy, bureaucratic
burglar
bus
business *(job)*, busyness *(being busy)*
cafeteria
calendar
camouflage
capital *(city)*, capitol *(state house)*
category
ceiling
cemetery
changeable
choose *(select)*, chose (past tense)
chord *(tones)*, cord *(rope)*
cite *(mention)*, sight *(view)*, site *(locale)*
climactic *(of a climax)*, climatic *(of a climate)*
coarse *(rough)*, course *(direction)*
commit, commitment
committee
competent
concomitant
conscience
conscious
consensus
consistent, consistency
consummate
control, controlled, controlling
controversy
coolly

corollary
correlate
corroborate
counterfeit
criticism, criticize
deceive
defendant
defense
definite, definitely
deity
dependent
descent *(lowering)*, dissent *(disagreement)*
desirable
despair
desperate, desperation
destroy
develop, development
die, dying *(expiring)*, dye *(color)*, dyeing *(coloring)*
dilapidated
dilemma
disastrous
discipline
dispensable
divide
divine
drunkenness
dual *(double)*, duel *(fight)*
duly
ecstasy
eighth
elicit *(draw forth)*, illicit *(unlawful)*
emanate
embarrass, embarrassed, embarrassing
envelop *(surround)*, envelope (for mailing)
environment
equip, equipped, equipment
evenness
exaggerate
exceed
excellent, excellence
exercise
exhilarate

existence
expel
extraordinary
fallacy
familiar
fascinate
fascist
faze *(daunt)*, phase *(period)*
February
fiend
fiery
finally
forbear *(refrain)*, forebear *(ancestor)*
forehead
foresee, foreseeable
foreword *(preface)*, forward *(ahead)*
forfeit
forgo
forty
fourth
friend
fulfill
fulsome
futilely
gases
gauge
glamour, glamorous
grammar, grammatically
greenness
grievance, grievous
gruesome
guarantee
guard
handkerchief
hangar (for airplanes), hanger (for coats)
harangue
harass
heroes
hindrance
hoping
idiosyncrasy
imagery
immediate

impel

inadvertent

incidentally

incredible

indestructible

indispensable

infinitely

innuendo

inoculate

interrupt

irrelevant

irreparable, irreparably

irreplaceable, irreplaceably

irresistible, irresistibly

jeopardy

judgment

knowledge, knowledgeable

laboratory

lead *(metal, conduct)*, led
(past tense of verb *lead*)

legitimate

leisure

length

lessen *(reduce)*, lesson
(teaching)

library

license

lightening *(getting lighter)*,
lightning *(flash)*

loath *(reluctant)*, loathe
(despise), loathsome

loneliness

loose *(slack)*, lose *(mislay)*,
losing

lying

maintenance

maneuver

manual

marriage

marshal (verb and noun),
marshaled, marshaling

material *(pertaining to
matter)*, materiel *(military
supplies)*

mathematics

medicine

memento

millennium

mimic, mimicked

miner *(digger)*, minor *(lesser)*

mischief, mischievous

missile

moral *(ethical)*, morale
(confidence)

mortgage

naval *(nautical)*, navel
(bellybutton)

necessary

nickel

niece

noncommittal

noticeable, noticing

occasion

occur, occurred, occurring,
occurrence

omit, omitted, omitting,
omission

opportunity

optimist

paid

pajamas

parallel, paralleled

paralysis, paralyze

parliament

passed *(went by)*, past
(previous)

pastime

peace *(tranquillity)*, piece
(part)

pejorative

perceive

perennial

perfectible, perfectibility

perform, performance

permanent

permissible

personal *(individual)*,
personnel *(employees)*

perspiration

phony

physical

physician

playwright

pleasant

pleasurable

possess, possession

practically

practice

pray *(implore)*, prey *(victim)*

principal (adjective, noun:
chief), principle (noun: *rule*)

privilege

probably

professor

pronunciation

propaganda

propagate

prophecy *(prediction)*,
prophesy *(predict)*

prostate *(gland)*, prostrate
(prone)

psychiatry

psychology

pumpkin

pursue, pursuit

putrefy

quizzes

rack *(framework)*, wrack *(ruin)*

rain *(precipitation)*, rein
(restrain), reign *(rule)*

rarefied

realize

receipt

receive

recognizable

recommend

refer, referred, referring

regretted, regretting

relevant, relevance

relieve

remembrance

reminisce

repellent

repentance

repetition

resistance

restaurant

rhythm

ridiculous

roommate

sacrilegious

said
schedule
secretary
seize
sergeant
sheriff
shining
shriek
siege
significance
similar
smooth (adjective and
    verb)
solely
soliloquy
sophomore
sovereign, sovereignty
specimen
sponsor
stationary (still), stationery
    (paper)
strength
stupefy
subtlety, subtly
succeed, success
succinct
succumb
suffrage

superintendent
supersede
suppose
suppress
surprise
symmetry
sympathize
tariff
temperament
temperature
tendency
than
their (belonging to them),
    there (at that place)
therefore
thinness
thorough
threshold
through
to (toward), too (also), two
    (one plus one)
track (path), tract (area)
traffic, trafficked, trafficking
tranquil, tranquillity
transcendent, transcendental
transfer, transferred,
    transferring
tries, tried

truly
unconscious
unmistakable, unmistakably
unnecessary
unshakable
unwieldy
vacillate
vacuum
vegetable
vengeance
venomous
vice
vilify, vilification
villain
waive (relinquish), wave
    (movement)
weather (state of the
    atmosphere), whether (if)
Wednesday
wield
wintry
withdrawal
withhold
woeful
worldly, unworldly
worshiped, worshiping
wreak (inflict), wreck (ruin)
writing

As you can see from examining this list, confusion of spelling and confusion of meaning often come to the same thing. To complete your survey of commonly misspelled words, you should review the paired definitions on pages 213–216.

Plurals

confusion with possessives Many spelling errors result from the fact that most nouns add *-s* to become *both* plural and possessive. Hastening through a draft, writers fail to mark the distinguishing feature, an *apostrophe for possessives only:*

plural	possessive
copies	copy's
trees	tree's
Kennedys	Kennedy's

Do not be surprised, then, to find some accidentally "possessive" plurals in your first drafts: x *three stereo's*, x *four cause's*, and so forth.

nouns ending in -o Some plural forms are especially tricky to spell. While most nouns ending in a *vowel* plus -o become plural by adding -s (*patios, studios*), most nouns ending in a *consonant* plus -o become plural by adding -es (*potatoes, vetoes*). Even so, some words flout the rules (*solos, pianos, sopranos*), and some others have alternative plurals: *cargos, cargoes; zeros, zeroes*. Where your dictionary lists two forms, always adopt the first.

compound nouns Most compound nouns—that is, nouns consisting of more than one word—form the plural by adding -s to the final word: *cross-examinations, fire fighters, head starts*. Although such words cause no problem in themselves, they may deceive you into pluralizing *all* compound nouns in the same way. Note that when the first word is the significant one, it takes the plural form: *mothers-in-law, men-of-war, secretaries-general, senators-elect*.

nouns ending in -ful Nouns ending in *-ful* become plural by adding -s to the end: *cupfuls, shovelfuls, spoonfuls*. Beware of the "genteel" but erroneous *cupsful*, and so forth.

nouns with foreign plural forms A number of words taken from foreign languages, especially from Greek and Latin, retain their foreign plural forms. Some have also acquired English plural forms, and thus have two plural spellings. The rule for deciding which plural to use is: look it up! But you should also be aware that some words take a foreign plural only in certain restricted uses. Thus:

singular	context	plural
appendix	abdomen	appendixes
	end of book	appendices *or* appendixes
index	alphabetical guide	indexes
	economic indicator	indices
antenna	television	antennas
	insect	antennae
formula	rule or method	formulas
	chemical composition	formulae
medium	séance	mediums
	news and entertainment	media

When in doubt, lean toward the English plural, which sounds less pretentious and is easier to spell: *cactuses, curriculums, maximums, minimums, radiuses, sanitariums, syllabuses*, etc. And when you do use an accepted foreign plural, make sure you do not have it confused with the singular. Many writers stumble over one or more of the following:

singular	plural
criterion	criteria
datum	data
kudos	kudos
phenomenon	phenomena
stratum	strata
vertebra	vertebrae

Although *datum* and *stratum* are rarely seen and the singular use of *data* is by now common, you would do well to keep both *data* and *strata* plural.

letters and figures   Letters and figures usually become plural by the addition of -'s:

- Hester was rapidly losing whatever fondness she might once have felt for capital *A*'s.
- Now that the postal rates have gone up again, do you think we can expect a closeout sale on 13's?

Some writers omit the apostrophe and give the plurals as *As, 13s.* But this can make for confusion; *As,* for example, looks too much like a two-letter word. It is better to use -'s consistently.

words considered as words   Whole words can be given the plural form -'s if you are trying to indicate that they *are* words:

- I hired you as my yes man, but in this memorandum of yours I find four *no*'s.

Note how the italicizing of the isolated word, but not of the -'s, helps to make the writer's meaning clear.

Possessives

You may find that your first drafts contain some would-be possessive nouns disguised as plurals: x *the boys education,* x *the camels back,* and so forth. (See p. 348.) Be sure you supply the necessary apostrophes: *the boy's education, the camel's back.*

optional -s   Singular nouns usually become possessive by the addition of -'s, whether or not the noun ends in an s sound: *day's, Camus's, Jones's,*

Keats's, Sis's, Snopes's, Wes's. But when a singular word has more than one syllable and ends with an *s* sound, the *s* after the apostrophe is optional:

pronounced -*s*	unpronounced -*s*
Dickens's	Dickens'
Demosthenes's	Demosthenes'

Whichever practice you follow, do so consistently.

unusual singular possessives Even if you intend to make all singular nouns possessive by using -'s, you should recognize certain exceptions. Where an -'s would make for three closely bunched -s sounds, the apostrophe alone can be used: *Moses', Ulysses', Xerxes'.* And certain fixed expressions violate the -'s rule: *for goodness' sake, for Jesus' sake.* Some writers even omit the apostrophe in these phrases.

Of course, singular nouns can also be made possessive by a preceding *of: the work of a day, the novels of Camus, the verse of Keats.* Be careful not to add an apostrophe in such cases. (For "double possessives" in which *of* and an apostrophe *are* combined, see p. 294.)

possessives of irregular plurals Plural nouns normally become possessive either by a preceding *of (the views of Americans)* or by the addition of an apostrophe alone:

- the Americans' views
- several days' work

But plural nouns that do not end in *s* become possessive in the same way that singular nouns do:

- the children's room
- those deer's habitat
- three mice's tails
- the alumni's representative

When such a plural possessive sounds awkward, change it to the *of* form: *the tails of three mice.*

plural possessives of time There is a growing tendency to drop the apostrophe in plural possessives of time: *two years parole, a six weeks holiday.* For the present, however, it might be wise to write *two years' parole, a six weeks' holiday.* The apostrophes serve a function in showing that the modified nouns in these phrases are *parole* and *holiday.*

compound possessives In "joint ownership" compound possessives, only the final name takes the possessive form:

- Bradley, Beatty, and Long's anthology
- Laurel and Hardy's comedies

But note that this applies only when the possession is truly collective. Compare:

- Bradley's, Beatty's, and Long's efforts were pooled in the task of compiling and editing the book.

> The possessive forms are correct here because three *separate* efforts are being discussed.

possessives in titles In some titles the expected possessive form is lacking: *The Authors Guild, The Merchants Bank, Finnegans Wake*. Do not "improve" such titles by adding an apostrophe.

possessives of pronouns Pronouns that are already possessive in meaning take no apostrophe: *his, hers, its, ours, yours, theirs, whose* (see the table on p. 257). Note especially the treacherous *it's*, which is the correct form for the contraction of *it is* but a blunder for the possessive *its*.

Some indefinite pronouns form the possessive in the same manner as nouns: *another's, nobody's, one's, somebody's*, and so on. But some other indefinite pronouns can only be made possessive in the *of* form: *of each, of all*, and so on.

awkward possessives Certain problems of spelling possessives cannot be satisfactorily resolved at all. For example, how should you form the possessive of a noun that is followed by a parenthesis? Is it *Mrs. Jones (née Davis)'s coat, Mrs. Jones's (née Davis) coat*, or what? All possible versions are awkward, except possibly *the coat of Mrs. Jones (née Davis)*.

Again, do not try to form the possessive of a word followed by quotation marks: *"The Dead"'s symbolism*. Resort to the *of* form: *the symbolism of "The Dead."*

And finally, watch out for unnatural separation of the *-'s* from the word it refers to. You can write *someone else's problem* or *the Queen of Sheba's tuba*, but you should not write *the house on the corner's roof*. In that phrase the *-'s* is just too far away from the word that "possesses" it, *house*. Once again, a timely recourse to *of* can rescue you: *the roof of the house on the corner*. And note that inanimate (nonliving) nouns often make awkward possessives. Instead of *the page's bottom*, write *the bottom of the page*.

Hyphenation

A hyphen sets off certain prefixes, separates the parts of certain compound words, connects the parts of compound modifiers and the words in certain compound phrases, and indicates that an uncompleted word at the end of a line will be completed at the beginning of the next line. Only your dictionary can tell you whether, and at what point, many terms should be hyphenated. The following survey of problems, however, offers some general guidelines.

word division at the end of a line   In a manuscript or typescript, where right-hand margins are uneven, the problem of hyphenation can be dodged. Just end each line with the last word that you can *complete*. Your reader will never know or care whether you are someone who finds it hard to divide words at the right junctures. But if you find that you must divide a word, do so only at one of the syllable (speech segment) breaks as marked in a dictionary.

Observe these further conventions:

---

1. Never divide a one-syllable word, even if you might manage to pronounce it as two syllables (*rhythm, schism*).
2. Do not leave one letter stranded at the end of a line (*o-ver, i-dea*), and do not leave a solitary letter for the beginning of the next line (*Ontari-o, seed-y*).
3. If a word is already hyphenated, divide it only at the fixed hyphen. Avoid *self-con-scious, ex-Pre-mier*.
4. You can anticipate what the dictionary will say about word division by remembering that:
   a. Double consonants are usually separated: *ar-rogant, inef-fable*.
   b. But when the double consonants come just before a suffix, the division falls *after* the double consonants: *stall-ing, kiss-able*.
   c. When a word has acquired a double consonant in adding a suffix, the second consonant belongs to the suffix: *bet-ting, fad-dish*.

---

prefixes   Hyphens are used to separate certain *prefixes*—letters that can precede the root or base form of a word to make a new word—from the root words to which they are attached:

all-, ex-, self-   Words beginning with *all-, ex-,* and *self-*, when these are prefixes, are hyphenated after the prefix:

all-powerful
ex-minister
self-motivated

Note that in *selfhood, selfish, selfless,* and *selfsame* the accented syllable *self* is not a true prefix, and no hyphen is called for.

prefixes with names

Prefixes before a name are always hyphenated:

pro-Kennedy
un-American
anti-Chinese

words like anti-intellectual and co-op

Prefixes ending with a vowel sometimes take a hyphen if they are followed by a vowel, especially if the two vowels are the same:

anti-intellectual
co-op
semi-invalid

exceptions: common terms

The hyphen prevents ambiguity and mispronunciation, as in *coop.* But prefixed terms that are very common are less likely to be mis-construed, and many double vowels remain unhyphenated:

cooperate
coordinate
preempt
reeducate

You will find good dictionaries in some disagreement with each other about such words. Some dictionaries prefer hyphens in most double-vowel situations; some have all but abolished the convention; and some recommend a dieresis mark over the second vowel to show that it is separately pronounced: *reëducate.* In contemporary prose, however, you will not come across many instances of the dieresis.

constructions like pre- and postwar

When a modifier occurs with two alternative prefixes, the first prefix often stands alone with a hyphen:

- There was quite a difference between *pre-* and postwar prices.
- *Pro-* and antifascist students battled openly in the streets of Rome.

Note that the first prefix takes a hyphen even if it would not have one when joined to the root word.

compound nouns Many compound nouns (nouns formed from more than one word) are hyphenated: *bull's-eye, city-state, poet-philosopher, point-blank, secretary-treasurer,* etc. Many others, however, are written as separate words (*fire fighter, head start, ice cream, oil spill,* etc.) or as single unhyphenated words (*earring, milkmaid, scofflaw, scoutmaster, underwriter,* etc.). As compound terms become familiar with long use, they tend to drop their hyphens. The dictionary can guide you in individual cases of doubt—though dictionaries themselves will differ somewhat over various words.

Among the compound nouns that are hyphenated, many contain prepositions: *good-for-nothing, jack-in-the-box, man-of-war, mother-of-pearl, son-in-law,* etc. The hyphenation shows that the prepositional phrase is part of the thing named, not part of the rest of the sentence. Compare:

- She had a *son-in-law.*
- She had a daughter in medicine and a *son in law.*

compound modifiers
before modified term:
<u>well-trained</u>

A compound modifier (containing more than one word) is usually hyphenated if it *precedes* the modified term:

a *well-trained* philosopher
an *out-of-work* barber

The hyphens are useful because they shift attention to the real noun: not a *well,* but a *philosopher.*

after modified term:
<u>well trained</u>

But no ambiguity is likely when a compound modifier *follows* the modified term, and in this position the hyphen usually disappears:

- The philosopher was *well trained.*
- A barber *out of work* is bound to resent people who cut their own hair.

modifiers like
<u>barely
suppressed</u>

When a compound modifier contains an adverb in the *-ly* form, it does not have to be hyphenated in any position. The adverb, clearly identifiable *as* an adverb, does the hyphen's work of signaling that the real noun comes later:

a barely suppressed gasp
an openly polygamous chieftain
the hypocritically worded note of protest

modifiers like
<u>fast-developing</u>

Adverbs lacking the *-ly* form are another matter: *the fast-developing crisis, a deep-boring bit,* etc.

modifiers with
<u>fixed hyphens</u>

If a modifier is hyphenated in the dictionary, it remains hyphenated in all positions:

- She was an *even-tempered* instructor.
- She was *even-tempered.*

avoidance of confusion

Certain words are sometimes hyphenated because they would otherwise look identical to very different words:

- If you don't *re-sort* the laundry, I will have to resort to buying new underwear at the resort.
- Mystic Mandala Village, an authentic *re-creation* of a hippie commune, is being advertised as a future center of recreation.
- Having run in the Olympics, she had a *run-in* with the Rules Committee about pep pills.

compound numbers   Numbers twenty-one to ninety-nine, when written out, are
numbers hyphenated, even when they form part of a larger number:
twenty-one to
ninety-nine   • Her waist was a perfect *forty-eight.*
          • Two hundred *seventy-five* years ago there was an Indian burial mound on the
            site of this beautiful Texaco station.

> Note that *and* is not a recognized part of any whole number.
> Strictly speaking, *two hundred and seventy-five years ago* would
> be incorrect.

fractions   Fractions are hyphenated only when they are used as modifiers:

AS MODIFIER:
• The jug of Thunderbird was *seven-eighths* empty at the end of the party.

> *Seven-eighths* modifies *empty.*

NOT AS MODIFIER:
• *Seven eighths* of all adults have experimented with such dangerous drugs as
  nicotine, caffeine, and alcohol.

> The fraction serves as the subject of the verb *have experimented.*

But many people ignore this rule, and by now it is debatable whether
the commoner fractions such as *two thirds* and *one quarter* ever need
to be hyphenated.
compound   Do not add an extra hyphen to compound fractions such as these:
fractions

three seventy-thirds
twenty-one forty-sevenths

> Hyphens after *three* and *twenty-one* would blur the distinction
> between the numerator and the denominator in each case.

connection of numbers   Hyphens are used to connect numbers expressing a range:

pages 136–98
the period September 11–October 4

> In such cases the hyphen means *between.* It is therefore redun-
> dant to write x *the period between September 11–October 4.*

EXERCISES

1. Go through all the previously graded papers (for this and other courses) that you have on
   hand, noting all the words that were marked as misspelled. Then carefully review the list on
   pages 345–348, checking the words you think you might misspell. From these two sources,

begin a spelling list such as the one shown on page 345. Submit ten entries from your list, using the three-column format ("Misspelling," "Remember," "Correct Spelling").

2. Write the plural forms of the following words:

A. ox	F. woman	K. wrong turn
B. ax	G. alloy	L. chairman-elect
C. datum	H. ferry	M. forkful
D. radio	I. Murphy	N. phenomenon
E. wish	J. tomato	O. analysis

3. Write the alternative possessive form for each of the following:

   A. of the victor
   B. of the bystanders
   C. for the sake of goodness
   D. of a Pisces
   E. of the children
   F. of the louse
   G. a journey of four days
   H. the wives of the Yankee pitchers
   I. the partnership of John, Paul, George, and Ringo
   J. the fault of somebody

4. If it were necessary to hyphenate these words at the end of a line, where would breaks be appropriate? Indicate possible breaks by vertical lines.

   A. overripe
   B. ex-Republican
   C. passionate
   D. butted
   E. penning

5. Correct any errors of hyphenation in the following items:

   A. selfsufficient
   B. antiAmerican
   C. semi-incapacitated
   D. redesign
   E. pre and postinflationary
   F. suicide leap
   G. father-in-law
   H. an ill schooled student
   I. The doctor was poorly prepared.
   J. Teachers are under-paid.
   K. a bad looking thunderhead
   L. a finely-tuned violin
   M. sixty-five days
   N. a hundred-thirty-one times
   O. a three sixteenths opening
   P. four-elevenths of those people
   Q. forty-three eighty-ninths
   R. a delay of between 8–10 hours
   S. between pages 45–50
   T. a completely unsettling experience

CAPITALS

first letters of sentences   The first letter of every sentence or independent sentence fragment should be capitalized:

- *Are* you a Pisces? *Certainly* not! *Too* bad.

sentences within sentences   Sentences within sentences customarily begin with capitals:

- Max asked Bessie, "*Why* don't we skip the tourist spots and just hang around American Express today?"
- I wondered, How am I ever going to finish this book?

But once in a while, words that might be construed as sentence openers are left uncapitalized:

- Max was curious. Who had invented that awful French coffee? *when? and why?*

  By leaving *when* and *and* in lower case, the writer emphasizes that Max was asking a three-part question, not three distinct questions. Capitals would have been equally correct and more usual.

Note that indirect questions are not capitalized:

- I wondered *how* I was ever going to finish that book.

sentences within parentheses   Sentences contained within parentheses should begin with capitals only if they stand between complete sentences:

CAPITALIZED:
- Max and Bessie had a fine time in Moscow. (*They* especially liked shopping for used blue jeans and drinking Pepsi with Herb and Gladys.) But in Bulgaria Max missed the whole World Series because no one would lend him a short-wave radio.

UNCAPITALIZED:
- Dr. Dollar's best seller, *Be Fat and Forget It* (*the* publisher decided on the title after a brainstorming session with his advertising staff), has freed millions of Americans from needless anxiety.

statements following colons   Some writers capitalize the first letter of a complete independent statement following a colon, but some readers regard this as an error. Play it safe and keep to the lower case.

- Dr. Dollar faced this dilemma: *should* he or shouldn't he appear on television and let people see that he weighed only 113 pounds?

quotations   Capitalize the first letter of a quotation only if (a) it was capitalized in the original, or (b) it represents the beginning of a complete remark, or (c) it begins your own sentence:

- Ben Jonson believed that *"Memory* of all *powers* of the mind, is the most *delicate* and *fraile; it is the first of our *faculties* that Age invades."

  Neither *Memory* nor *Age* would ordinarily be capitalized in the positions they occupy here, but the writer wants to reproduce Jonson's text exactly. (The italics, too, are Jonson's.)

- What Shelley considered immortal was "Thought / Alone, and its quick elements. . . ."

  The capitals are found in Shelley's poem.

- Bessie told Max, *"There's* nothing like a good American cup of freeze-dried coffee."

  The beginning of Bessie's sentence must be capitalized, even though it does not begin the writer's own sentence.

- *"Citizen's* band radio" was the phrase Max kept muttering to himself as he walked through Paris, wondering how a civilization could have survived so long without the bare necessities of technology.

  Max's phrase is not a complete statement, but it begins the *writer's* sentence.

uncapitalized quotation   When a quotation does not meet any of the three tests for capitalization, leave its first letter in the lower case:

- Bessie said that she didn't mind the coffee's tasting like lentil soup, *"if* only they would make it hot."

  The quotation is a subordinate clause, not a full statement.

representations of thoughts   When you are "quoting" an unspoken thought, as in *I wondered, How am I ever going to finish this book?*, capitalize the first letter of the represented thought.

titles of works   In citing titles written in English, you should capitalize the opening letters of the first word, the last word, and other important words. If articles, conjunctions, or prepositions do not occur in the first or last positions, leave them in the lower case.

- *Dr. Dollar Raps with the Newborn*

The same rules hold for subtitles in English. Note also that the first letter of a subtitle is always capitalized:

- *Working within the System: A Guide to Sewer Repair*

Foreign titles tend to follow different conventions; if you do not translate the title, use the capitalization as you find it on the title page.

historical terms Specific events, movements, and periods are often known by capitalized names:

- the Bronze Age
- the Civil War
- the War between the States
- the Romantic poets
- the Depression

times Days, months, and holidays are capitalized, but seasons and the numerical parts of dates are not:

CAPITALIZED:
- next Tuesday
- May, 1985
- Christmas
- Columbus Day

UNCAPITALIZED:
- next fall
- a winter storm
- July twenty-first
- the third of August

groups versus groupings Organized groups and nationalities require capitals, but looser groupings do not:

CAPITALIZED:
- Christian
- Hungarian
- Republican
- Women for Peace

UNCAPITALIZED:
- the upper class
- the underprivileged
- the peace movement

abbreviations   Abbreviations after a name are usually capitalized: *Jr., Sr., M.A., Ph.D., Esq., U.S.N. (Ret.).* In contrast, *a.m.* and *p.m.* are usually left uncapitalized.

directions versus places   Geographic directions are left uncapitalized, but specific places take capitals. When faced with a word like *northwest,* think whether it refers in this case to a compass point *(northwest of here)* or to a fixed place or route *(Northwest Territories, Northwest Passage).*

CAPITALIZED:
- Southeast Asia
- the winning of the West

UNCAPITALIZED:
- southeast of Tucson
- go west until you meet the oily surf

specific institutions   Specific institutions are capitalized, and so are their formal subdivisions:

- Museum of Modern Art
- University of Chicago
- the Department of Business Administration
- Franklin High School

Subsequent, shortened references to the institution or department are sometimes left uncapitalized:

- She retired from the *university* last year.

   But *University* would also be correct here.

   Note that articles, brief prepositions, and conjunctions appearing in the names of institutions or departments are left uncapitalized, just as they are in titles of publications.

general institutions   Institutions meant in a general sense are not capitalized:

- a strife-torn *museum*
- Every *university* is threatened by anarchy.
- His *department* fired him because the students were too fond of him.
- He dropped out of *high school* to give all his time to chess.

courses versus branches of learning   Specific courses of study are capitalized, but general branches of learning are not:

CAPITALIZED:
- Physics 1A
- Social Welfare 203

UNCAPITALIZED:
- He never learned the rudiments of *physics.*
- Her training in *social welfare* didn't prepare her for this.

names   Names of people, places, businesses, and organizations are capitalized:

- William Wordsworth
- Louisville, Kentucky
- Marvelous Max's Junktiques
- American Broadcasting System

family relations versus names   Family relations should be capitalized only when they are part of a name or when used in direct address:

CAPITALIZED:
- Everyone has seen posters of *Uncle Sam.*
- Oh, *Mother,* you're so old-fashioned!

UNCAPITALIZED:
- My *uncle* Sam wasn't the same man after the Dodgers moved to Los Angeles.
- You are the only *mother* on this block who objects to pierced noses.

sacred names   Sacred names are conventionally capitalized, whether or not the writer is a believer:

- The Old Testament
- the Bible
- God
- the Lord
- He, Him, His [referring to the Judeo-Christian deity]
- the Virgin Mary
- the Koran
- the Upanishads

ranks and titles   A rank or title is capitalized when joined to a name or when it stands for a specific person, but it is often left uncapitalized in other circumstances:

CAPITALIZED:

* General R. R. Junket

UNCAPITALIZED:

* Two *generals* and a *colonel* were reprimanded for mislaying the B-52's.

Note, however, that some high offices are uniformly capitalized: *the Queen of England, the President of the United States, Secretary of Defense, Chief Justice of the United States.* (There is no such office as *Chief Justice of the Supreme Court.*)

adjectives derived from names Most adjectives derived from names are capitalized:

* Shakespearean
* American
* Maoist
* the French language

foreign words and titles Foreign conventions of capitalization are too various to summarize. The general rule, however, is that in giving a foreign word or title, you should follow the practices of that language rather than your own. Be careful to reproduce the capitals exactly as you find them in the original.

different meanings Sometimes a word has quite different meanings in its capitalized and uncapitalized forms:

* The Pope is a *Catholic.* [He belongs to the Church.]
* George has *catholic* tastes. [His tastes are wide-ranging.]
* He became a *Democrat* after the President declared a national day of prayer for the Redskins. [He joined the party.]
* Tocqueville saw every American farmer as a *democrat.* [He believed that they all supported the idea of equality.]

EXERCISE

6. Correct any errors of capitalization:

   A. Our most musical president was Harry Truman, who, after reading a review of one of his Daughter Margaret's concerts, threatened to beat up the critic.
   B. Each year the Pelicans fly south to build their nests near the outfall pipe.
   C. Realizing that her marriage was in trouble, Susan went straight to the lingerie department and asked if she could try on a Freudian slip.
   D. She wondered Whether it was really necessary for the management to frisk people who lingered near the meat counter.
   E. Stanley believed that the People, guided by himself and a few trusted friends, knew more about their true interests than any politician did.

ITALICS

Ordinary typeface is known as **roman**, and the thin, slightly slanted typeface that stands apart from it is called **italic**—as in *these three words*. In manuscript or typescript, underlining is the equivalent of italic type. The conventional symbols *Rom* and *Ital*, when used in correction of a manuscript or typescript, mean respectively "do not underline" and "underline."

Italics are used for certain titles, foreign words, scientific names, names of ships, words considered *as* words, and words bearing a special rhetorical emphasis.

titles Titles of books, plays, films, newspapers, magazines, journals, and other works that form complete publications are usually italicized:

- *Mademoiselle*
- *The Golden Notebook*
- *A Streetcar Named Desire*
- *Philadelphia Inquirer*
- *Paradise Lost*

Note that:

a. In the names of newspapers, the *place* of publication is included in the italicized title.
b. A single poem, if it was first published as a whole volume, is named in italics; if it formed only part of the volume, it is named in roman type, within quotation marks. So are the titles of chapters, essays, and short stories.
c. A work that was first published in a magazine may later be expanded into a whole book; or, if the book is itself a collection, it may bear the title of the story, article, or poem. Remember that when you give the title in italics (i.e., underline it on your typewriter) you are always referring to the complete volume, not to the item that gave the volume its title.
d. Newspapers and magazines have their own conventions for identifying titles. Some publications use italics sparingly or not at all. If you know that your writing will be printed by a given magazine or newspaper, follow its own rules. Student papers, scholarship, and writing that may be submitted to various publications should observe the rules given here.
e. The Bible and its divisions are left in roman type: the Bible, the Old Testament, Leviticus.
f. When one title contains another one that would normally be italicized, that second title becomes roman—that is, you should not underline it. Citing a book called *The Meaning of* A Streetcar Named Desire, for example, you would underline only *The Meaning of.*

foreign versus "domesticated" terms Foreign words that have not yet been adopted as routine English expressions should be italicized:

- Dr. Dollar's *Weltanschauung* was a mixture of Dale Carnegie and P. T. Barnum.
- After four best sellers he was assured of *la dolce vita*.

But compare the following borrowed words, which are familiar enough to be printed in roman:

ad hoc	de facto
bourgeois	genre
cliché	junta

Consult your dictionary for doubtful cases.

Use foreign terms sparingly; they often sound affected.

Latin abbreviations Latin abbreviations are often italicized, but the tendency is now to leave them in roman. There is no need to italicize the following, for example:

cf.	i.e.
e.g.	q.v.
et al.	viz.
f., ff.	vs.

See pages 366–367 for the meanings of these and other abbreviations.

translations When translating foreign words, it is customary to put the foreign term in italics and the English one in quotation marks.

- The Italian term for "the book" is *il libro*; in French it is *le livre*.

See also page 338 for the use of single quotation marks in translation.

scientific names Technical scientific names should be italicized:

- Don't mess around with the threadtailed stonefly *(Nemoura venosa)*.

ships Names of ships are italicized: *Queen Elizabeth*, *Cristoforo Colombo*.

words considered as words Words considered *as* words are often italicized:

- Bessie could not think of the Spanish word for *indigestion*.

Quotation marks serve this function equally well.

emphasis Italics can be used to impart emphasis to a word or group of words, but this device, if used too frequently, becomes a form of shouting.

Try to resort to emphatic italics only when clarity demands them. When you add your italics to quoted words, follow the quotation with a parenthetical acknowledgment:

- The author writes mysteriously of a *"rival* system of waste management" (emphasis added).

ABBREVIATIONS

Abbreviations are useful devices for saving space. Knowing their meaning, however, is only half the battle; you must also know where they do and do not belong.

main text The words for certain things are generally *not* abbreviated in the main body of an essay:

a. titles: *the Reverend, the Honorable, Senator, President, General.*
b. given names: *George, Richard, Martha.*
c. months, days of the week, and holidays: *October, Monday, Christmas.*
d. localities, cities, counties, states, and countries: *Point Reyes National Seashore, Philadelphia, Westchester, Alabama, Bangladesh.*
e. *Street, Lane, Avenue, Boulevard,* etc.
f. courses of instruction: *Botany, Physical Education.*
g. units of measurement: *inches, meters, pounds, hours, pints.*

citations Certain abbreviations do frequently appear in essays, but only in footnotes, parenthetical references, and bibliographies. These abbreviations are tools for referring to consulted works in the briefest space:

abbreviation	meaning
anon.	anonymous
b.	born
bibliog.	bibliography
©	Copyright
c. or ca.	about (with dates only)
cf.	compare (not *see*)
ch., chs.	chapter(s)
d.	died
diss.	dissertation
ed., eds.	editor(s), edition(s), edited by
e.g.	for example (not *that is*)
esp.	especially

et al.	and others (people only)
etc.	and so forth (not interchangeable with *et al.*)
f., ff.	and the following (page, pages)
ibid.	the same (title as the one mentioned in the previous note)
i.e.	that is (not *for example*)
introd.	introduction
l., ll.	line(s)
loc. cit.	in the place cited (in the same passage mentioned in a recent note)
ms., mss.	manuscript(s)
n., nn.	note(s)
N.B.	mark well, take notice
n.d.	no date (in a book's imprint)
no., nos.	number(s)
op. cit.	in the work cited (in a recent note; but the page number here is different; cf. *loc. cit.*)
p., pp.	page(s)
pl., pls.	plate(s)
pref.	preface
pt., pts.	part(s)
q.v.	see elsewhere in this text (literally *which see*)
rev.	revised, revision; review, reviewed by (beware of ambiguity between meanings; if necessary, write out instead of abbreviating)
sc.	scene
sec., secs.; sect., sects.	section(s)
ser.	series
st., sts.	stanza(s)
tr., trans.	translator, translation, translated by
viz.	namely
vol., vols.	volume(s)
vs.	verse, versus

Note that *passim,* meaning *throughout,* and *sic,* meaning *thus,* are full Latin words and are not followed by a period. (For the use and abuse of *sic,* see p. 332.)

acceptable in main text Some other abbreviations, however, are considered standard for any piece of writing, including the main body of an essay:

a. *Mr., Mrs., Dr., Messrs., Mme., Mlle., St.,* etc., when used before names. Some publications now refer to all women as *Ms.,* and this title has rapidly gained favor as a means of avoiding designation of marital status.

b. *Jr., Sr., Esq., M.D., D.D., D.D.S., M.A., Ph.D., LL.D.,* etc., when used after names.

c. abbreviations of, and acronyms (words formed from the initial letters in a multi-word name) for, organizations that are widely known by the shorter name: *CIA, FBI, ROTC, NOW, NATO, UNESCO,* etc. Note that very familiar designations such as these are usually written without periods between the letters.

d. *B.C., A.D., a.m., p.m., m.p.h.* These abbreviations should never be used apart from numbers (x *in the p.m.*). *B.C.* always follows the year, but *A.D.* precedes it: *252 B.C.,* but *A.D. 147.*

e. places commonly known by their abbreviations: *U.S., D.C., U.S.S.R.,* etc.

titles with names In abbreviating titles attached to people's names, watch for two problems. First, beware of redundancy. You can write *Dr. Lincoln Dollar* or *Lincoln Dollar, M.D.,* but do not write *Dr. Lincoln Dollar, M.D.;* that says the same thing twice. And do not allow the abbreviation to stray from the name it is supposed to accompany:

x There were two famous Jameses, Henry and *Wm.*

x As the collection plate was being passed, the *Rev.* described how misers are everlastingly chained to the burning lake.

technical terms Abbreviations of complex technical terms, or of terms that will be used many times in one essay, can spare monotony. *ACTH* is better in every way than *adrenocorticotropic hormone,* provided it has been sufficiently identified. It is customary to give one full reference before relying only on the abbreviation:

• The best investment Dr. Dollar ever made was in Holiday International Tours (HIT). The corporate philosophy of HIT agreed with his own views in several respects.

spacing When the letters of abbreviations are separated by periods *(M.D.),* no space should be left between a period and the next letter. The one exception is the initials of a name *(O. J. Anderson).*

NUMBERS AND FIGURES

numbers versus figures No universally applicable rules govern the choice between written-out numbers *(sixty-seven)* and figures *(67).* In scientific and technical writing, figures are generally preferred; newspapers customarily use figures for all numbers higher than ten; and in nontechnical books and journals, the usual rule is that figures are to be used only for numbers that cannot be expressed in one or two words or a brief phrase. For your own essays, this last rule is the best one to follow. Thus you should write *forty-three pounds of lard*, but not x *seventy-one dollars and twenty-eight cents* (write $71.28). There may be *eighteen counties* and *sixty-eight precincts* involved in an election, but the winning candidate's tally should not be given as x *two hundred ten thousand three hundred ninety-seven votes*.

Note, however, that a mixture of figures and written-out numbers can be confusing if they all refer to quantities of the same thing. If *any* figures are necessary in such circumstances, *all* the numbers should be expressed in figures:

- The initial orbit was 39–125 miles from the surface of the earth.
- The astronauts' heart rates varied between 55 and 120.
- It was later discovered that they had hidden between 25 and 347 trinkets in the capsule for later sale as souvenirs.

A number beginning a sentence should always be written out. But if the number is a long one, find a way of recasting the sentence so that the number comes later; then it can be stated as a figure.

normal use of figures   Figures are regularly used for the following:

a. apartment numbers, street numbers, and zip codes: *Apt. 17C, 544 Lowell Ave., Palo Alto, Calif. 94301.*
b. tables of statistics.
c. numbers containing decimals: *7.456, $6.58.*
d. dates (except for extremely formal communications such as wedding announcements): *October 5, 1974; 5 October 1974; October 5th.*
e. hours, when they precede *a.m.* or *p.m.*: *8 a.m., 12 p.m., 2:47 p.m.* Whole hours, unmodified by minutes, are usually written out before *o'clock*: *eight o'clock.* Do not write *twelve-thirty o'clock.*
f. page numbers: *page 76, p. 76, pages 76–78, pp. 76–78.* All these forms are correct, but the abbreviated ones should be saved for footnotes and parenthetical references.
g. volumes, books (e.g., of the Bible), acts, scenes, and lines. (See p. 420.)
h. percentages: *2 percent, 100 percent.*

Figures can be made plural by the addition of either *-s* or *-'s: two 7's, many 10's; two 7s, many 10s.* Note that no apostrophe is used when the number is written out: *many tens.* Thus the name of a decade can be written as either *the 1950s* or *the 1950's*; just be consistent about it. The shorter name for a decade is usually written out and given a capital letter: *the Fifties.*

Roman numerals   In general, the only reason for using Roman numerals *(XI, LVIII)* is that together with Arabic numerals *(11, 58)* they can distinguish one set of numbers from another. (See p. 420 for typical situations.) Lower-case Roman numerals are also used to indicate page numbers preceding the main text of a book *(Preface, p. xi)*.

The following list will remind you how Roman numerals are formed:

1	I	10	X	50	L	200	CC
2	II	11	XI	60	LX	400	CD
3	III	15	XV	70	LXX	499	CDXCIX
4	IV	19	XIX	80	LXXX	500	D
5	V	20	XX	90	XC	900	CM
6	VI	21	XXI	99	XCIX	999	CMXCIX
7	VII	29	XXIX	100	C	1000	M
8	VIII	30	XXX	110	CX	1500	MD
9	IX	40	XL	199	CXCIX	3000	MMM

cardinal versus ordinal numbers   Numbers like *one, two,* and *three (1, 2,* and *3)* are called **cardinal numbers**; numbers like *first, second,* and *third (1st, 2nd,* and *3rd)* are called **ordinal numbers**. The choice between the cardinal and ordinal systems is usually a simple one, but differences between written and spoken usage do arise. You say *Louis the Fourteenth* but should write *Louis XIV;* you say *July seventh, 1984,* but should write *July 7, 1984,* or *7 July 1984.* When the year is omitted, however, you should write the date as an ordinal number: *July 7th* or, preferably, *July seventh.*

Note, finally, that ordinal numbers can serve as adverbs without the addition of *-ly:*

- Let me say, first, that . . . Second, . . .

The *-ly* forms are not incorrect, but they are unnecessary. The only plainly wrong choice would be a mixture of forms: *Firstly, . . . Second, . . .*

EXERCISES

7. Correct any errors in the use of italics, abbreviations, and numbers:
    A. Most drunk drivers would find it difficult to count backward from 135 to twenty-one by threes.
    B. He had only one reason for not wanting to ride—e.g., he was afraid of horses.
    C. 40 dollars will buy an adequate dinner for 1 at that restaurant.
    D. Four six'es are twenty-four.
    E. The attack was planned for precisely 7:42 o'clock.
    F. "Gone with the Wind" was the film that introduced profane language to the Hollywood screen.
    G. Alimony was never an issue for the ex-wives of King Henry the VIIIth.

H. *The Falmouth Enterprise* is a typical small-town newspaper.
I. You can still get a sporty sedan, fully equipped with roll bars, seat belts, impact-absorbing bumpers, and collision insurance, for nine thousand eight hundred forty-four dollars.
J. Melody thought that *A Midsummer Night's Dream* was the most realistic play she had ever seen.
K. She made an appointment with Dr. Calvin Gold, D.D.S.
L. The Titanic at its launching was the world's largest, and soon thereafter the world's wettest, ocean liner.
M. Over the loudspeaker came an urgent and repeated request for a dr.
N. Criminals are treated leniently in Rome if they committed their offenses during lo scirocco, the hot, dry wind that supposedly makes people behave irrationally.
O. He won the primary election on June 8th, 1976.

8. The following paragraph contains errors in the use or absence of capitals, italics, abbreviations, and numbers. Find the errors and make a list of your corrections.

No piece of criticism has ever been harsher or funnier than Mark Twain's essay, *Fenimore Cooper's Literary Offenses,* which can be found in a vol. called "Selected Shorter Writings of Mark Twain." Twain asserts that Cooper, in novels such as *the Deerslayer, The Last of the Mohicans,* et al., has committed one hundred fourteen offenses against literary art out of a possible 115. "It breaks the record," says Twain. He proves that Cooper's Natty Bumppo, the indian Chingachgook, etc., perform physically impossible deeds and speak wildly different kinds of english from 1 page to the next. The attack is hilarious, but on a 2nd reading it can also be taken as seriously indicating Twain's allegiance to the literary realism of the later XIXth Century.

PART V
RESEARCH

14

USING THE LIBRARY

If you are asked to write a research paper, or if you see that another paper will require some knowledge that lies beyond arm's reach, you will have to get acquainted with your college library. The sooner you do so, the better. Whether you intend to be in college for two years, four years, or the necessary time to earn an advanced degree, the library can offer you an almost limitless extension of your power to gather information and write from a position of authority. Knowing how to put a library to work for you, furthermore, is a capacity that can serve you for a lifetime of business or research projects.

Perhaps your college library strikes you as mysterious or even vaguely threatening. If so, bear in mind that:

a. You do not have to understand the whole system — just some procedures for retrieving the books and articles you need;
b. free library tours and information packets are probably available; and
c. a *reference librarian* is ready to answer your questions and help you get started efficiently on any given project.

As for the fear of being "scooped" by library sources, you can cope with it by simply plunging in. By the time you run across your original idea in somebody else's book, you will have gotten several further ideas and a different, more precisely focused, sense of what you want to accomplish.

In essence the library is a vast information-retrieval system. As with a computer, the knack of using it successfully consists in knowing the right questions to present it with. Rummaging through the stacks without any questions at all would be as senseless as fishing blindly in the computer's memory bank. You have to know at least some of the overlapping ways in which sources can be found, and you have to keep narrowing your search as you get a clearer and clearer idea of the way your project is developing.

As you do more research, you will gradually develop a better sense of the difference between a promising lead and a blind alley. The majority of available books on any topic, you will find, have already been superseded by others; the more recent the work, the more eager you should be to lay hands on it. This is doubly true because an up-to-date work may contain a selective **bibliography**—a list of key books and articles for further reference—that can save you many hours of scrounging and many mistakes of judgment. An experienced researcher does not have to run through *all* the types of information-seeking described in the following pages; he or she finds a few key works as early as possible and then allows those works to suggest further moves.

PARTS OF THE LIBRARY

Although no two libraries are alike, your college library probably has at least seven places for essential functions:

1. *Stacks.* These are shelves on which most books and bound periodicals are stored. In the "open stack" system, all users can enter the stacks, find materials, and take them to a check-out desk. If your library has "closed stacks," access to the stacks is limited by status; see the next item.

2. *Circulation desk.* In a closed-stack library, you can check out a book or bound periodical by submitting a **call slip**—a card identifying what you need—to the circulation desk, to which a clerk will return either with the book or with an explanation that it is on reserve (see item 4), out to another borrower, or missing. If it is out to another borrower, you can "put a hold" on it—that is, indicate that you

want to be notified as soon as the book has been returned. Since you may have to wait as long as two weeks for some items, it is important to begin your research early.

3. *Reference room.* In the reference room (or behind the reference desk) are stored sets of encyclopedias, indexes, dictionaries, bibliographies, and similar multi-purpose research tools. You cannot check out reference volumes, but you can consult them long enough to get the names of promising-looking books and articles that you *will* be able to get from the main collection. The reference room usually doubles as a reading room, enabling you to do much of your reading near other sources of information.

4. *Reserve desk.* Behind the reserve desk (or in the reserve book room) are kept multiple copies of books that are essential to current courses. The distinctive feature of reserved books is that they must be returned quickly, usually within either an hour or a day or a week. When you learn that a book is "on reserve," even for a course other than your own, you can be reasonably sure of finding an available copy.

5. *Periodical room.* In the periodical room you can find magazines and journals too recent to have been bound as books. Thus, if you do research on a topic of current interest, you are certain to find yourself applying to the periodical room for up-to-date articles.

6. *Newspaper room.* Take your call slips to this room to get a look at newspaper articles and editorials. Most newspapers are stored on microfilm, which can only be read within a microfilm reader. Ask a clerk to show you how the machine works.

7. *The catalog.* Near the circulation desk you will find cabinets full of alphabetically filed cards, listing all the library's printed holdings (books, periodicals, pamphlets, and items on microfilm, but not manuscripts, phonographs, or tapes). This is the **card catalog**. In some libraries the card catalog has been supplemented or replaced by a **microfiche catalog**, consisting of miniaturized photographic entries on plastic cards that can be read when placed in a microfiche reader, available nearby. Your library may even have an **on-line catalog**—that is, a continually updated computer file. If so, you will see computer terminals, accompanied by appropriate instructions, near the circulation desk. Whatever its form, the catalog is your open sesame to the stacks, for it gives you call numbers enabling you or a clerk to locate the books you need (see p. 380).

Thus your research is likely to take you back and forth between various sites:

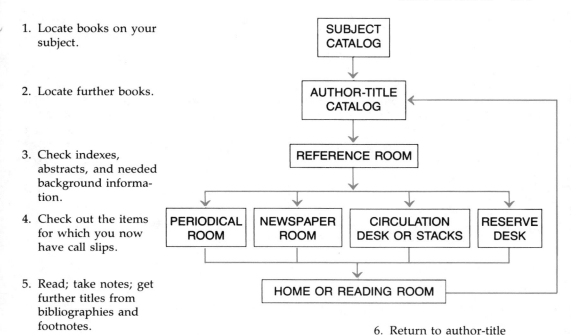

1. Locate books on your subject.

2. Locate further books.

3. Check indexes, abstracts, and needed background information.

4. Check out the items for which you now have call slips.

5. Read; take notes; get further titles from bibliographies and footnotes.

6. Return to author-title catalog to get further call numbers, and resume cycle.

At some point, obviously, this cycle has to be interrupted; the first draft beckons. But even as you write successive drafts, you may find yourself dipping back into library sources to check new leads and follow up ideas that now look more fruitful than they did at first.

SEARCHING FOR BOOKS

Subject Catalogs

If you are searching for a topic within a general subject area, the first thing you want to do is check your library's holdings within that area. You can do so by consulting the **subject catalog**, which is arranged not by authors and titles of books but by fields of knowledge, problems, movements, schools of thought, and so forth. Once you locate an array of relevant titles, you should fill out call slips for the most recent appropriate-looking works. If you get hold of just one recent book that has a bibliography in the back, you may discover that you already have the names of all the further books and articles you will need.

guide to subject headings   But how do you know which headings your subject catalog uses to classify the entries you will want to review? You can try your luck, sampling a number of alternative phrases, or you can take a more systematic and reliable approach. Your subject catalog probably follows the headings adopted by the Library of Congress in Washington, D.C. Ask your reference librarian where a book called *Library of Congress Subject Headings* is to be found. That book is heavily **cross-indexed**; in other words, if you look up a plausible-sounding phrase, you will not only learn whether it constitutes a Library of Congress subject heading, you will also be directed to other phrases that do serve as headings.

Thus the student who wanted to investigate computer crime for his research paper (pp. 448–456) began by going to the pages of the *Library of Congress Subject Headings* referring to *Computers*. There he found the following valuable listing:

```
                                                    1
                                                    |
                            Computer crimes   (Indirect)   (HV6773)
2  ─────────────────────────────────   sa  Computers – Access control
                                            Electronic data processing departments
                                               – Security measures
                                            Privacy, Right of
3  ─────────────────────────────────    x  Computer fraud
                                            Computers and crime
4  ─────────────────────────────────   xx  Computers – Access control
                                            Crime and criminals
                                            Privacy, Right of
                                            White collar crimes
```

Observe in this typical entry:

1. The Library of Congress call number of a key book on the subject – an authoritative government study containing a bibliography.
2. The symbol *sa* ("see also") introduces three related headings that can be consulted to locate titles that may not be covered under the main heading *Computer crimes.*
3. The symbol *x* tells the reader not to bother looking up *Computer fraud* or *Computers and crime*; since these are not Library of Congress headings, they will not be headings in the campus library catalog, either.
4. The symbol *xx* introduces four *broader* headings that will cover some works on computer crime. By checking these phrases in the subject catalog the reader can see the chosen problem in several wider perspectives.

shelf list   Armed with this much information, the student researcher could make use of the subject catalog without a single wasted step. And already possessing a key call number, he could also inspect the related cards in his library's **shelf list** – still another catalog, this one arranged in order of call numbers. Since his library followed the Library of Congress system of numbering, and since call numbers in any library are ordered by subject, he could be sure of finding relevant material near card HV6773.

on-line catalog The student was aware, however, that his library had recently begun to compile an on-line (computer) catalog which would eventually replace the card catalog. Though this catalog was still fragmentary, he knew it would be more up-to-date than any of the others. Following the instructions listed beside a terminal, he told the computer to retrieve all titles about computer crimes listed in the on-line catalog. Here is what he read on the display and copied out:

Your search for: subject words COMPUTER CRIMES retrieved: 9 books.

1. Bequai, August. COMPUTER CRIME. 1978

2. Deighton, Suzan. THE NEW CRIMINALS: A BIBLIOGRAPHY OF COMPUTER . . . 1978

3. Leibholz, Stephen W. USERS' GUIDE TO COMPUTER CRIME: ITS . . . 1974

4. Lin, Joseph C. COMPUTER CRIME, SECURITY, AND PRIVACY: A SELECTED . . . 1979

5. McKnight, Gerald. COMPUTER CRIME. 1973

6. McKnight, Gerald. COMPUTER CRIME. 1974

7. McNeil, John. THE CONSULTANT: A NOVEL OF COMPUTER CRIME. 1978

8. THE NEW CRIMINALS: A BIBLIOGRAPHY OF COMPUTER RELATED CRIME . . . 1979

9. Parker, Donn B. CRIME BY COMPUTER. 1976

Like most examples of computer retrieval, this list contained some obviously false leads. Items 6 and 8 were simply reprints of items 5 and 2, respectively, and item 7 was a work of fiction. But items 1, 2, and 9 turned out to be centrally important; the researcher already had an avenue of access to more information than he could possibly use in his paper.

Author-Title Catalog

If you know that your paper will deal with a certain author, you can bypass the various subject catalogs and go directly to the **author-title catalog**, which lists works alphabetically by both author and title. The last entries in that listing, after the author's own works, may be useful books of biography, criticism, and commentary. Thus the author-title catalog is itself a kind of subject catalog, with prominent authors as the subjects.

Even if you are writing about a general problem, you can pick up likely references by browsing for books listed in the author-title catalog under possible key terms (*Computer*, *Crime*, etc.). And if you have already found, through a subject search, that certain writers are authorities in your field, you may want to check the author-title catalog for further works of theirs. Once again, if your library has an on-line catalog, it will cover works too recent to have found their way into the card catalogs.

The most important piece of information on any catalog card is the **call number** in the upper left corner; it tells exactly where the book or bound journal is shelved. But you can also get several other kinds of information from a card. Consider, for example, an author card actually encountered by the writer of the UFO research paper on pages 429–445:

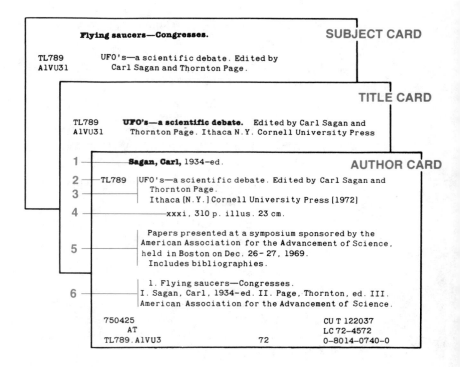

In addition to some coded information chiefly of interest to librarians, this author card conveys six potentially useful kinds of knowledge:

1. The name of one editor of the book.
2. The call number, enabling someone to apply for the book at the circulation desk or to locate it in the stacks.
3. The title of the book, both editors' names, the place of publication, the

publisher, and the date of publication. These are facts a researcher would want to get down on a bibliography card (p. 396).

4. Physical features of the book. It consists of 31 pages of prefatory material and 310 pages of main text; it contains illustrations; and it is 23 centimeters in height. The substantial length of this book makes it more worth looking into than, say, a 40-page pamphlet would be.

5. Notes on the context and contents of the book. The AAAS sponsorship suggests a high standard of quality; the date is recent enough to suggest some historical perspective on the UFO controversy; and the mention of "bibliographies" suggests that this book could lead someone to other pertinent materials.

6. A list of all the headings under which this book is filed in the card catalog. By going to "Flying saucers—Congresses," a researcher might find several further cards of related interest. In this manner the card catalog itself can function as a bibliography.

Once in a while you may come across a reference to an apparently indispensable book that is not listed in your library's catalog. Since there are some sixty thousand new volumes published each year in English alone, no library but the Library of Congress itself could acquire more than a minority of them. You can get essential information about the book's author, title, publisher, and date from the *National Union Catalog*, which reproduces the Library of Congress Catalog and includes titles from other libraries as well. If you cannot visit a library that has the book, you can probably borrow it through *interlibrary loan* arrangement. The same holds for journals as well. By consulting the *Union List of Serials in Libraries of the United States and Canada* you can discover which libraries own sets of hard-to-find journals.

EXERCISES

1. Find out—if necessary by asking a reference librarian—what catalogs your main campus library has, where they are located, and whether they are equally up-to-date. Submit a paragraph that supplies these pieces of information.

2. Choose a sample research project dealing with any promising subject other than UFO's (pp. 429–445) and computer crime (pp. 448–456). Go to the *Library of Congress Subject Headings* (p. 378) and find what appears to be the main heading for your subject. Copy out a passage beginning from that heading (as on p. 378) and submit it along with an explanation of the symbols accompanying the entries.

3. Using one or more of the headings located through Exercise 2, consult your library's subject catalog, its author-title catalog, and its shelf list (if any), looking for key books on your subject. Submit a paragraph or two explaining the steps of your search and the relative usefulness of the catalogs you examined.

4. List what you take to be the three most important books to consult for the sample research project you undertook for Exercise 2. For each book, explain which information on the entry card (or in the microfiche or on-line entry) made you eager to see that book.

5. If you have free access to the stacks, locate and check out the three books you discussed in Exercise 4. If you do not have stack privileges, submit call slips for the books at the circulation desk. When you have been able to scan two of those books, submit a paragraph about each of them, explaining how acquaintance with that book could influence the direction of your sample research project. Are you closer than before to having a precisely focused topic? What sources would you want to investigate next?

SEARCHING FOR ARTICLES AND REVIEWS

If you have chosen a topic of current interest—the spread and control of a new disease, say, or the changing American family structure —you will want to review the latest available information. You cannot find it in even the most recently published books, which will necessarily be a year or two behind the times. *Newspaper* articles will be best for following events as they occur; *magazine* articles will give you a general, unspecialized perspective that may be just right for the audience and level you wish to establish; and articles in professional *journals* will give you specialized knowledge and theory that may not have appeared yet in hard covers. You may also want to check *reviews* of books you hope to use. If a book is more than a few months old, you can easily find reviews (or, more efficiently, summaries of reviews) that will suggest how much trust you should place in it.

indexes and abstracts   Obviously, you would be wasting your time poring over the handiest newspapers, magazines, and journals in the hope of finding relevant items. The efficient thing is to consult *indexes* and *abstracts*, which you will find shelved together in your library's reference room. Indexes are books, usually with a new volume each year, containing alphabetically ordered references to articles on given subjects. And abstracts are summaries of articles, allowing you to tell whether or not a certain article is important enough to your project to be worth tracking down. It is the reference room, then—not the newspaper room or the periodical room—that holds the key to your search for pertinent articles and reviews.

Newspapers

The only newspaper index you may ever need to consult is the *New York Times Index* (1913–), which covers a vast array of news and commentary having national or international importance. Since it is issued every two weeks before being bound into annual volumes, you can be sure of staying current with developments in your subject. For coverage of newspapers in Chicago, Los Angeles, New

Orleans, and Washington, D.C., try the *Newspaper Index* (1972–). And for international and especially British coverage, consult the *Index to the* [London] *Times* (1906–).

Magazines

If you want to find an article in a general-interest magazine, go to the *Reader's Guide to Periodical Literature* (1900–), which covers about 160 magazines on a twice-monthly basis. Indeed, the *Reader's Guide* is so useful for the typical research paper that many students begin their entire investigation there, saving the subject catalog until they have seen whether their topic has engaged the public lately. If you draw a blank from *Reader's Guide,* ask yourself whether your topic is too broad, too narrow, too specialized, or too threadbare to merit a paper.

A typical segment of a column in *Reader's Guide* looks like this:

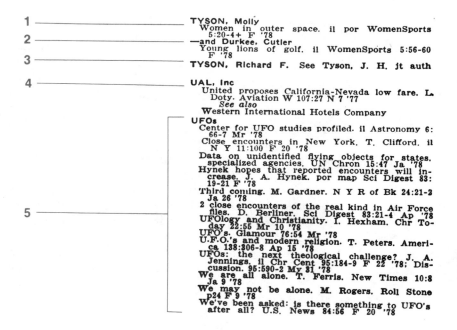

Here you see:

1. *An entry by author.* Molly Tyson's article, "Women in Outer Space," including an illustration and a portrait, appeared in the February 1978 issue of *WomenSports* (volume 5), on pages 20–24 and some later pages.

2. *An entry by two authors.* In the same issue of *WomenSports,* Molly

Tyson wrote another article, this time in collaboration with Cutler Durkee.

3. *A cross-indexed item.* If you are looking for an article by Richard F. Tyson, you are told that you can find it listed under the name of the joint author, J. H. Tyson.

4. *An entry about a corporation.* Here we see that L. Doty, in volume 107 of *Aviation Week* (7 Nov. 1977), page 27, has a brief article about United Air Lines.

5. *Entries about a subject.* Here are references to thirteen articles about unidentified flying objects—the subject of the sample research paper on pages 429–445.

Journals

Journals, which are on the whole more scholarly and technical than magazines, may contain articles of vital concern to your topic. Although you probably want to keep a general-interest focus, you also want to be aware of relevant discoveries and controversy. For most purposes, the key indexes for access to journal articles are the *Humanities Index* (1974–) and the *Social Sciences Index* (1974–). The *Humanities Index* should be your first choice for post-1973 articles in archaeology, area studies, classics, folklore, history, language and literature, literary and political criticism, performing arts, philosophy, religion, and theology. Use the *Social Sciences Index* for post-1973 articles in anthropology, economics, environmental science, geography, law and criminology, medicine, political science, psychology, public administration, and sociology. For years before 1973, consult the *International Index* (1907–65) and the *Social Sciences and Humanities Index* (1965–74); these are the parents of the new *Humanities Index* and *Social Sciences Index*.

There are a great many further indexes and abstracts that intensively cover single fields. The following titles are self-explanatory:

Abstracts in Anthropology (1970–)
America: History and Life: A Guide to Periodical Literature (1964–)
Applied Science and Technology Index (1913–)
Art Index (1947–)
Arts and Humanities Citation Index (1978–)
Bibliographic Index (1933–)
Biography Index (1947–)
Biological Abstracts (1926–)
Bioresearch Index (1967–)
British Humanities Index (1962–)
Business Periodicals Index (1958–)
Chemical Abstracts (1907–)

Child Development Abstracts and Bibliography (1927–)
Current Index to Journals in Education (1969–)
Education Abstracts (1936–)
Education Index (1929–)
Engineering Index (1920–)
Essay and General Literature Index (1934–)
Film Literature Index (1973–)
General Science Index (1978–)
Historical Abstracts (1955–)
Index to Legal Periodicals (1908–)
MLA Abstracts of Articles in Scholarly Journals (1971–)
MLA International Bibliography (1969–)
Monthly Catalog of United States Government Publications (1895–)
Music Index (1949–)
Philosopher's Index (1967–)
Psychological Abstracts (1927–)
Public Affairs Information Service Bulletin (1915–)
Religious and Theological Abstracts (1958–)
RILA Abstracts (International Repertory of Art Literature) (1975–)
RILM Abstracts (International Repertory of Music Literature) (1967–)
Science Abstracts (1898–)
Science Citation Index (1961–)
Social Sciences Citation Index (1973–)
Sociological Abstracts (1977–)

Book Reviews

If you want to know how reliable a certain book is, you can quickly learn what some of the book's original reviewers had to say by consulting *Book Review Digest* (1905–). Thus, for example, the writer of the research paper on pages 429–445 needed to decide how much trust to place in Philip J. Klass's 1974 book *UFOs Explained*. By looking in *Book Review Digest* in the period following publication, she was able not only to find citations of reviews, but also to get a capsule idea of whether the book deserved to be taken seriously:

KLASS, PHILIP J. UFOs explained. 369p pl
$8.95 '74 Random House
    001.9 Flying saucers
    ISBN 0-394-49215-3   LC 74-9054
    The author examines a sampling of UFO
cases and seeks to show that when such cases
are examined objectively and scientifically
rational explanations other than the existence
of extraterrestrial spaceships or other phenomena can be found. Index.

————

    "The hobby of Mr. Klass, Senior Avionics
Editor for Aviation Week & Space Technology,
is tracking down and demolishing reports of
unidentified flying objects. Sight saucer, sink
same is his motto, and he backs it with gingery,
well-argued accounts of the process. He demon-
strates, among other engaging facts, that flight
crews from Venus and environs are infallibly
drawn to earthlings who happen to need some
quick cash." Phoebe Adams
            Atlantic 235:122 F '75 80w
    "[The author] argues in this work that there
is no scientific evidence to support belief in the
existence of UFOs. He devises ten UFOlogical

Principles by means of which he explains the various types of attitudes and beliefs which have developed in the personalities of UFO believers. . . . In thirty-one chapters describing investigations of various categories of UFO reports there appears to be no lack of rigor whatever. The author denies validity of the vast majority of UFO sightings. The description of his investigations is intensely interesting." R. E. O'Brien

> Best Sell 34:537 Mr 1 '75 350w
>
> Choice 12:863 S '75 200w

"Klass thinks that UFO's can be explained as terrestrial phenomena and not as intelligently guided ships. He is a painstaking investigator and has the technical competence to understand and to be able to explain, for example, a piece of equipment and how it can malfunction. . . . [However] his explanations for UFO's seem thin on occasion. . . . One unfortunate thing is the impression Klass conveys that he alone is right; although irritating, it is a not infrequent attitude in this field. . . . Probably not for small libraries." Robert Molyneux

> Library J 100:491 Mr 1 '75 90w
>
> Reviewed by A. C. Clarke
>
> N Y Times Bk R p4 Jl 27 '75 500w

"No UFO author has taken such a look at radar as Klass, whose decade of experience in the field as an engineer has been augmented by a later career as a knowing technical reporter covering the aerospace industry. . . . This is a good-sized, meaty, rather contentious work. It treats very successfully many of the classic 'sightings' of the past, making a strong prima facie case of fraud in several of the best-known. . . . There is no more explicit and insightful account of UFO's than this one. . . . The reader can profit a great deal, even though the tone is sometimes rather more indignant than seems wise." Philip Morrison

> Sci Am 232:117 My '75 900w

For other guides to book reviews, see *Book Review Index* (1965–), *Current Book Review Citations* (1976–), and *The New York Times Book Review Index, 1896–1970*.

On-Line Searching

In increasing numbers, printed indexes, abstracts, reports, conference proceedings, and government documents are being gathered in the alternative form of **databases**—that is, computer files that can be instantly scanned. If your library has an on-line catalog (p. 376), then that catalog is itself a database. But that is just the beginning. If your library subscribes to such databases as, say, *Pharmaceutical News Index, Population Bibliography,* and *Pollution Abstracts,* you can instruct the computer to retrieve every relevant article from one or more of those sources.

Such "on-line searching" can save time, catch very recent references, and ferret out specific topics that do not constitute subject headings in the index itself. Suppose, for example, you are interested in the connection between child abuse and alcoholism. Instead of asking for all items within each of those large subjects, you can tell the computer to display only those items whose titles refer to *both* problems. The outcome will be a relatively short but highly efficient list, fairly free of "dumb mistakes" on the computer's part.

On-line searching can produce dramatic results if you have a well-defined topic in mind. But there are serious disadvantages as well:

1. You will be charged a fee—possibly a steep one—for the search.
2. You will need the assistance of a trained technician.
3. It is hard to "browse" in computer files; if your chosen keywords do not appear in the title of a relevant article, the computer will probably overlook it.

On the whole, then, for the purposes of a college paper it is better to do your searching in printed sources. But at least you know that on-line searching is available if you should need it. A reference librarian can tell you whether your project is one that lends itself readily to a computer search.

EXERCISES

6. Resume the sample research project you began for Exercise 2, or begin a new one. Using the *New York Times Index*, locate two relevant articles or editorials in the *Times*. Find those items (probably on microfilm) in your library's newspaper room, and take notes on their content. Submit a paragraph or two in which you give precise references to those items, and summarize what you learned from them.

7. Repeat Exercise 6, this time using magazine articles traced through the *Reader's Guide*. One of your two articles should be so recent that it can be found in an unbound copy of a magazine; the other should be at least two years old.

8. Repeat Exercise 6, this time using journal articles traced through one or more of the indexes and abstracts named on pages 384–385. As in Exercise 7, retrieve one of your two items from an unbound issue of a journal.

9. Use *Book Review Digest* to find summaries of the reviews of any one book that looks promising for your sample research project. Submit a paragraph or two referring specifically to some of the reviews and explaining how they have affected your assessment of the book.

BACKGROUND SOURCES

The steps we have already covered should be enough to give you all the information you need for a typical research paper. Sometimes, however, you may want an out-of-the-way bit of knowledge or a broad introduction to the field you are going to treat. Where should you turn? Most of the works listed below can be found in the reference room.

Booksellers' Bibliographies

If you know an author's name but not the title of the book, if you have the title but not the author, if you want to see whether new books on a certain topic appeared in a certain year, or if you want to know whether a book is still in print or has appeared in a paperback edition, then you should consult one of the following:

Books in Print (1948–)
Cumulative Book Index (1898–)
Paperbound Books in Print (1955–)
Subject Guide to Books in Print (1957–)

The last of these volumes can give you a quick idea of what you could hope to find under a given subject heading of your card catalog. If you see essential items in the *Subject Guide* that do not appear in your card catalog, you can send for them through interlibrary loan (p. 381).

Guides to Reference Works

Reference works—that is, books that survey a field and tell you how to find materials within that field—are now so numerous that you may need to consult an even more general book that lists reference works and explains their scope:

Basic Reference Sources: A Self-Study Manual, ed. Margaret Taylor (1973)
Best Reference Books: Titles of Lasting Value Selected from American Reference Books Annual 1970–1976, ed. Bohdan S. Wynar (1976)
Guide to Reference Books, comp. Eugene P. Sheehy (1976)
Guide to the Use of Books and Libraries, by Jean Kay Gates (1979)
Reference Books: A Brief Guide, by Marion V. Bell and Eleanor A. Swidan (1978)
Reference Books: How to Select and Use Them, ed. Saul Galin and Peter Spielberg (1969)
The Use of Books and Libraries, by Raymond H. Shove et al. (1963)
A World Bibliography of Bibliographies, comp. Theodore Besterman (1965–66)
A World Bibliography of Bibliographies, 1964–1974, comp. Alice F. Toomey (1977)

Of these works, the most widely used is Sheehy's *Guide to Reference Books,* whose first eight editions were compiled by Constance M. Winchell. By going to Sheehy and looking up your field of interest, you can quickly see which are the important reference works—and indexes and bibliographies as well.

General Encyclopedias

An up-to-date edition of a general encyclopedia can provide initial orientation to a field or problem and a limited amount of bibliographic guidance. See especially:

Chambers's Encyclopedia (1973)
Collier's Encyclopedia (1974)
Encyclopaedia Britannica (1974)
Encyclopedia Americana (revised annually)
The New Columbia Encyclopedia (1975)
The Random House Encyclopedia (1977)

Special Encyclopedias, Reference Works, Handbooks, and General Histories

If you want to locate more facts about a field than you could find in a general encyclopedia article, you can consult a work that surveys the field or a significant portion of it. Such books are helpful both for locating a technical or historical fact and for acquiring a sense of the whole field before working on narrow problems.

The following titles, arranged by field, represent a sampling of useful sources. Dates of publication refer to the most recent editions.

art
American Painting: A Guide to Information Sources, by Sydney Starr Keaveney (1974)
Britannica Encyclopedia of American Art (1973)
Encyclopedia of Painting, ed. Bernard S. Myers (1970)
Encyclopedia of World Art (1959–68)
Fine Arts: A Bibliographic Guide to Basic Reference Works, Histories, and Handbooks (1975)
Larousse Encyclopedia of Byzantine and Medieval Art (1963)
Larousse Encyclopedia of Modern Art (1965)
Larousse Encyclopedia of Prehistoric and Ancient Art (1966)
Larousse Encyclopedia of Renaissance and Baroque Art (1964)
The McGraw-Hill Dictionary of Art, by Bernard S. Myers and Shirley D. Meyers (1969)
The Oxford Companion to Art, ed. Harold Osborne (1970)
Phaidon Dictionary of Twentieth-Century Art (1978)
The Praeger Encyclopedia of Art (1971)

business and economics
A Dictionary of Economics, by Harold S. Sloan and Arnold J. Zurcher (1970)
Dictionary of Economics and Business, ed. Erwin E. Nemmers (1979)
Economic Education (1977)
Encyclopedia of Banking and Finance, ed. Glen G. Munn (1973)
The Encyclopedia of Management, ed. Carl Heyel (1973)
International Bibliography of Economics (1952–)
The McGraw-Hill Dictionary of Modern Economics, by Douglas Greenwald (1973)
Sources of Business Information, by Edwin T. Coman, Jr. (1964)
University Dictionary of Business and Finance, ed. Donald T. Clark and Bert A. Gottfried (1972)

drama
Annals of English Drama, 975–1700, by Alfred Harbage (1966)
Crowell's Handbook of Contemporary Drama, by Michael Anderson et al. (1971)
Cumulated Dramatic Index, 1909–1940, ed. Frederick W. Faxon (1965)
Dramatic Criticism Index, ed. Paul F. Breed and Florence M. Sniderman (1972)
How to Locate Reviews of Plays and Films, by Gordon Samples (1976)
McGraw-Hill Encyclopedia of World Drama (1972)
Modern World Drama: An Encyclopedia, by Myron Matlaw (1972)
New York Times Directory of the Theater (1973)
The Oxford Companion to the Theatre, ed. Phyllis Hartnoll (1967)
The Reader's Encyclopedia of World Drama, ed. John Gassner and Edward Quinn (1969)

education A Dictionary of Education, by Derek Rowntree (1982)
The Encyclopedia of Education (1971)
Encyclopedia of Educational Research, ed. R. L. Ebel (1969)
How to Locate Educational Information and Data, by Carter Alexander and A. J. Burke (1958)
International Encyclopedia of Higher Education, ed. Asa K. Knowles (1977)
Resources in Education (1975–   )
Second Handbook of Research on Teaching, ed. R. M. Travers (1973)
The Teacher's Handbook, ed. Dwight Allen and Eli Seifman (1971)

film Film Research: A Critical Bibliography, by Peter J. Bukalski (1972)
International Encyclopedia of the Film (1972)
New York Times Film Reviews, 1913–1974
The World Encyclopedia of the Film, ed. Tim Cawkwell and John Milton Smith (1972)

folklore and mythology Encyclopedia of Classical Mythology, by A. Van Aken (1965)
Funk & Wagnalls Standard Dictionary of Folklore, Mythology and Legend (1949–50)
The Golden Bough: A Study in Magic and Religion, by Sir James G. Frazer (1907–15)
Larousse World Mythology (1968)
Motif-Index of Folk-Literature, by Stith Thompson (1955–58)
The Mythology of All Races, ed. Louis Herbert Gray et al. (1916–32)
The Study of American Folklore, by Jan Harold Brunvand (1978)

history The Cambridge Ancient History (1970–75)
The Cambridge Medieval History (1911–36)
The Cambridge Modern History (1902–26)
Dictionary of American History, ed. James Truslow Adams (1976)
Encyclopedia of American History, by Richard B. Morris and Jeffrey B. Morris (1976)
An Encyclopedia of World History, ed. William L. Langer (1972)
Guide to Historical Literature, ed. George F. Howe et al. (1961)
Harper Encyclopedia of the Modern World, ed. Richard B. Morris and Graham W. Irwin (1970)
Harvard Guide to American History, ed. Frank Freidel and Richard K. Showman (1974)
The Historian's Handbook, by Helen J. Poulton and Marguerite S. Howland (1977)
International Bibliography of Historical Sciences (1930–   )
Larousse Encyclopedia of Ancient and Medieval History (1972)
Larousse Encyclopedia of Modern History (1972)
The University of Michigan History of the Modern World, ed. Allan Nevins and Howard Ehrmann (1958–   )

literature American Authors, 1600–1900, ed. Stanley J. Kunitz and Howard Haycraft (1952)
American Fiction 1900–50: A Guide to Information Sources, ed. James Woodress (1974)
Annual Bibliography of English Language and Literature (1921–   )

Articles on American Literature, 1900–1950, by Lewis Leary (1954)
Articles on American Literature, 1950–1967, by Lewis Leary (1970)
Bibliography of American Literature, by Jacob Blanck (1955–   )
Black American Literature, by Roger Whitlow (1973)
British Authors before 1800, by Stanley J. Kunitz and Howard Haycraft (1952)
British Authors of the Nineteenth Century, by Stanley J. Kunitz and Howard Haycraft (1936)
The Cambridge Guide to English Literature (1983)
Cassell's Encyclopedia of World Literature, ed. John Buchanan-Brown (1973)
Columbia Dictionary of Modern European Literature, ed. Jean-Albert Bede and William Edgerton (1980)
Concise Bibliography for Students of English, ed. Arthur G. Kennedy and Donald B. Sands (1972)
Dictionary of World Literature, ed. Joseph T. Stipley (1972)
Guide to American Literature and Its Backgrounds since 1890, by Howard Mumford Jones and Richard M. Ludwig (1972)
A Handbook to Literature, by Clarence Hugh Holman (1980)
Harvard Guide to Contemporary American Writing, ed. Daniel Hoffman (1979)
A Literary History of England, by Albert C. Baugh (1967)
Literary History of the United States, by Robert E. Spiller et al. (1974)
Masterplots (1954–   )
New Cambridge Bibliography of English Literature (1969–77)
The Oxford Companion to American Literature, by James D. Hart (1965)
The Oxford Companion to Classical Literature, by Paul Harvey and J. E. Heseltine (1937)
The Oxford Companion to English Literature, by Paul Harvey (1967)
The Oxford History of English Literature, by Percy Wilson and Bonamy Dobrée (1945–63)
The Penguin Companion to World Literature (1969–71)
The Reader's Companion to World Literature, ed. Lillian H. Hornstein et al. (1973)
A Reference Guide to English Studies, by Donald F. Bond (1971)

music *Dictionary of Music and Musicians,* by Sir George Grove (1955)
Everyman's Dictionary of Music, by Eric Blom and Jack A. Westrup (1972)
Harvard Dictionary of Music, by Willi Apel (1969)
International Cyclopedia of Music and Musicians, by Oscar Thompson (1975)
Music Reference and Research Materials: An Annotated Bibliography, comp. Vincent Harris Duckles (1974)
The New College Encyclopedia of Music, by Jack A. Westrup and F. L. Harrison (1976)
New Grove Dictionary of Music and Musicians, ed. Stanley Sadie (1980)
The New Oxford History of Music (1974–   )
The Oxford Companion to Music, by Kenneth McLeish and Valerie McLeish (1982)

philosophy *The Concise Encyclopedia of Western Philosophy and Philosophers,* ed. J. O. Urmson (1960)
Dictionary of Philosophy and Psychology, by James M. Baldwin (1925)
Dictionary of the History of Ideas, ed. Philip P. Wiener (1973–74)
The Encyclopedia of Philosophy, ed. Paul Edwards (1973)

A History of Philosophy, by Frederick C. Copleston (1947–75)
A History of Western Philosophy, by Bertrand Russell (1945)

psychology *Annual Progress in Child Psychiatry and Child Development* (1968)
Annual Review of Psychology (1950–)
A Comprehensive Dictionary of Psychological and Psychoanalytical Terms, by Horace B. English and Ava C. English (1958)
Dictionary of Psychology and Related Fields, by Hugo G. Beigel (1974)
The Encyclopedia of Human Behavior, by Robert M. Goldenson (1970)
Encyclopedia of Psychology, ed. H. J. Eysenck et al. (1972)
Guide to Library Research in Psychology, by James E. Bell (1971)
Psychological Research: An Introduction, by Arthur J. Bachrach (1965)

religion *The Concise Encyclopedia of Living Faiths,* ed. Robert C. Zaehner (1959)
A Dictionary of Non-Christian Religions, by Geoffrey Parrinder (1973)
Dictionary of the Bible, by John L. McKenzie (1965)
Encyclopedia Judaica (1972)
Encyclopedia of Religion and Ethics, ed. James Hastings (1955–58)
Exhaustive Concordance of the Bible, by James Strong (1894)
Faiths of Mankind, by Geoffrey Parrinder (1965)
Handbook of Denominations in the United States, by Frank Spencer Mead (1975)
Nelson's Complete Concordance of the Revised Standard Version Bible, comp. John W. Ellison (1978)
The New Catholic Encyclopedia (1967)
The Oxford Dictionary of the Christian Church, by F. L. Cross and Elizabeth A. Livingstone (1974)
Philosophy of Religion, ed. John Hick (1983)
A Reader's Guide to the Great Religions, ed. Charles J. Adams (1977)

science and technology *Biology Data Book,* ed. Philip L. Altman and Dorothy S. Dittmer (1972–74)
Cambridge Encyclopedia of Astronomy (1977)
Dictionary of Electronics, by Harley Carter (1972)
A Dictionary of Geology, by John Challinor (1974)
Dictionary of Mathematics, by Cyril C. Baker (1970)
Dictionary of Science and Technology, ed. T. C. Collocott (1972)
A Dictionary of Science Terms, ed. George E. Speck and Bernard Jaffe (1965)
Encyclopedia of Chemistry, ed. Clifford A. Hampel and Gessner G. Hawley (1973)
Encyclopedia of Computers and Data Processing (1978–)
Encyclopedia of Ecology, ed. Bernhard Grzimek (1976)
Encyclopedia of Environmental Science, ed. Daniel N. Lapedes (1974)
Encyclopedia of Physics, ed. Robert M. Besancon (1974)
The Encyclopedia of the Biological Sciences, ed. Peter Gray (1970)
Grzimek's Animal Life Encyclopedia (1972–75)
The International Dictionary of Physics and Electronics, ed. Walter C. Michels (1961)
McGraw-Hill Encyclopedia of Science and Technology (1982)
Science and Engineering Literature, ed. Harold R. Malinowsky (1976)
Science and Technology: An Introduction to the Literature, by Denis Joseph Grogan (1982)

Science Reference Sources, by Francis B. Jenkins (1969)
Technology, by Theodore Besterman (1971)
Universal Encyclopedia of Mathematics (1964)
Van Nostrand's International Encyclopedia of Chemical Science (1964)
Van Nostrand's Scientific Encyclopedia (1976)

social and political science

The American Negro Reference Book, ed. John P. Davis (1966)
The American Political Dictionary, by Jack C. Plano and Milton Greenberg (1967)
Annual Review of Anthropology (1972–   )
Annual Review of Sociology (1975–   )
Dictionary of American Politics, ed. Edward C. Smith and Arnold J. Zurcher (1968)
Dictionary of Political Analysis, by Jack C. Plano (1972)
A Dictionary of the Social Sciences, ed. Julius Gould and William J. Kolb (1965)
Encyclopaedia of the Social Sciences, ed. Edwin R. A. Seligman and Alvin Johnson (1930–34)
Encyclopedia of American Foreign Policy, ed. Alex DeConde (1978)
The Encyclopedia of Human Behavior, ed. Robert M. Goldenson (1970)
Encyclopedia of Sociology, ed. Gayle Johnson (1974)
Encyclopedia of the Third World, by George Thomas Kurian (1978)
International Encyclopedia of the Social Sciences, ed. David L. Sills (1968–   )
Literature and Bibliography of the Social Sciences, by Thelma K. Freides (1973)
A Reader's Guide to the Social Sciences, ed. Bert F. Hoselitz (1972)
Reference Encyclopedia of the American Indian, ed. Barry T. Klein (1978)
Research Materials in the Social Sciences, by Jack A. Clarke (1967)
Sources of Information in the Social Sciences, ed. Carl M. White et al. (1973)
Worldmark Encyclopedia of the Nations, ed. Moshe Y. Sachs and Louis Barron (1976)

Almanacs, Yearbooks, and Compilations of Facts

These volumes can be consulted for miscellaneous facts and statistics:

The Americana Annual (1923–   )
Britannica Book of the Year (1938–   )
CBS News Almanac (1976–   )
Collier's Yearbook (1939–   )
Demographic Yearbook (1948–   )
Facts on File (1940–   )
Information Please Almanac (1947–   )
International Yearbook of Education (1948–   )
The Negro Almanac (1967–   )
Political Handbook and Atlas of the World (1927–   )
The Statesman's Year-Book (1864–   )
Statistical Abstract of the United States (1878–   )
The World Almanac and Book of Facts (1868–   )
Yearbook of the United Nations (1946–   )
Year Book of World Affairs (1947–   )

Atlases and Gazetteers (Geographical Dictionaries)

Geographical knowledge can be located in:

Atlas of World History, ed. R. R. Palmer (1957)
Britannica Atlas: Geography Edition (1974)
Commercial Atlas and Marketing Guide (1981)
Cosmopolitan World Atlas (1978)
Historical Atlas, ed. William R. Shepherd (1964)
The National Atlas of the United States of America (1970)
National Geographic Atlas of the World (1975)
The New York Times Atlas of the World (1981)
The Oxford Bible Atlas, by Herbert G. May and G. H. Hunt (1974)
The Oxford Economic Atlas of the World (1972)
The Times Atlas of the World (1980)
The Times Index Gazetteer of the World (1966)
Webster's New Geographical Dictionary (1980)

Dictionaries and Thesauri

Dictionaries for everyday reference are discussed on page 209. For synonyms and research into the origins and changing meanings of words, see:

A Comprehensive Etymological Dictionary of the English Language, by Ernest Klein (1979)
A Dictionary of American English on Historical Principles, ed. Sir William A. Craigie and James R. Hulbert (1938–44)
Dictionary of American Slang, by Harold Wentworth and Stuart B. Flexner (1975)
Dictionary of Foreign Terms, by Mario Pei and Salvatore Ramondino (1975)
A Dictionary of Slang and Unconventional English, by Eric Partridge (1970)
March's Thesaurus Dictionary, by Francis A. March (1968)
Modern Guide to Synonyms and Related Words, by S. I. Hayakawa (1971)
A New English Dictionary on Historical Principles (also called *The Oxford English Dictionary*) (1888–1933)
Origins: A Short Etymological Dictionary of Modern English, by Eric Partridge (1977)
The Oxford Dictionary of English Etymology, ed. C. T. Onions (1966)
Roget's International Thesaurus (1977)
Webster's Collegiate Thesaurus (1976)
Webster's New Dictionary of Synonyms (1978)
Webster's New Third International Dictionary (1961)

Biography

Names can be identified and lives studied in the following:

Chambers's Biographical Dictionary, ed. J. O. Thorne and T. C. Collocott (1968)
Contemporary Authors (1962–)

Current Biography (1940–)
Dictionary of American Biography (1928–)
Dictionary of National Biography [British], ed. Leslie Stephen and Sidney Lee
  (1885–1963)
Dictionary of Scientific Biography (1970–80)
International Who's Who (1935–)
The McGraw-Hill Encyclopedia of World Biography (1973)
The National Cyclopaedia of American Biography (1893–)
Notable American Women 1607–1950 (1971)
Webster's American Biographies (1975)
Webster's Biographical Dictionary (1980)
Who's Who [British] (1849–)
Who's Who in America (1899–)
Who's Who in the World (1976)

Quotations

Your best hope of tracking down an unattributed quotation lies with one of these sourcebooks:

The Apollo Book of American Quotations, ed. Bruce Bohle (1970)
Dictionary of Quotations, by Bergen Evans (1968)
Familiar Quotations, by John Bartlett and E. M. Beck (1968)
The Home Book of Quotations, Classical and Modern, ed. Burton E. Stevenson
  (1967)
A New Dictionary of Quotations, by H. L. Mencken (1942)
The Oxford Dictionary of Quotations (1979)

EXERCISES

10. For each of the following proposed topics, list two or three sources (a dictionary, a bibliography, the subject catalog, etc.) that you would *begin* by consulting:

    A. The reception of Philip Roth's 1979 novel *The Ghost Writer*.
    B. Should abortions be automatically granted on demand?
    C. Pickett's Charge.
    D. How the decontrol of domestic oil prices was achieved.
    E. Recent advances in semiconductor memory systems for computers.
    F. The development of logical positivism as a philosophical school.
    G. Beethoven's reputation today.
    H. Beethoven's childhood.
    I. The origin and evolving meaning of the word *wit* in English.
    J. Who wrote the line "The proper study of mankind is man"?

11. Which of the following books are still in print? Which ones are available in paperbound editions? (See pp. 387–388.)

    A. Milan Kundera, *The Book of Laughter and Forgetting*
    B. Oliver Perry Medsger, *Edible Wild Plants*
    C. James Herndon, *Sorrowless Times: A Narrative*

    D. Maria Lemnis and Henryk Vitry, *Old Polish Traditions in the Kitchen and at the Table*

    E. Flannery O'Connor, *The Habit of Being*

12. Read one encyclopedia article (p. 388) about the general problem treated in your sample research project (Exercise 2 and/or Exercise 6), and look up the same problem in any two of the reference sources listed on pages 389–393. Submit two or three paragraphs identifying the three sources you used and indicating what you have learned from them.

13. Check several biographical sources (pp. 394–395) for information about any one prominent figure in the field of knowledge that includes your sample research project. Submit a paragraph or two identifying the sources you checked and comparing their usefulness in this one instance.

TAKING NOTES FROM READING

A typical library book or journal will be available to you for a few hours or days or weeks, depending on its importance to other borrowers. When you try to get it again, you may find that it is on loan to someone else, or sent to the bindery, or even misplaced or stolen. Thus you have to be sure to get everything you need from the work on your first try, and your notes must be clear and full enough to be your direct source when you write. Although it is always a good idea to keep the work before you and recheck it for accurate quotation and fair summary, you should assume that this will not be possible. Your notes should contain all the information necessary for full citations (pp. 410–427), and you should make sure your notes are error-free before you let the book or article out of your hands.

bibliography cards versus content cards   The notes you take from reading will serve two distinct purposes: to keep an accurate list of the works you have consulted and to record key information you have found in them. Sooner or later, most researchers understand that these purposes demand different kinds of notecards. To compile a bibliography, one card per entry is ideal; but content (or informational) notes may run through many cards, only one of which will contain the needed bibliographical facts. To avoid confusion, use 3″ × 5″ **bibliography cards** to identify the works you have consulted, and larger (usually 4″ × 6″) **content cards** for quotations, summaries, and miscellaneous comments.

    Observe the following sample cards:

BIBLIOGRAPHY CARD

TL 789
H 91

Hynek, J. Allen
The U F O Experience:
A Scientific Inquiry
Chicago: Henry Regnery,
1972.
(Hynek's early critique of Condon)

CONTENT CARD

Hynek, p. 225   reliability of
                                 reports

"A great wealth of data, highly variable
in quality, has been gathered over the
past two decades. In its present
form it is much akin to low grade
ore, which must be processed and refined
before it is of value."

    Interesting analogy. But we process
ore only when we have a reasonable
expectation of extracting something
profitable. Does the history of U F O
investigations yield that expectation?

Note that once a separate bibliography card has been prepared, the researcher can give the briefest of references on a content card: *Hynek, p. 225.*

The more systematic you are about note taking, the less likely you will be to misquote, summarize unfairly, or supply inaccurate references. Here are some tips about form:

---

form of notecards

1. Use cards of one uniform size for all your bibliography notes, and cards or sheets of another uniform size for all your content notes. This will make for easy filing and reshuffling.

2. Write in ink. Penciled notes smudge when pressed against other notes.

3. Never put entries from different sources on one card or page, and never write on the reverse side. Otherwise you will probably lose track of some of your work.

4. Include the call number of any book or magazine you have found in the library. You never know when you may want to retrieve it for another look.

5. Quote exactly, including the punctuation marks in the original, and check each quotation as soon as you have copied it.

6. Use quotation marks only when you are actually quoting verbatim, and check to see that the marks begin and end exactly where they should. Use the dots known as ellipses (pp. 332–333) to indicate where you have skipped some material within a quotation.

7. Be attentive to oddities of spelling and punctuation in quoted material. If, for instance, the original text omits a comma that you would have included, you can place a bracketed [*sic*], meaning *this is the way I found it,* at the questionable point in your notes; this will remind you not to improve the quotation illegitimately when reproducing it in your essay. But do not retain the [*sic*] in your paper unless it refers to an obvious blunder.

8. Supply page references for all quotations, paraphrases, and summaries.

9. Do not allow any ambiguities in your system of abbreviations. If two of your symbols mean the same thing, change one of them.

10. Distinguish between your own comments and those of the text you are summarizing. (See pp. 404–406.) Slashes, brackets, or your initials can be used as signals that the following remarks are yours, not those of the author.

11. When copying a passage that runs from one page to another, mark where the first page ends: *"The district attorney is a vigilant enemy of crime in the / sheets" (pp. 34–35).* If you finally quote only a portion of the excerpt in your paper, you will want to know where it ended in the original.

12. Use a portion of the card or page to evaluate the material and to remind yourself of possibilities for further study. You might say, for example, *This looks useless—but reconsider chapter 13 if discussing astrology.*

13. Leave some space in the margin or at the top for an indexing symbol.

EXERCISE

14. Using any books or articles you have handy, submit two sample bibliography cards and two content notes. One of your notes should quote a passage; the other should summarize that same passage. Be sure your two bibliography cards give full and exact citations.

COMPLETING THE PROJECT

Let us assume that you now have access to all the books and articles you need for a research paper and that you feel sure you could locate further background information in reference works. At this point your problem is no longer one of worrying that you may end with nothing to say. On the contrary, the danger is that you will think of yourself as a mere conveyer belt, feeding information from certain unanswerable sources to your reader without interposing a perspective of your own.

Remember, then, that a good research paper is simply an essay written on the basis of library materials the writer has sought out and carefully considered. It should offer exact citations of those materials (Chapter 15), but the paper itself need not be dull or impersonal. Even though you may feel awed by some of the authorities you cite, you must not let them dominate you. Make sure that your own voice stays in control, and quote only where the quotation will serve *your* purpose of explanation or argument.

If you do find that a published work anticipates what you hoped to say, your first impulse may be to give up and begin from a completely new subject area. But in most cases that would be an overreaction. The reading you have already done with one topic in mind will alert you to several closely related topics, one of which ought to prove satisfactory. As you take notes, then, you should keep exploring ways of shifting the topic, either to resolve unforeseen difficulties or to make room for new ideas and evidence you want to include. Before settling finally on one topic, you should review all possibilities together, looking for the best way to be original, challenging, and convincing. The majority of good research papers are about topics somewhat different from the writer's first idea.

Thus the writer of the UFO paper on pages 429–445, knowing in a vague way that she doubted the existence of unidentified flying objects, began by expecting to write about "the UFO cult" as an expression of mass psychology. As her research advanced, however, she realized that this "cult" encompassed the majority of her fellow citizens. If she had gone ahead and treated the UFO issue as already settled, she would have been begging a question (pp. 63–64) that readers might regard as still debatable. She therefore turned her attention to the primary issue of whether or not a belief in UFO's is justified by the present state of knowledge. Instead of writing an explanatory paper, she ended by constructing an argument.

The writer of the paper on computer crime (pp. 448–456), on the other hand, started with an argumentative idea and ended with an explanatory one. Having read a famous *Esquire* article about "phone phreaks" who had discovered how to tap into long-distance telephone connections without being charged, he expected to argue that "ripping off the monopoly" was just as criminal as robbing individuals. But as soon as he saw how little research material was available on that one form of piracy, he turned his attention to electronic crime in general. And at a certain point he decided that an explanatory survey of computer crime — still a fairly unfamiliar matter — would be more engaging than a sermon against it.

But if it is inadvisable to press ahead with a project when you are getting no encouragement from the subject catalog and the standard indexes, it is also a mistake to give up as soon as you have hit one dead end. Even negative results can sometimes be instructive. Thus the writer of the UFO paper began by going to the *Applied Science and Technology Index,* where, to her surprise, she found no references at all to UFO's. Instead of abandoning her topic, she began to grasp a key element of the UFO controversy — namely, that UFO's have thus far left behind no scientifically credible evidence of their existence.

You should also be prepared to reapportion your research time when you have come across decisively important works. The writer on computer crime found that he could hang his paper from two very different hinges, an authoritative government document and a "human interest" case history. As for the UFO project, the student sifted quickly through many books and articles before committing much time to any of them. She was looking for the best representatives of both sides — the authorities who were cited most often by others and who seemed to take the most comprehensive positions. For the pro-UFO side she settled on J. Allen Hynek's *The Hynek UFO Report,* and for the negative, Philip J. Klass's *UFOs Explained.* Instead of continuing to pile up miscellaneous bibliography cards (p. 396) and rushing between the reference room and the card catalog, she sat down with those two books and made extensive notes comparing their ways of handling evidence and logic. For example:

Hynek — evading the question

Hynek keeps blasting Air Force and Condon for taking UFO reports lightly. Fair enough — but this turns us away from asking the really hard questions. Are there any _good_ cases — i.e., ones that are proof against suspicion of fraud or error?

Hynek vs. Klass — rival methods

Note that while Hynek just piles up sightings — implying that they must add up to something — Klass deals with principles of explanation. They're writing at cross-purposes.

Hynek vs. Klass — assumptions required

If Klass is right re UFO's, no extra assumptions have to be brought in. If Hynek is right, gravity and gravitation don't seem to affect certain unique vehicles; we have to believe in time machines or something; and we have to supply motives for aliens to travel quadrillions of miles to visit us - without really introducing themselves! Note that H. lacks a general hypothesis to cover sightings. (But he _was_ chief technical consultant to _Close Encounters_!)

> *Hynek vs. Klass — dealing w/ objections*
> *Hynek's book comes 3 yrs. after Klass's,*
> *but doesn't refer to it or deal w/ any of*
> *the objections it raises. Interesting! — esp.*
> *since Hynek is a leading character*
> *in Klass's book. See, e.g., the comical*
> *Pascagoula case (K, pp. 347-369). Use?*
> *Anyway, if H. could have replied to K,*
> *why didn't he?*

By the time she had finished intensively comparing the books by Hynek and Klass, the student had a firm point of view and the makings of a thesis. Then she returned to her other sources with a much clearer idea of which items to pursue and which to discard.

If you feel uncertain about finding a thesis for your research paper, organizing it, or putting it into a technically correct final copy, review Chapters 5 and 6. For citation form, see the chapter on documentation following this one.

15

DOCUMENTATION

The Obligation to Document

If you have done any research for a paper, there are several reasons why you should document the source or sources you consulted, using a standard form of citation. In the first place, you naturally want credit for the trouble you have taken. Second, your citations will help to show a reader that your ideas are consistent with facts and expert judgments that have already appeared in print. If you happen to express considered disagreement with one of your sources, all the better; a thoughtfully posed challenge can demonstrate your independence of mind. And documentation is also a courtesy to your reader, who ought to be able to check your sources to see if you have used them responsibly or to pursue an interest in your topic.

avoiding plagiarism   A further reason for providing documentation is to avoid **plagiarism**—the serious ethical violation of presenting other people's words and ideas as your own. We all know that plagiarism does

404

tempt some student writers who feel too rushed or insecure to arrive at their own conclusions. Yet systematic dishonesty is only part of the problem. For every student who buys a term paper or copies a whole article without acknowledgment, there are dozens who indulge in "little" ethical lapses through thoughtlessness, haste, or a momentary sense of opportunity. Though perhaps ninety percent of their work is original, they too are plagiarists—just as someone who robs a bank of $2.39 is a bank robber.

Unlike the robber, however, some plagiarists fail to realize what they have done wrong. Students whose schoolteachers asked them to copy encyclopedia articles may never have learned the necessity of using quotation marks and citing sources. Others may think that by paraphrasing a quotation or summarizing an idea—that is, by putting it into their own words—they have turned it into public property. Others acknowledge the source of their idea but fail to indicate that they have borrowed authors' words as well as thoughts. And others plagiarize through sloppy note taking (pp. 396–399). Since their notes fail to distinguish adequately between personal observations and the content of a consulted book, their essays repeat the oversight. And finally, some students blunder into plagiarism through failing to recognize the difference between fact and opinion. They may think, for example, that a famous critic's opinion about a piece of literature is so authoritative that it belongs to the realm of common facts—and so they paraphrase it without acknowledgment. All these errors are understandable, but none of them constitutes a good excuse for plagiarism.

Consider the following source and three ways that a student might be tempted to make use of it:

SOURCE:

The joker in the European pack was Italy. For a time hopes were entertained of her as a force against Germany, but these disappeared under Mussolini. In 1935 Italy made a belated attempt to participate in the scramble for Africa by invading Ethiopia. It was clearly a breach of the covenant of the League of Nations for one of its members to attack another. France and Great Britain, as great powers, Mediterranean powers, and African colonial powers, were bound to take the lead against Italy at the league. But they did so feebly and half-heartedly because they did not want to alienate a possible ally against Germany. The result was the worst possible: the league failed to check aggression, Ethiopia lost her independence, and Italy was alienated after all.[1]

VERSION A:

Italy, one might say, was the joker in the European deck. When she invaded Ethiopia, it was clearly a breach of the covenant of the League of

Nations; yet the efforts of England and France to take the lead against her were feeble and half-hearted. It appears that those great powers had no wish to alienate a possible ally against Hitler's rearmed Germany.

Comment: Clearly plagiarism. Though the facts cited are public knowledge, the stolen phrases are not. Note that the writer's interweaving of his own words with the source's does *not* leave him innocent of plagiarism.

VERSION B:

Italy was the joker in the European deck. Under Mussolini in 1935, she made a belated attempt to participate in the scramble for Africa by invading Ethiopia. As J. M. Roberts points out, this violated the covenant of the League of Nations.[1] But France and Britain, not wanting to alienate a possible ally against Germany, put up only feeble and half-hearted opposition to the Ethiopian adventure. The outcome, as Roberts observes, was "the worst possible: the league failed to check aggression, Ethiopia lost her independence, and Italy was alienated after all."[2]

------

[1] J. M. Roberts, *History of the World* (New York: Knopf, 1976), p. 845.
[2] Roberts, p. 845.

Comment: Still plagiarism. The two correct citations of Roberts serve as a kind of alibi for the appropriating of other, unacknowledged phrases.

VERSION C:

Much has been written about German rearmament and militarism in the period 1933–39. But Germany's dominance in Europe was by no means a foregone conclusion. The fact is that the balance of power might have been tipped against Hitler if one or two things had turned out differently. Take Italy's gravitation toward an alliance with Germany, for example. That alliance seemed so very far from inevitable that Britain and France actually muted their criticism of the Ethiopian invasion in the hope of remaining friends with Italy. They opposed the Italians in the League of Nations, as J. M. Roberts observes, "feebly and half-heartedly because they did not want to alienate a possible ally against Germany."[1] Suppose Italy, France, and Britain had retained a certain common interest. Would Hitler have been able to get away with his remarkable bluffing and bullying in the later Thirties?

------

[1] J. M. Roberts, *History of the World* (New York: Knopf, 1976), p. 845.

Comment: No plagiarism. The writer has been influenced by the public facts mentioned by Roberts, but he has not tried to pass off Roberts' conclusions as his own. The one clear borrowing is properly acknowledged.

What to Acknowledge

There *is* room for disagreement about what to acknowledge; but precisely because this is so, you ought to make your documentation relatively ample. Provide citations for all direct quotations and paraphrases, borrowed ideas, and facts that do not belong to general knowledge.

Ask yourself, in doubtful cases, whether the point you are borrowing is an opinion or a fact. Opinions are by definition ideas that are not yet taken for granted; document them. As for facts, do not bother to document those that could be found in any commonly used source — for example, the fact that World War II ended in 1945. But give references for less accessible facts, such as the numbers of operational submarines that Nazi Germany still possessed at the end of the war. The harder it would be for readers to come across your fact through their own efforts, the more surely you need to document it.

If you are quoting or paraphrasing statements or literary passages that are not generally familiar, cite the source. A phrase from Lincoln's Gettysburg Address could get by without a citation, but a remark made in a presidential news conference could not.

DO NOT DOCUMENT	DOCUMENT
the population of China	the Chinese balance of payments in 1984
the existence of a disease syndrome called AIDS	a possible connection between AIDS and the virus that carries cat leukemia
the fact that Dickens visited America	the supposed effect of Dickens' American visit on his subsequently written novels
the fact that huge sums are wagered illegally on professional football games	an alleged "fix" of a certain football game
a line from a nursery rhyme	a line from a poem by Elizabeth Bishop

How to Document

A note, although it is the most common means of documentation, is not always the most convenient or considerate one. A reader who has to keep skipping to your notes after every few lines of text will have difficulty concentrating on your essay itself. When most of your references are to one source, you can mention that fact in a brief statement or note, announcing that page references will be inserted parenthetically into the text (pp. 419–420). But you will find that running away from notes can sometimes be clumsier than using them. It is better to refer your reader to a note than to stuff a sentence full of trivial data. Otherwise you will get clumsy effects like this:

x Mao Zedong, as J. M. Roberts remarks on page 823 of his *History of the World* (New York: Knopf, 1976), turned his attention from the cities to the countryside in the 1920's.

All this reference information is necessary, but here it interrupts a substantive remark. The writer should get the merely technical data into a note, freeing the main text to dwell on essentials:

• As J. M. Roberts remarks, Mao Zedong's attention turned from the cities to the countryside in the 1920's.[3] Furthermore, ...

Substantive Notes

The purpose of most notes is simply to provide citations for quoted material and borrowed ideas. Occasionally, though, you can use a note to expand or qualify your main discussion. A point may strike you as worth making, but also potentially distracting. By placing it in a note, you give the reader a choice between skimming it, ignoring it, or pausing to consider it fully.

Most often, a substantive note develops *from* a citation. The book or article being cited raises further issues that bear on your thesis in a challenging way. After giving the reference, you add a sentence or even a whole paragraph dealing with this challenge.

Bear in mind, however, that notes are supposed to remain subordinate elements. The time a reader spends poring over your notes amounts to a loss of concentration on your thesis. If you find, in rereading a draft, that you have given too much weight to commentary in the notes, try to condense the material as much as possible. Get rid of casual remarks, and incorporate key statements into the body of your paper. The notes you decide to keep should be clear, concise, and plainly subordinate to your main text.

Styles of Documentation

Conventions for citing sources differ widely between disciplines. In general, the humanities have favored versions of "footnote/endnote" style, whereas the sciences have preferred "reference list" style. The key distinctions are these:

FOOTNOTE/ENDNOTE STYLE	REFERENCE LIST STYLE
Note numbers appear in text, usually at ends of sentences.	Except for substantive notes (p. 408), no note numbers are used.
Notes at foot of pages or at end of text give citations corresponding to the note numbers in text.	No notes are used to cite works.
Parenthetical citations within text are used only for "subsequent references" (pp. 419–420) to frequently cited works.	All references are made through parenthetical citations within text.
No reference list is supplied.	A reference list, identifying only works cited, must appear after text. The listed works match the parenthetical citations in the text.
A bibliography, identifying both works cited and works consulted, may appear after all notes.	No bibliography is supplied.

Traditionally, essays written for composition courses have followed "MLA Style" (pp. 410–422), the footnote/endnote system recommended by the Modern Language Association of America. Recently, however, an MLA advisory committee has declared a preference for reference list style. We will explain both alternatives, using the specifications of the American Psychological Association to typify the reference list approach (pp. 423–427).[2] In illustration, the sample research papers on pages 429–445 and 448–456 have been cast, respectively, in MLA and APA style.

EXERCISE

1. If you intended to make the following statements in college papers, which ones would require documentation? What kind of documentation, if any, would be appropriate in each case? Briefly explain each of your decisions.

   A. The "black hole" hypothesis, once generally dismissed, has been steadily gaining favor among astronomers in recent years.
   B. To be or not to be: that is indeed the central question for anyone who experiences suicidal feelings.
   C. There can be no denying the fact that industrialization and lung disease are inseparable twins; where you find the first, you are bound to find his grim brother.
   D. The oppressed people of the world must often feel like those who cried out, "How long, O Lord, holy and true, dost thou not judge and avenge our blood . . . ?"
   E. The first direct act of atomic warfare occurred at Hiroshima in August 1945.

MLA CITATION FORM

Placement and Numbering of Notes

The word **footnote** is loosely used to cover both a footnote proper, which appears at the bottom of the page on which the reference occurs, and an **endnote**, which appears in a consecutive series with all other notes at the end of an essay or article. You can choose either system if you follow it consistently, but within MLA style endnotes are now usually preferred for research papers and for articles submitted for publication.

Wherever you decide to put your notes, you should follow these rules for handling the note numbers within your text:

1. Number all the notes consecutively (1, 2, 3, . . .).
2. Elevate the note numbers slightly, as `here.`[8]
3. Place the numbers after, not before, the quotations or other information being cited: not x `As Rosenhan says,`[11] `"the evidence is simply not compelling,"` but `As Rosenhan says, "the evidence is simply not compelling."`[11]
4. Place the numbers after all punctuation except a dash; even parentheses, colons, and semicolons should precede note numbers.

endnotes versus footnotes   Type endnotes on a new page after your main text, but before a bibliography if you are supplying one. Here is the standard form:

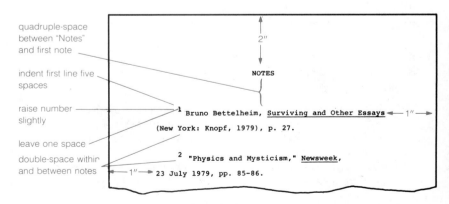

when only 1″ remains at the bottom of the page, continue notes on a following page

See pages 440–443 for endnotes in an actual research paper.

Handle footnotes just like endnotes except for these differences:

1. On each page where you will have notes, stop your main text high enough to leave room for the notes.
2. Quadruple-space between the end of the text and the first note on a page.
3. Single-space within the notes, but double-space between them.
4. If you have to carry a note over to the next page, type a solid line a full line below the last line of text on that new page, quadruple-space, and continue the note. Then continue any new notes.

Thus, footnotes at the bottom of a page look like this:

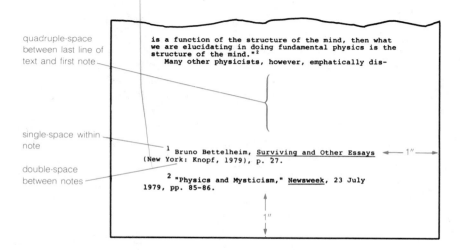

And here is a footnote carried over from a preceding page:

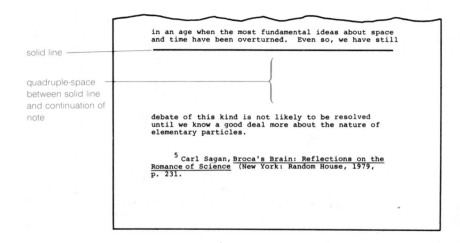

First Notes

As the thirty-eight examples on pages 412–418 will indicate, footnote form can become rather tricky. The principle behind all handling of citations, however, should be the efficient communication of a *necessary minimum* of information. Thus, for example, if you supply a bibliography (pp. 420–422) containing very full references, you can keep your notes relatively simple; a reader can use the bibliography entries to learn a book's subtitle or the fact that its first edition was published so-and-so many years before the edition you are citing. Again, once you have given one full reference to a work, you can make your later citations much briefer. We will even see that you can do away with "second notes" altogether, getting those later citations into parenthetical references within your main text.

For now, however, we will concentrate on full notes, those giving all the information that would be needed to distinguish one item from the same work published by a different house or in an earlier edition. Observe that despite all the small differences of form, every note proceeds from the author or editor (if any) to the title to the place and/or date of publication to the specific pages being quoted or cited. And observe as well that the punctuation of most notes tends to be the same; you should become familiar with the way commas, parentheses, and colons regularly separate key elements of the note.

Here, then, are "first" endnotes—double-spaced—covering a variety of circumstances:

books   A FIRST EDITION:

¹ Robert Langbaum, <u>The Modern Spirit: Essays on the Continuity of Nineteenth- and Twentieth-Century Literature</u> (New York: Oxford Univ. Press, 1970), p. 107.

If the same work appeared in your bibliography, you could shorten the footnote by dropping the book's subtitle.

AN EDITED BOOK:

² George Abbott White and Charles Newman, eds., <u>Literature in Revolution</u> (New York: Holt, 1972), p. 14.

The publisher's full name is Holt, Rinehart and Winston, but *Holt* is sufficient.

A BOOK EDITED BY MORE THAN THREE PEOPLE:

³ Frank Kermode et al., eds., <u>The Oxford Anthology of</u>

English Literature, 2 vols. (New York: Oxford Univ.

Press, 1973).

The title page says that New York, London, and Toronto are the places of publication. When more than one place is listed, you need only supply the first.

A PAGE REFERENCE TO THE SAME BOOK:

[4] William Hazlitt, "My First Acquaintance with Poets,"

in The Oxford Anthology of English Literature, ed. Frank

Kermode et al. (New York: Oxford Univ. Press, 1973), II,

705.

Instead of giving the number of volumes as in note 3, you provide the volume number of the passage being cited. With a Roman numeral for the volume number and an Arabic numeral for the page number, there is no need to write *p.* before *705.*

A TRANSLATION:

[5] Marcel Proust, Swann's Way, trans. C. K. Scott

Moncrieff (New York: Random House, 1928), pp. 203-05.

A LATER EDITION OF A BOOK WITH CORPORATE AUTHORSHIP:

[6] Sunset Western Garden Book, 3rd ed. (n.d.; rpt.

Menlo Park, Calif.: Lane, 1967), p. 79.

The date of the first edition should come first in the parentheses, but this book gives no indication of when the first edition appeared; *n.d.* means "no date." If the place of publication is not given, replace it with *n.p.* for "no place." Note that both the city and state—or in some cases the city and country—should be given if the city is not widely familiar.

A BOOK THAT FORMS PART OF A SERIES:

[7] Thomas S. Kuhn, The Structure of Scientific

Revolutions, International Encyclopedia of Unified

Science, 2nd series, No. 2, 2nd ed. (1962; rpt. Chicago:

Univ. of Chicago Press, 1970), pp. vii-viii.

Kuhn's book is the second item in the second series issued by the editors of the International Encyclopedia. The lower-case Roman page numbers indicate prefatory pages.

A BOOK REVISED BY SOMEONE OTHER THAN THE AUTHOR(S):

[8] Edward F. Ricketts and Jack Calvin, <u>Between Pacific Tides</u>, rev. Joel W. Hedgpeth, 4th ed. (1939; rpt. Stanford: Stanford Univ. Press, 1968), p. 295n.

The cited passage appears in a footnote on page 295.

A BOOK WHOSE VOLUMES WERE PUBLISHED IN DIFFERENT YEARS:

[9] All quoted poems are based on the <u>Poetical Works of William Wordsworth</u>, ed. E. de Selincourt and H. Darbishire, 2nd ed., 5 vols. (Oxford: Oxford Univ. Press, 1952–59).

The dates of the earliest- and last-published volumes are given.

A PAGE REFERENCE TO THE SAME WORK:

[10] <u>Poetical Works of William Wordsworth</u>, ed. E. de Selincourt and H. Darbishire, 2nd ed., I (Oxford: Oxford Univ. Press, 1952), 217.

The one volume being cited is indicated along with its date of publication.

AN ESSAY PUBLISHED IN A BOOK:

[11] Josephine Miles, "What We Compose," in <u>Rhetoric and Composition: A Sourcebook for Teachers</u>, ed. Richard L. Graves (Rochelle Park, N.J.: Hayden, 1976), pp. 183–92.

The title of the article included in the book belongs within quotation marks.

A NOTE CITING MORE THAN ONE BOOK:

[12] See Susan Isaacs, <u>The Nursery Years: The Mind of the Child from Birth to Six Years</u> (1929; rpt. New York:

Schocken, 1968); Géza Róheim, <u>Magic and Schizophrenia</u>

(1955; rpt. Bloomington: Indiana Univ. Press, 1962); and

R. D. Laing, <u>Self and Others</u>, 2nd ed. (1961; rpt. New

York: Pantheon, 1969).

articles in magazines, journals, and newspapers Footnote form is slightly different for periodical publications, as these samples indicate:

AN ARTICLE IN A JOURNAL WITH CONTINUOUS PAGINATION THROUGH EACH YEAR'S VOLUME:

[13] Davis S. Boyer, "Ontario: Canada's Keystone,"

<u>National Geographic</u>, 154 (1978), 760-95.

> After a year or so, library copies of magazines and journals are bound into single annual volumes. If the page numbers for each year's volume run continuously, you do not have to specify the month or week of publication; just give the volume number, the year in parentheses, and the page number(s), without *p.* or *pp.* You *should* supply the full date of publication, however, if the journal is too recent to have been bound.

AN ARTICLE IN A MAGAZINE WITH SEPARATE PAGINATION FOR EACH ISSUE:

[14] Robert Begiebing, "Twelfth Round: An Interview with

Norman Mailer," <u>Harvard Magazine</u>, March-April 1983, pp.

40-50.

> If the paging starts anew with each issue, the volume number can be omitted. This eliminates the parentheses around the date, but it also means that *p.* or *pp.* should be supplied.

AN ARTICLE IN A JOURNAL THAT DOES NOT IDENTIFY THE EXACT DATE OF EACH ISSUE:

[15] Richard P. Wheeler, "Poetry and Fantasy in Shake-

speare's Sonnets 88-96," <u>Literature and Psychology</u>, 22,

No. 3 (1972), 151-62.

> The number of the issue in the yearly series is given after the volume and/or issue number.

A BOOK REVIEW:

16 Jean Strouse, rev. of <u>Stieglitz</u>, by Sue Davidson Lowe, <u>Newsweek</u>, 14 Mar. 1983, p. 70.

Note the preferred form for giving the date.

AN UNSIGNED MAGAZINE ARTICLE:

17 "Drugs That Don't Work," <u>New Republic</u>, 29 Jan. 1972, pp. 12-13.

A SIGNED NEWSPAPER ARTICLE:

18 Peter Weisser, "Governor Reagan on Grass," <u>San Francisco Chronicle</u>, 29 Jan. 1972, Final Ed., p. 6, cols. 1-5.

It is not essential to give either the edition or the columns, but both can be helpful. Occasionally a story will appear in one edition of a day's paper and not in others. Note that the city where the paper is published is part of the underlined title.

AN UNSIGNED NEWSPAPER ARTICLE OR EDITORIAL:

19 "School Desegregation, Commuter Style," <u>New York Times</u>, 6 Mar. 1983, Sec. 4, 20.

The writer of this note has chosen to omit the edition and column numbers. The editorial appears on page 20 of section 4 in the many-sectioned Sunday *Times.*

encyclopedia entries

20 L[awrence] K. L[ustig], "Alluvial Fans," <u>Encyclopaedia Britannica</u>, 1974, Macropaedia.

The author's initials appear at the end of the entry; they are identified elsewhere. Note that volume and page numbers are unnecessary when items appear in alphabetical order. But since the *Britannica* from 1974 onward has three sets of contents, the note should indicate which one is intended—in this case the "Macropaedia."

pamphlets

SIGNED:

21 H. H. Koepf, <u>Compost: What It Is/How It Is Made/What</u>

It Does, rpt. from Bio-Dynamics, No. 77 (Stroudsburg,
Pa.: Bio-Dynamic Farming and Gardening Assn., 1956).

Because pamphlets are hard to locate in libraries, any extra information about their origin should be supplied. The reader of
this note could track down the magazine from which the pamphlet was taken or write to Stroudsburg for a copy.

UNSIGNED:

[22] Dye Plants and Dyeing--A Handbook, rpt. from Plants
and Gardens, 20, No. 3 (Baltimore: Brooklyn Botanic
Garden, 1964).

dissertations   [23] Henry Morton Boudin, "The Ripple Effect in Classroom Management," Diss. Univ. of Michigan, 1970, p. 89.

public   [24] U.S. Constitution, Art. I, sec. 2.
documents   [25] Environmental Quality Committee of the Governor's
Science Advisory Council, Some Technology Considerations
for Environmental Quality in Maryland (Jan. 1971).

[26] "Shipments and Unloads of Certain Fruits and
Vegetables, 1918-1923," U.S. Dept. of Agriculture
Statistical Bulletin, No. 7 (Apr. 1925).

[27] "Actual Revenues from Taxes and Monopolies in
Taiwan District," Monthly Statistics of the Republic of
China, No. 96 (Dec. 1973), Table 27.

published   [28] Steve Allen, Letter, Popular Photography, June
letters   1978, p. 4.

[29] "To Joel Warren Norcross," 11 Jan. 1850, Emily
Dickinson, Selected Letters, ed. Thomas H. Johnson
(Cambridge, Mass.: Harvard Univ. Press, 1971), pp. 31-34.

unpublished letters

[30] Letter received from Gerald Graff, 20 May 1983.

mimeographed materials

[31] Willie Sutton, "Writing Effective Letters of Recommendation," mimeographed (Ossining, N.Y., 1936), p. 8.

theatrical performances

[32] Douglas Johnson, dir., <u>Wait Until Dark</u>, by Frederick Knott, with Juliet Mills, Alcazar Theatre, San Francisco, 23 Sept. 1979.

films

[33] Don Siegel, dir., <u>Escape from Alcatraz</u>, with Clint Eastwood and Patrick McGoohan, Paramount, 1979.

[34] <u>Metrics for Measure</u> (Santa Monica, Calif.: BFA Educational Media, 1975), 16 mm., 12¼ min., color.

radio or television programs

[35] <u>The World's Worst Air Crash</u>, narr. Bill Moyers, PBS, Los Angeles, 27 July 1979.

If the program is local, you should identify it by station and city. You can also supply the names of the producer, director, and writer if such information is important to your paper.

recordings

[36] Desmond Dekker, "Shanty Town," on Jimmy Cliff, <u>The Harder They Come</u>, Mango Records, MLPS-9202.

lectures

[37] E. D. Hirsch, Jr., "Frontiers of Critical Theory," Wyoming Conference on Freshman and Sophomore English, Laramie, 9 July 1979.

interviews

[38] Personal interview with Jennifer Sutherland, 18 Nov. 1983.

Subsequent Notes and Parenthetical Citations

shortened notes   If you have several references to one work, your first note to it can be the only full one you supply:

> ¹ Donald McQuade, ed., <u>Linguistics, Stylistics, and the</u>
> <u>Teaching of Composition</u>, Studies in Contemporary Language
> #2 (Akron, Ohio: Dept. of English, Univ. of Akron,
> 1979), Preface, p. xii.

Then in later notes you can identify the book simply by the author's or editor's name:

> ² Richard L. Larson, "Language Studies and Composing
> Processes," in McQuade, pp. 182-90.

If your paper cites two or more works by the same author or editor, you will have to add a shortened title to prevent confusion:

> ⁵ See McQuade, <u>Linguistics</u>, p. 48.

And if the book lacks a single author or editor and has a cumbersome title, you may choose to abbreviate that title in your subsequent notes. If you do so, you may want to announce what the abbreviation will be:

> ¹ <u>The McGraw-Hill Encyclopedia of World Biography</u>, 12
> vols. (New York: McGraw-Hill, 1973), I, 804; hereafter
> cited as <u>MEWB</u>.

Then a subsequent note might simply read:

> ³ <u>MEWB</u>, II, 489.

References to names, titles, or abbreviated titles are now generally preferred to Latin abbreviations like *ibid., loc. cit.,* and *op. cit.* (see pp. 366–367), which often cause momentary confusion.

eliminating unnecessary notes   If you will be citing the same work more than a few times, you can spare your reader unnecessary trips to your endnotes or footnotes by putting the later citations between parentheses in your main text:

• Good journals, as Macrorie says, have something in common: "They do not speak privately" (Macrorie, p. 131).

Or again:

• A variety of assumptions tend to color our use of the term "humanism" (see Smith and Preston, pp. 12-13).

citing plays and long poems Once you have established the author and full title of a play or long poem and have specified the edition you are using, you can cite lines by using a combination of Roman and Arabic numerals:

citation	meaning
<u>Lear</u> I.ii.56-59	Shakespeare's *King Lear*, Act one, scene two, lines 56–59
<u>Aen</u>. III.201	Vergil's *Aeneid*. Book Three, line 201
<u>P.L.</u> IV.32-33	Milton's *Paradise Lost*, Book Four, lines 32–33
II Kings iv.6	The Bible, Second Book of Kings, Chapter Four, verse 6

Note that the Bible and its books are not customarily italicized.

Shortened references to lines or verses can appear either in notes or in parenthetical references. Whenever you cite a work more than a few times, however, you should try to get all citations but the first one into parentheses:

FIRST NOTE:

[1] Shakespeare, <u>The Merchant of Venice</u>, ed. Louis B. Wright and Virginia A. LaMar (New York: Washington Square Press, 1957), II.iii. 43.

PARENTHETICAL REFERENCE:

Portia tells Nerissa that she will do anything "ere I will be married to a sponge" (I.ii.90-91).

Bibliographies

A bibliography is a list of works that you have consulted, or that you recommend to your readers for further reference. Research papers, dissertations, and scholarly books that do not follow a reference list style of citation (pp. 408–409) typically contain bibliographies at the end, but in shorter or more informal writing they are less commonly seen. Apart from your instructor's preference, you can decide whether or not to include a bibliography by asking yourself whether your notes have given a sufficient idea of your sources. If you want to show that you have taken account of unmentioned works, the extra effort of compiling a bibliography may be worthwhile.

placement of bibliography entries Your bibliography should come last, after your footnotes, and it should begin on a new page. Follow this pattern:

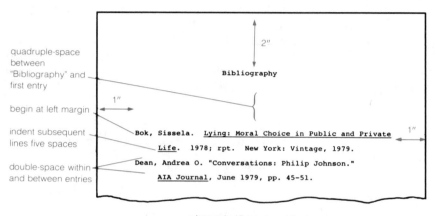

bibliography form Observe that:

1. Most bibliographies follow the alphabetical order of the authors' or editors' last names, with anonymous items inserted in the alphabetical order of the first *significant* word in each title (excluding articles like *A* and *The*):

    The Penguin World Atlas. Harmondsworth, England:

        Penguin, 1974.

    Plumb, J. H. The Growth of Political Stability in

        England 1675-1725, 1967; rpt. Harmondsworth,

        England: Penguin, 1973.

2. If an entry has more than one author or editor, invert the normal order of first and last names only for the first name you find on the title page:

Sagan, Carl, and Thornton Page. <u>UFO's--A Scientific</u>

<u>Debate</u>. Ithaca: Cornell Univ. Press, 1972.

3. In nonscientific writing, bibliography entries are generally not numbered.
4. Bibliography entries, unlike footnotes, begin at the left margin and then show a five-space indention on each subsequent line of the entry.
5. In bibliography entries, periods rather than commas follow the author's or editor's name and the title of the work.
6. In bibliography entries, information about the place, publisher, and date of publication is not surrounded by parentheses, as it is in notes.
7. If you include more than one work by the same author or editor, supply the name(s) only in the first entry. In subsequent entries, type ten hyphens and a period, skip two spaces, and supply the next alphabetically ordered title:

Popper, Karl R. <u>The Open Society and Its Enemies</u>.

2 vols. Fifth ed.; Princeton: Princeton Univ.

Press, 1966.

----------. <u>The Poverty of Historicism</u>. Third ed.,

1961; rpt. New York: Harper & Row, 1964.

The following note and bibliography entry show the essential differences of form:

NOTE:

[8] Jane Jacobs, <u>The Death and Life of Great American</u>

<u>Cities</u> (New York: Vintage, 1961), p. 208.

BIBLIOGRAPHY ENTRY:

no number

last name first

first line not indented

Jacobs, Jane. <u>The Death and Life of Great American</u>

<u>Cities</u>. New York: Vintage, 1961.

periods after main divisions

subsequent lines indented

no parentheses

For a complete sample bibliography at the end of a research paper, see pages 444–445.

EXERCISES

2. Write sample first endnotes (double-spaced) giving the usual amount of information about the following sources:

    A. A quotation from page 228 of this present book.

    B. A book by Herman Ermolaev called *Soviet Literary Theories 1917–1934: The Genesis of Socialist Realism.* The book was published in 1963 by the University of California Press, whose offices are in Berkeley and Los Angeles, California.

    C. A 1940 pamphlet issued by the United States Department of the Interior, Bureau of Indian Affairs, called *Navajo Native Dyes: Their Preparation and Use.* The pamphlet was published by the U.S. Government Printing Office in Washington, D.C.

    D. A story by Philip Roth called "On the Air," published in Number 10 of *New American Review,* on pages 7 through 49. This magazine did not carry dates, and its pagination began anew with each issue.

    E. A two-volume book called *American Literary Masters,* edited by Charles R. Anderson and seven other people. The work was published in 1965 by Holt, Rinehart and Winston, whose places of publication are listed on the back of the title page as New York, Chicago, San Francisco, and Toronto.

3. If you are now working on a research project, supply first notes to five items you have examined, including at least one article in a magazine or newspaper. In addition, supply a subsequent note or a parenthetical reference for each item.

4. For each item you used in Exercise 3, submit a bibliography entry in standard MLA form.

APA CITATION FORM

The virtue of a reference list style of citation (pp. 408–409) is that it does away with note numbers that can keep a reader yo-yoing between text and notes—only to find, in many cases, that a work cited earlier is being cited again. In some disciplines—for example, mathematics, chemistry, physics, biology, and engineering—the textual citations are simple Arabic numerals corresponding to numbered items in the reference list:[3]

SENTENCE IN TEXT:

It appears that female choice is frequently involved in the evolution of the conspicuous acoustic signals that precede mating (*2, 3*).

ITEMS IN REFERENCE LIST:

    2. L. Fairchild, *Science 212,* 950 (1981); R. D. Howard, *Evolution 32,* 850 (1978); M. J. Ryan, *Science 209,* 523 (1980).

3. R. D. Alexander, in *Insects, Science, and Society*, D. Pimentel, Ed. (Academic Press, New York, 1975), p. 35; P. D. Bell, *Can. J. Zool. 58*, 1861 (1980); W. Cade, *Science 190*, 1312 (1975); in *Sexual Selection and Reproductive Competition in Insects*, M. S. Blum and N. A. Blum, Eds. (Academic Press, New York, 1979); D. J. Campbell and E. Shipp, *Z. Tierpsychol. 51*, 260 (1979); A. V. Popov and V. F. Shuvalov, *J. Comp. Physiol. 119*, 111 (1977); S. M. Ulagaraj and T. J. Walker, *Science 182*, 1278 (1973).

In other disciplines—for example, botany, geology, zoology, economics, and sociology—the parenthetical citations include the author(s) and date of publication: *(Comstock & Fisher, 1975)*. We will take one such author-date style, that of the American Psychological Association, as a model of reference list form.

Citations

A WORK WITH ONE AUTHOR:

There appears to be no significant correlation between stress and depression (Garcia, 1983).

> The name and date correspond to an item in the reference list at the end of the paper.

Garcia (1983) found no significant correlation. . . .

> If the author's name already appears in the sentence, it is not repeated in the citation.

Garcia's 1983 article reports no significant correlation. . . .

> If both the name and the date already appear, no citation is called for.

A WORK WRITTEN BY MORE THAN ONE AUTHOR:

Preston and Martino (1967) examined the backgrounds of 234 schizophrenic patients.

> If there are two authors, mention both of them in every citation.

This hypothesis has recently received compelling support (De Mille, Yushenko, & Horwitz, 1984).

No matter how many authors a work has, give all of their surnames in a *first* citation. (Note the use of the ampersand (*&*) within a parenthetical citation but not in the main sentence: *Preston and Martino.*

See, however, the contrary findings of De Mille et al. (1984).

In a *subsequent* citation of a work by *more than two* authors, give only the first surname plus *et al.* (Latin 'and others').

A WORK BY AN AUTHOR WHO IS REPRESENTED BY MORE THAN ONE ITEM FROM THE SAME YEAR:

Karsh (1981b) has proposed a rival explanation.

In the reference list Karsh's two articles are identified as *1981a* and *1981b.*

A PAGE REFERENCE:

Manteca's explanation has been disputed as "based on altogether inconclusive data" (Karsh, 1981b, p. 891).

Quotations require citation of the pages where they were found. Page or chapter references are helpful whenever you mean to call attention to one part of the cited work: *(Karsh, chap. 4).*

The Reference List

After your text, including any substantive notes (p. 408), supply a list titled *References.* If you keep to APA style, your reference list will look like the one on pages 455–456.

Order your list alphabetically by the authors' surnames. A work not attributed to any author should be positioned according to the first significant word in its title. (Disregard *A* and *The.*) If the author is an agency or institution—for example, SRI International—list it by the first significant word in the corporate name.

Within each entry, give first the author(s), then the title, and finally the facts of publication, with periods after each of these major divisions and other punctuation as shown below:

1. *The author(s):*

2. *The title:*

capital letters only for first letters of title and subtitle

White-collar crime: A twentieth-century crisis.

title underlined   period

3. *Facts of publication:*

place   publisher   date

Lexington, Mass.: Lexington Books, 1978.

colon   comma   period

Study the following sample entries for variations of form:

A BOOK:

first line not indented ———— Parker, D. B.   Crime by computer.   New York:

subsequent lines ———————— Scribner's, 1976.
indented three
paces

AN ARTICLE IN A JOURNAL WITH CONTINUOUS PAGINATION THROUGH EACH YEAR'S
VOLUME:

no quotation marks

Kolata, G.   Students discover computer threat.

Science, 1982, 215, 1216-1217.

underlined   year of   volume   page numbers
journal   journal   number   without *pp.*
name   volume   underlined

AN ARTICLE IN A MAGAZINE WITH SEPARATE PAGINATION FOR EACH ISSUE:

Gomes, L.   Secrets of the software pirates.

Esquire, January 1982, pp. 58-65.

no volume   *pp.* for
number   page numbers

AN ARTICLE WITH TWO OR MORE AUTHORS:

names joined by &   all surnames first

Henderson, G., & Young, J.   The heist.

Esquire, May 1981, pp. 36-47.

AN UNSIGNED ARTICLE:

<pre>
    Locking the electronic file cabinet. Business

Week, October 18, 1982, pp. 123-24.
</pre>

EXERCISES

5. Submit five sentences containing APA citations of real or imaginary works (pp. 424–425). The five citations should be to:

   A. A book written by three authors.
   B. A book written by four authors.
   C. A quotation from an unsigned article.
   D. A work written by an author who appears more than once in the reference list.
   E. An article in a journal that uses continuous pagination through each year's volume.

6. Write a sample APA reference list (pp. 425–427) covering the five items described in Exercise 2 (p. 423).

NOTES

[1] J. M. Roberts, *History of the World* (New York: Knopf, 1976), p. 845.

[2] See *MLA Handbook for Writers of Research Papers, Theses, and Dissertations* (New York: Modern Language Assn., 1977); "Report of the Advisory Committee on Documentation Style," *PMLA*, 97 (1982), 318–24; and *Publication Manual of the American Psychological Association*, 2nd ed. (Washington, D.C.: American Psychological Assn., 1974).

[3] The example is taken from Christine R. B. Boake and Robert R. Capranica, "Aggressive Signal in 'Courtship' Chirps of a Gregarious Cricket," *Science*, 218 (1982), 580–82.

16

SAMPLE RESEARCH PAPERS

To illustrate the fruits of library research, here are two student papers. Taken together, they cover several variations of mode and form:

	UFO Paper	Computer Crime Paper
Mode	Argument (pp. 60–78)	Explanation (pp. 42–58)
Thesis Statement	Included (pp. 100–103)	Not included
Outline	Included (pp. 105–109)	Not included
Documentation Form	MLA (pp. 410–422)	APA (pp. 423–427)
List of Sources	Bibliography (pp. 420–422)	Reference list (pp. 425–427)
Sample Handwritten Page	Included (p. 446)	Not included

For information about the two writers' research procedures, see pages 378–381, 383–386, 397, 400–402.

AN ARGUMENTATIVE RESEARCH PAPER ON UFO'S

Kate Englander

Professor Keogh

English 1A

December 13, 1978

UFO's: Should Seeing Be Believing?

Thesis statement: Although many private citizens, scientists, and government officials continue to be seriously concerned about Unidentified Flying Objects, belief in UFO's must rest on faith, not science, because no sound reasons for that belief have yet been presented.

The writer forms a complete thesis statement (pp. 100–103) by surrounding her core thesis with *although* and *because* clauses that remind her to consider the opposing position and to supply evidence.

Outline

I. The UFO Hypothesis Remains Popular

   A. Thousands of sightings have been reported over a thirty-year period

   B. The American public and many astronomers take UFO's seriously

   C. So do some members of the government

II. The Quality of the Evidence, Not the Number of Eyewitnesses, Should Decide the Issue

III. No Sound Reasons for Believing in UFO's Have Yet Been Presented

She uses a full-sentence outline (pp. 107–108) showing the subordination of some ideas to others.

Outline 2

A. Decades of investigations have failed to convince
officially chosen experts

B. The case for UFO's rests on reports that are open to
challenge

1. The reports never provide independent chains of
evidence

2. The reports do not exclude alternative explanations

C. The UFO hypothesis is the least likely of available
explanations for reported sightings

1. Interstellar visitation--the only way of accounting for the alleged flight capabilities of UFO's
--is highly improbable

2. When a plausible alternative is brought into view,
a UFO report typically falls apart

IV. Belief in UFO's Must Therefore Rest on Faith, Not
Science

UFO's: Should Seeing Be Believing?

For more than thirty years now, a controversy has raged over the existence or nonexistence of Unidentified Flying Objects (UFO's). Sightings have been reported continually since the first "flying saucers" caused panic in the 1940's, and in some periods, such as 1965-67 when nearly three thousand reports descended on the Air Force, waves or epidemics of alleged sightings have kept UFO's near the center of public concern.[1] And the UFO phenomenon shows no signs of letting up. In the past few weeks alone, my morning newspaper has covered sightings in West Virginia, Australia, and the oil fields of Kuwait.[2] To quote the title of one recent article on the subject, "UFO's Just Will Not Go Away."[3]

The center of controversy is not, of course, whether many people have been alarmed by strange sights in the sky, but whether any of the objects seen should be considered vehicles showing extraordinary, indeed unearthly, propulsion capabilities. By a narrow margin, the American public's answer to that question appears to be yes. A Gallup poll of 1973 showed, for example, that fifty-one percent of the respondents considered UFO's "real,"[4] and

The paper begins with three paragraphs granting the popularity of the idea it will oppose.

The writer has chosen to use endnotes rather than footnotes. See p. 410.

by 1978 Gallup found that the percentage of believers had increased to fifty-seven.[5] More strikingly, a 1977 survey of the American Astronomical Society disclosed that fifty-three percent of the membership believed that UFO's merited scientific study. Of the 1,356 members who completed the survey, sixty-two reported having personally seen UFO's.[6]

In view of such widespread interest, it is not surprising to learn that worry about the reality and significance of UFO's extends to the highest levels of government. Responding to an increasing flow of UFO reports, the Presidential science advisor approached the National Aeronautics and Space Administration in 1977 about the possibility of a new federal investigation.[7] During the same period, a special U.N. committee began discussing a proposal that an agency within the UN be established to study UFO's.[8] Although NASA eventually rejected the White House's request that it begin another study, stating that such an inquiry would be "wasteful and probably unproductive,"[9] the idea of UFO's clearly makes some of our leaders uneasy. Indeed, American concern over UFO's goes straight to the top--to President Carter, who, one evening in 1969 when he was Governor of Georgia, looked up and saw a large bright object which, he reported, "came close, moved away--came close,

3

then moved away . . . then disappeared."[10]   As late as 1976
Mr. Carter maintained in an interview that his experience
had proved to him the reality of UFO's.[11]

In the face of so much testimony from varied sources,
we might be inclined in advance to favor the UFO hypothesis
--the notion that some astonishingly advanced vehicles have
veered and vanished in our skies. But an awareness of
history should make us recall that large numbers of people
can be wrong about what they saw; perceptual expectations
such as a belief in witches, demons, or ghosts have caused
whole societies to "see things." UFO's could be merely what
one critic calls "the modern myth"--a quasi-religious fan-
tasy rather than a physical actuality.[12] The only way to
settle the issue is to appeal, not to popular belief or even
to the number of eyewitnesses, but to the quality of the
evidence that has been produced so far. When we do, we
will have to conclude that the present state of our knowledge does not justify a belief in UFO's.

Before saying for sure that some controversial phenomenon exists, we would do well to find out what the most
tough-minded and knowledgeable experts think about it. No
such phenomenon has ever been as thoroughly investigated as
have UFO's--and the results have been entirely negative.

Here she pivots from pro-UFO considerations to her own point of view.

From here on, every paragraph will build support for the thesis.

4

During the period 1947-1966, when the Air Force was officially responsible for checking UFO reports, not one among
thousands of cases was found to be substantial. When the
Air Force, under criticism from UFO supporters, handed
the investigation over to a group of civilian scientists,
the outcome was the same. Edward U. Condon, the civilian
project director, stated the group's joint position in
these words:

For a prose quotation of
more than four typed lines,
the writer uses the ex-
tracted form, indenting by
ten spaces and omitting
quotation marks, but con-
tinuing to double-space.

> As indicated by its title [Scientific Study of
> Unidentified Flying Objects], the emphasis of
> this study has been on attempting to learn from
> UFO reports anything that could be considered as
> adding to scientific knowledge. Our general con-
> clusion is that nothing has come from the study
> of UFOs in the past 21 years that has added to
> scientific knowledge. Careful consideration of
> the record as it is available to us leads us to
> conclude that further extensive study of UFOs
> probably cannot be justified in the expectation
> that science will be advanced thereby.[13]

Although believers in UFO's have dismissed the Condon
Report as little better than a coverup,[14] even they

5

generally admit that the case for UFO's rests only on unveri-
fied stories, not on physical data that an outsider would
have to consider authentic. When those stories <u>are</u>
checked, furthermore, they never yield the minimum requirement for proof, namely what one physicist calls "independent and multiple chains of evidence, each capable of
satisfying a link-by-link test of meaning."[15] Many people
in an area may think they have seen a UFO, but the alleged
flying object never flies <u>to</u> a second area where its features can be corroborated or where the intentions of its
supposed occupants can be guessed at.

 Even reports that look unusually reliable always turn
out to lack the necessary elements of corroboration. Consider the much-publicized case, dating from the late
sixties, of a gleaming object that was actually recorded on
16-mm. film as it repeatedly appeared and disappeared outside a window of a passenger plane. After carefully study-
ing the film, a leading aeronautical expert affirmed that
the object was metallic and that its rate of approach and
recession far exceeded that of any known aircraft. To
millions of Americans who saw the film on television, here
was proof positive that UFO's are real. But this "UFO,"
like others generally, had made itself known in only one

Here and on p. 7 of her paper, the writer lends concreteness to her argument by getting down to cases.

way and to only one set of observers, all of whom--including
the movie camera--could have been registering a signal from
an ordinary but concealed source. As it happens, investi-
gators eventually proved that the object sighted was not
a separate vehicle but the tilting tail of the airplane
itself, captured by the astigmatic lens of the plastic
window.[16]

In the case just cited, the flaw in the original report
was not simply the lack of a second, independent, set of
observers, but a failure to search vigorously for alternative explanations. Unfortunately, this failure appears to
be an inevitable feature of UFO reports. When people with
alien spacecraft on their minds glimpse something that seems
to be flashing through the sky, they rarely pause to ask
themselves whether they may have seen only a reflection, a
meteor, or a bright planet.[17] And UFO enthusiasts, instead
of holding off from crediting a report until doubters have
probed it for mistakes, treat the most plausible-looking
new reports as if they corroborated the thousands of previous ones. The result is a very long, hastily formed
chain of testimony, every link of which is seriously weak.

The neglect of alternative explanations becomes fatal
when we realize that the UFO hypothesis is always the least

7

likely explanation of a given sighting. When people state
that they have seen a vehicle defy gravity, they are talking about a technology that must almost certainly have been
devised outside our solar system. If the UFO came to us
from the nearest stellar system, Alpha Centauri, it must
have traveled about 4.3 light-years, or 25,318,400,000,000
miles. If its speed during that journey had been a million
miles per hour, it would have been launched some twenty-
nine centuries ago, at about the time King David was unit-
ing the tribes of Israel.[18] The prospect is hard to imagine.
It is also quite unnecessary to consider until less extreme
possibilities have been ruled out.[19]

    To see how the UFO hypothesis collapses as soon as any
rival explanation has been proposed, let us return to the
celebrated case that made a believer of Governor Jimmy
Carter. The Governor's report states that the luminous
object in the Georgia sky appeared to him around 7:15 p.m.
on January 6, 1969, at about 30° elevation in the western
sky. At that hour of that clear evening, the planet Venus
was in the west-southwest at an elevation of 25° and was
nearly 100 times brighter than a first-magnitude star.
Venus does not, of course, advance and retreat or change its
size, but whenever it becomes brilliant, hundreds of people

The writer reconsiders a famous UFO case, which she had deliberately used as "bait" on pp. 2–3.

8

think it is a UFO in motion. Indeed, during World War II
U.S. planes frequently tried to shoot it down, mistaking
it for an enemy aircraft.[20] In view of these facts, how
likely is it that Governor Carter saw a UFO rather than
Venus? The first hypothesis requires us to believe in time
machines or absurdly prolonged voyages lasting through the
life spans (in our terms) of perhaps sixty generations of
alien beings; the other hypothesis conforms to what we
already know about unexpected sightings of Venus.

Although the idea of UFO's carries a vaguely scientific
aura, science clearly offers no encouragement to believers.
"We may even have to face the fact," writes the most
knowledgeable spokesman for UFO's, "that the scientific
framework, by its very internal logic, excludes certain
classes of phenomena, of which UFO's may be one" (Hynek, The
UFO Experience, p. 261). But the logic of science is simply
the logic of determining, as best we can, whether something
actually happened or will happen in a specified way. Hynek's
statement thus leads to a drastic conclusion: UFO's make
so little empirical sense that we must choose between
believing in them on the one hand and reasoning from available facts on the other.

That is indeed the choice we face, or ought to face.

A parenthetical citation (p. 419) of a previously cited work eliminates the need for still another note.

9

"The facts" do not disprove the existence of UFO's; they
simply point in another, less miraculous, direction. Perhaps the miracle is true and the apparent facts are wrong.
Until the miracle reveals itself more plainly, however, I
must continue to think that the absence of evidence for
UFO's stems from one cause only: an absence of UFO's themselves.

Notes

For the form of notes, see pp. 410–418.

[1] See David Michael Jacobs, <u>The UFO Controversy in America</u> (Bloomington: Indiana Univ. Press, 1975). Although sympathetic to the pro-UFO camp, this study is historically comprehensive.

[2] <u>San Francisco Chronicle</u>, 24 Oct. 1978, p. 16 and pp. 1, 16; 14 Nov. 1978, p. 10.

[3] See D. Shapley, "UFO's Just Will Not Go Away," <u>Science</u>, 198 (1977), 1128.

[4] "Is There Something to UFO's After All?" <u>U.S. News & World Report</u>, 20 Feb. 1978, p. 56.

The writer combines a citation with a substantive note (p. 408).

[5] George Gallup, "Most Americans Believe in UFOs," <u>San Francisco Chronicle</u>, 25 May 1978, p. 2. The same article reveals that between 1966 and 1978, the percentage of people who believe that there are "people somewhat like ourselves living on other planets" increased from 34 to 51. Belief in humanoid aliens still lags behind belief in angels, however, by three percentage points: see George Gallup, "UFO's, Ghosts and True Believers," <u>San Francisco Chronicle</u>, 15 June 1978, p. 2.

Notes 2

A shortened citation of a work already cited in note 4.

[6] "Is There Something . . . ?," p. 56.

[7] Boyce Rensberger, "U.F.O. Interest Rising, Stirred by Science Fiction Films," New York Times, 9 Dec. 1977, Sec. II, p. 1.

[8] Rensberger, p. 1.

[9] "NASA Refuses to Reopen Investigation of U.F.O.'s," New York Times, 28 Dec. 1977, Sec. I, p. 14.

[10] Shapley, p. 1128.

[11] The interview is cited in "Is There Something . . . ?," p. 56.

[12] See Donald H. Menzel, "UFO's--the Modern Myth," in Carl Sagan and Thornton Page, eds., UFO's--a Scientific Debate (Ithaca: Cornell Univ. Press, 1972), pp. 123-182. See also, in the same volume, Carl Sagan, "UFO's: The Extra-terrestrial and Other Hypotheses," pp. 265-275. The most negative view of UFO belief as a substitute religion is expressed by Martin Gardner, "The Third Coming," New York Review of Books, 26 Jan. 1978, pp. 21-22.

[13] Edward U. Condon, <u>Scientific Study of Unidentified Flying Objects</u> (New York: Bantam, 1969), p. 1.

[14] For the case against the Condon Report, see J. Allen Hynek, <u>The Hynek UFO Report</u> (New York: Dell, 1977). Hynek himself served as a scientific consultant to the Air Force's UFO investigation. He believes that the Condon Committee was biased against the UFO hypothesis from the beginning.

[15] Philip Morrison, "The Nature of Scientific Evidence: A Summary," in Sagan and Page, p. 280.

[16] For discussion of this case, see Morrison, pp. 281-282. Needless to say, the media covered the original mystery much more extensively than its solution. UFO's are newsworthy; debunkings of UFO's are not. That fact is worth remembering when we try to weigh the importance of opinion surveys showing a wide belief in UFO's.

[17] For an understanding of the kinds of events that typically set off UFO reports, see Philip J. Klass, <u>UFOs Explained</u> (1974: rpt. New York: Vintage, 1976).

Notes 4

[18]These figures can be checked in <u>The Random House Encyclopedia</u> (New York: Random House, 1977), pp. 1900 (Alpha Centauri), 2346 (light-year), and 982 (reign of David).

[19] In view of interstellar distances, we can understand why UFO backers tend to be vague about explanations, even while they continue to flirt with the idea of alien visitors. Thus J. Allen Hynek admitted in 1972 that "after more than twenty years' association with the problem, I still have few answers and no viable hypothesis" (J. Allen Hynek, <u>The UFO Experience: A Scientific Inquiry</u> [New York: Ballantine, 1972], p. 258.) If there is really "no viable hypothesis" on one side of the UFO debate, that is a rather telling handicap.

[20] All the information in this paragraph comes from Robert Sheaffer, "President Carter's 'UFO' Is Identified as the Planet Venus," <u>Humanist</u>, July 1977, pp. 46-47. It is now widely agreed that Governor Carter saw Venus rather than a UFO; see also Shapley, p. 1128, and "Is There Something . . . ?," p. 56. Nonetheless, UFO supporters continue to cite the Carter incident as a pro-UFO example.

Bibliography

For bibliography form, see pp. 420–422.

Condon, Edward U. <u>Scientific Study of Unidentified Flying Objects</u>. New York: Bantam, 1969.

Emenegger, Robert. <u>UFO's Past, Present, and Future</u>. New York: Ballantine, 1974.

Gallup, George. "Most Americans Believe in UFOs." <u>San Francisco Chronicle</u>, 25 May 1978, p. 2.

The right form for a second bibliography entry by the same author.

----------. "UFO's, Ghosts and True Believers." <u>San Francisco Chronicle</u>, 15 June 1978, p. 2.

Gardner, Martin. "The Third Coming." <u>New York Review of Books</u>, 26 Jan. 1978, pp. 21-22.

Hynek, J. Allen. <u>The Hynek UFO Report</u>. New York: Dell, 1977.

----------. <u>The UFO Experience: A Scientific Inquiry</u>. New York: Ballantine, 1972.

"Is There Something to UFO's After All?" <u>U.S. News & World Report</u>, 20 Feb. 1978, p. 56.

Jacobs, David Michael. <u>The UFO Controversy in America</u>. Bloomington: Indiana Univ. Press, 1975.

Klass, Philip J. <u>UFOs Explained</u>. 1974; rpt. New York: Vintage, 1976.

                              Bibliography 2

----------, and J. Allen Hynek. "The Great UFO Debate."

     Christian Science Monitor, 24 Aug. 1977, pp. 11-13.

"NASA Refuses to Reopen Investigation of U.F.O.'s." New

     York Times, 28 Dec. 1977, Sec. I, p. 14.

Rensberger, Boyce. "U.F.O. Interest Rising, Stirred by

     Science Fiction Films." New York Times, 9 Dec. 1977,

     Sec. II, p. 1.

Sagan, Carl, and Thornton Page, eds. UFO's--a Scientific

     Debate. Ithaca: Cornell Univ. Press, 1972.

San Francisco Chronicle, 24 Oct. 1978, pp. 1, 16; 14 Nov.

     1978, p. 10.

Shapley, D. "UFO's Just Will Not Go Away." Science, 198

     (1977), 1128.

Sheaffer, Robert. "President Carter's 'UFO' Is Identified

     as the Planet Venus." Humanist, July 1977, pp. 46-47.

Vallee, Jacques. UFO's in Space: Anatomy of a Phenomenon.

     1965; rpt. New York: Ballantine, 1977.

A Sample Handwritten Page

3

then moved away...then disappeared."[10] As late as 1976 Mr. Carter maintained in an interview that his experience had proved to him the reality of U.F.O.'s. [11]

In the face of so much testimony from varied sources, we might be inclined in advance to favor the UFO hypothesis -- the notion that some astonishingly advanced vehicles have veered and vanished in our skies. But an awareness of history should make us recall that large numbers of people can be wrong about what they saw; perceptual expectations such as a belief in witches, demons, or ghosts have caused whole societies to "see things." UFO's could be merely what one critic calls "the modern myth"-- a quasi-religious fantasy rather than a physical actuality.[12] The only way to settle the issue is to appeal, not to popular belief or even to the number of eyewitnesses, but to the quality of the evidence that has been produced so far. When we do, we will have to conclude that the present state of our knowledge does not justify a belief in U.F.O.'s.

Before saying for sure that some controversial phenomenon exists, we would do well to find out what the most tough-minded and knowledgeable experts think about it. No such phenomenon has ever been as thoroughly investigated as have U.F.O's -- and the results have been entirely negative. During the

EXERCISES

1. How would you characterize the tone of the UFO paper? Has the writer dealt fairly with the position she opposes?

2. Why did the writer begin with three full paragraphs detailing the extent of current interest in UFO's? What different effect would she have created by revealing her thesis in the opening paragraph?

3. The writer's note cards (pp. 401–402) reveal an interest in head-to-head comparisons between the two leading spokesmen in the UFO controversy. Why do you suppose she omitted such comparisons from the final draft of her paper?

4. Why do you think the writer chose to discuss the "gleaming object" case (p. 5) and the Carter case (pp. 2, 7), as opposed to others? Did these cases give her argument more weight than it would have had without them? If so, how?

5. A key assumption behind this paper is made explicit in the two closing paragraphs: we should not affirm the existence of something that cannot be detected by scientific investigation. Do you agree? Why, or why not?

6. If you find the writer's argument convincing, prepare a brief summary of the way she has handled evidence effectively. If you disagree, prepare a brief critique of the paper. Deal with specific points that you think the writer neglected or mishandled. Be sure, however, that your position is more, not less, comprehensive than the writer's if you are challenging it.

AN EXPLANATORY RESEARCH PAPER ON COMPUTER CRIME

Barry Lewis

English 101

Mr. Swenson

13 May 1983

Computer Theft: Crime Wave of the Future?

It is hardly a secret these days that computers are quickly becoming an indispensable feature of our lives. The Internal Revenue Service, the Census Bureau, Social Security, banks, insurance companies, corporations, universities, hospitals, small businesses, farmers, families, and students all use computers to maintain files, solve problems, and perform many other vital operations. Our checking accounts, taxes, bills, school registration, and grades are all routinely handled by computer. With personal computer sales

for 1982 estimated at 2.8 million units as compared with 724,000 in 1980 ("The Computer Moves In," 1983, p. 14), the age of universal data processing is at hand. It is little wonder that _Time_'s "Man of the Year" for 1982 was no man at all but a machine, the computer ("The Computer Moves in," 1983).

But if our number one hit is now the computer, its flip side is bound to be computer crime. In the new

2

cybernetic world, just how safe from theft and misuse will
our records and money be? How well can access to sensitive
data be controlled? Will computer fraud become, as The
Futurist magazine predicted back in 1976, "the dominant mode
of criminal conduct" in America ("Crime in a Cashless Society,"
1976, p. 132)?

The problem of computer crime is such a novelty that we
must still consult experts to learn just what the phenomenon
is. We must go, for example, to the U.S. Department of
Justice's publication Computer Crime: Criminal Justice
Resource Manual, which divides the field into the introduction of fraudulent records or data into a computer system;
unauthorized use of computer-related facilities; the alter-
ing or destroying of information or files; and the stealing
of money, financial instruments, property, services, or valuable data (SRI International, 1977, p. 5). And if that
sounds too abstract, the manual also gets down to specific
capers, including "data diddling," "salami techniques" (such
as rounding down on accounts and depositing the fractions of
a cent in a favored account), and "scavenging" to obtain procedures, codes, and proprietary secrets (SRI International,
1977, pp. 9-29).

Though computer crime is in its infancy, outlaws have

Through division (pp. 45–47), the writer surveys the various types of computer crime.

3

Examples of current and potential crimes render the topic more concrete.

already disabled computers, held them for ransom, destroyed essential files, stolen equipment, pirated programs, created huge insurance frauds, and "borrowed" company time to develop

Several items from the reference list are combined in one citation.

gambling systems (Bartimo, 1983; Gomes, 1982; Parker, 1976; Whiteside, 1978). Nevertheless, bigger game may lie ahead. Recent articles have speculated about the advent of electronic terrorism and war, whereby extremists or enemy powers may create riots by crippling the computers that process welfare checks or black out the air-traffic-control computers across the country. Donn Parker (1976), a Stanford Research Institute computer security expert and the author of <u>Crime by Computer</u>, has outlined several possible battle plans that might cause national or even international computer failures.

Whether or not such scenarios are exaggerated, there is no doubt that computer theft is already lucrative, relatively easy, and on the rise. Donn Parker believes that wrongdoers will find the computer a more and more attractive target. The average computer bank robbery, he points out, nets

To indicate the widening scope of the problem, the writer calls on authorities and numerical data.

$500,000 as opposed to $2500 for the conventional version. Estimated annual losses from computer crime already range from $300 million to $5 billion (Ball, 1982). Everyone knows, furthermore, that those figures are unrealistically low. "Much chicanery goes undetected, and even when culprits

4

are caught, the victimized company often tries to hush up the scandal and absorb its losses rather than admit to having poor computer security" (Alexander, 1982, p. 60).

It is a mistake, furthermore, to think that only a handful of evil geniuses are capable of computer fraud.   The robbers, according to one expert's profile,

> tend to be relatively honest and in a position
> of trust; few would do anything to harm another
> human, and most do not consider their crime to
> be truly dishonest. . . .   Between the ages of
> 18 and 30, they are usually bright, eager,
> highly motivated, adventuresome, and willing
> to accept technical challenges.   Actually,
> they sound like the type of person managers
> would like to employ.   (Ball, 1982, p. 23)

One typical, if spectacular, case can illustrate how the odds on computer theft presently favor the criminal. On October 25, 1978, Stanley Mark Rifkin, a 32-year-old computer consultant who still phoned his mother every day, managed to steal $10.2 million from Security National Bank in Los Angeles--with three telephone calls and a computer code number.   The theft went unnoticed for eight days and

Standard form for an extracted quotation (p. 335)

One case dramatically illustrates lax computer security.

5

was discovered then only because Rifkin's lawyer had revealed
it to an unsuspecting agent of the FBI's white-collar crime
unit in Los Angeles. Nor did Rifkin have to draw on much
of his expertise to carry out the plan. The bank's passwords were reportedly posted on a bulletin board, and Rifkin
obtained the code for transferring funds simply by posing as
a Federal Reserve Bank consultant (Henderson & Young, 1981).

The Rifkin story makes it clear that we are still in
the horse-and-buggy stage of computer security.[1] Such conventional safeguards as identification cards, keys, badges,
code numbers, and passwords would cause little trouble for
an alert, strategically placed thief. Moreover, there is a
natural tendency for bright, inquisitive people to test
their wits against a computer's "electronic fences"--and
for the winning secret to be passed around.

In 1981, for example, undergraduates at the University
of California at Berkeley found an astonishingly simple way
to invade other users' programs within the university's
computer network. Luckily, the students had no criminal

[1]"Most managers," observes Herman MacDaniel, president
of Management Resources International, "have the misconcep-
tion that the technology is so sophisticated that it doesn't
need to be protected. But most of the frauds have been [com-
mitted] by people who were not technically [sophisticated]"
("Locking the Electronic File Cabinet," 1982, p. 123).

Marginal notes:

Form for citing coauthors of a single article

A second long example reinforces the writer's point.

Substantive footnotes can be combined with reference list citation.

6

intent; they planted anonymous messages within the computer
explaining its vulnerability (Petit, 1982). Not so luckily,
the January 11, 1982, issue of <u>InfoWorld</u>, a computer trade
newsletter, divulged the incident. Appalled officers of the
Stanford Research Institute, the Computer and Business Equipment Manufacturers Association, and the National Security
Agency only managed to spread the tantalizing news to potential thieves (Kolata, 1982).

Needless to say, the would-be computer crook will face
tougher obstacles in the future. New programs are being
developed to trace internal transactions (Levin, 1983).
Transactions outside banks are now increasingly protected
by "encryption," a mathematical scrambling procedure
(Meinel, 1982). Furthermore, fingerprint identification
devices, retina scanners, and "signature dynamics" machines
may soon be used to control access to data and equipment
(Yulsman, 1982).

Even with better management and technology, however,
the forces of crime prevention will be handicapped until
the law itself is brought up to date. As of now, specific
legal deterrents to computer fraud exist only at the state
level--and in only eleven states (Frenkel, 1982). As Alan
G. Merten, professor of computer and information systems at

Having sketched the present situation, the writer turns to recent developments that could make computer crime difficult.

But in one important area —the law—reform has scarcely begun.

7

the University of Michigan, acknowledges, "There just aren't laws out there yet" ("Locking the Electronic File Cabinet," 1982, p. 124). And though the FBI has established a school to train special agents in investigating computer crime, under current standards of evidence conviction is difficult and sentencing light. "Our legal system," says August Bequai in White-Collar Crime: A Twentieth-Century Crisis, "has fallen behind our technology" (1978, p. 109).

The writer concludes by hazarding a general pre-diction about the future of computer crime.

It seems safe to predict that in the longer run, neither side will permanently gain the upper hand. This struggle, like the nuclear arms race, will be one of moves and counter-moves based on inside knowledge of the other party's latest advances. How can we be sure that the government, the banks, and the corporations will not find a way to make their sys-tems absolutely crimeproof? The answer is that the security

The writer has saved two striking quotations for the end of his paper.

devices will be invented, of course, by computer experts-- experts "just like Stan Rifkin" (Henderson & Young, 1981, p. 47). As one analyst has concluded with a sigh, "the only completely secure computer would be one that nobody could use" (Conniff, 1982), p. 94).

8

References

Alexander, C. Crackdown on computer capers. Time, February
8, 1982, pp. 60-61.

Ball, L. D. Computer crime. Technology Review, April 1982,
pp. 21-27; 30.

Bartimo, J. Three WP typists at Ford named in betting operation. Computerworld, January 10, 1983, p. 11.

Bequai, A. White-collar crime: A twentieth-century crisis.
Lexington, Mass.: Lexington Books, 1978.

The computer moves in. Time, January 3, 1983, pp. 14-24.

Conniff, R. Computer war. Science Digest, January 1982,
pp. 14-15; 26; 28; 94.

Crime in a cashless society. The Futurist, June 1976,
p. 132.

Frenkel, K. A. Computers in court. Technology Review,
April 1982, pp. 28-29.

Gomes, L. Secrets of the software pirates. Esquire, January 1982, pp. 58-65.

Henderson, B., & Young, J. The heist. Esquire, May 1981,
pp. 36-47.

Kolata, G. Students discover computer threat. Science,
1982, 215, 1216-1217.

References 9

Levin, S. E.   Security possible in communications networks. _Computerworld_, January 31, 1983, pp. 5-10.

Locking the electronic file cabinet.   _Business Week_, October 18, 1982, pp. 123-124.

Meinel, C.   Encryption: Can spies and thieves break it? _Technology Review_, November/December 1982, pp. 72-74.

Parker, D. B.   _Crime by computer_.   New York: Scribner's, 1976.

Petit, C.   UC students' computer trick worries experts.   _San Francisco Chronicle_, March 2, 1982, p. 6.

SRI International.   _Computer crime: Criminal justice resource manual_.   Washington, D.C.: U.S. Department of Justice, 1977.

Whiteside, T.   _Computer capers: tales of electronic thievery, embezzlement, and fraud_.   New York: Crowell, 1978.

Yulsman, T.   Amazing laser locks.   _Science Digest_, June 1982, pp. 26; 28.

EXERCISES

7. Why did the writer begin with remarks about the growing importance of computers in our society? Would the paper have been more, or less, effective without that opening paragraph? Think of possible reasons for either answer.

8. The writer's first idea (p. 400) was to write about a much narrower topic: the breaking of long-distance telephone codes. Was he well-advised to tackle the whole field of computer crime instead? What aspect of that field makes his choice look more sensible than it otherwise would?

9. What is the writer's attitude toward lawbreaking? Would his paper have been more, or less, engaging if he had carried out his early intention (p. 400) of denouncing computer criminals?

10. Compare this writer's use of reference list citation form to the UFO writer's use of MLA form. Which system is more efficient? more informative? less distracting?

PART VI
PRACTICAL WRITING

17

THE EXAMINATION ESSAY

All the skills you are learning in a composition course will help you in answering so-called "essay questions" on examinations. Obviously, though, the high-pressure exam situation calls for certain adjustments of method. Having little time to plan an essay and even less time to revise it, you must make quick, sensible decisions and abide by them. Also, you should bear in mind that the grader of your blue book will be reading rapidly, looking not for subtleties but for signs that you have grasped the relevant material and stated a coherent, well-supported position. If the subtleties are there to be perceived, so much the better; but your first job is to ensure that the grader cannot miss your main ideas.

Here, then, are ten essential principles, the first of which can be put into operation weeks before the exam:

1. *Try to anticipate questions.* Students who consistently write successful examination essays do not just get lucky when they see what the question is. Throughout the term they have been reading, listening, and note-taking with attention to broad patterns of meaning, and they arrive at the exam with ideas that *tie together* the assigned

material. Some of those ideas ought to prove useful if they reflect the instructor's own notion of what deserves emphasis.

2. *Read the question with care.* Pressure, haste, and a wish to make use of memorized information can mislead you into writing answers to questions that were not asked. You *must* pause and study the wording of the question. If you are to contrast X with Y, do not give ninety percent of your emphasis to X. If you are to state the relationship between A and B, do not throw in C for good measure. And if the question tells you to analyze the content and style of a quoted passage, remember that a double effort on content alone will be wasted. Break the question into its natural parts and attend to all of them.

3. *Gauge your available time.* Every question on an exam has a point value which you can quickly translate into a time value. A 30-point question in a 50-minute, 100-point exam should not take much more of your time than 15 minutes (30 percent of 50). If you find yourself running over, stop and leave some blank space while you get something written on *all* other questions.

4. *Plan your essay.* For longer answers, take the necessary time to draw up a scratch outline (p. 105), and check the outline against the question to make sure it covers the required ground. This will enable you to write confidently and quickly.

5. *Do not waste time restating the question.* A grader can only be annoyed by a hollow introductory paragraph that merely announces your willingness to address the topic. The grader is already looking for ideas.

6. *State your thesis in the opening paragraph.* Fairly or unfairly, graders tend to decide after one or two paragraphs whether a student has a clear thesis to present. Perhaps a negative impression will be erased later—but do not count on it. Rather, use the opening paragraph to *announce your main point* and *establish the structure of everything that follows.* You cannot make your strategy too obvious. The more obvious the better, provided your thesis directly answers the question that has been posed.

7. *Keep to the point.* Digressions, or passages that stray from the case being made, are of questionable value in any essay. In an examination essay you simply have no time for them. Refrain from trying to befriend your grader with humorous asides, pleas for sympathy, or reflections about the swift hands of the clock. If you can imagine the mental state of someone who has been reading, say, fifty consecutive essays on the same topic, you will realize that this is no one to be trifled with.

8. *Be emphatic.* Your ideas may be complex, but your way of presenting them should be direct and plain. If you like, underline your leading points to ensure that they will not be overlooked.

9. *Support your generalizations.* Most essay questions are broad enough to allow for a variety of "right" answers. An experienced

grader will be looking, not for a single, all-important idea, but for evidence that you have done the reading and have thought about it carefully. Your own ideas, backed by detailed references to the assigned material, will be much more impressive than unsupported statements taken directly from lectures and textbooks.

10. *Read through your completed answer.* If time permits, go over your exam essay as if you were the grader and try to catch inconsistencies, incoherent sentences, illegible scribbles, and mistaken predictions about what follows. Cross out whole paragraphs if necessary, sending your grader to an extra page in the back of the blue book.

To get a further idea of the way an examination answer should go straight to the point, look at these excerpts from an English final.

Question: Who would you say is the central character in *Heart of Darkness*, Kurtz or Marlow? Justify your choice by detailed reference to the text.

Answer: The central character in *Heart of Darkness* is surely Marlow, not Kurtz. Three considerations make this choice necessary. In the first place, Marlow as the storyteller is constantly in front of us, talking about his own experience and ideas. Kurtz, by contrast, is scarcely seen or heard at all. Second, it is Marlow, not Kurtz, who survives with a changed attitude. And third, Marlow is portrayed with much more psychological complexity than Kurtz.

thesis first

a preview of the main supporting points

Let us look first at Kurtz's actual appearances in the story, and note how rare and brief they are. . . .

It is generally true that the central character of a story undergoes some significant change during the time covered by the narrative. Although Kurtz has indeed changed dramatically, the entire change has occurred *before* the action of *Heart of Darkness* begins. Marlow, by contrast, emerges *from the narrated events* a different man. Note, for example, ...

each of the previewed points receives a paragraph of its own

Finally, no one doubts that the central character of a story ought to be the most psychologically complex figure. At first glance, we might regard Kurtz as extremely complex—a would-be savior who has turned into a fiend. Note, however, that the whole process of development has been omitted; Kurtz is simply *declared* to have lost all of his Christian principles. Compared to Marlow, whose excited perceptions and confused moralizing engage us throughout the story, Kurtz is essentially two-dimensional. . . .

18

THE BUSINESS LETTER

To write an effective business letter you must come across as "all business." Your reader will not expect to be charmed by oddities of phrasing, sarcastic gibes, novelties of spelling and punctuation, or displays of your ability to change your mind in the middle of a paragraph. The likelihood of a good reception for your letter will be raised by neatness, accuracy, consistency, courtesy, efficiently concise and unpretentious statement, and adherence to standard form.

CONVENTIONS

Customary Elements

Examine the following sample business letter:

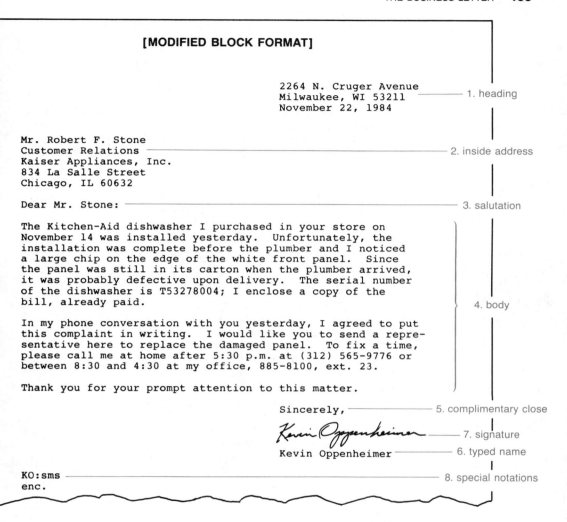

[MODIFIED BLOCK FORMAT]

2264 N. Cruger Avenue —————— 1. heading
Milwaukee, WI 53211
November 22, 1984

Mr. Robert F. Stone
Customer Relations ——————————————————— 2. inside address
Kaiser Appliances, Inc.
834 La Salle Street
Chicago, IL 60632

Dear Mr. Stone: ———————————————————— 3. salutation

The Kitchen-Aid dishwasher I purchased in your store on
November 14 was installed yesterday. Unfortunately, the
installation was complete before the plumber and I noticed
a large chip on the edge of the white front panel. Since
the panel was still in its carton when the plumber arrived,
it was probably defective upon delivery. The serial number
of the dishwasher is T53278004; I enclose a copy of the
bill, already paid.

In my phone conversation with you yesterday, I agreed to put
this complaint in writing. I would like you to send a representative here to replace the damaged panel. To fix a time,
please call me at home after 5:30 p.m. at (312) 565-9776 or
between 8:30 and 4:30 at my office, 885-8100, ext. 23. } 4. body

Thank you for your prompt attention to this matter.

Sincerely, —————————— 5. complimentary close

Kevin Oppenheimer ——————— 7. signature
Kevin Oppenheimer ———————— 6. typed name

KO:sms ———————————————————————— 8. special notations
enc.

Here you see:

1. *The heading.* It contains your address and the date of writing. Notice the absence of end punctuation.
2. *The inside address.* Place this address high (or low) enough so that the body of the letter will appear centered on the page. Include the name of the addressee, that person's title or office, the name of the company or institution, and the full address:

Joan Lacey, M.D.   Mr. Kenneth Herbert
Pioneer Medical Group   Director of Personnel
45 Arrow Avenue   Cordial Fruit Cooperative
Omaha, NE 68104   636 Plumeria Boulevard
                                    Honolulu, HI 96815

3. *The salutation.* This formal greeting appears two lines lower than the inside address:

```
Dear Dr. Lacey:            Dear Ms. Diaz:

Dear Mr. Herbert:          Dear Reverend Melville:
```

Ms. is now the preferred form for addressing a woman who has no other title such as *Dr.* or *Professor.* Use *Miss* or *Mrs.* only if your correspondent has put that title before her own typed name in a letter to you: *(Mrs.) Estelle Kohut.* And unless you see otherwise, you should assume that a woman wishes to be known by her own first name, not her husband's.

When writing to an institution or a business, you can avoid the possibly offensive *Dear Sir* or *Dear Sirs* by choosing a neutral salutation:

```
Dear Personnel Manager:     Dear Editor:

Dear Sir or Madam:          Dear Macy's:

Dear Bursar:                To Whom It May Concern:
```

Note that business salutations end with a colon. Only if the addressee happens to be a friend should you strike a more informal note: *Dear Estelle, Dear Andy, ...*

4. *The body.* Use the body of your letter to explain the situation and to make your request or response in a straightforward, concise way. You can write briefer paragraphs than you would use in an essay. Prefer middle-level diction, avoiding both slang and legalese: not × *You really put one over on me* or × *The undersigned was heretofore not apprised of the circumstances cited hereabove* but *I was not aware of the problem.*

Single-space the paragraphs of your letter, but leave a double space between one paragraph and the next.

5. *The complimentary close.* Type the complimentary close three lines below the last line of the body. The most common formulas are:

```
Sincerely,                  Yours sincerely,

Sincerely yours,            Very truly yours,

Yours truly,                Cordially,
```

Of these tags, *Cordially* is the only one that hints at actual feeling.

6. *Your typed name.* Leave four lines between the complimentary close and your typed name as you intend to sign it. If you have a professional title or role that is relevant to the purpose of the letter, add it directly below your name:

```
Nicole Pinsky               Jackson Marley
Assistant Manager           Lecturer
```

In general, such titles are appropriate when you are using letterhead stationery.

7. *Your signature.* Always use blue or black ink. Match your signature and your typed name; a briefer signature is a sign of impatience.

8. *Special notations.* Lowest on the page, always flush left, come notations to indicate the following circumstances if they are applicable:

NOTATION	MEANING
cc: A. Pitts F. Adler	"Carbon copies" (probably photo-copies) are being simultaneously sent to interested parties Pitts and Adler.
enc.	The mailing contains an enclo-sure (always mentioned in the body of the letter).
att.	A document has been attached to the letter.
BR:clc	The writer (initials *BR*) has used the services of a typist (initials *CLC*).

Alternative Formats

There are three recognized ways of handling the arrangement of a business letter's elements on the page. You can choose any of the three, but they make somewhat different impressions. For extreme impersonality, **block format** works best. A middle style, very commonly used, is **modified block format**. And if you want your business letter to have some of the flavor of a personal letter, **indented format** is available.

Here are the three formats in a nutshell:

	BLOCK FORMAT	MODIFIED BLOCK FORMAT	INDENTED FORMAT
Heading	Flush left	Toward right margin	Toward right margin
Inside Address	Flush left	Flush left	Flush left
First Lines of Paragraphs	Flush left	Flush left	Indented 5–10 spaces
Complimentary Close, Name, and Signature	Flush left	Toward right margin	Toward right margin
Special Notations	Flush left	Flush left	Flush left

("Flush left" means that the lines begin at the left margin. "Toward right margin" means that the lines should end at or near the right margin but not beyond it.)

These differences may sound complicated, but they are easy to see in examples:

Block Format: p. 469
Modified Block Format: pp. 465, 470
Indented Format: p. 471

Note that indented format is simply modified block format plus indentions for the first lines of paragraphs.

The Envelope

Make the address on your envelope identical to the inside address. In the upper left corner, type your own address as it appears in the heading:

```
Kevin Oppenheimer
2264 N. Cruger Avenue
Milwaukee, WI 53211



                    Mr. Robert F. Stone
                    Customer Relations
                    Kaiser Appliances, Inc.
                    834 La Salle Street
                    Chicago, IL 60632
```

PURPOSES

Asking for Information

Make your inquiry brief, and limit your request to information that can be sent in a brief reply or an available brochure. Be specific, so that there can be no doubt about which facts you need.

Ordering Merchandise

Begin by stating which items you are ordering, using both product names and stock or catalog page numbers. Tell how many units of each item you are ordering, the price per item, and the total price. If you want to receive the shipment at a different address, say so. Mention that you are enclosing payment, ask to be billed, or indicate a credit-card number:

[BLOCK FORMAT]

```
36 Hawthorne Hall
University of the North
Bridgewater, CT 06413
January 15, 1984


NF Systems, Ltd.
P. O. Box 76363
Atlanta, GA 30358

Dear NF Systems:

Please send me the following software items for use on the
IBM Personal Computer as described on page 40 in the December
1983 issue of Softalk magazine:

    1 "Household Aids," a group of six programs,
         total package,                          $49.95
    1 "Check Register," includes 40 ledger/
         budget headings,                         39.95

Kindly ship this merchandise to the address shown above.  I
enclose my check #186 for $89.90.  Since your advertisement
does not specify shipping costs, please bill me for them
separately if they are not included in the prices.

Sincerely yours,

Lily Marks

Lily Marks
```

Stating a Claim

Take a courteous but firm tone, setting forth the facts so fully and clearly that your reader will be able to act on your letter without having to ask for more information. If you are complaining about a purchase, supply the date of purchase, the model and serial number, and a brief description. If you have been mistakenly billed twice for the same service or product, state what that service or product is, the date of your payment, and the check number if you paid by check. If possible, enclose a photocopy of the canceled check (both sides). In a second paragraph, calmly and fairly state what adjustment you think you are entitled to.

Making an Application

Tailor your letter to the particular job, grant, or program of study you are applying for. Name the opening precisely. If you are asking to be considered for a job, explain how you heard about it. If a person in authority recommended that you apply, say who it was. Tell how you can be reached and express your willingness to be interviewed.

When applying for a job, include your résumé (pp. 472–474) and mention that you have included it. Emphasize those elements in the résumé that qualify you for *this* position. Avoid boasting and false modesty alike. The idea to get across is that the facts of your record make such a strong case for your application that no special pleading is necessary.

The following letters illustrate how an applicant can state qualifications in different ways for different opportunities:

[MODIFIED BLOCK FORMAT]

137-20 Crescent Street
Flushing, NY 11367
August 17, 1984

Mr. Patrick Lyons
974 CHOB
Washington, DC 20510

Dear Mr. Lyons:

Professor Alan Gibson of the Political Science Department at Queens College (City University of New York) has suggested I write to you about working as a correspondent in Representative Schiavo's Washington office beginning this fall. I have completed my second year at Queens as a Political Science major with a minor in English and plan to take a year off from school to supplement my education with relevant work away from the classroom. At the same time, I hope to earn some money for the remaining two years of college.

From my enclosed résumé, you can see that I have experience in writing and editing. Writing editorials for The Phoenix, a student-run newspaper, has sharpened my political sense; I enclose an editorial and an article as a writing sample. As the Assistant Editor of the theater guide, A Budget Guide to Broadway (Queens Press, 1984), I corresponded with readers, researchers, and various entertainment organizations; I also did some research, hired personnel, and edited copy. I can type 65 words per minute and can use a word processor. I believe these skills will help me learn the ins and outs of corresponding for the Representative.

Professor Gibson has offered to write you about me, and a transcript of my grades, which I understand you require, is being sent to you by the Queens College Registrar. I would be happy to appear for an interview either in New York or in Washington, at your convenience.

Please call me at (212) 317-1964 between 9 a.m. and 5:30 p.m.

Sincerely yours,

Louise Lenahan

Louise Lenahan

LL/gs
encl.

[INDENTED FORMAT]

137-20 Crescent Street
Flushing, NY 11367
August 17, 1984

Ms. Augusta Sterling
Dept. AT-952
P. O. Box 6614
Grand Central Station
New York, NY 10163

Dear Ms. Sterling:

I am applying for the position of Market Research Project Assistant to Law Firm, which was advertised in the New York Times, August 16. I have completed my second year at Queens College as a political science major with an English minor and plan to take a year off from school to supplement my education with relevant work. At the same time, I hope to earn some money for the remaining two years of college.

This summer I have been working as Assistant Editor of The Budget Guide to Broadway (Queens Press, 1984). In addition to my editorial duties, I research a number of questions about the theater and the entertainment industry in New York and regularly use such facilities as the New York Public Library, the Columbia University Library, and the Library of the Performing Arts. Last year I worked as a part-time research assistant to Professor Alan Gibson of the Queens College Political Science Department, who is writing a book on a history of voting practices among operators of small businesses in the United States. In both instances, the work required familiarity with reference materials and special collections, strong writing and typing skills, accuracy, and patience.

Since I plan to attend law school after I graduate from Queens, I am especially interested in spending next year with a law firm. I can send you the names of several references in addition to Professor Gibson, and would be grateful for the chance to be interviewed. Please write to me at the above address or call me at (212) 317-1964 between 9 a.m. and 5:30 p.m.

Sincerely yours,

Louise Lenahan

Louise Lenahan

LL:gs
encl.

19

THE RÉSUMÉ

Your résumé is a brief (usually one-page) record of your career and qualifications. Along with your letter of application (pp. 469–471), it can land you a job interview. To that end it should be clear, easy on the eye, and totally favorable in emphasis. Have your résumé typed by a professional if you are unsure of your typing skills.

Divide your résumé into the following sections:

1. *Personal information.* Provide only what is necessary: name, present address, permanent address, phone numbers. Add your age, marital status, and condition of health only if you believe they are relevant to the job you want.
2. *Education.* Begin with the college you currently attend or have attended most recently, and work backward to high school. (If you have already graduated from college, omit high school.) Give dates of attendance, degrees attained, major and minor areas of study, and memberships in special societies. Briefly explain any outstanding projects or courses. Include your gradepoint average only if it happens to be high.
3. *Work experience.* Begin with your current or most recent employment and list all relevant jobs since high school. Try not to leave suspicious-

A SAMPLE RÉSUMÉ

LOUISE LENAHAN

Current Address:
137-20 Crescent Street
Flushing, NY 11367
(212) 317-1964

Permanent Address:
28 Pasteur Drive
Glen Cove, NY 11542
(516) 676-0620

EDUCATION: Queens College, Flushing, New York 11367
Majoring in Political Science with emphasis on
Government.
Minoring in English. Additional course sequence
in Writing for the Law.
B.A. expected June 1986.

Locust Valley High School, Locust Valley, New
York.
Received Regents Diploma with Distinction, June
1982.

EXPERIENCE:

Summer, 1984   Assistant Editor, <u>A Budget Guide to Broad-</u>
<u>way</u>. Widely sold entertainment guide to
New York. Written by Queens College
students for the Queens Press. Performed
a variety of editorial, research, and
clerical functions.

1982-84   Research Asssistant to Professor Alan
Gibson, Political Science Department,
Queens College. Research tasks included
documentation, following statistical
trends, drawing graphs, corresponding
with government and university libraries,
editing copy. Part-time.

1983-84   Features Editor, <u>The Phoenix</u>, a weekly
newsmagazine. Wrote editorials and a
weekly feature on undergraduate issues.

1982   Volunteer tutor of Chinese immigrants.
Conducted conversations in English (as a
Second Language). Helped accustom new
immigrants to American society. Fall
semester.

HONORS: Elected President of Queens College Pre-Law
Society, 1984.

SKILLS: Type 65 wpm.
Use word processor.
Speak French.

REFERENCES: Placement Office
Queens College
Kissena Boulevard
Flushing, NY 11367

looking gaps of time. Give the name and address of each employer, the dates of employment, and a brief description of your duties. Include part-time or volunteer work that may be relevant. Remember that you can mention relevant skills learned on a job that seems unrelated. If you are seeking a teaching position, consider beginning this part of your résumé with a section called *Teaching Experience* and following it with another called *Other Work Experience.*

4. *Special skills, activities, and honors.* Include special competencies that make you a desirable candidate, such as proficiency in a foreign language, ability to operate equipment, or skill in unusual procedures or techniques. Mention any honors, travel, or community service.

5. *References.* Supply the address of your college placement office, which will send out your dossier (dáhss-ee-ay) upon request. The dossier is a complete file of your credentials, including all letters of recommendation and transcripts. You may wish to give the names, positions, and addresses of three people you can trust to write strong letters in your behalf. Be sure you have their permission, however.

Further advice:

1. *Keep the format clear and the text concise.* Single-space within each section and double-space between sections. Try to keep your résumé to one page; do not exceed two pages.

2. *Do not mention the salary you want.* You will be considered for more openings if you stay flexible on this point.

3. *Update your résumé periodically.* Do not hesitate to ask for new letters of recommendation.

4. *Rewrite your résumé for a particular job opening.* Rewriting allows you to highlight those elements of your background that will suit the job you are aiming for.

GLOSSARY OF TERMS

The glossary offers simple definitions of terms used in this book. Words appearing in **boldface** have separate entries which you can consult if the term is unfamiliar. The abbreviation *cf.* means "compare"—that is, note the difference between the term being defined and another. And *e.g.* means "for example."

abbreviation A shortened word, with the addition of a period to indicate the omission *(Dr.)*. Cf. **acronym**.

absolute *(n.)* An **adjective** or **adverb** that does not lend itself to qualification or comparison, since it already contains an idea of the highest degree: *infinite, uniquely,* etc. Since something *unique* stands by itself, it would be illogical to write *the most unique experience* or *She performed more uniquely than ever.* Cf. **absolute phrase**.

absolute phrase A **phrase** that, instead of modifying a particular word, acts like an **adverb** to the rest of the sentence in which it appears:

ABS PHRASE
- *All struggle over,* the troops lay down their arms.

ABS PHRASE
- *Time out having been called,* four commercials were shown.

Absolute phrases are not considered mistakes of usage. Cf. **absolute, dangling modifier,** and **misrelated modifier.**

abstract   A concise summary of an article, often printed at the head of the article or collected in a book covering the year's research in a certain field. Cf. **index.**

abstract language   Words that make no appeal to the senses: *aspect, comprehensible, enthusiasm, virtuously,* etc. Cf. **concrete language.**

acronym   A word formed from the initial letters of words in a name—e.g., *NOW,* formed from the National Organization for Women. Cf. **abbreviation.**

active voice   See **voice.**

ad hominem reasoning   A form of **evading the question** whereby someone tries to discredit a position by scorning the person, party, or interest that supports that position.

adjectival clause   See **clause.**

adjective   A **modifier** of a **noun, pronoun,** or other **nounlike element**—e.g., *strong* in *a strong contender.* Most adjectives can be compared: *strong, stronger, strongest.* See **degree.**

adverb   A word **modifying** either a **verb,** an **adjective,** another adverb, a **preposition,** an **infinitive,** a **participle,** a **phrase,** a **clause,** or a whole **sentence:** *now, clearly, moreover,* etc. Any one-word **modifier** that is not an adjective or an **article** must be an adverb.

adverbial clause   See **clause.**

agreement   In **grammar,** the matching of **subjects** and **verbs** in **number** and **person.** In *I stumble,* e.g., the verb *stumble* "agrees with" the subject *I;* both are singular and first-person in form. Cf. **pronoun reference.**

allusion   A passing reference to a work or idea, either by directly mentioning it or by borrowing its well-known language. Thus, someone who writes *She took arms against a sea of troubles* is alluding to, but not mentioning, Hamlet's most famous speech. Shakespeare is directly alluded to in the sentence *He did it with Shakespearean flair.* Quotation through allusion differs from **plagiarism** in that readers are expected to notice the reference.

ambiguity   Uncertainty of meaning between two or more possible interpretations. The sentence x *He wants nothing more than fame* is ambiguous. Is fame *all* he wants, or does he want fame more than he wants other things?

analogy   In general, a similarity of features or pattern between two things: *The nearest analogy to human speech may be the songs of whales.* In **rhetoric,** an analogy is an extended likeness purporting to show that the rule or principle behind one thing also holds for the quite different thing being discussed. Thus, someone who disapproves of people leaving their home towns might devise this analogy: *People, like trees, must find their nourishment in the place where they happen to grow up; to seek it elsewhere is as fatal as removing a tree from its roots.* Like most analogies, this one starts with an obvious resemblance and proceeds to a more debatable one.

analysis The breaking of something into its parts or functions and showing how those smaller units go to make up the whole.

annotated bibliography A **bibliography** including brief comments on the content and value of the separate entries.

antecedent The word for which a **pronoun** stands:

> ANT   PRO
> • *Jane* was here yesterday, but today *she* is at school.

> ANT PRO
> • *John, who* is twenty-one, ...

anticipation In narration, the telling of later events before earlier ones. Many effective narratives begin with anticipation and then supply the events that led up to the rendered episode.

anticipatory pattern A structure, such as *both x and y* or *not x but y*, which gives an early signal of the way it will be completed.

APA form The citation style preferred by the American Psychological Association, featuring parenthetical citations and a reference list. Cf. **MLA form**.

aphorism A memorably concise **sentence** conveying a very general assertion: *If wishes were horses, beggars would ride. Aphoristic* and **epigrammatic** are close in meaning.

appositive A word or phrase whose only function is to identify or restate an immediately preceding **noun, pronoun**, or **nounlike element**:

> APP
> • Mike *the butcher* is quite a clown.

> APP
> • We *the people* hope to keep the government in check.

> APP
> • What she wanted, *a cheetah purse,* would be hard to acquire.

Arabic numerals Numerals like *1, 5,* and *12*, as opposed to **Roman numerals** like *I, V,* and *XII*.

argument See **essay**.

article An indicator or determiner immediately preceding a **noun** or **modi-**

fier. Articles themselves may be considered modifiers, along with **adjectives** and **adverbs**. The *definite article* is *the*; the *indefinite articles* are *a* and *an*.

attributive noun   A **noun** serving as an **adjective**: *Massachusetts* in *the Massachusetts way of doing things,* or *gun* in *a gun lover.*

auxiliary   A **verb** form, usually lacking **inflection**, that combines with other verbs to express possibility, likelihood, necessity, obligation, etc. The commonly recognized auxiliaries are *can, could, dare, do, may, might, must, need, ought, should,* and *would,* as in *She can succeed* and *He could become jealous. Is, have,* and their related forms act like auxiliaries in the formation of **tenses**: *He is coming; They have gone.*

baited opener   An introductory **paragraph** which, by presenting its early **sentences** "out of context," teases its reader into continuing to read.

balance   The effect created when a whole **sentence** is controlled by **matching**, as in a *A stoic never cries; a coward never tries.* A balanced sentence typically repeats a grammatical pattern and certain words in order to highlight important differences.

base form of verb   An **infinitive** without *to*: *see, think,* etc. Base forms appear with **auxiliaries** *(should see)* and in the formation of present and future **tenses** *(I see, I will see).*

begging the question   The **fallacy** of treating a debatable idea as if it had already been proved. If, in a paper favoring national health insurance, you assert that only the greedy medical lobby could oppose such an obviously needed program, you are begging the question by assuming the rightness of your position instead of establishing it with **evidence**.

bibliography   A list of consulted works presented at the end of a book, article, or **essay**. Also, a whole book devoted to listing works within a certain **subject area**.

bound element   A word, **phrase**, or **subordinate clause** falling within a **main assertion**. All bound modifiers are also **restrictive**. Cf. **free element**.

bureaucratese   The inflated, important-sounding language often used in government reports—e.g., *finalize* for *complete*.

call number   The number at the upper left corner of every card in the **card catalog** of a library. The call number is the key to locating the item in the **stacks**.

call slip   A card which, when properly filled out, can be submitted to the **circulation desk** of a library, enabling the needed item to be retrieved from the **stacks**.

card catalog   An alphabetical index of a library's printed holdings, with a separate card for each entry. Cf. **microfiche catalog** and **on-line catalog**.

cardinal numbers   Numbers like *one (1)*, *two (2)*, and *three (3)*. Cf. **ordinal numbers**.

case   The **inflectional** form of **nouns** and **pronouns** indicating whether they designate actors (*subjective* case: *I, we, they*), receivers of action (*objective* case: *me, us, them*), or "owners" of the thing or quality modified (*possessive* case: *his* toy, *their* indecision, *Biff's* endorsement). **Personal pronouns** also have **second possessive** forms: *mine, theirs,* etc. See also **double possessive**.

catchall explanation   The **fallacy** of ascribing one cause to phenomena that may have many causes—for example, claiming that unemployment is due entirely to the unreasonable demands of union leaders.

circular reasoning   Reasoning that **begs the question** by reasserting an assumption instead of supporting it. Suppose you wanted to show that prayer in public schools is really constitutional, despite recent Supreme Court decisions to the contrary. If you wrote *The fact that school prayer doesn't violate the Constitution shows that the Supreme Court has been wrong on this issue,* you would be engaging in circular reasoning—using the point to be proved as evidence for a further contention.

circulation desk   The part of a library that accepts **call slips** and delivers books that have been retrieved from the **stacks**.

circumlocution   Roundabout expression—e.g., *when all is said and done* in place of *finally.*

clause   A cluster of words containing a **subject** and a **predicate**. All clauses are either independent or subordinate (dependent). An *independent* clause makes a complete statement and thus can stand alone: *Biff held the cologne in front of the camera.* A *subordinate* clause, which does not make a complete statement, cannot stand alone: *before I go out on the field.* In *I splash myself with this he-man preparation before I go out on the field,* the subordinate clause modifies the main **verb** *splash.*

Among subordinate clauses, an *adjectival* clause serves the function of an **adjective**:

ADJ CLAUSE
* The model, *who was gorgeous,* pretended to faint in ecstasy.

The adjectival clause modifies the noun *model,* as in *the gorgeous model.*

An *adverbial* clause serves the function of an **adverb**:

ADV CLAUSE
* She swore at Biff *when he tried to help her up.*

The adverbial clause modifies the verb *swore,* as in *she swore then.*

And a *noun* clause serves the function of a **noun**:

NOUN CLAUSE
- *That a little cologne could cause such extreme reactions* surprised him.

The noun clause serves as the subject of the verb *surprised,* as in *reactions surprised him.*

cliché   A trite, stereotyped, overused expression: *an open and shut case*; *a miss is as good as a mile.* Most clichés contain **figurative language** that has lost its vividness: *get the lead out, bring the house down,* etc.

collective noun   A **noun** that is singular in form but designates a group of members: *band, family,* etc.

comma splice   See **run-on sentence.**

common gender   The intended sexual neutrality of **pronouns** used to indicate an indefinite party. Traditionally, indefinite *(one)* and masculine personal *(he)* pronouns were used, but the masculine ones are now widely regarded as **sexist language.**

comparative degree   See **degree.**

complement   Usually, an element in the **predicate** that identifies or describes the **subject.** A single-word complement is either a *predicate noun* or a *predicate adjective.*

PRED N
- He is a *fool.*

PRED ADJ
- He is *foolish.*

In addition, a **direct object** can have a complement, known as an *objective complement:*

D OBJ OBJ COMPL
- They consider him *unteachable.*

Infinitives, too, can have complements:

INF COMPL INF
- They beg him to be *serious.*

compound (adj.)   Consisting of more than one word, as in a *compound noun (ice cream)*, a *compound preposition (in spite of)*, or a *compound subject (He and she* were there).

concession **(conceding)**   In argument, the granting of an opposing point, usually with the purpose of showing that it does not overturn one's own **thesis.**

conciseness   Economy of expression. Not to be confused with simplicity; conciseness enables a maximum of meaning to be communicated in a minimum of words.

concrete language   Words describing a thing or quality appealing to the senses: *purple, car, buzz, dusty,* etc. Cf. **abstract language**.

conjunction   An un**inflected** word that connects other words, **phrases**, or **clauses**: *and, although,* etc.
    A *coordinating conjunction* joins grammatically similar elements, without turning one into a **modifier** of the other: *and, but, for, nor, or, so, yet.*
    A *subordinating conjunction* joins grammatically dissimilar elements, turning one of them into a modifier and specifying its logical relation to the other —e.g., *Although* in *Although you are sad, I am cheerful.*
    Correlative conjunctions are matched pairs with a coordinating function: *either/or, neither/nor,* etc.

conjunctive adverb   See **sentence adverb**.

connective   A sentence element that joins and relates parts of a sentence. All **conjunctions** and **sentence adverbs** are connectives. So are transitional phrases such as *to be sure, on the other hand.*

connotation   An association that a word calls up, as opposed to its **denotation** or dictionary meaning. Thus, the word *exile* denotes enforced separation from one's home or country, but it *connotes* loneliness, homesickness, and any number of other, more private, thoughts and images.

consonant   A speech sound involving the blockage or diverting of breath: *b, c, d, f, g,* etc. The consonants consist of all the letters of the alphabet that are not **vowels**.

continuity   The felt linkage between consecutive **sentences** or **paragraphs**.

contraction   The condensing of two words to one, with an apostrophe added to replace the omitted letter or letters: *isn't, don't,* etc.

convention   A rule established by custom; also, accepted usage in general. By following the conventions of **standard written English**, writers can allow full attention to be given to their ideas.

coordinating conjunction   See **conjunction**.

coordination   The giving of equal grammatical value to two or more parts of a **sentence**, usually connected by a coordinating **conjunction**: *Apples and eggs are scarce*; *He tried, but he failed.* Cf. **subordination**.

correlative conjunction   See **conjunction**.

cross-indexing   The listing of an item in more than one entry of a catalog or **index**.

dangling modifier   The **modifier** of a term that has been wrongly omitted:

DM
x *Not wishing to be bothered,* the telephone was left off the hook.

> The person who did not wish to be bothered goes unmentioned, and is thus absurdly replaced by *telephone.*

database   A computer file of information. In an **on-line catalog** the library's holdings have been listed as a database. Also, a file of references to, or **abstracts** of, articles, dissertations, documents, etc., that can be retrieved through on-line searching.

dead metaphor   See **metaphor**.

declarative sentence   A **sentence** that makes a statement: *Lambs are woolly.*

definite article   See **article**.

degree   The form of an **adjective** or **adverb** showing its quality, quantity, or intensity. The ordinary, uncompared form of an adjective or adverb is its *positive* degree: *quick, quickly.* The *comparative* degree is intermediate, indicating that the modified term surpasses at least one other member of its group: *quicker, more quickly.* And an adjective or adverb in the *superlative* degree indicates that the modified term surpasses all other members of its group: *quickest, most quickly.*

   Note that the three degrees show increasing extremeness or coverage, but not necessarily increasing size or value: *little, less, least; bad, worse, worst,* etc.

demonstrative adjective   A **demonstrative pronoun** form serving as a **modifier**—e.g., *those* in *those laws.*

demonstrative pronoun   A **pronoun** that singles out what it refers to: *this, that, these,* or *those,* when not used as a **modifier**. *Those* is a demonstrative pronoun in *Those are the laws.* Cf. **demonstrative adjective**.

denotation   The primary, "dictionary," meanings of a word. Cf. **connotation**.

dependent clause   See **clause**.

description   See **essay**.

dialect   A variety of a language distinguishable by the way it is spoken within a certain group or region. Cf. **grapholect**.

dialogue   In narration, the direct representation of speech between two or more persons. Cf. **indirect discourse**.

diction   The choice of words, especially insofar as they contribute to different **tones** or occupy different levels:

FORMAL	MIDDLE	INFORMAL
impecunious	bankrupt	broke
appellation	name	handle
deranged	crazy	nuts
livelihood	job	racket

Extremely informal diction of a faddish character is called *slang*: *a together dude, Your threads gross me out*, etc.

direct object A word naming the item directly acted upon by a **subject** through the activity of a **verb**:

      S   V   D OBJ
- She hit the *jackpot*.

Cf. **indirect object** and **object of preposition**.

direct paragraph See **paragraph development**.

double possessive A possessive form (see **case**) using both *of* and *-'s*: *an idea of Linda's*. Cf. **second possessive**.

either-or reasoning Depicting one's own position as the better of an artificially limited and "loaded" pair of alternatives—e.g., asking readers to favor a certain air-pollution measure as the only possible way of avoiding mass asphyxiation.

ellipsis The three or four dots used to indicate material omitted from a quotation: *"about the . . . story."* Longer rows of ellipses are used to indicate omission of lines of verse.

emotionalism The quality of overwrought feeling communicated by someone who is too upset to think clearly. Not to be confused with strong emotion, which can be communicated without any sacrifice of logic.

endnote A **footnote** placed in a consecutive series with others at the end of an article, chapter, or **essay**.

enumeration The device of highlighting key points in a piece of writing by assigning numbers to them.

epigrammatic Ingeniously concise and pointed in phrasing. Professor Spooner's famous slip, *Work is the curse of the drinking classes*, accidentally struck an epigrammatic note.

essay A fairly brief (usually between three and twenty typed pages) piece of nonfiction that tries to make a point in an interesting way.
    The standard modes of the essay are *description*, in which the writer tries to acquaint the reader with a place, object, character, or group; *narration*, recounting something that has happened; *explanation* (often called *exposition*),

presenting information or analyzing something; and *argument,* attempting to convince the reader that the writer's position on a certain issue is well-founded.

euphemism A vague or "nice" expression used in place of a more direct one; e.g., *rehabilitation facility* for *prison,* or *disincentive* for *threat.*

evading the question Avoiding the issue at hand, usually by shifting to a related point that is easier to maintain. Thus, someone who favors sharply limiting the number of immigrants to the United States is evading the question if he dwells on the government's right to pass immigration laws; that right is not the point being contested. **Ad hominem reasoning** and the **straw man** are forms of evading the question.

evidence Facts and informed opinions tending to support a **thesis**. One statement can be used as evidence for another only if there is a high likelihood that readers will accept it as true.

explanation See **essay**.

expletive The word *it* or *there* when used only to postpone a **subject**:

EXPL   S
- *It* will be a cold *day* when she arrives.

EXPL   S
- *There* are many *reasons* to doubt his story.

exposition An alternative name for the mode that is called *explanation* in this book. See **essay**.

extracted quotation A quoted passage set apart from the writer's own text. Prose quotations of more than four typed lines and verse quotations of more than two or three lines are customarily extracted. Such passages are **indented** by ten spaces, and quotation marks at the beginning and end are dropped. Cf. **incorporated quotation**.

fallacy A formal error or illegitimate shortcut in reasoning. See **begging the question, catchall explanation, either-or reasoning, evading the question, faulty generalization,** *post hoc ergo propter hoc,* and **straw man**.

familiar essay An **essay** that deals informally and lightly with a **topic** lying within the writer's personal experience. Also called *personal essay.*

faulty generalization The **fallacy** of drawing a general conclusion from insufficient **evidence**—e.g., concluding from one year's drought that the world's climate has entered a long period of change.

faulty predication See **predication**.

figurative language Language that heightens expressiveness by lending imaginative coloration to the thing described—e.g., *the hungry maw of the* *grave* for *death* or *laughing water* for *creek.* See especially **metaphor** and **simile**. Cf. **literal language**.

focused freewriting   See **freewriting**.

footnote   In general, any citation or comment set below or after a main text. More narrowly, a note at the bottom ("foot") of a page. Cf. **endnote**.

formal diction   See **diction**.

free element   A word, **phrase**, or **subordinate clause** falling outside a **main assertion**. Cf. **bound element**.

freewriting   The practice of writing continuously for a fixed period in order to stimulate thought. In *focused freewriting,* the writer begins with a specific topic and tries to stay within its bounds.

funnel paragraph   A **paragraph** beginning with a broad assertion and gradually narrowing to a specific subject.

fused sentence   See **run-on sentence**.

gazetteer   A geographical dictionary.

gender   The concept of sexual classification determining the forms of masculine *(he),* feminine *(she),* and neuter *(it)* **personal pronouns** and the feminine form of certain **nouns** *(actress).* Cf. **common gender**.

general language   Words that are not **specific**: *suburbia,* as opposed to *Chestnut Hill*; *bird,* as opposed to *scarlet tanager.*

gerund   A **nounlike** form derived from a **verb**—e.g., *Skiing* in *Skiing is dangerous.* Gerunds take exactly the same form as **participles**, and they are capable of having **subjects** (usually possessive in **case**) as well as **objects**:

    S GER   GER   OBJ GER
 • *Nancy's making* the *putt* was unexpected.

Cf. participle.

gerund phrase   See **phrase**.

grammar   The formal features of a language; also, the rules for fashioning "grammatical" or technically correct sentences in that language. Cf. **usage**.

grapholect   A variety of language distinguishable by the way it is written (not spoken). Cf. **dialect**. English has many dialects but only one widely used grapholect, **standard written English**.

imperative mood   See **mood**.

implied subject   A **subject** not actually present in a **clause**, but nevertheless understood: [*You*] *Watch out!*

incorporated quotation   A quotation placed within quotation marks and not set off from the writer's own prose. Cf. **extracted quotation**.

indefinite article   See **article**.

indefinite pronoun   A **pronoun** that leaves unspecified the person or thing it refers to: *anybody, one,* etc.

indefinite relative pronoun   An apparent **relative pronoun** lacking an **antecedent**—e.g., *what* in *She says what she thinks.*

indention   The setting of the first word of a line in from the left margin, as in a new **paragraph** (5 spaces) or an **extracted quotation** (10 spaces).

independent clause   See **clause**.

independent sentence fragment   See **sentence fragment**.

index   A book, usually with a new volume each year, containing alphabetically ordered references to articles (and sometimes books) in a given field. Also, an alphabetical list of subjects and the page numbers where they are treated in a nonfiction book. Cf. **abstract**.

indicative mood   See **mood**.

indirect discourse   Reporting what was said, as opposed to directly quoting it. Not *She said, "I am tired,"* but *She said she was tired.* Cf. **dialogue**.

indirect object   A word designating the person or thing *for whom or which,* or *to whom or which,* the action of a **verb** is performed. Note that an indirect object never appears without a **direct object** occurring in the same **clause**:

> IND OBJ   D OBJ
- She sent *him* a discouraging *letter.*

Note that when a seeming indirect object is preceded by a **preposition**, it is in fact an **object of a preposition**:

> OBJ PREP
- She sent a discouraging letter to *him.*

indirect question   The reporting of a question without use of the question form—not, e.g., *She asked, "Where should I turn?"* but *She asked where to turn.*

infinitive   The **base form** of a **verb**, usually but not always preceded by *to: to win; prove, to prove.*

infinitive phrase   See **phrase**.

inflection   A change in the ending or whole form of a word, without turning it into a new word. Thus, *he* can be inflected to *his, George* to *George's, go* to *went,* etc. The word is recognizably the same, but the inflection has placed it in a new state.

informal diction   See **diction**.

intensifier   A "fortifying" expression like *absolutely, definitely,* or *very.* Habitual use of intensifiers weakens the force of assertion.

intensive pronoun   A **pronoun** like *myself* or *themselves,* when used for emphasis: *I myself disagree with that.* Cf. **reflexive pronoun**.

interjection   A word that stands apart from other constructions in order to command attention or show strong feeling: *aha, hey, wow,* etc.

interrogative adjective   An **interrogative pronoun** form serving as a **modifier** that introduces a question—e.g., *Whose* in *Whose socks are these?*

interrogative pronoun   A **pronoun** serving to introduce a question: *who, whom, whose, which,* and *what,* as in *Which is it?*

intransitive verb   A **verb** expressing an action or state without connection to an **object** or a **complement**—e.g., *complained* in *They complained.* Cf. **transitive verb** and **linking verb**.

irony   A sharply incongruous effect, as when an advocate of holy poverty is found to have been collecting Rolls-Royces.
   In **rhetoric**, irony is the saying of one thing in order to convey a different or even opposite meaning: *Let us continue this noble war, by all means; when the best young men of their generation have all been killed or maimed, the rest of us can congratulate ourselves on having upheld the national honor.* Cf. **sarcasm**.

irregular verb   A **verb** that does not simply add *-d* or *-ed* to form its past **tense** and its past **participle**: *go (went, gone), swim (swam, swum),* etc.

italic type **(italics)**   The thin, slightly slanted typeface of *these three words,* represented in typing and handwriting by underlining: good , *good* . Cf. **roman type**.

jargon   Technical language used in inappropriate, nontechnical contexts— e.g., *upwardly mobile* for *ambitious, positive reinforcement* for *praise, paranoid* for *upset.*

journalese   **Jargon** borrowed from the language of newspapers—e.g., *gets the nod* for *wins the decision, the blaze rages* for *the fire is out of control.*

level of diction   See **diction**.

limiting sentence   A **sentence** that addresses a possible limitation, or contrary consideration, to the **theme**, or leading idea, of a **paragraph**.

linking verb   A **verb** connecting its **subject** to an identifying or **modifying complement**:

- They *were* Mormons.

LV

- She *became* calmer.

LV

Cf. **transitive verb** and **intransitive verb**.

literal language   Words that factually represent what they describe, without poetic embellishment: *dog, car, landscape.* Cf. **figurative language**.

lower case   The ordinary, uncapitalized form of letters, as in *hello.*

main assertion   The core of statement in a **sentence**, consisting of an independent **clause** and any **bound** (or **restrictive**) **modifiers**. Elements set off by commas fall outside the main assertion.

matching   The placing into grammatical association of elements that are related in meaning. Matching is an act of **coordination**, creating an effect of **parallelism**.

merged verb   A **verb** combined with a **preposition** to make a new unit— e.g., *knock down,* as in *He knocked down the challenger.*

metaphor   An implied comparison, whereby the thing at hand is **figuratively** asserted to be something else: *He was a tower of strength.* Cf. **simile**.
   A *dead metaphor* is one that has become so common that it usually does not call to mind an image: *a devil of a time, rock-bottom prices,* etc. When overworked, a dead metaphor becomes a **cliché**.
   A *mixed metaphor* is one whose elements clash in their implications: *Let's back off for a closer look*; *He's a straight arrow who shoots from the hip.*

microfiche catalog   A listing of a library's printed holdings on sheets of **microfilm** that can be read only in a special machine known as a microfiche reader.

microfilm   Film bearing a miniature photographic copy of printed or other graphic matter. In libraries, all but the most recent newspapers can be read only in a machine called a microfilm reader.

middle diction   See **diction**.

misrelated modifier   A **modifier** that might modify either of two terms, or that stands too distant from its modified term, or that unnecessarily interrupts another construction:

MOD TERM?   MM   MOD TERM?

x The proposal that he rejected *utterly* amazes me.

MM   MOD TERM
x *Laughing* so hard, it was extremely difficult for Alice to keep control of the wheel.

              MM
x They chose to *finally and decisively* end their relationship.

See also **split infinitive** and **squinting modifier**. Cf. **dangling modifier**.

mixed construction   The use of two clashing structures within a sentence, as in x *I gave him for his birthday it was a necktie.*

mixed metaphor   See **metaphor**.

MLA form   The citation style preferred by the Modern Language Association, featuring either **footnotes** or **endnotes**. Cf. **reference list**.

modifier   A word, **phrase**, or **clause** that limits or describes another element:

   M
• the *gentle* soul

   M
• *When leaving,* turn out the lights.

    M
• *Before you explain,* I have something to tell you.

mood   The manner or attitude that a speaker or writer intends a **verb** to convey, as shown in certain changes of form. Ordinary statements and questions are cast in the *indicative* mood: *Is he ill? He is.* The *imperative* mood is for commands: *Stop! Get out of the way!* And the *subjunctive* mood is used for certain formulas *(as it were),* unlikely or impossible conditions *(had she gone),* that **clauses** expressing requirements or recommendations *(They ask that she comply),* and *lest* clauses *(lest he forget).*

narration   See **essay**.

nominal   See **nounlike element**.

nonrestrictive element   A **modifier**, often a **phrase** or **clause**, that does not serve to identify ("restrict") the modified term:

            NONRESTR EL
• That woman, *whom I met only yesterday,* . . . .

            NONRESTR EL
• The man, *brushing the dust from his suit,* . . . .

Cf. **restrictive element**.

note   See **footnote**.

noun A word like *house, Jack,* or *Pennsylvania,* usually denoting a person, place, or thing, capable of being **inflected** for both plural and possessive forms *(houses, house's, houses'),* and of serving a variety of sentence functions.

noun clause See **clause**.

nounlike element (nominal, substantive) A word or group of words having the same function as a **noun**—e.g., *what you mean* in *He knows what you mean.*

number In **grammar**, the distinction between *singular (boat)* and *plural (boats)* words.

object A **noun**, **pronoun**, or **nounlike element** representing a receiver of an action or relation. See **direct object**, **indirect object**, and **object of preposition**. In addition, **infinitives**, **participles**, and **gerunds** can take objects:

OBJ INF
* to hit the *ball*

OBJ PART
* Hitting the *ball,* he heard the bat crack.

OBJ GER
* Hitting the *ball* is gratifying.

object of preposition A **noun**, **pronoun**, or **nounlike element** following a **preposition** and completing the prepositional phrase—e.g., *November* in *throughout November,* or *siesta* in *during a long siesta.*

objective case See **case**.

objective complement See **complement**.

on-line catalog A computer file of a library's printed holdings. Users can read the catalog by typing instructions into a computer terminal. Cf. **card catalog**, **microfiche catalog**.

ordinal numbers Numbers like *first (1st), second (2nd),* and *third (3rd).* Cf. **cardinal numbers**.

outline A concise, consecutive list of the points an **essay** will make, usually with **indention** and sets of numbering and lettering to show **subordination**, or the relation of major to minor points.

A *scratch outline* simply lists the points to be made in order, without use of categories and subcategories. A *topic outline* is one whose headings are words or **phrases**. In a *sentence outline,* the headings—except perhaps for the most general ones—are full **sentences**.

paradox A seeming contradiction that may nevertheless be true: *That country is the richest—and the poorest—in the world.* (Perhaps the country has the highest per-capita income but the poorest mass of peasants.)

paragraph   One or more **sentences** marked as a unit, usually by the **indention** of the first line. A typical effective paragraph develops one central idea, or **theme**, in a consistent manner.

paragraph block   A group of **paragraphs** addressing the same part of a **topic**, with strong continuity from one paragraph to the next.

paragraph development   The order in which the main types of **sentences** appear in a **paragraph**. In this book, three types of paragraphs are recognized:

1. *Direct.* The **theme sentence** comes at or near the beginning, and the remaining sentences support it, sometimes after a **limiting sentence** or two.

2. *Pivoting.* The paragraph begins with one or more limiting sentences but then makes a sharp turn to its theme sentence, which may or may not be followed by **supporting sentences**.

3. *Suspended.* The paragraph builds toward a theme sentence at or near the end.

parallelism   The structure that results from **matching** two or more parts of a **sentence**—e.g., the words *Utica, Albany,* and *Rye* in the sentence *He went to Utica, Albany, and Rye,* or the three equally weighted **clauses** that begin this sentence: *That he wanted to leave, that permission was denied, and that he then tried to escape—these facts only became known after months of official secrecy.* Cf. **coordination** and **balance**.

paraphrase   Sentence-by-sentence restatement of the meaning of a passage.

parenthetical citation   A page reference to a work, given not in a **footnote** but in parentheses within a main text—e.g., *(Meyers, pp. 241–75).* In **MLA form**, parenthetical citations are usually given only after a full footnote (or **endnote**) citing the same work has been supplied. In **reference list** form, parenthetical citations are the sole means of citing works.

parenthetical element   A word or group of words that interrupts the main flow of a **sentence**:

> PRTHL EL
> • You, *alas,* are not the one.

Parenthetical elements should always be set off by punctuation, usually commas.

part of speech   Any of the major classes (**noun, verb, conjunction,** etc.) into which words are customarily divided, depending on their dictionary meaning and their **syntactic** functions in **sentences**. Since many words belong to several parts of speech, you must analyze the sentence at hand to see which part of speech a given word is occupying.

participial phrase See **phrase**.

participle An adjectival form derived from a **verb**—e.g., *Showing* in *Showing fear, he began to sweat.* Participles can be *present (showing)* or *past (having shown),* and *active* or *passive (being shown, having been shown).* Like **gerunds**, they can also have *objects* (*fear* in the sentence above), but they do not generally have possessive-case **subjects**, as in *George's showing fear.* Cf. **gerund**.

passive voice See **voice**.

past participle See **participle**.

person In **grammar**, a characteristic of **pronouns** and **verbs** indicating whether someone is speaking *(first person: I go, we go),* being spoken to *(second person: you go),* or being spoken about *(third person: he, she, it goes; they go).*

personal essay See **familiar essay**.

personal pronoun A **pronoun** traditionally used in the conjugation (tense formation) of **verbs**—*I, you, he, she, it, we,* or *they.* Personal pronouns also have objective and possessive forms: *me, my, mine, your, yours,* etc.

phrase A cluster of words functioning as a single **part of speech** and lacking a **subject-predicate** combination.

A noun and its modifiers are sometimes called a *noun phrase (the elliptical billiard balls),* and a verb form consisting of more than one word is sometimes called a *verb phrase (had been trying).* But the types of phrases most commonly recognized are *prepositional, infinitive, participial, gerund,* and *absolute.*

A *prepositional phrase* consists of a **preposition** and its **object**, along with any **modifiers** of those words:

$$\underbrace{\overset{\text{PREP}}{among} \quad \overset{\text{M}}{the} \quad \overset{\text{M}}{many} \quad \overset{\text{M}}{fine} \quad \overset{\text{OBJ PREP}}{things}}_{\text{PREP PHRASE}}$$

An *infinitive phrase* consists of an **infinitive** and its **object**, along with any **modifiers**, and it may also include a **subject** of the infinitive:

$$\text{They asked } \underbrace{\overset{\text{S INF}}{John} \quad \overset{\text{INF}}{to \; hit} \quad \overset{\text{M}}{the} \quad \overset{\text{M}}{tiny} \quad \overset{\text{M}}{red} \quad \overset{\text{OBJ INF}}{target.}}_{\text{INF PHRASE}}$$

A *participial phrase* consists of a **participle** and its **object** and/or **modifiers**:

$$\underbrace{\overset{\text{M}}{Quickly} \quad \overset{\text{PART}}{reaching} \quad \overset{\text{M}}{the} \quad \overset{\text{M}}{correct} \quad \overset{\text{OBJ PART}}{decision,}}_{\text{PART PHRASE}} \text{ he pressed the button.}$$

A *gerund phrase* consists of a **gerund** and its **object**, along with any **modifiers**, and it may also include a **subject** of the gerund:

S GER   GER OBJ GER   M
* *Their sending him away* was a bad mistake.
                GER PHRASE

An *absolute phrase* may contain an infinitive or a participle, but it always modifies a whole statement. See **absolute phrase**.

Phrases are often confused with clauses; cf. **clause**.

pivoting paragraph   See **paragraph development**.

plagiarism   The taking of others' thoughts or words without due acknowledgment. Cf. **allusion**.

plural   See **number**.

possessive case   See **case**.

post hoc ergo propter hoc   A **fallacy** whereby the fact that one event followed another is wrongly taken to prove that the first event caused the later one.

predicate   In a **clause**, the **verb** plus all the words belonging with it:

                PRED
* He *had a serious heart attack.*

Cf. **subject**.

predicate adjective   See **complement**.

predicate noun   See **complement**.

predication   The selection of a **predicate** for a given **subject**. The problem of *faulty predication* appears when subjects and predicates are mismatched in meaning: ˣ *The purpose of the film wants to challenge your beliefs.*

prefix   One or more letters that can be attached before the root or base form of a word to make a new word: *pre-, with-,* etc. Cf. **suffix**.

preposition   A function word introducing a **prepositional phrase**—e.g., *to* in *to the lighthouse.* Cf. **conjunction**.

prepositional phrase   See **phrase**.

principal parts   The **base** or simple **infinitive form** of a **verb**, its past **tense** form, and its past **participle**: *walk, walked, walked; grow, grew, grown.*

process analysis   The **analysis** of a series of steps constituting a complete activity (cooking, driving, skiing, etc.).

pronoun   One of a small class of words, mostly used in place of **nouns** for a variety of purposes. See **personal pronoun, intensive pronoun, reflexive pronoun, reciprocal pronoun, indefinite pronoun, indefinite relative pronoun, demonstrative pronoun, relative pronoun,** and **interrogative pronoun**.

pronoun reference   The matching of **pronouns** with their **antecedents**, with which they should agree in **number, person,** and **gender**. Thus, in the sentence *When they saw Bill, they gave him a warm welcome,* the pronoun *him* properly refers to the singular, third-person, masculine antecedent *Bill*. Cf. **agreement**.

proofreading   Checking the final copy of a piece of writing for small errors.

psychologese   Psychological **jargon**—e.g., *superego* for *conscience, schizophrenic* for *undecided*.

punctuation marks   Marks used to bring out the meaning of written **sentences**. They are:

period .	parentheses ( )
question mark ?	brackets [ ]
exclamation point !	ellipses . . .
comma ,	apostrophe '
semicolon ;	hyphen -
colon :	quotation marks " "
dash —	slash (virgule) /

readability   The ease with which a reader can grasp the meaning of a writer's prose. Not to be confused with simplicity; if the meaning is complex, its formulation may have to be complex as well.

rebuttal   An opposing argument, intended to overturn an argument already made by someone else. Rebuttals do not always succeed; cf. **refutation**.

reciprocal pronoun   A **pronoun** expressing mutual relation: *each other, each other's, one another, one another's.*

redundancy   The defect of unnecessarily conveying the same meaning more than once; also, an expression that does so—e.g., *retreat back, ascend up.*

reference list   A list, supplied at the end of a paper or article, showing where and when the cited materials appeared. The **parenthetical citations** within the text refer to the reference list. The reference list style explained in this book is **APA form**. Cf. **MLA form**.

reference room   The part of a library where sets of encyclopedias, **indexes**, dictionaries, **bibliographies**, and similar **reference works** are stored. A reference room often doubles as a reading room, where library users can do "homework" without leaving the library.

reference works Books that survey a field of knowledge and tell how to locate materials within that field.

reflexive pronoun A **pronoun** like *myself* or *themselves,* used to indicate that the **subject** of a **verb** is also its **direct** or **indirect object**: *They killed themselves; I gave myself a treat.* Cf. **intensive pronoun**.

refutation The disproving of an argument already made. Cf. **rebuttal**.

relative adjective An **adjective** serving to introduce a relative or adjectival **clause** — e.g., *whose* in *the one whose picture you saw.*

relative adverb An **adverb** serving to introduce a relative or adjectival **clause** — e.g., *where* in *the place where he lives.*

relative clause In this book, any adjectival **clause**. (Some grammarians would say that only a **relative pronoun** can introduce a relative clause.)

relative pronoun A **pronoun** introducing a relative or adjectival **clause** — e.g., *that* in *This is the one that he chose.* Relative pronouns have **antecedents**, such as *one* in the example above. But see also **indefinite relative pronoun**.

reserve desk The part of a library where books and articles are kept "on reserve" (with limited borrowing times) for currently taught courses.

restrictive element A **modifier**, often a **phrase** or **clause**, that "restricts" (establishes the identity of) the modified term:

- The woman *whom I met* has disappeared.
  <small>RSTR EL</small>

- The man *in the black suit* is following you.
  <small>RSTR EL</small>

Cf. **nonrestrictive element**.

rhetoric The strategic placement of ideas and choice of language, as in *His rhetoric was effective* or *His ideas were sound but his rhetoric was addressed to the wrong audience.* Note that the unmodified noun *rhetoric* need not mean *deception* or *manipulation.*

rhetorical question A question posed for effect, without expectation of a reply: *How often have we seen this same pattern of betrayal?*

Roman numerals Numerals like *I, V,* and *XII.* Cf. **Arabic numerals**.

roman type The ordinary typeface of printed words, equivalent to what is produced by the keys of most typewriters. Cf. **italic type**.

run-on sentence   A **sentence** in which two or more **independent clauses** are improperly joined. One type of run-on sentence is the *comma splice,* in which independent clauses are joined with a comma but without a coordinating **conjunction**: x *She likes candy, she eats it every day.* The other type of run-on sentence is the *fused sentence,* in which independent clauses are joined without any punctuation or conjunction: x *She likes candy she eats it every day.*

sandwiched modifier   A **modifier** standing between two parts of a modified term:

• His first, hastily assembled, draft of the paper was a mess.

The comma after *assembled* indicates that *hastily assembled* modifies *first draft*, not just *draft.*

Cf. **squinting modifier**.

sarcasm   Abusive ridicule of a person, group, or idea, as in *What pretty phrases these cold-hearted traitors speak!* Cf. **irony**.

scratch outline   See **outline**.

second possessive   The **case** forms of possessive **pronouns** used when the **modified** term does not immediately follow the pronoun: *mine, yours, ours, theirs,* as in *The blame is ours.* Cf. **double possessive**.

self-evident thesis   A **thesis** saying little or nothing more than is already implied in the meaning of its terms—e.g., *If we fail to solve our transportation problems, congested traffic will continue to plague us.* Cf. **begging the question**, **circular reasoning**.

sentence   A complete unit of thought, usually containing at least one **independent clause**, beginning with a capital letter, and ending with a period, question mark, or exclamation point. See also **sentence fragment**.

sentence adverb   An **adverb** that also serves to indicate a logical connection between the modified **clause** or whole **sentence** and a previous statement—e.g., *therefore* in *He took the job; therefore, he had to resign his fellowship.*

sentence element   One of the functional parts of a **sentence**: **appositive**, **complement**, **connective**, **direct object**, **indirect object**, **modifier**, **objective complement**, **subject**, and **verb**.

sentence fragment   A set of words punctuated as a **sentence**, but lacking one or more of the elements usually considered necessary to a sentence:

FRAG
x *When they last saw her.*

In general, sentence fragments are regarded as blunders. But an *independent sentence fragment*—one whose context shows that it is a shortened sentence rather than a dislocated piece of a neighboring sentence — can sometimes be effective:

IND FRAG

- How much longer can we resist the enemy? *As long as necessary!*

sentence outline See **outline**.

series A set of more than two **parallel** items within a **sentence**:

SERIES
- He liked to sniff *bananas, apples, and banapple gas.*

sexist language Expressions that can give offense by implying that one sex (almost always male) is superior or that the other sex is restricted to certain traditional roles: *lady doctor, a man-sized job,* etc.

simile An explicit or open comparison, whereby the object at hand is **figuratively** asserted to be *like* something else: *She ran like the wind; it happened as if in a dream.* Cf. **metaphor**. Both similes and metaphors are called metaphorical or figurative language. Also cf. **analogy**.

slang See **diction**.

slash The punctuation mark /, also called *virgule*. Slashes are used to separate alternatives *(either/or)* and to indicate line endings in **incorporated quotation** of verse.

sociologese **Jargon** taken from sociology — e.g., *peer group* for *friends.*

specific language Words dealing in particulars — e.g., the *200-meter high hurdles,* as opposed to *the race.* Cf. **general language**.

split infinitive An **infinitive** interrupted by at least one **adverb**: *to firmly stand.* When such an adverb makes an awkward effect, it is considered a **misrelated modifier**.

squinting modifier A **misrelated modifier** trapped between sentence elements, either of which might be regarded as the modified term:

SQ M
- Why he collapsed *altogether* puzzles me.

Cf. **sandwiched modifier**.

stacks The shelves on which most books and bound periodicals in a library are stored.

stance The rhetorical posture a writer adopts toward an audience. This book recognizes two stances, *forthright* and *ironical.* See **irony**.

standard written English The only widely recognized **grapholect** in English **usage**.

straw man   A misrepresentation of an opponent's position so that it will appear weaker than it actually is. In this unfair form of argument an irrelevant point is attacked and easily dismissed.

subject   The part of a **clause** about which something is **predicated**:

S
- *Ernest* shot the tiger.

The subject alone is called the *simple subject*. With its modifiers included it is called the *complete subject*—e.g., *The only thing to do* in *The only thing to do is compromise.* The simple subject here is *thing.*
  Not only **verbs**, but also **infinitives** and **gerunds** can have subjects:

S INF
- They wanted *him* to be king.

S GER
- *His* refusing upset them.

subject area   A wide range of concerns, from which the **topic** of an **essay** may be extracted. Cf. **topic**, **thesis**.

subjective case   See **case**.

subjunctive mood   See **mood**.

subordinate clause   See **clause**.

subordinating conjunction   See **conjunction**.

subordination   In general, the giving of minor emphasis to minor elements or ideas. In **syntax**, making one element grammatically dependent on another, which the subordinate element limits or supports or explains. Thus, in *They were relieved when it was over,* the subordinate **clause** *when it was over* limits the time to which the verb *were relieved* applies.

substantive (n.)   See **nounlike element**.

suffix   One or more letters that can be added at the end of a word's root or base to make a new word: *-ship, -ness,* etc. Cf. **prefix**.

superlative degree   See **degree**.

supporting sentence   A **sentence** that restates, elaborates, or provides evidence or context for some aspect of a **paragraph's theme** or leading idea.

suspended comparison   A comparison proposing two possible relations between the compared items, and in which the second item is stated only at the end of the construction: *Taco Bell is as good as, if not better than, Pizza Hut.*

suspended paragraph   See **paragraph development**.

synonym A word having practically the same meaning as another word—e.g., *car, auto.*

syntax The pattern of word order in a **sentence**.

tense The time a **verb** expresses: present *(see),* future *(will see),* etc.

theme The leading idea of a **paragraph**. Every sound paragraph has a theme, whether or not that theme is spelled out in a **theme sentence**. Also, the most prominent idea in a work of art or literature. Cf. **thesis**.

theme sentence The **sentence** in a **paragraph** that conveys its leading idea. Often called a *topic sentence.* Cf. **thesis statement**.

thesis The point, or one main idea, of an **essay**, article, book, etc. Cf. **theme, subject area, topic**.

thesis statement A one-**sentence** statement of the **thesis** or main idea of an **essay**. In this book, a thesis statement is considered complete only if it contains enough elements of support (or support and limitation) to give organizing guidance to the essay. Cf. **theme sentence**.

tone The quality of feeling conveyed by something. Words like *factual, sober, fanciful, urgent, tongue-in-cheek, restrained, stern, pleading,* and *exuberant* may begin to suggest the range of tones found in **essays**. Cf. **stance, voice**.

topic The specific subject of an **essay**; the ground to be covered or the question to be answered. Cf. **subject area, thesis**.

topic outline See **outline**.

topic sentence See **theme sentence**.

transitional paragraph A whole paragraph devoted to announcing a major shift in focus.

transitive verb A **verb** transmitting an action to a **direct object**:

TR V
- They *cast* the dice.

Cf. **intransitive verb** and **linking verb**.

trial thesis A possible **thesis**, or main idea, considered before a final thesis has been chosen.

understatement A device of **rhetoric** whereby the writer conveys the importance of something by appearing to take it lightly: *Being a paraplegic has its inconvenient moments.*

usage   The practices of word choice and sentence formation typically accepted by a group of speakers and writers. Cf. **grammar, standard written English**.

verb   A word or words like *goes, saw,* or *was leaving,* serving to convey the action performed by a **subject**, to express the state of that subject, or to connect the subject to a **complement**.

verb phrase   See **phrase**.

verbal   A form derived from, but different in function from, a **verb**. Verbals are either **infinitives**, **participles**, or **gerunds**.

virgule   See **slash**.

voice   The form of a **verb** indicating whether the **subject** performs *(active* voice: *we strike)* or receives *(passive* voice: *we are struck)* the action. Also, the "self" projected by a given piece of writing. This book recognizes two voices in this latter sense, the *personal* and *impersonal.*

vowel   An unblocked speech sound, marked by one of the letters *a, e, i, o, u,* or *y* as in *try* (not as in *yellow*). Cf. **consonant**.

INDEX

NOTE: Where more than one page number is given, begin by looking up the *italicized* one. A **boldface** number refers to a definition in the Glossary of Terms.

A

a vs. *an*, 266–267
a while vs. *awhile*, 213
abbreviation, *366–368*, **475**; capitalization of, 361; in citation, 366–367; in main text of essay, 366, 367–368; italics in, 365; Latin, 366–367; of technical term, 368; of title accompanying name, 368; punctuation of, 312; redundancy in, 368; spacing of, 368; when to avoid, 366; with time, 368
absolute: adjective or adverb, **475**; comparison of, 300–301; phrase, 271, 273, 294, **475**
abstract: diction, 23–24, 25, *225–227*, **476**; noun, as subject of gerund, 295; of published article, 382, 384–385, 386, **476**
accept vs. *except*, 213
acknowledgment of sources, 404–407; *see also* documentation
acronym, **476**; punctuation of, 368

action, revealing: in description, 26; in narration, 32
active voice, 249–251, **500**; in distinct assertion, 179, *181–182*; of infinitive, 269; of participle, 270; tense forms of, 250–251
A.D., 368
ad hominem reasoning, 64, **476**
adapt vs. *adopt*, 213
addition, and agreement problems, 284
address: public, footnote citing, 418; street, punctuation of, 325
adjectival clause, 275, **479**
adjectival noun, *see* attributive noun
adjective, *263–264*, **476**; comparison of, 263–264, 302; demonstrative, *167*, 290, **482**; derived from name, 363; interrogative, 259, **487**; irregular, 263; predicate, 243, 263, 265, **495**; relative, 254; vs. adverb, 264–265
adopt vs. *adapt*, 213
adverb, *264–266*, **476**; comparison of, 265;

G

H

I

ABOUT THE AUTHOR

Frederick Crews, Professor of English at the University of California, Berkeley, received the Ph.D. from Princeton University. Throughout a distinguished career he has attained many honors, including a Guggenheim Fellowship, appointment as a Fulbright Lecturer in Italy, and recognition from the National Endowment for the Arts for his essay, "Norman O. Brown: The World Dissolves." His writings include highly regarded books on Henry James, E. M. Forster, and Nathaniel Hawthorne, the best-selling satire *The Pooh Perplex*, and a recent volume of his own essays entitled *Out of My System*. Professor Crews has published numerous articles in *Partisan Review, New York Review of Books, Commentary, Tri-Quarterly*, and other important journals. He is Chairman of Freshman Composition in the English Department at Berkeley.

SYMBOLS FOR REVISION

When commenting on your essays, your instructor may use some of the following marks:

✓	Good point; well expressed
✗	Delete this expression
⌒	Close up space
#	Insert a space
∧	Omission
∼	Transpose (reverse the order of two elements)
X	Obvious error
¶	Paragraph break needed here, *p. 173*
¶ con	Paragraph continuity lacking, *pp. 165–170*
¶ dev	Paragraph development lacking, *pp. 153–160*
¶ unity	Paragraph needs more unity, *pp. 161–164*
‖	Parallel construction faulty or missing, *pp. 295–299*
'	Apostrophe, *pp. 333–334*
[/]	Brackets, *pp. 331–332*
:	Colon, *pp. 328–329*
,	Comma, *pp. 313–325*
—	Dash, *pp. 329–330*
/.../	Ellipses, *pp. 332–333*
!	Exclamation point, *p. 313*
=	Hyphen, *pp. 353–356*
(/)	Parentheses, *pp. 330–331*
⊙	Period, *pp. 311–312*
?	Question mark, *pp. 312–313*
"/"	Quotation marks, *pp. 334–341*
;	Semicolon, *pp. 327–328*
Ab	Faulty abbreviation, *pp. 366–368*
Abst	Too abstract, *pp. 225–227*
Agr	Faulty subject-verb agreement, *pp. 283–286*
Amb	Ambiguous expression
Awk	Awkward expression
Bibl	Faulty bibliography form, *pp. 421–422*
Ca	Wrong pronoun case, *pp. 287–288*
Cap	Capital letter required, *pp. 358–363*
CF	Comma fault, *pp. 313–325*
Chop	Choppy sentences, *pp. 198–205*
Circ	Circumlocution, *p. 223*
Cl	Cliché, *p. 227*
Coh	Coherence lacking
Colloq	Colloquial expression, *pp. 218–219*